DATE DUE

BRODART, CO.

Leaps in the Dark

UNIVERSITY PRESS OF FLORIDA

Florida A&M University, Tallahassee
Florida Atlantic University, Boca Raton
Florida Gulf Coast University, Ft. Myers
Florida International University, Miami
Florida State University, Tallahassee
New College of Florida, Sarasota
University of Central Florida, Orlando
University of Florida, Gainesville
University of North Florida, Jacksonville
University of South Florida, Tampa
University of West Florida, Pensacola

Leaps in the Dark
Art and the World

Agnes de Mille, edited by Mindy Aloff

University Press of Florida
Gainesville · Tallahassee · Tampa · Boca Raton
Pensacola · Orlando · Miami · Jacksonville · Ft. Myers · Sarasota

Copyright 2011 by Jonathan de Mille Prude
Printed in the United States of America on acid-free paper

16 15 14 13 12 11   6 5 4 3 2 1

Library of Congress Cataloging-in-Publication Data
De Mille, Agnes.
Leaps in the dark : art and the world / Agnes de Mille ; edited by Mindy Aloff.
p. cm.
ISBN 978-0-8130-3570-3 (alk. paper)
1. Modern dance. I. Aloff, Mindy, 1947– II. Title.
GV1783.D43 2011
792.8—dc22   2010042342

Frontis: Courtesy *Life* magazine.

The University Press of Florida is the scholarly publishing agency for the State
University System of Florida, comprising Florida A&M University, Florida Atlantic
University, Florida Gulf Coast University, Florida International University, Florida State
University, New College of Florida, University of Central Florida, University of Florida,
University of North Florida, University of South Florida, and University of West Florida.

University Press of Florida
15 Northwest 15th Street
Gainesville, FL 32611-2079
http://www.upf.com

For Bob Gottlieb,
Who championed the usefulness of
this book and my participation in it.
M.A.

One can't go through life on
one's hands and knees.
One leaps in the dark.

"Rhythm in My Blood"
And Promenade Home

Contents

sively revised version of The Who's rock opera, as different from the shows of Broadway's "Golden Age" as it was then possible to get and still attract some part of Broadway's middle-class audiences. (Among other differences, the opera—or oratorio—had been given its world première, in 1969, not as a live staging but rather as a two-record LP, that is, as a self-contained musical experience, whose action was, of necessity, imagined by its listeners.)

Despite her suffering over professional and romantic rejection early in her career, her exhaustion at having to weather huge cultural changes in her art and in her audiences in middle age, and her terrors as well as her epic frustrations in laboring to overcome the effects of a massive stroke in her later years, the author of the essays in this volume lived a huge, often satisfying life. Her knack for ruffling feathers and bruising egos, thanks to her lifelong penchant for brute candor, cost her jobs and sometimes friendships; yet for those who could take her personality in stride, she was a pillar of fire, and they repaid her with unwavering loyalty and support. Choreographer, wife, dancer, mother, writer: de Mille, indeed, "had it all"—as she wrote in her essay "The Milk of Paradise" she greedily set out to acquire—including membership in several close-knit families. There was the one she grew up in, with her parents and sister, Margaret. There was the one she constructed with her husband, Walter Prude, and their son, Jonathan. And there was the one that evolved as de Mille bonded with other dancers and theatrical collaborators—those for whom she performed (Antony Tudor, Lucia Chase), those with whom she performed and worked (such as Frederic Franklin, Oliver Smith, and Trude Rittmann), those she admired (Martha Graham, La Argentina, the Alicias Markova and Alonso, Carmelita Maracci), and those whom she taught, encouraged, and/or inspired (Bambi Linn, Diana Adams, Joan McCracken, Dania Krupska, James Mitchell).

In the year of this writing, two individuals from the last group—the widely respected Gemze de Lappe (de Mille's frequent assistant) and the choreographer Liza Gennaro (daughter of the choreographer Peter Gennaro)—collaborated with the New York Theatre Ballet and its founding artistic director, Diana Byer, on *Dance/Speak: The Life of Agnes de Mille*. That show, written by novelist and former dancer Anderson Ferrell (who also serves as director of the licensing organization for de Mille's stage work), features reconstructions of choreography from many of those long-gone Broadway productions, as well as from de Mille's early years as a performing choreographer on the concert stage. During an era when choreographers are finding it difficult to reinvent techniques for telling stories through movement alone, de Mille's resurrected Broadway dances—imprinted with the pride of classic ballet and full of social detail, exactingly delineated psychological texture, and expert use of pared-down folkdance material—seem like an unexpected endowment, miraculously excavated from the hold of a sunken galleon.

And yet, as accomplished a choreographer as de Mille was, her gifts as a writer were greater. Her natural genre was the memoir, a form that often teeters on the brink of fiction. Still, bathed as they may be in theatrical lighting, many of her indelible word portraits of her contemporaries have been validated as accurate (if, sometimes, scathingly so) by readers who also knew the subjects. Occasionally, the memoirs glide into Shavian critical analysis that pulls no punches while retaining de Mille's hallmark humor and undercurrents of sympathy. As it happens, with the exception of de Mille's biography of Martha Graham, her some dozen books have been permitted by her publishers to go out of print over the past couple of decades. The collection here draws on all but one of the memoirs. (Since the focus of this book is professional dancing and the contexts for it to thrive, there is no excerpt from *Where the Wings Grow*, de Mille's entirely offstage remembrance of a childhood summer home.) I've also included a morsel of theory from *The Book of the Dance*, one of her two volumes of brilliantly illustrated and highly personal dance history.

In typing the collection you hold into the computer, I made one discovery that concerns the author's masterful technique of contrast between long and short sentences. Among leading dance writers in English, not even Edwin Denby bettered her in wresting full value from this element of style, so that the short sentence is now the rosette that brings the ensemble into focus, now the bullet from nowhere that shatters your heart. I also discovered a small yet pervasive group of words on which she relied: "enormous," "build" as a verb, "gay" in the sense of "merry" or "light-hearted" (i.e., without reference to sexual orientation), "quiet." As her paragraphs flowed onto the computer screen, I watched her keen deployment of repetition elevate entire pages from personal memoir into essay. I saw how, in her accounts from the 1940s, World War II inserted itself into the most unexpected aspects of dancing and daily living. I marveled at the speed with which she could open herself up to deep feeling in one phrase and then, in the next, reestablish her formidably self-possessed, gleefully patrician, tough, responsible character as an observer. I also noticed that she (and/or her publishers) practiced austerity when it came to punctuation. Admiring as I was of their Modernism in that regard, in places where the meaning of a sentence was potentially ambiguous, I have added a comma or semicolon. (I also corrected misspellings of names.) Occasionally, I have written a headnote to an essay to give background information about dancers whose names may no longer be familiar, or about unusual venues or terms. One word about format: de Mille employed few footnotes, and I have retained them all. Long ones are indicated in the text by asterisks; short ones are incorporated into the text with curly brackets.

Agnes George de Mille was the daughter and granddaughter of writers, the wife of a writer, the mother of a writer, and the close friend of such writers as Elizabeth Bowen and Rebecca West. She belongs to American literary nobility. It is my hope that this collection will stimulate new interest in her complete literary estate and prompt the republication, in its entirety, of at least her first book, *Dance to the Piper*, on which several generations of star-struck dance audiences and dancers were dazzlingly nurtured.

Mindy Aloff

Portraits and Self-Portraits

Agnes de Mille Takes Her Own Measure
(Excerpt from *Speak to Me, Dance with Me*)

Although the following chapter—the first in de Mille's 1973 *Speak
to Me, Dance with Me* and republished here almost in its entirety—
comes from one of the author's later memoirs, it sets up the context
of her early life so fully that it leads off this collection. The subject
of *Speak to Me, Dance with Me* is the period between 1932 and 1935,
when the young de Mille was prey to humiliating professional disappointments in New York, as she attempted to fire up her dancing
career; she also endured a piercing disappointment of the heart in
London, where she seems to have been reasonably content professionally, studying and performing at the Mercury Theatre, run by
the capricious visionary Marie Rambert. De Mille saw Frederick
Ashton and Antony Tudor choreograph and the young Alicia
Markova and Margot Fonteyn perform during this fertile and
thrilling period that has come to be considered the birth of British
ballet. The author's marriage and child and her international success on the commercial and concert stage would be some ten years
in the future; however, since the book is reflecting on its material
several decades after the fact, its tone incorporates the knowledge
of what would happen without actually recounting it.

I was born in New York City, where my father was a successful playwright. He went to Hollywood at the urging of his younger brother, Cecil, when I was very young, and I grew up there, acquiring a sound, even excellent, schooling. Since I loved the life and environs and my family, I had a happy childhood.

Many people have written about Hollywood, but very few natives, and very few who like it. The writers, usually those who went out to make a quick financial killing, and did or did not succeed, invariably regretted that the atmosphere found was not that of their college libraries.

My family lived quietly and apart, but the values maintained in my father's business, which was moving pictures, did have a shaping influence on all our lives. It was my home, after all, and although I later went far away and tried for other goals, I used the yardstick I had grown up with to measure my failures. The Hollywood point of view was that one must be a success, successful in worldly terms, that is: recognized universally and paid largely. There was no other kind of success. My father was an educated man, and my mother was the daughter of Henry George, one of American's greatest economists and philosophers, who died poor. My parents tried to counteract and modify the local attitude, but we lived in Hollywood and we lived by Hollywood, and success was success.

In Hollywood one put on a tremendous front; one associated with the powerful; if a woman, one was pretty and sexy. This was not only helpful, this was obligatory. Other attributes were not essential: talent, for instance. Not in those days. This was why Hollywood was so attractive: the untalented and vulgar need not be disqualified. People the world over recognized the opportunity and for that reason there was magic there, the magic of pure luck. It became almost a mystic quality.

Hollywood, in terms of the movies, is now no more than a ruined capital; nevertheless, every time the plane circles down over the vast stretches of look-alike cottages, one recognizes, almost as an odor, the latent power. It trembles in the air. It is there, present as it is in baseball arenas or racetracks or gambling casinos, or for that matter, in Kremlin Square, life-and-death attention by adult men and women to something that concerns them nearly, without diversion, without alloy, without consideration for any other value or interest, something to kill for. In the case of Hollywood, it was and is—money. One had the feeling that the gardens of Hollywood reached to Moscow. One had the sense that Hollywood could buy the world, and often did.

The artistic market was centered in London, Paris and New York, but Hollywood was the ultimate reward.

Behind the writing of every play, every song, every acting or dancing lesson, was the dream of a Hollywood contract. It was not so expressed. Quite the contrary. The more sophisticated the artist, the greater the proclaimed contempt. But artists came, and a lot stayed, and they lived very well, better than they could elsewhere. The ones that failed, and this includes some immortals, were bitterly scornful.

We natives knew that the city contained more colleges and universities than any other place of comparable population in the West. We were acquainted with the academic faculties and we knew librarians and doctors and architects in vine-covered cottages on hillsides with home-tended gardens and rare books and choice cuisines. We knew that conversation could be quite as good as anywhere else and the music nearly as good. So we didn't mind the scorn. Whether the transients sat around in expensive Moroccan villas with whirling sprinklers on the vast uneventful lawns, luxuriating in the prostitution of their gifts, made not a whit of difference beside the fact that after all they were there. It was a worldwide compulsion.

They had come, and mostly they grumbled because they were not immune to being sent away again. If under the system it was possible for quite mediocre people to live like dukes, it was equally possible for them to have their status reversed without warning. Only the producers who owned controlling shares of stock were impervious—and Charlie Chaplin.

At the forefront of this strange and potent community there had marched since 1913 my Uncle, Cecil Blount De Mille. He rode the fluctuating business deeps as on a surfboard, with gaiety and bravado. If he had any doubts as to his own ability or scope, he never expressed them. He had doubts about his colleagues; he expected the worst in business dealings and was always ready. He was himself a phenomenally shrewd man who augmented an instinct for popular taste with bold and astonishing business coups. His success was a world success, and he enjoyed every minute of it, and it lasted. He kept sex, sadism, patriotism, real estate, religion and public relations dancing in midair like jugglers' balls for fifty years.

He was particularly known for his dicta on the beauty of women. If he found a young woman attractive, she might very well turn out to be Gloria Swanson. If he found her unattractive, she had a long, long road to go before she could again approach a camera. Styles have changed since, but C.B.'s dream of beauty set the standard in early Hollywood. None of his family women looked like his dream. It mattered to none but me. His daughter, Cecilia, very handsome, but not pretty, chose to raise horses, an eminently wise decision, however expensive. She has been for fourteen years the only woman on the

Board of the California Thoroughbred Breeders' Association (the largest in North America) and the only woman president, 1963–66.

He was the most glamorous figure of my youth and probably the most powerful. I did not always admire Cecil's later pictures, but I never got over wondering what he would think of me. He was a kind of monarch, and although a younger son, he was the head of the clan.

Not as famous, but perhaps more subtly influential, was his older brother, my father, William de Mille, whose forte was gentle domestic drama which foreshadowed the present school of English comedy and French genre. He concerned himself with domestic relations and character revelation. Cecil thought all this rather dull and commonplace. It was as common as humanity and it was not dull. But it did not, like Cecil's style, appeal to the Arabs and the Chinese. It did not set every little shopgirl to doing her hair differently. In fact, Pop's pictures were often about shopgirls, which was no news to them. Pop's co-workers have said they thought he was years ahead of his time. He wrote and directed over fifty pictures.

I considered my father a very great artist and I adored him. He was all that meant excitement and reaffirmation in my life. His praise was everything I sought and his disapproval was a dimming of my sun. Therefore, any conflict of will became an agony. That I had a will of my own I consider rather surprising, my infatuation was so deep and so dependent.

Both men were rich, Cecil very rich. Father considered himself moderately paid, but in the 1920's he earned a steady four thousand a week with almost no taxes the year around until he had to take the dreadful adjustment of a renewed contract and was reduced to two thousand. Mother maintained a comfortable but restrained household and saved out of her housekeeping budget ($200 per week), against the day which she felt must surely arrive when all this affluence would cease. Why she felt this I do not know. Perhaps she wished it. She feared and disliked the atmosphere of the studios and wanted Pop to return to the East and to playwriting without financial guarantees. This had been the background of their early marriage when they had been happy. Those household savings of my mother were what was to give me a career.

Both men wanted boys. Their wives gave them nothing but girls. We were a family of women, with spinster aunts and dependent widows. The men never expressly said they wanted sons, but Cecil determined to name his only child after himself and was stopped at the fount by his mother, who persuaded him to let the baby be baptized Cecilia and give it some sex. (He later adopted two boys as well as a girl, Katherine.) My sister and I were named quite femininely, Agnes and Margaret, after members of the de Mille clan, but Pop referred to us for the first eight years of our lives as "the boys." "How are my fellers?" he wrote Mother; "How are the boys doing? Kiss my boys good-night." Sometimes he addressed my beautiful little sister as "old man." He wished me to become a tennis champion. He wanted me to learn fencing and boxing. He took me fishing. He taught me photography. Above all, he wanted me to write plays. He wrote my mother from New York: "Incidentally, I showed him [John Erskine] Agnes's sonnet and the Miracle Play and he was really delighted. Of course, he had some criticism—but he thinks the kid really has 'It.'

"Don't talk to her too much about it for she is inclined to think her own opinion is nearly always the right one, but I was very much pleased with the effect of her work on John."

I wanted to act. It's all I wanted to do. I was a good actress. Certainly not, he said. Why? Well, first I was gap-toothed, then I was spotty and gawky— no, that I never was. But I developed an unfashionable bosom, aggressive and somehow so unsexy. "Your sister is so dainty and appealing," everyone said. She was flat as a pancake and therefore chic in the clothes of the twenties—and she was neat; I came apart at every seam. Then it turned out I was ugly. No one ever expected this, but they accepted it and proclaimed it. And in time I came reluctantly to believe them. Were the de Milles not expert? Crooked teeth and that awful Jewish nose inherited straight from my Jewish grandmother. If there was one certain thing no Jewish producer in Hollywood would put a camera on, it was a female who looked Jewish. I was doomed. But I was a good actress, I said. That was not the point. Barbra Streisand was to change all that, but so very much later.

So I said I would dance. Uncle Cecil thought this interesting. He'd seen some dancers he found attractive and provocative. Father had seen none and was appalled. Tennis, yes. Dancing, no. "You see," said Mother, "your father knows you will be accepted anywhere if you play fine tennis."

"I can go a lot of places if I dance well," I muttered. So I was turned back to Chopin, Dumas, my mother's garden and long, long daydreams. I was a very moody girl, sullen in the parlor and mean in school. Mother said I entered any social gathering on the defensive with the expression, "I dare you to like me." My sister was a raving little beauty and sweet-natured, with a string of beaux from the time she was eleven. She flirted outrageously with my father's colleagues—even Walter Wanger. They loved it. I was amazed at her boldness. Mother was shocked. Margaret continued and Father found her amusing—I wasn't amusing; I was rock-passioned.

But, being incapable of any unfilial disloyalty or violence, there was for me no thought of a Duncan-type revolt. All I wanted was to dance beautifully, but unlike Duncan, I wasn't sure I could. Nor did I believe, as she did, that I had been sent to change the world. I was the granddaughter of one who had. I knew that pattern; it was a tough one. People could be responsive enough to emotional vagaries, but not to blueprints; I could not be vague; I had learned to count exactly.

Since it had been established that I wasn't pretty and was no housekeeper, obviously then it was to be my talents which would make men find me adorable, my brilliant, active, successful talents. Ah, me—the learning ahead!

Father wrote in my autograph book:

My first-born child you are
But that's nothing.
I'd rather love you
For what you do
Than because you're mine.
So go to it.

And Mother wrote beneath:

I who have always been known as the daughter of my father,
and the wife of my husband, pray that some day I will be
known as the mother of my daughter.

There are two birth processes. The biological one, which is so brutal and traumatizing that doctors say certain individuals never recover, and the rupturing of the invisible net spun around our world by parental prejudices. Fathers are there to help break through, but some fathers are not patient. Some fathers abandon us.

Mother and Father got divorced and we moved away. It was a terrible divorce. Father was never the same man after, although he remarried and married happily. Mother was shattered, and I elected not to speak to Father for two years in an effort to help her reestablish a life.

My dancing career was begun, therefore, totally without de Mille help. And this imposed a dreadful handicap. There was not an office, not an agent, not a manager I addressed who did not ask the simple question, "Why don't your folks give you a job?" Since they were the fountainheads, the answer must be obvious.

The affluence did fade. Father's work had entered a period of long diminuendo and he began having excruciating tax problems. In fact, his tangled finances, the divorce settlement, and the usual Hollywood dodgings about these matters grew into a nationally known case which lawyers across the land followed with grim interest. Cecil faced all the same problems but came through unscathed. His bookkeeping had been dazzling and he'd had no divorce to make fiscal complications. Slowly during the years, the government bankrupted Pop and took away all his savings, every penny. He suffered a heart attack over the troubles and only his staunch wife pulled him through. At the beginning of this sad decline the depression hit and Hollywood disintegrated.

When Pop first saw me dance two years after I started, he offered to give me six thousand dollars to further my work. I wanted an appearance in Paris. John Erskine, Father's classmate at Columbia and head of the Juilliard School of Music, persuaded him that I was being conned by a European racketeer and the offer was withdrawn. Later, Pop had no six thousand to give me.

At the time of the divorce he made my sister and me very generous allowances because, as he explained, he wanted us to be free. But Mother was in collapse and freedom was out of the question. Not that she lay around or sulked; she was still powerful and active, but her heart, that is, her pride, had been broken. She was a desperate woman.

She married me and as a wedding gift she gave me my career.

My sister, who was an honor student in both history and English, ran away from Barnard to go on the stage. Father and Mother deplored the decision. I, who had learned how jolly a cum laude could make one, cheered her on. Her final interview with Dean Virginia Gildersleeve was brief. "Oh, don't go, my dear," begged the dean, "The last girl to make this dreadful mistake and spoil all her chances was Helen Gahagan!"

Margaret went. Shortly afterwards she married, against Mother's dire warnings, a moving-picture producer, Bernard P. Fineman, then my father's boss. Both men handled this delicate situation with tact.

After several years of tentative theatrical efforts, my mother and I elected to storm Europe and London without Pop's six thousand. It seemed imperative to get away from New York. I had just been fired as choreographer from my first big job, *Flying Colors*, book and lyrics by Howard Dietz, music by Arthur Schwartz.

The theater in that period was very rough—particularly the musical theater; all of the musical producers were tough and hard, except Winthrop Ames, whom I never met. The musical theater was controlled mainly by the brothers Shubert, and what the Shuberts and their friends or rather, their associates, looked for in a young woman was well known. I didn't have it. The English producers, on the other hand, I'd heard, were willing to look for something else.

The Shuberts owned thirty theaters in New York City, and landlorded approximately one hundred and fifty theaters in key cities right across the continent. In fact, they held what was virtually a monopoly on the few theaters that had not been taken over by movies. This made them influential. They would present anything the law permitted if they thought there was cash in the project. And in the course of fifty years and over five hundred productions, they sponsored almost everything, including a few very good shows. It was always difficult, however, to approach them with a new idea because they bought only what had been proven salable.

The barrier of cold and calculating appraisal that a young artist had to pierce was practically impenetrable and if one were shy, as I was, and uncertain, as I was, it was final. One time when Uncle Cecil was negotiating with Lee Shubert, I asked him for a word of help. He explained, as he refused, that his word would do no good. It would have, of course; Lee recognized power. What Lee's henchman simply asked was, "So, why doesn't your uncle give you a job himself?" Nevertheless, I got to Mr. Lee.

Mr. Lee must have been very old during my Shubert era, but his appearance defeated calculation. His hair was black, shiny and flat. He was sunburned to a somber mahogany and so embalmed with unguents and oils that his skin had lost mobility and texture. Indeed, few ever saw an expression of any sort cross his face. He had cultivated the ability to speak without moving his lips. His voice was an old man's, high and querulous, which came oddly from that dark, foreboding mask. His eyes were black and brilliant and burned with watchful steadiness in the gummy skull. He seemed not to hear or take any notice, but no one was fooled. There are animals that sit unmoving in this fashion with unblinking eyes, apparently lost in inner thought until something edible passes. Mr. Lee knew everything that happened in theatrical New York, every click of every cash register in every box office, every complaint of every chorus girl about salary or dressing-room plumbing. He didn't know much about music or manuscript, but that was of no consequence. He could buy taste. He could not buy watchfulness. Not of that sort. This is the dark, primeval, digestive instinct that means survival. This is the shellfish opening and closing in Pleistocene waters. This is the eye in the jungle. I think Mr. Lee would rather have lost a leg than a bargain. There was magic about him. Like any witch doctor, he knew just where the life-blood trickled. And the young and helpless gazed on him as on a fetish or object of powerful taboo. And there was magic about the great maroon car and its liveried chauffeur that waited in Shubert Alley. When that awful receptacle blocked the passage, the taboo, we knew, was inside working. Little girls sweated through their mascara as they passed by.

Today David Merrick attempts the same effect, but he has a sense of humor, and this spoils everything.

The other New York managers may have been physically less spectacular, but they were equally tough, if not as powerful—Ziegfeld, Gordon, Brady. And the agents were the same, but rabid because dependent and frightened. It was from a Gordon production that I had just been fired, but Shubert had fired me, too. New York was dead for me. And, so, of course, was Hollywood. There were no ballet companies. This firing was drastic.

Mother knew about this. What she did not know about was that I had at the same time been jilted. The ordinary experience of being courted, completely won, and then discarded was to me so astonishing, so overwhelming, that my pride could not adjust. I grieved as my mother had and for much the same reason. I failed to understand how people so sincere and charming as we simply wouldn't do. Looking back, it seems easy to grasp, but then, no! I never knew why men didn't want me for a wife. It's plain as a pike staff. I would have been a dreadful wife. I didn't give a rap about a house or domesticity, and very little about anyone else's problems except my own. I was extremely interested in me. Men hanker after something else. It is really not the wife's career they mind. They would accept a career if she would get on with it successfully but unnoticeably while keeping her best attention for the husband's needs and work. I was capable of devoted love. I was not capable of domesticity. And I did not intend household chores to limit my activities. The basic needs of a man or a child would be something else again, but these did not include marketing or sweeping floors.

The artist is a devourer and cannot accommodate. That is why so few creative women can marry, unless it is with a colleague. Passion, character—even love, deep love—do not modify the flaw of divided attention. It's that simple. The only easy solution would have been to be as light in love as a bachelor boy. But I was trained not to be, nor was I inclined to be.

At least I kept my mouth shut. Mother didn't know I'd had a romance.

We went in October 1932 to Europe, Mother and I, quite alone, and we launched a brief season in Paris, Brussels and London without management, public relations, patronage or money, the budget for the season being as I recall (exclusive of passage, board and keep) $1,200. This financed seven public appearances in three foreign capitals. The concerts in London were sufficiently well received to elicit an invitation from Ashley Dukes, the writer, and his wife, Marie Rambert, reinforced by the critic, Arnold Haskell, to repeat the series the following June in the Dukeses' private theater, the Mercury, at Notting Hill Gate.

I was to take classes from Rambert and give my concerts in her theater, which Ashley proposed to rent to me for ten pounds a performance. It was against the Lord Chamberlain's regulations to perform publicly in English theaters on Sunday but various theatrical organizations got around this by forming clubs and selling subscriptions, hence the name "Ballet Club," which catered to a subscribing audience every Sunday night. During the week, Ashley Dukes produced experimental theater pieces, some noteworthy, and on odd nights the theater was let to visiting transients. I was to have one night a week, either a Tuesday or a Thursday.

I was to pay my way on every level, but I was used to paying my way and it would be cheaper than in New York or Los Angeles, where the name de Mille invited exploitation. The name de Mille was not so awfully regarded in London. . . .

The plan was that I was to be only informally attached to Ballet Club, but I was to be in the middle of it. I could never have managed to be in the middle of any state company. I was about to get an education in big style, hard correct Cecchetti technique, hard good rehearsals and public, professional performances.

The family, of course, thought I was running away from failure and con-sorting with ineffective Bohemians. They thought I was one myself because I couldn't get a job. My relatives always talked of audiences in the millions. Ballet Club seated one hundred and ten, and compared to the West End, New York, or Hollywood, its febrile activity seemed very small, but this, whether we knew it or not, was where the action was—here and in a few barren studios in Greenwich Village, New York.

If I have one sure gift, it is to be at the place where great things happen, or rather, in that wonderful fermenting prelude to greatness wherein movement and power form. Planning has nothing to do with it, nor has foresight, nor in-telligence. Unwilling, resentful, and unknowing, simply I am there. This is the story of someone who got not what she wanted, but better than she deserved. (1–17)

Choice of Vocation
(Excerpt from "New York," *Dance to the Piper*)

Adeline Genée (1878–1970), who so affected the young Agnes, was a native of Denmark who became a principal dancer at Copenhagen's Royal Opera House and then went on to triumph as a ballerina in the United States, Australia, and England, where, prior to World War I, her dancing was regarded as a standard of technique and style and where, after her retirement from the stage, she remained tremendously influential as a model of classical schooling. The Orchestrelle that Mrs. de Mille played was a reed organ, built similarly to a player piano and popular at the turn of the last century.

Since Father was a playwright, I determined to be an actress. . . . It was only after seeing the matinee performance of Adeline Genée, dainty, doll-like and impeccable, that I altered my choice of vocation. I declared on coming home that henceforth I would be a ballet dancer, and that Mother might arrange about lessons for the next day. There were, however, no lessons. But nevertheless I danced, and sometimes I was permitted to improvise dances for dinner guests, and I was encouraged by Mother to improvise nightly while she accompanied me on the Orchestrelle, these exercises becoming as much a part of the evening's program as brushing teeth. (4–5)

Uncle Ce (Cecil B. De Mille, 1881–1959)

People Mover
(Excerpt from "The Brothers," *Dance to the Piper*)

Certainly, as a director of mass movement, this century has not seen his like. I have worked with many, including Reinhardt, Mamoulian, Cukor and Kazan, and I know. He surpassed in this respect by long odds D. W. Griffith, who many think invented and developed the technique of screen spectacle. The sense of rhythm, the eye for detail, the dynamic power with which he hypnotized a mob standing for hours in the open sun, kept them from sitting down, scattering, chewing gum or even growing mechanical in their response at the end of the exhausting rehearsals; his faculty for invention; his endless patience despite weather or wear to stop the whole enormous mechanism, as elaborate as an advancing army in attack, because some fool man on a balcony in the middle distance had thrown off his toga and put on his pince-nez; his courage to re-rehearse the whole scene, hearten his assistants, whip up the actors again to performance pitch and straighten out all technical difficulties before the sun dropped and the shadows changed, knowing that every five minutes the cash register ticked up thousands, were a source of never-ending astonishment to me. The power to dominate the mob came out of his guts, the very core of his nervous life. When I began to direct I recognized what went into these spectacular displays of endurance. He talked to me about it. "If one takes one's focus off the crowd for the space of even a few sentences to an assistant, if one leaves the set for five minutes, to go to the bathroom for instance, it takes an hour and a half to get the crowd back to where one broke off." I might have added from depths of my own experience, "Or if one is doubtful or afraid or uncertain." But such ideas never occurred to him in his whole career. The strength for this domination came from his undeviating belief in what he was doing and from his enormous pride of position. (35–36)

The Bull in the China Shoppe
(Excerpts from *Speak to Me, Dance with Me*)

In 1934, Cecil B. De Mille—who, for most of his niece's girlhood, had disparaged her looks, insofar as any ambition she had to appear in movies was concerned—finally gave her a chance. He was filming one of his historical spectaculars, *Cleopatra*, and he invited her to choreograph and perform a *pas de deux* in it—with a (drugged) bull. In her third memoir, published well after Cecil's death, in 1959, Agnes included an account of her hair-raising experience on the *Cleopatra* set through the reproduction of letters that she wrote to her mother at the time, followed by a coda composed decades later. In the letters, some of which are excerpted below, de Mille refers to her uncle in a variety of ways: as "The Boss," "Uncle Ce," "C.B.," and "Cecil." "Aunt Con" is a reference to Constance Adams De Mille, wife of Cecil, an erstwhile actress eight years older than her husband. "Lastex," which revolutionized corsets, is, as the *American Heritage Dictionary* puts it, "a trademark used for a yarn having a core of elastic rubber wound with rayon, nylon, silk, or cotton threads." "Ramon" is the brilliant British writer Ramon Reed, stricken as a teenager with a disease that seems to have been multiple sclerosis, which put him in a wheelchair and which eventuated in his death by his mid-20s. It was during a trip across America with Agnes that a physician cruelly raised Reed's hopes with the prospect of a cure. These hopes were dashed by new and definitive test results, an event referred to in one of the letters here. De Mille's ballet *Three Virgins and a Devil*—given its world première in 1934, in London, and taken into Ballet Theatre in 1941—follows a libretto whose story Reed adapted for her from Boccaccio.

Dearest Mum,

I'm in Bullocks Wilshire being marcel-waved.

Aunt Con met me at Pasadena with chauffeur Ulysses S. Poe and a group of newspaper photographers. They held the train while I was taken on the steps, getting off the steps, getting back on the steps, resting beside the steps. A curious ring of passengers gathered about the cameras. Imagine their disappointment when I stepped into the center of the circle.

We drove straight to the studio, Chauffeur Poe proudly pointing out the flowering lupine to me.

The Boss stopped murdering Caesar to give me one of his really best embraces. I had just time to recognize with disappointment that Calpurnia was one of the regulation de Mille cuties when he halted again, and coming up to me surveyed me from top to toe with his quizzical jeweler's eye and then said, "Lift your skirts, baby. I want to see if your legs have thickened."

Now, my legs always have been all right. I passed that test.

Then he said, "Now, when the great net is dragged up from the Nile full of naked dripping women and they extend their hands toward Antony, in their hands are shells. But what is in the shells?"

"Babies," I said.

He only just smiled. He does not like his ideas joked about. I failed test two.

"I want to do dances for the camera and not for the proscenium arch," I said rather too smartly.

"What's the difference?" he asked.

That question he failed. Our score was now even. Uncle Cecil got back to the Ides.

I don't know whether it was the lights, the excitement, the nervousness caused by his staring, but I suddenly decided if I did not go home I would probably faint. Aunt Con and I went precipitously. She stretched me out on the sofa and flung hot tea at me, coming in every so often from a children's hospital board meeting to make soothing sounds. . . .

I was really wilting but I had to wait up and get some matters settled with the Boss. He came home at his usual hour—eleven. Aunt Con had his little table before the living-room fire and his dinner hot in double boilers and his German wine cold. And I, who was both hot and cold, tried to make sense. He listened very kindly and attentively—away from the set he's a different man.

He was delighted with my ideas, or professed to be, and then I told him I would like not to do a dance of a man whipping half-naked girls dressed as leopards. He said he'd been absolutely ravished by my *Ouled Naïl*, and he wanted something like that with the bull.

I said, "But that's a belly dance from a café, a dirty, angry prostitute, spitting betel-nut juice all over the stage."

"It was pretty effective."

"In its place it was, but it would not be fit for a queen on a barge like a silver shallop, nor for Mark Antony, who'd seen a lot everywhere. He should have something mysterious and exotic dished up for him." I was thinking of Martha Graham's *Aztec Suite*, and I told him about it with fervor.

"Well, I haven't seen her Aztecs, and I have seen your desert girl."

"Oh, I should so love to do something mysterious, beautiful, new. Beautiful movement, not belly grinds and bumps. I can do those as you well know, but I do them with a point of view, not to be seductive. *Ouled* is a raging, filthy whore."

"You use strong language, baby."

"Sure, but I don't dance dirty."

"I don't want you to. Anyone can do that; that is why I sent for you from London."

"Oh Uncle Ce, we'll make history together."

"All right, baby, but some of the things that have already been done are very, very effective."

Then I said he must decide who was to be in command, LeRoy Prinz, his regular dance director, or me. He said he understood my point and would clarify later.

Aunt Constance has installed me in the west wing, where she can watch over my convalescence. Once more I look to the mountains over arbors of waving roses. Once more the tall, beautiful Norwegian Frederik serves me breakfast in the Italian patio and flatters and reminisces and gossips. This is very nice for me personally, but may not be good professionally. I enter the house as a distinguished European artist. How long will it take Uncle Ce to realize I'm only his niece? Three days? Will he recognize he's got a little nepot who can't earn a decent wage and is not certain she is the best choreographer in the world? But it's so seductive here, and such fun—and I'm so tired!

And I must save money! But I do hope I'm not making a mistake in policy.

Tuesday: The morning after I arrived I showed Ramon's medical charts to Dr. Sidney Burnap, who studied them carefully and said the disease was of too long duration to permit of any cure. The body has been invaded and taken over forever. Ramon's doppelgänger is multiple sclerosis and he must live harnessed—until his death. The illness is not progressive, but it is incurable.

This sad interview readied me for the studio, where trouble has already begun. The resident de Mille dance director is a man with the aristocratic name of LeRoy Prinz, a fibrous toughy with a Renaissance past. If he has not himself been a gangster, he has mixed with the worst in Chicago, has been taken for a Ride, has had his arm deliberately broken against the front right wheel of the car, and has witnessed more bloody, murky trafficking than most survivors. He has the quieting air of an Italian bravo and something of the gallows humor. But aside from the fact that I believe he will stop at absolutely nothing he is a likable enough guy. One of his amusements is to watch my eyes grow round at his stories of debauchery and horrid brutality, which Cecil affects to believe he invents. I believe he invents very little. He has photographs to illustrate the worst of his tales—lynched Negroes, drilled bootleggers, knifed prostitutes—and several hours, which were better spent in constructive work, have been whiled away in storytelling. But he does not let amusement or good nature dull his wits. He has survived gangsterism; he is not going to be cowed by de Mille's niece.

When I saw Prinz on the set today, he said, after elaborate greetings, that we must keep together so that he could tell me what I had to do. He also informed me that he begged Uncle Ce to send for me, that Uncle Ce did not know where to find me, and LeRoy told him London. It's transpired subsequently that I'm to do the dances I suggested, and, I think, a bacchanal in falling rose petals at the finish, though I haven't been officially given this last one yet. But I'll be called in to help, I know; LeRoy does Uncle Ce's ideas: the clams—the girls in the net fished from the Nile; a dance between a man with a whip and two women dressed as leopards; a dance in which a goat butts young naked girls around the hall. There seems to be a dearth of clothes in this dance production.

I get along beautifully with the staff. They are all cheering me on. "If only C.B. will let you," they say. Apparently they're all raring to go and they're held back only by the Boss's technique of work. He asks everyone's opinion about everybody else's business, and afterwards does what he's made a custom of doing during the last twenty years. This is the Belasco method, I've been told, and C.B. copies Belasco in very many things—the entire manner, the show for any audience around, the style, the "act." It's sort of nerve-racking for us little pros who would just like to get on with our own business. Yesterday, he asked me about Cleopatra's litter—the designer's business, surely. I told him what I thought. Then he asked everyone else on the set and eventually did what I'd suggested; it was, however, two prop boys who had convinced him.

The musician, Rapp, is cheap and commonplace, but he sighed wistfully when I told him I wanted alternating bars of 3/4 and 4/4, and two rhythms at once.

"He won't let you," he said, "and I can't have the instruments I want. But we'll see what we can put over on him."

Then there's a Russian on salary for his opinion, which is seldom heeded, who is frantic to have the dances done in an unusual way. If I can only persuade C.B. to let me have one print cut the way I want as an experiment, I know I could persuade him.

Friday: Well, Prinz this afternoon gave the Boss an ultimatum which was duly relayed to me over Cecil's midnight supper. Cecil asked me very levelly if, in the event he let Prinz go, did I think I could handle all dance movement to his satisfaction. I was not sure: to my satisfaction certainly, but not necessarily to his. He acknowledged my candor and decided to keep Prinz on.

So, we enter the job in double harness, outwardly friendly and gay.

Uncle Ce keeps a killing schedule. Up at 6:30 A.M., he has breakfast at 7 with Aunt Con in her beautiful east bedroom, the sun pouring through the climbing roses. Off in his own car at 8:00, he drives through the Paramount gate at 8:10 and is on the set between 8:30–9:00—lunches at 12:30 in the commissary. He is the only producer-director that doesn't demand a private dining room. Of course, his table is in the center and on a raised platform and all his staff sits with him.

Back on the set at 1:30—shooting until 7:00—five straight hours of the most intense concentration and unbroken responsibility. He does everything (sets every camera angle, for instance, carrying a light gauge around his neck and a portable lens. His cameramen, although the best, take instructions from him). He breaks at 7:00. Rushes—the daily laboratory prints—for an hour or so and decisions as to selection for the cutter (Ann Bauchens), who keeps right up to the daily shooting with her rough cuts. The office conferences and business decisions until 10:30. Home alone at 11 P.M.—dinner (kept hot by Aunt Con in double boilers) in front of the fire and conversation with her until 1:00 A.M. This is the time he catches up on family business, and he does. He knows about everything and cares very much. He personally locks up the whole house, speaks to the night watchman, and goes to bed. I think he reads a little before sleep. Sometimes new scripts, more often the Bible—there's one by his bedside. He never gets more than five hours' sleep.

It is a working program which would kill a young man of twenty-five. He never smokes, and he takes only a little wine, German preferably, at his late supper. He needs no exercise, for he is on his feet all day and the energy he gives out is that of a general in full battle. He amazes me. No wonder his staff calls him "Chief." And I think I understand the yes-men phenomenon. They're his protection. If he wasted energy in self-questioning, he couldn't keep up the pace. This is the unflagging zeal, the undivided strength of the prophet, the fanatic—or alternately, the absolute monarch.

They all send love constantly—most particularly Uncle Ce—

Devotedly,

A.

1010 de Mille Drive
April 13, 1934

Dearest Mum,

Things get thicker and thicker, but not, on the whole, more satisfactory. I wear my feet out tramping, tramping, tramping over the cement from the costume department to the makeup, to the music, to the business offices, to the still galleries, to the stage and back to the costumes. I suppose this is unavoidable with affairs in such confusion, but the waste of energy is distressing and exhausting.

I don't know who countermands orders, or if Cecil knows what is happening and watches to see if I can fight my way through, or whether he is too busy to notice. But I've been most deliberately served with procrastination. I've been sent to rehearse in the studio carpenter shops, where the electric saws splitting wood make it impossible to hear a piano. On my protesting strongly, I was put in an empty set (by Prinz) with no piano and no space. The costume sketches have never been prepared, the scenic designs never attempted. No music is forthcoming. I've worn myself out walking all day from one department to another, on cement walks, upstairs and down, and always I've met with great courtesy (except from the business manager, Burns, an ex-waiter, and the Boss) and always nothing had been done.

The crux of the matter is that C.B. trusts no one and does not seem to take the deciding voice with expedition and certainty. Yet he insists on okaying every single item from hairpins to the still photographs that are released for my personal publicity, also all estimates of cost. You can imagine the entailed amount of waiting. He must be shown. Cecil always has to see everything finished out and completed: every eyelash drawn on his costume sketches, every muscle, particularly muscles. And if showing him necessitates the use of drapes or props his businessman, Roy Burns, holds up all outlay until C.B.'s O.K. is obtained.

As far as the cooperation of the other subordinates is concerned, I am being treated like a beloved sister. I get willing, enthusiastic and friendly help at every hand. But the producer's attitude is not protective.

After our first talk, I have never been able to get his attention sufficiently to make him understand my ideas or get a decision. He has ignored my presence on the set, using the script girl for the setting of business or positions while I, a trained dancer, stand by offering suggestions to deaf ears. He has deferred right over my head to Prinz on everything to do with action. He has forbidden me to hire any girls for rehearsal so that I could work out and show him the dances. At the same time he has continually announced his doubts as to the suitableness and effectiveness of my projected numbers, not in private, but in front of any members of his staff who happen to be present when his fears assail him. The psychological effect on me I needn't go into, and on the staff, which has been quick to take its tune from him.

And so we come to last Monday. On Monday afternoon Ralph Jester, the designer, brought a colored girl on the stage in one of the Lastex dresses we made as an experiment. It was not a successful one, and both of us knew it. I begged him not to show the costume, but C.B. insisted, so it was exhibited. Well, he didn't like it a bit (nor did we), or the idea which had prompted me to suggest it (which we did—I wanted something that looked carved in granite, a frieze against which I would be absolutely gorgeous). He knitted his brows; he gnawed his fist; he rocked back and forth in his chair; he snapped out questions at me. What did I think the girls could do in such a rig? He could visualize nothing. I wanted to reply that if he could visualize all they were going to do there would be no need for me around. He cut short all my explanations and continued, "It has neither beauty nor richness nor seductiveness. What will they carry in their hands?"

"Nothing," I said, "they are dancers. They use their hands for dancing."

Well, he bit his lip and shook his head and his face went stone. He demanded to see what they were going to do right then and there. I said he couldn't. I hadn't had one girl to rehearse with, not even for half an hour. (They are paid for rehearsals $5.00, by the day.) Then he ordered me to have the dance ready to show him the next day. I said that was impossible. He was angry. I stood my ground.

Christ, he said, how long was he going to be kept in the dark about what I was up to? I told him he was unreasonable, that no dance director in the world would show his work without rehearsal. Well, he said, jingling the money in his pockets, come over on the barge set and tell him about what I wanted to do there. Over there, he frowned and shook his head before I had completed the first sentence. It wouldn't be effective. I said I was convinced it was excellent else I wouldn't have suggested it. He said it wasn't, and that he was the director. Maybe I'd have my chance someday. So in desperation I myself showed him the steps. "That looks rotten," said Roy Burns, who always stands at the director's elbow whenever I wish to talk to him. "It looks dangerous," said Cecil.

I thought it did, too. It was to be a carpet of naked rolling girls through which stepped daintily the bull on whose back was to be me—naked and rolling. So far have I progressed into the spirit of things.

Well, he asked everybody's ideas on the subject until someone suggested youths pole-vaulting over the back of the bull. Then he'd had enough fun with the conversation and he went off to projection. And yet he says on all occasions that Isadora Duncan and I are the only dancers who have interested him.

I told Burns to get me ten white girls the next day so that I could show the Boss what I meant. He said I could have two girls. I appealed to C.B. He said I could have two, no more (that's $10). And that I could show him any kind of a dance in the world with two girls. "And what," I asked, "if the ten girls all did different things?"

Show them to him separately and he would visualize the assembled effect.

I sat in tears of exasperation and fatigue. Ralph Jester, the designer, kneeled on the floor beside me and begged me to alter the dance to something C.B. would know how to photograph, that he simply had no conception of what I was after. I realized that as I couldn't possibly get what I wanted I must work out something quickly that would suit his needs—and his tastes. Ralph took me out to dinner and was understanding and kind. I stayed up all night and did a new dance.

A frivolous footnote to the above distressing scene was the moment when Cecil, in the middle of the argument, had suddenly yelped, "Ouch!" The leopard which lay beside Cleopatra's bed, drugged on perfume, came to and playfully closed his jaws on Cecil's calf. The beast is kept so doped we all grew careless. Only the thick leather puttee saved Ce's leg. Even so, the teeth grazed the skin. Cecil was amused, but the keeper sternly rebuked his charge and hastened to administer another large dose of Arpège.

Friday: Well, now Colbert is playing sick (or so C.B. claims—indeed she may not be playing; in fact, the poor girl may be gravely ill), but the entire company has to lay off until she is ready to work again. This illness involves a possible loss of $10,000 (as C.B. crossly and ungallantly expresses the situation, "She always was a bitch"), the complete rearrangement of the shooting schedule, and a two-day holdup—which I feel may be good for everyone's nerves. They might be more relaxed by the time we get to the barge.

Yesterday on the set, LeRoy Prinz called me over and said, "Agnes, can you find out what goes on about the barge?"

"No," I answered, "I cannot. Not anything."

"Well, shake on it," and we shook. "It's not," he continued, "as though you could call what I do dancing." ("That will be the general criticism," I almost put in, but didn't, Mom, didn't.) "But I do like to know what I'm expected to have ready."

I've made the acquaintance of the bull. He lives in the back lot, tethered in a pen. As I have always been unreasonably afraid of cows, I could see that this chore was going to present unusual tensions. At first I contented myself with hanging over the fence, making sounds that were soothing and, I hoped, bovine. But as matters have deteriorated up on the stages and workshops, I take to going to the back lot for comfort. And, yesterday, before I was aware, I was even climbing up and down his sides and leading him around (Ralph Jester had the courage and kindness to show me how). Since then I've been clinging to his enormous neck daily in a kind of animal sympathy for the strange predicament we both find ourselves in. He is a great dark tawny brute with a strangely subdued manner. It was suggested that he may be an ox. I am no expert, but as far as I can tell from a casual nonagrarian survey, he is indeed a bull, but perhaps he has been in pictures before; I think he's lost his spirit.

Yesterday, they made a camera test of me. Cecil directed. I mustn't move my head to right or left on account of my nose. I mustn't open my mouth on account of my teeth.

My bald Russian pianist (Chaliapin's accompanist, and don't you forget it) has pasted together bits of Rachmaninoff and Rimsky-Korsakov and I've finally assembled a dance. I don't believe it's very good, but like the bull, I have lost my viewpoint.

A.

Kenmore Drive, Hollywood
April 21, 1934

Dearest Mum,

Plenty has happened since last I wrote, and that's the reason I haven't written. It's like this—

I'm out of the picture. Walked out. And thank God, too! Never in all my life have I been subjected to greater rudeness, humiliation, ignominy, and indifference. Cecil has been unlike Cochran at his worst only in regard to money because, while not generous, he has been scrupulously honest.

Yesterday, the time at last came to show him the number—in full panoply, like a performance, at half-past eight in the evening, after the shooting was over. Two hours before the audition, the makeup department went into high gear. Ignoring bones and organs they started from scratch and worked up something quite new. As Cecil thought of things during the afternoon's shooting he phoned up his orders.

"Pull out her eyebrows." I was straightaway rendered as bald as an egg.

"Grease her hair black." (Roy Burns very shrewdly had withheld authorization for a wig until he learned whether or not I and my dance were to be retained.) "Change her lower lip." Two women and two men worked, sweating, in the little makeup room, with grim mouths. Suddenly the head cosmetician, a Westmore, said, "My God, the body makeup is streaked. Strip her and do it over." He looked stricken. "My God, if de Mille sees that!" The photographing, you will remember, was not to take place for another five days. This was only an audition I was being groomed for. Westmore looked up from my legs with a brown sponge in his hand. "You mustn't mind me, honey. Think of me as a doctor. This has got to be done. I'm the best at it. And there's no time."

There was a good deal of me to be repainted. The costume was extremely brief and affixed to me at strategic points by surgical tape.

"Hurry up. Send her down," came the call. The dressers moaned and swore and hurried. Their hands began to shake. I felt as though I were being prepared for an electrocution.

The costume was beautiful, eight yards of pleated white gauze that fanned around my painted legs exactly like the great skirts on any lotus girls in a sunbaked relief. The skirt was affixed to a jeweled halter around the groin; a wide, flat Egyptian collar and very large eyes completed the outfit. For obvious reasons, the collar had to be rendered immovable, and this took some doing. Three times the dressers wrenched the jewels off my resisting flesh and adjusted it anew. The third time gouts of blood sprang out all over my back and shoulders. (The trained nurse took this last taping off me. And today I had to be given treatment for second-degree burns. All's well now. I add this detail because I simply can't resist it.) But "Hurry" rang the phone. They wiped the blood away without apology and glued to fresh exposure. And I thought only of pleasing a man who found me not beautiful enough to permit the turning of my head or the opening of my mouth.

Done at last and breathing imprecations and prayers, we bundled over to the stage, where the day's shooting had just ended. Cecil sat in Cleopatra's great black marble throne at the top of a flight of steps, the Sun of Horus behind his head. On his right sat Claudette Colbert, most rebukingly lovely. On his left, the public censor to remind him not to break the decency laws. In serried ranks on either hand, behind, below, ranged the cast and staff and technical force—about fifty. Better so, I thought. Fifty is an audience. No audience I have ever faced has remained altogether unfriendly. The prop boys wheeled a Steinway grand onto the black marble floor. I walked to the end of the great hall and spread my white, winged skirt behind me. It was reflected white in the polished black marble. I knew I could walk beautifully. That's one thing I can do better than almost anyone. I can walk greatly. I started toward the throne and made the first abrupt gesture.

Twice the jeweled collar broke and I had to stop for repairs. The costume department had no conception of the strength in the muscles of a dancer's back.

During the second halt, Cecil spoke quietly through the stillness. "I think the costume department owes you an apology."

"Forgive me, darling," whispered Ralph Jester, who was working at my shoulder with safety pins.

On the third try I got through. I mounted the steps to Cecil's knees and dropped the hibiscus flower I was holding into his hand, Mark Antony's hand.

Then I waited and looked up. An audience? I have faced them in four countries, in every kind of theater, big and little, intelligent and dull, but here I faced a jury. This was a new experience. No one moved. No one breathed. No one held a thought. They all suspended, waiting; a row of plates on a shelf would have made a livelier assemblage. Suddenly, the line of disks stirred, the unfaces focused, the core, the nucleus had gathered life and moved. Like ripples on a pool they circled back the decision.

Cecil was shaking his head. "Oh, no! Oh, no!" he said very slowly. "I am so disappointed! This has nothing. It may be authentic, but it has no excitement, no thrill, no suspense, no sex."

"It had beauty," said Jester, quietly. Cecil wheeled to the censor, "Would that rouse you?"

"It sure wouldn't!" said the censor heartily.

"It wouldn't rouse me," said Cecil, "nor any man. What about the bull? What's happened to the bull?"

I was standing naked under army searchlights and angry.

"What I would like is something like the Lesbian dance in *The Sign of the Cross*," he continued.

"Boy!" said the censor, "If he hadn't had the Christians singing hymns like crazy all throughout that dance we never would have got away with it."

The dance in question was in my mind a piece of the cheapest pornography. I felt I had taken enough. I blazed. "That dance was one of the funniest exhibitions I ever saw."

"That is then precisely the kind of humor we are after, baby," said Cecil, climbing down from the throne, and then remembering, he stopped and threw back over his shoulder as he left the stage, "LeRoy Prinz, take this number and make something out of it we can photograph."

With that sentence he broke my contract. Five minutes later I was off the payroll. Thank God I have a prepaid berth to go home in.

LeRoy Prinz moaned, "Oh honey, honey, that belly dance!" Cecil also said, very levelly on the edge of the stage: "We'll have to be very careful about the press release. This could be awkward. Try not to talk, baby, until I do; you can hurt yourself."

So the announcement in the *Los Angeles Times* today read that we had disagreed over the length of my number, and that what he had in mind was a beautiful naked woman dancing sensually on the back of a milk-white bull.

And, Mom, that just wasn't true. The bull is not milk white.

In justice to the truth let me repeat that the dance is not my best. It may be lousy for all I know. I'm bewildered. He had meant to help me and I had let him down publicly. One thing I am sure of, it could have been fixed with a quiet discussion. I knew very well what he wanted, but have tried perversely to give something that interested me. Something that Martha Graham or Arnold Haskell would have praised.

Then the heavens opened and Bernie Fineman came to take me to dinner. "Good God, Agnes," he said. "You're naked! If your father could see you!"

This morning I told C.B. over breakfast that I was getting out of the picture. He said that if Prinz could not furnish the dance he wanted he would call on me again and stage the number himself. So against this contingency, I went to the studio and made up another dance which I knew was a skilled handling of what he wanted but which was also filthy. I called Jester in to watch. He said he knew it would please C.B. but he hoped to God I wouldn't do it. I told C.B. I had a dance. He's never asked to see it. I didn't think he would. He'd described the dance he wanted to a member of his staff as an orgasm, a copulation between an animal and a girl. Only he wanted it with "class" and that's why he'd sent for me.

Today, I received congratulations. "You're well out of this, Aggie. I've never seen such an exhibition in my life. He was shameful to you," said Ralph Jester.

"I'da liked to've punched his head in," said Wally Westmore, the makeup man. "The way he talked to you! That dance had sex all right. I sat up and took notice! Only it wasn't dirty. If you ask me, it was too good for him."

"You won't do it for him, will you, honey?" said the wig girl. "You won't be that vulgar. You got class."

"He wasn't fair," said the assistant director.

"The bastard!" said Bernie. "If your father had been here!"

I'm no longer in the west wing—I've left his house forever. I'm staying with Dr. Lily Campbell while I decide what to do. Write me here—

My love,
A.

Poor man, he was never to get the dance he was after. They hung my bull with silk carpets and ropes of roses and led him staggering under the too-hot lights through the path of rolling girls, while naked women pulled his ears and fondled his muzzle and rubbed against his flanks. At the height of proceedings he just shut his eyes. At no point did he show the slightest interest. "It only goes to show," said a visiting Englishman, "how good a cow is."

The next night after my fiasco, I went to the back lot in search of a pair of work shoes I'd left in the bullpen. I was alone and I hung over the rails and stared at my late partner. There he sat, darkly couched in sweet-smelling hay, giving an odor of male assurance. He quietly chewed something healthy and simple.

"Good-bye," I said, as I picked at a splinter. The tears stuck on my enormous false lashes. "And good luck with the sexy girls." He chewed and breathed out a great snuffle of warm air.

On the edge of the lot stood a young man I had known for years. "I hear there's been trouble," he said. "I've come to take you to dinner. The gang's waiting. And we've got a bottle of wine."

"You know," he put his arm around me in the car, "this is all not very important and what he said is not accurate."

I came to believe him.

The next day I took my new money and bought a very pretty dress and two fine hats, had my hair and nails done, then paraded around the Paramount stages. "How well you look!" everyone remarked. "Why, you're pretty!"

I met Roy Burns outside the commissary. "Well, so long," he jauntily said. "Good luck!"

"Roy," I answered levelly, "I came here from London a trained professional and with hits in a Charles Cochran show. I came in all eagerness, mad to please, adoring my uncle and believing in him; I have been flouted and cut off on every side deliberately. I go back without a foot of film shot. Figure out what I have cost all around and what you got for it and tell me if that's good business. And then figure out the utter wastage of talent that many people think first-class and ask yourself why."

He threw his arms around me. "Forgive me, I'm nervous. You don't know the Boss. I couldn't help myself. You're well out of this."

"Good-bye, Roy, I don't wonder you're nervous. Does anyone have any fun in this place?"

He shook his head. "I'm getting ulcers."

"Back to London!"

He kissed me. He did look regretful. He did get ulcers.

What Cecil got was not the dance he wanted.

He also got a very bad press. I don't know about the financial returns. Claudette Colbert got big stardom.

Thereafter, Cecil was always unhappy and self-conscious about this episode. He stipulated when my first book was considered for a movie that *Cleopatra* never be referred to in any way. (It hadn't been mentioned in the book.) He had sincerely wanted to help me and he had truly been very rough. Much later, after my six Broadway hits, he greeted me fulsomely with, "Baby, you are now the greatest choreographer in the world."

"No," I said. "I certainly am not, but just possibly I am one of the best paid."

"Ah, baby," he said, looking at me with great spirituality, "there's more to it than that. You must think of other aspects. You can't take it with you, you know."

Before I left Hollywood I treated myself to a superb fling with a wonderful young man. I had earned it in blood. And, although no one except he and I know anything about it, I want to say in these words, which he will probably never read, that I owe him one of the very fine times in my life—unforgettable, dazzling. (217–234).

Uncle Ce Weighs In
(Excerpt from *Empire of Dreams: The Epic Life of Cecil B. De Mille*, by Scott Eyman)

The following remarks by de Mille's Uncle Cecil were included in a letter he wrote in response to one by his brother, de Mille's father, the playwright and teacher William C. de Mille. On May 4, 1934, William wrote to his younger brother: "Very sorry you and Agnes

could not see eye to eye. Of course, there is no artist as positive as
a young artist, unless perhaps it is an old artist. I am sorry for I had
hoped she could be of real help."

I was amused by your comments relative to Agnes, but I must confess that
I was not greatly amused by Agnes. Apparently in her mind, motion picture
companies are just great big foster-fathers created for the purpose of furnish-
ing little girls with funds gratis. I was particularly sorry because of the relative
angle, which, of course, put me in a rather foolish light with the Company . . .
   (Quoted by permission of Scott Eyman)

Anna Pavlova (1881–1931)

"Pavlova"
(*Dance to the Piper*)

Anna Pavlova! My life stops as I write that name. Across the daily preoccupation of lessons, lunch boxes, tooth brushings and quarrelings with Margaret
flashed this bright, unworldly experience and burned in a single afternoon a
path over which I could never retrace my steps. I had witnessed the power of
beauty, and in some chamber of my heart I lost forever my irresponsibility. I
was as clearly marked as though she had looked me in the face and called my
name. For generations my father's family had loved and served the theater.
All my life I had seen actors and actresses and had heard theater jargon at the
dinner table and business talk of box-office grosses. I had thrilled at Father's
projects and watched fascinated his picturesque occupations. I took a propri-
etary pride in the profitable and hasty growth of "The Industry." But nothing
in his world or my uncle's prepared me for theater as I saw it that Saturday
afternoon.

   Since that day I have gained some knowledge in my trade and I recognize
that her technique was limited, that her arabesques were not as pure or clas-
sically correct as Markova's, that her jumps and *batterie* were paltry, her turns
not to be compared in strength and number with the strenuous durability of
Baronova or Toumanova. I know that her scenery was designed by second-rate
artists, her music was on a level with restaurant orchestration
definitely inferior to all the standards we insist on today, and
phy mostly hack. And yet I say that she was in her person the
theatrical excitement.

   As her little bird body revealed itself on the scene, either imr bling mystery or tense in the incredible arc which was her lift, her instep stretched ahead in an arch never before seen, the tiny bones of her hands in ceaseless vibration, her face radiant, diamonds glittering under her dark hair, her little waist encased in silk, the great tutu balancing, quickening and flashing over her beating, flashing, quivering legs, every man and woman sat forward, every pulse quickened. She never appeared to rest static, some part of her trembled, vibrated, beat like a heart. Before our dazzled eyes, she flashed with the sudden sweetness of a hummingbird in action too quick for understanding by our gross utilitarian standards, in action sensed rather than seen. The movie cameras of her day could not record her allegro. Her feet and hands photographed as a blur.

Bright little bird bones, delicate bird sinews! She was all fire and steel wire. There was not an ounce of spare flesh on her skeleton, and the life force used and used her body until she died of the fever of moving, gasping for breath, much too young.

She was small, about five feet. She wore a size one and a half slipper, but her feet and hands were large in proportion to her height. Her hand could cover her whole face. Her trunk was small and stripped of all anatomy but the ciphers of adolescence, her arms and legs relatively long, the neck extraordinarily long and mobile. All her gestures were liquid and possessed of an inner rhythm that flowed to inevitable completion with the finality of architecture or music. Her arms seemed to lift not from the elbow or the arm socket, but from the base of the spine. Her legs seemed to function from the waist. When she bent her head her whole spine moved and the motion was completed [down] the length of the arm through the elongation of her slender hand and the quivering reaching fingers. I believe there has never been a foot like hers, slender, delicate and of such an astonishing aggressiveness when arched as to suggest the ultimate in human vitality. Without in any way being sensual, being, in fact, almost sexless, she suggested all exhilaration, gaiety and delight. She jumped, and we broke bonds with reality. We flew. We hung over the earth, spread in the air as we do in dreams, our hands turning in the air as in water—the strong forthright taut plunging leg balanced on the poised arc of the foot, the other leg stretched to the horizon like the wing of a bird. We lay balancing, quivering, turning, and all things were possible, even to us, the ordinary people.

I have seen two dancers as great or greater since, Alicia Markova and Margot Fonteyn, and many other women who have kicked higher, balanced longer or turned faster. These are poor substitutes for passion. In spite of her flimsy dances, the bald and blatant virtuosity, there was an intoxicated rapture, a focus of energy, Dionysian in its physical intensity, that I have never seen equaled by a performer in any theater of the world. Also she was the *first* of the truly great in our experience.

I sat with the blood beating in my throat. As I walked into the bright glare of the afternoon, my head ached and I could scarcely swallow. I didn't wish to cry. I certainly couldn't speak. I sat in a daze in the car oblivious to the grown-ups' ceaseless prattle. At home I climbed the stairs slowly to my bedroom and, shutting myself in, placed both hands on the brass rail at the foot of my bed, then rising laboriously to the tips of my white buttoned shoes I stumped the width of the bed and back again. My toes throbbed with pain, my knees shook, my legs quivered with weakness. I repeated the exercise. The blessed, relieving tears stuck at last on my lashes. Only by hurting my feet could I ease the pain in my throat.

It is a source of sadness to me that few of our contemporary ballet dancers ever saw Anna Pavlova. At the time of which I write, her name was synonymous with the art—Pavlova, the Incomparable, was [an] internationally known slogan. She was as famous as Caruso and her position as unique. No one today approaches her power over the popular imagination. She half-hypnotized audiences, partaking almost of the nature of a divinity.

My life was wholly altered by her—so I wonder, casting about in vain for similar dazzling influences, what first drove Kaye, Alonso, Fonteyn, Toumanova and Helpmann to the barre.

Anna Pavlova was born in St. Petersburg of a Jewish mother and an unknown father, reputedly a laundress and a peasant. She was a graduate of the Imperial School and one of the last five ranking ballerinas of the Maryinsky Theater. Pavlova was the first great star to leave the Czarist confines and toured Scandinavia one summer with Adolph Bolm. They forfeited their pensions for doing so. The Scandinavians had never before seen any dancing like it.

Years later Bolm used to sit on the long Pullman jumps of his last American tour beguiling beginners like me with tales of the great days. There were dinners, banquets, torchlight processions, horses unhitched from the carriage, mobs outside the hotel windows, flowers thrown down on their heads. And in the winter, in the snows, when they went touring through the Russian provinces, trainloads of balletomanes followed them from city to city, rich and enthusiastic young men bringing their own servants and wine and horses, and in some cases furniture, along with them, and laughing with a flask of vodka in their hands and the snow matted on their fur coats, to see the darling, the great new ballerina, Anna Pavlova, rolling like a kitten in the snow, frost glinting on her dark curls, frost on her fur cap, frisking and waving her incredible little feet like deer's hoofs.

The short tour through Scandinavia gave her a taste for the outer world and in 1905 she followed Diaghilev to Paris and danced opposite Nijinsky in the initial, legendary season at the Théâtre du Châtelet. I am told their waltz in *Les Sylphides* was the lightest, most aerial and brilliant dancing ever seen by living eye. She shortly broke away, however, to become [the] star in her company and thereafter toured the world, back and forth, around and around, and never stopped.

In 1910, she came to New York partnered by the first great male star this country had ever seen, Michael Mordkin, and aroused a popular response no one this century had commanded. When she tore across the Metropolitan Opera stage that first midnight performance in *Coppélia* and then in the *Autumn Bacchanal* and *The Swan* women wept and ripped the violets out of their muffs and hurled them on the stage.

Few Americans had seen great dancing before they saw her, although they have always been responsive to foreigners. When Fanny Elssler came in the forties of the last century the members of Congress unhitched the horses of her carriage and dragged her through the capital cheering. Bonfanti, a plump, unimportant Italian, danced with acclaim at Niblo's Garden in the mid-sixties and there were a few more visiting fatties, both French and Italian, but dancing consisted mainly of skirt dancing or twiddling about on toes. In 1898, Isadora Duncan, the great revolutionist, unknown and nearly starving, left via a cattle boat to try her fortunes abroad. St. Denis, only a little less neglected, followed soon after. They did not return for a long time and not until after their reputations had been firmly established in Paris and London. When they came back years later, their influence within their craft proved deep, lasting and incalculably productive. Under their leadership the dance once more was put to high purpose. But they never commanded the audience that flocked to see Pavlova.

When she had gone back to the mysterious regions whence she came, and the memory of her was less immediate and more indulgent, I turned to action. It seemed imperative that we give dance pageants. I summoned the gang and announced this to them. I don't think it particularly relevant to remark that not one of us had dancing lessons. We wrote down a program on a piece of yellow paper and informed my mother how many costumes we should need, and the date of the performance—eight days later to be precise. With remarkable ingenuity and a minimum of purchase my mother coped, and very creditable and suitable little outfits they turned out to be, although the assembling cost her many weary walks, up and down hill in the neighborhood. "Have you got anything around the house that my child could wear as an Egyptian crown of the middle dynasty?" she would say, sinking into a chair and sipping a welcome cup of tea as Aunt Mildred Smith leaned forward all breathless eagerness to sacrifice any part of her furnishings or wardrobe, her dear face puckered in consideration. From Aunt Mildred Smith she got three deerskin rugs to clothe the shepherds in the Pastorale.

The dance program or pageant was performed under the banana tree in the back yard. The audience (ten- and fifteen-cent admissions) sat in the lee of the house. Mother stayed upstairs frantically changing the little girls. Since Anna Pavlova always began her *divertissements* with a Slavic folk dance, I accordingly opened with a polka, presumably of Polish origin, in an Italian dress borrowed from Luigina and a great wreath made of real poppies and straw about the size and consistency of a partridge nest. There followed minuets, shepherd dances, Ruth St. Denis's yogi dance, St. Denis's Japanese geisha, a Duncan finale with tossed oranges and a classic *pas de deux* done on point in unblocked shoes on the grass. (I could stay on point, with pain, of course, only as long as I walked in the grass.) There was also a sea nymph danced by Eleanor Worthington, a dazzlingly pretty child, who hadn't given a thought to anything but her costume before running out on the lawn, but whose beauty elicited audible pleasure from the audience. This made me mad. It was the first time I had run up against biology in my professional life and I found it unreasonable.

Aunt Mildred Smith sat in a corner by the fuchsia bush with a small portable Victrola and a catholic selection of records. There having been no music or dress rehearsal, some strain was entailed during performance as I shot her signals from mid-stage. At any mistake, all action suspended and the aggregate stare of the cast turned on her in angry dismay until she grasped what was wanted next. At afternoon's close she confessed the need of a strong cup of tea.

Since Mother refused lessons, all I learned about dancing I learned through reading and looking at pictures. I cut out photographs of every dancer I could find and pasted them in a scrapbook. The Diaghilev Ballets Russes came to Los Angeles. Mother went and even had supper with them, afterwards, mentioning it to me in an offhand way when the week was nearly up. It seems she had been seated next to a very nice gentleman named Adolph Bolm who was interested to hear her little girl liked to dance. I was as staggered as though she had casually announced breakfast with the President of the United States. I set up a clamor to be taken to every remaining performance. But they were at night and of course I couldn't stay up for them. Besides, Mother said, they were very disappointing, full of silly things. The Butterfly in *Carnaval* wore white kid gloves, idiotically enough, with blue ribbons on her wrists. And there was something about *Afternoon of a Faun* which was, morally speaking, not quite fine. However, we were all taken to the Saturday matinee. *Sylphides* proved exquisite. Mother said if she had known they could do graceful and pretty things like this, she would have taken us more often. She urged me to look at all the colors and costumes in *Schéhérazade*, hoping no doubt that the point of the piece would escape me. She was quite right. I grew so confused by the concentric circles of the debauchees, the platters of fruit, the turbans and the glitter, that I lost track about why the Shah got so mad at his wife that he killed everyone within reach. That afternoon I saw Nijinsky. I have nothing to say of that. He whirled and moved his head like a cat and the audience applauded. I was too young to know what I was looking at.

I saw Duncan shortly after. She likewise held no interest for me. A fat, cross-eyed woman in dull costumes made of material like portieres, she resembled not one little bit Anna Pavlova. Mother explained that the reason she looked so sad was because her little children had been drowned in an automobile accident. Mother said she found her dull too, but I noticed she sat with the tears streaming down her cheeks as she watched. "Why are you crying?" I asked. "I don't know," said Mother, "this dance is very long" (it was an entire Beethoven symphony) "but I can't bear to think of her losing her children." Isadora came before the curtain at the end and urged us all to run barefoot over the hills. I did the next afternoon, and Mother sat for some time picking cactus spines out of me.

But when the plays and pageants were done, when Mother's friends had stopped talking and had gone home filled with her tea and cookies, when the costumes were put away, then what? Then I spent an evening twisting before the truth. My dance pageants were only makeshifts. Father came home to dinner and talked of the real theater. His work went on and on, month by month, undisturbed by these nursery flurries. I wanted so much to study. I wanted to be part of a real professional company where grown-ups worked. But Mother and Father were obdurate; Father did not wish me to get involved any further with dancing. And Mother, living in an age where self-expression was considered paramount, was afraid of the stultifying effect of training. It was then the proudest boast a mother could make—"Entirely self-taught, my dear, never had a lesson in her life."

Once Ruth St. Denis was invited to the house to look me over. With gigantic *sang-froid* I performed one of her own dances for her. She paid me the serious compliment of growing exasperated, kicked off her shoes and sat on the carpet beside me going through the entire routine twice correctly. She then left recommending that I be trained at once, preferably in her own school. But it came to nothing. St. Denis and Shawn, however, grew to be devoted and close friends of my parents. Father repeatedly said that, although dancers, they were very intelligent people indeed. But he refused to attend a single performance.

Matters might have gone on this way for years if my sister's arches hadn't providentially fallen. She was taken to a great orthopedist who advised, of all things, ballet dancing. He advised it for her, not for me, but what one sister did in our family the other always shared. We went straight away to the Theodore Kosloff School of Imperial Russian Ballet. (42–50)

"The Swan"
(*Dance to the Piper*)

Pop was too smart to forbid me outright to continue with my chosen work. He knew that direct frontal attack would only serve to crystallize my determination; he bored from within. He sought to make me doubt the validity of the art itself. And I listened to him in anguish because he was an artist, in my eyes—a genius. He counted on this deference. He refused to go to my classes, to go to any performance of dancers, to read about them or look at pictures. At mention of any incident in the ballet school and the daily doings there, ice would form on his mouth and he would sit silently sipping his cocktail until the subject had been dropped.

Occasionally we settled right down and talked problems through. One night in his study with brandy in one hand and a cigar in the other, he asked quietly, "Do you honestly think, my daughter, that dancing has progressed since the time of the Greeks?"

"No," I replied snappily. "Do you think you write any better than Euripides?" That ought to hold him, I figured.

He looked at me long and slow. "No, my dear," he said, "but we have Euripides's plays. They have lasted. A dancer ceases to exist the minute she sits down."

As Father spoke I understood death for the first time. I was a child of fourteen but I realized with melancholy that oblivion would be my collaborator no matter how fine my work. Mankind had never developed a reliable way of recording dances. Well—so much the worse for me. I was born a dancer.

Those days when I was called upon to dance in school plays I froze with inhibition. What if I should reveal myself as not truly great? I never showed off any more for Mother's guests. Showing-off also meant exposing. I sought refuge in study and daydreaming, and unconsciously all my private extracurricular resources led to the unnamable goal.

Uncle Cecil had a fine reference library in which he gave me permission to browse whenever I liked. So on Saturday afternoons when I was free from study, I used to walk up through the beautiful gardens and sit in the large room with the mullioned windows among his trophies, suits of armor and knives, silverwork, French battle flags, the Crown of Thorns on a red velvet pillow, and pore over the extraordinary volumes of old prints—Shakespeare, Doré—the entire portrait gallery of Versailles. How quiet and enriching those afternoons were to me! Hollywood lay below sparkling, here and there [a] window reflecting fire in the late day, the Italian cypress blackening in the lucent air. The garden suddenly intensified as it always does before dark, all the odors breathing out more poignantly with anticipatory pungent chill exhaling from the leaves, the great sky deepening and streaming with banners and banks of fire. And all of these, the Italian garden, the Renaissance sky, the glint on the armor and the warm radiance cast by the blood-red curtains and the bowls of Uncle Cecil's dark roses, as I sat bowed over the books attempting to learn and memorize forever every detail of every costume, filled me with an enormous sense of excitement and latent power. I felt in truth I should amount to very much. The high excitements of the Renaissance were present again—whom might I not meet at the turn of the road or come upon standing in the garden as I went home through the dew? What had the great nights following upon other great baroque sunsets meant to these men and women under my hands? What pomp? What daring? What clashing of lives? What might the night mean to me who was alive, not dead, and very young and ready?

The night meant supper, trigonometry and bed at nine o'clock. Or just possibly a corner movie with Margaret and Rita, the housemaid, in attendance.

About this time, Anna Pavlova came back. I heard of the return with a mixture of excitement and dread. What if she was not as I remembered her? What if I looked at her and saw her as Father would see her? I knew a great deal more about technique now; I would look at her with a critical eye.

Mr. Kosloff, Miss Fredova and the leading girls of the studio went on opening night. I was not permitted to go, of course, until the matinee. "Watch carefully," I said to the girls after class. "Tell me everything. Every little detail." And the next time when I was in the studio I fairly gasped my curiosity, "How was she?"

Miss Fredova spoke with moderation. "Well, of course, there is only one Anna Pavlova. She is very graceful and lovely, but there is something not quite in order with her knees. And the joint of her right foot has enlarged with all this touring. Mr. Kosloff was very sorry to see that."

"Does she show signs of growing older?"

"Oh my, yes, how could it be otherwise?"

"She does not dance so perfectly as she used to?"

"Oh my goodness, no. She probably has not had the time to practice her barre carefully every day. And then—she is getting older. Still, she is very lovely."

My heart felt like iron.

We were excused from school for the Thursday afternoon matinee. I ate scarcely any lunch. I saw to it that we were in our seats twenty minutes before the curtain rose, Mother's first experience of the kind. The ballet was *Autumn Leaves* composed by Madame herself to music by Chopin. The curtain went up on a park scene. Two slim girls ran out chased by the autumn wind in a blue wig, and were whirled to the floor. Volinine played a poet with his left foot pointed behind and his right well turned out, showing that he was saddened by the indifference of his lady love who was paying him no mind in *demi contretemps* and *jetés battus*. He grew more and more disconsolate and finally sank on a bench in a *fondu*. This was plain ham, but I turned to Mother with glistening eyes. "It's wonderful, isn't it."

"Hmm," said Mother. I waited.

She came on. What did she do? Does it matter? She was gone. The audience stirred. She was back and dancing. Right there in front of me in flesh and nerve. Oh, holy life! How could I have doubted her? She changed us while we sat there that Thursday afternoon; she made us less daily. I don't know what she did. I know and remember what she meant. The upturned face, the waiting listening face, the exposed heart, the shared rapture.

A friend touched my shoulder. "Would you like to meet her? I know her well." Mother answered for me. I was unable to speak. "She would. Yes." We filed backstage. I remember the dress I wore, dark blue silk taffeta, my first silk dress. I had a little blue hat to match with petals that curled up against the crown. My sister was an exact replica two sizes smaller. Madame had finished the program with a Russian dance. She stood in full Boyarina costume in the dressing room talking to friends. She spoke in light, twittering sounds and her dark eyes flashed incessantly with enormous alertness and inner excitement. Her clawlike hands played nervously with the pearls at her throat. They were the veined hands of an old woman or of an instrumentalist. I noticed her insteps jutting up under the straps of her buttoned slippers. The rocky arch was like a bird claw. There seemed to be no flesh on the foot; it was all bone and tendon. The toe was clubby, broadened and coarse. Her little thin shoulders lifted from the gathered peasant blouse. What was gross had been burnt and wasted off her. She had kept no part of her body that was not useful to her art, and there was about her the tragic aura of absolute decision. The high pale brow, her front against the world, the somber eyes, the mobile lips shut with humorous tolerance on God knows what tumult and violence caged within the little skull, marked her as one apart. She had the fascination of a martyr. We drew aside and looked at her with both reverence and relief, smug in our own freedom. Possibly I am reading back into her face the wisdom of my own bitterness learned later. Possibly as a girl I saw only the glory. But I think not. I knew enough to understand the cost of the beauty she achieved and to be terrified at the price.

"This is Kosloff's best pupil," said my friend, pushing me forward. An exaggeration, of course, but I was incapable of speech. Kosloff had undoubtedly presented his own candidate nights before.

"Ah! Brava! Brava!" chirped Madame. "Would you like some flowers?" She tore a handful of pink carnations and cherry blossoms from a basket that had just been handed to her across the footlights. Then she leaned down and kissed me. Anna Pavlova kissed me.

I wept.

Someone led me kindly from the room, maybe Mother. Someone stood beside me and lent me a pocket handkerchief while I fought to regain control of myself among the hurrying stagehands. Someone helped me into the car and asked no questions. I was weeping silently by this time.

"Well," said Margaret, "I must say I don't see what there is to cry about."

"Be quiet!" said Mother with the greatest severity I had ever heard her use in addressing my little sister.

When we reached home I ran through the garden without stopping to take off my coat and threw myself on the ground under the orchard trees.

O Father in Heaven make me worthy!

I kept the flowers she gave me for ten years in a box, shaming myself at last into throwing the little mummies away. Dear Madame, she kissed all the little girls that were brought backstage to her, gave them all flowers and altered their lives. One out of every dozen dancers of my generation has confessed to the same experience. This does not make it any less impressive—more so, I should say. She was an apostle. She had the power of conversion. That it may have come in time to seem a touch routine to members of her company does not mitigate the miracle. The recipients bear stigmata.

She returned again three years later, her last tour. By this time, my taste and judgment were forming. I looked with a professional eye. She had begun to develop real crotchets and mannerisms. For example, she held each pose until she got applause like a circus performer. It was this abominable trick that led one of our ablest critics to call her an acrobat. She roughhoused and savaged the music for any effect she wished. And the choreography—oh God, the choreography! Her own inventions, *California[n] Poppy*, *Autumn Leaves*, *Blue Danube Waltz*, were probably the silliest and most tasteless items I have ever seen. She was incapable of creative imagination. And in the dances tailored for her, the Gavotte, *Coquetteries of Columbine*, *Don Quixote*, *Dragonfly*, she made use over and over again of a barren string of five ballet steps. I sat shocked. But then, after folding the orange silk petals of the poppy about her head and flopping over sideways to simulate sleep, she began to take bows and therewith performed a theatrical miracle. While bowing, not while dancing, she built a paltry hand to bravos and calls. She was known for this enchanted teasing; no one else has ever approached her technique in curtain calls. The applause never diminished. It rose instead to climactic screaming. The applause was purely for her, not so much for what she did. At the end of three bows, the audience had fallen in love.

Among these idiot pieces were three important works—*The Bacchanal*, *The Swan*, and *The Indian Suite*, the first choreography of an eighteen-year-old Hindu named Uday Shankar. Everyone has seen pictures of her in *The Bacchanal*, composed in 1904 by Fokine. She wore her hair fuzzed out in black curls, grapes over the ears, and a white tunic flecked with red. Her partner's arm about her, she entered skipping, the knees working like pistons to the chest and the feet driving through the earth. The dancers carried over their heads a scarlet veil, and the man held a large bunch of red paper roses with which he pelted her. Occasionally, she chewed a paper rose with her teeth. Corn? Thunder and fire. The working knees, the feet tearing the earth, the wild glance, the flamelike thrust and contraction of her back, the abandoned arms, her body broken and contorted on his thigh, the exhausted flame against the earth as he stood over her, the head moving, moving, in restless joy, the hands torn, stretching, fainting, unresting. Oh ancient ecstasy, passion beyond promise!

She danced *The Dying Swan*. Everyone had danced *The Swan*. What was it? A series of *pas de bourrées* around and around the stage with flutterings and undulations of the arms interspersed with broken staggers until the final collapse and folding away. Nothing else. Fokine composed it in half an hour for a charity performance, and it is probably the most famous solo in the history of dancing. When she trembled onto the stage it was a death agony, the voice in the dark, the final anonymous cry against annihilation. And when she lay doubled up and the last shudder passed through feathers and broken bones, drawing as an afterbeat when all was finished the shivering inert hand across her face in a gesture of final decency, everyone sat stricken. Death was upon each of us.

Death came to Anna Pavlova in 1931, when she was fifty. She had not stopped touring for a single season. Her knees had sustained some damage, but she would not rest, and she was in a state of exhaustion when the train that was carrying her to Holland was wrecked. She ran out into the snow in her nightgown and insisted on helping the wounded. When she reached The Hague she had double pneumonia. Her last spoken words were, "Get the *Swan* dress ready."

Standing on Ninth Avenue under the El, I saw the headlines on the front page of the *New York Times*. It did not seem possible. She was in essence the denial of death. My own life was rooted to her in a deep spiritual sense and had been during the whole of my growing up. It mattered not that I had only spoken to her once and that my work lay in a different direction. She was the vision and the impulse and the goal.

Her death touched off a worldwide hysteria among adolescent girls that is without precedent. Several young dancers identified themselves so completely with the star as to believe in fact that her soul had transmigrated into their own bodies. Each one felt that she had got the original or genuine soul and looked upon the other claimants as impostors. One poor girl went into a decline, shut herself in her room and refused to eat. She finally pressed confusion to the point where she failed to note the legal difference between Pavlova's dances and her own and wound up in a Paris law court with Madame's exceedingly angry husband and a dozen of Madame's indignant colleagues pointing it out. The Paris press had a bean feast.

Nor was this odd mania confined to mere fools. Alicia Markova, one of our two greatest living classic dancers, believes that Pavlova's spirit takes possession of her body when she dances and has said so many times, and despite the merciless teasing of her colleagues—"The spirit is doing fine tonight, eh, Alicia?"—persists in the belief and draws reaffirmation and comfort from it.

"It is doing fine, isn't it?" she says with perfect sweetness, flirts out her tutu and runs back on stage to dance peerlessly.

Pavlova's ashes were laid in the Golder's Green cemetery near her home, Ivy House, Hampstead Heath. All the glory of the last great Imperial days stood by. Karsavina was there, Lopokova, Massine.

But also in New York, in Los Angeles, in Paris, Berlin, Rome, San Francisco, wherever there was a Russian Orthodox Church, the dancers gathered, those that knew her and many more that didn't. I went in New York and all the dancers of the city were there. My mother came. She said she wished to, that she owed her a debt of many hours of joy. We stood. The Russians held lighted candles; the choir chanted with a high tonal insistency that wore down like rain on rock. The priest passed in and out of his painted, holy screens. A friend leaned to me. "They are singing," she whispered. "Receive the soul of Anna. Cherish our Anna. Bless and protect Anna." But I put my handkerchief to my mouth and heard the drums and the beating of feet and the cries she gave as she leaped. At the conclusion of the service, Fokine as senior friend, colleague, and Russian, received our condolences. He knew very few of us. We walked up silently, strangers, and shook his hand. His wife, Vera Fokina, in black from head to foot with sweeping veils, stood beside him.

We went out into the day. Wherever Pavlova had passed, hearts changed, flames sprang in the grass and girls ran out to a strange, wild, ancient dedication.

(72–79)

Theodore Kosloff (1882–1956)
(Excerpts from "The Kosloff School," *Dance to the Piper*)

Theodore Kosloff graduated in 1901 from the Moscow Imperial Theater School. He danced briefly with Diaghilev's Ballets Russes in its inaugural year, 1909, and was brought to Los Angeles the same year by the dancer Gertrude Hoffman, for whom he staged several dances. After touring one of the vaudeville circuits, he was hired as an actor in the silent films of Cecil B. De Mille and continued to perform in and choreograph for the movies. Among the students in his L.A. school was Cecil B. De Mille's niece Agnes de Mille, who, like her father, spelled her name with a lower-case "d." Kosloff's two assistants at the school were the British dancer Vera Fredova, née Winifred Edwards, who would go on to be an important teacher at the school of The Royal Ballet, and Winifred Hudnut, who, renamed Natacha Rambova, eventually married Rudolph Valentino. Kosloff took on Agnes and Margaret de Mille as pupils who—owing to "courtesy to Uncle Cecil"—paid nothing for tuition "for as long or as often as we wished to go to his school."

When I first saw Kosloff he was naked in feathers, leaning on a feathered spear. He had painted himself horned eyebrows in the Russian Ballet style, and his gestures were real classic pantomime, involving clenched fists and the whites of the eyeballs, a positive style which gave the camera something substantial to focus on. Here was passion and here certainly was sincerity in amounts. Every expression was performed with a force that could have carried him across the room and over the wall. I was awestruck. I went home and doubled the number of kneebends I performed every night before bed. . . .

I gave my audition in a bathing suit. Kosloff himself put me through the test. He did not say how talented I was or how naturally graceful. He said my knees were weak, my spine curved, that I was heavy for my age and had "no juice." By this he meant, I came to learn, that my muscles were dry, stubborn and unresilient. . . . We were sent off to buy blocked toe slippers, fitted right to the very ends of our toes, and to prepare proper practice dresses.

The first lesson was a private one conducted by Miss Fredova. Miss Fredova was born Winifred Edwards and had received her training in London from Anna Pavlova. She was as slim as a sapling and always wore white like a trained nurse. She parted her dark hair in the center and drew it to the nape of her neck in glossy wings, Russian style. She was shod in low-heeled sandals. She taught standing erect as a guardsman, and beat time with a long pole. First she picked up a watering can and sprinkled water on the floor in a sunny corner by the barre. This she explained was so that we should not slip. Then she placed our hands on the barre and showed us how to turn out our feet ninety degrees from their normal walking stance into first position. Then she told us to *plier* or bend our knees deeply, keeping our heels as long as possible on the floor. I naturally stuck out behind. I found the pole placed rigidly against my spine. I naturally pressed forward on my insteps. Her leg and knee planted against my foot curbed this tendency. "I can't move," I said, laughing with winning helplessness.

"Don't talk," she said. "Down-ee, two-ee, three-ee, four-ee. Down the heels, don't rock on your feet."

At the end of ten minutes the sweat stuck in beads on my forehead. "May I sit down?" I asked.

"You must never sit during practice. It ruins the thigh muscles. If you sit down you may not continue with class." I of course would have submitted to a beating with whips rather than stop. I was taking the first steps into the promised land. The path might be thorny but it led straight to Paradise. "Down-ee, two-ee, three-ee, four-ee. *Nuca.* Give me this fourth position. Repeat the exercise."

So she began every lesson. So I have begun every practice period since. It is part of the inviolable ritual of ballet dancing. Every ballet student that has ever trained in the classic technique in any part of the world begins just this way, never any other. They were dreary exercises and I was very bad at them but these were the exercises that built Taglioni's leg. These repeated stretches and pulls gave Pavlova her magic foot and Legnani hers and Kchessinska hers. This was the very secret of how to dance, the tradition handed down from teacher to pupil for three hundred years. A king had patterned the style and named the steps, the king who built Versailles. Here was an ancient and enduring art whose technique stood like the rules of harmony. . . .

I bent to the discipline. I learned to relax with my head between my knees when I felt sick or faint. I learned how to rest my insteps by lying on my back with my feet vertically up against the wall. I learned how to bind up my toes so that they would not bleed through the satin shoes. But I never sat down. I learned the first and all-important dictate of ballet dancing—never to miss the daily practice, hell or high water, sickness or health, never to miss the barre practice; to miss meals, sleep, rehearsals even but not the practice, not for one day ever under any circumstances, except on Sundays and during childbirth. . . .

The plain truth is I was the worst pupil in the class. Having grown into adolescence feeling that I was remarkably gifted and destined to be great (I remember a friend asking Mother, "But do you want her to be a professional dancer?" and Mother's cool reply, "If she can be a Pavlova—not otherwise"), I now found I could not hold my own with any of the girls standing on the floor beside me. So I crept about at the rear of the group, found matters wrong with my shoes, with my knees, with my hair, resorted to any device to get away from the dreadful exposure.

Furthermore, the Kosloff method of teaching rather accentuated my dilemma. The accent was placed on force and duration instead of harmony. He was intent on disciplining the feet and legs, and paid almost no attention to the co-ordination of arms and facial expression. The girls grew as vigorous as Cossacks, leaping prodigiously, whirling without cease, flailing and thrashing as they went and contorting their necks and faces in a hideous effort to show the master how altogether hell-bent for beauty they were. The exercises he devised were little miracles of perverse difficulty, muscle-locking gut-busters, all of them. I have never since seen healthy girls faint in class, but in Kosloff's class they went down quite regularly and were dragged off with their heels bumping on the floor behind them. Kosloff barely stopped counting. He used to sit in a great armchair facing the room, stamping and roaring, whacking a cane in measure to the music. In the corner sat the man with the balalaika barely audible through the noise. All the girls adored the master and gladly fainted for him. It was Miss Fredova, however, who gave me my private lessons, quietly, patiently, kindly. Kosloff occasionally walked in, looked for a minute, said, "No juice, no juice. More *plié*. Do you know? More expression, more sowl," grinned suddenly with Tartar glee and lost interest. "Don't be discouraged," said the angel Fredova, "I wish though you could practice more regularly." . . .

At Christmas there was a table covered with gifts, photographs for the first year pupils, gold pins for the second year, and pins with additional diamonds and wreaths and bars for the veterans. We were called out singly by name and given our gift. We then made a reverence, said "thank you" in Russian and retired. Kosloff kept open house on Christmas with magnificent Russian food and boundless Russian welcome.

There were books on a side table in the studio filled with pictures of the great ballerinas. We pored over them between classes. As I stood shifting from one weary foot to the other trying to ease my cramped muscles, Miss Fredova used to tell about Legnani, the great Italian ballerina, who brought the *fouetté* pirouette to Russia—how a ruble used to be placed on the floor and a circle drawn around it—how she placed the toe of her left foot in this mark and then performed sixty-four consecutive *fouetté* pirouettes, stopping in perfect fifth position, the toe of her left foot exactly in the ruble mark; how her turnout was so extraordinary that she could balance a glass of wine on the flat of her instep as she revolved in second position—how her balance was so peerless that she could perform a complete adage, thirty-two measures long, standing in the middle of the floor on one point without support of any sort. "Will I be able to do this?" I asked breathlessly. "I doubt if you will be that good," she said smiling. "Oh," I sighed with deep disappointment, not realizing that no one else has ever been able to duplicate this feat, not realizing that it is unlikely indeed that Legnani herself performed it. But the legend spurred me on. "*Nuca*," said Miss Fredova, "give me this one pirouette and stop in some recognizable position." (52–61)

Adolph Bolm (1884–1951) and Louis Horst (1884–1964)
(Excerpt from "The Profession," *Dance to the Piper*)

At the end of the summer, Adolph Bolm invited me to be a guest soloist on his autumn tour. I was to replace Ruth Page and perform three of my own pieces, an agreeable arrangement. The company numbered about fifteen and there was a small orchestra conducted by Louis Horst.

Bolm had been the great character dancer of the original Diaghilev season in Paris. He had created leading roles in *Prince Igor*, *Thamar*, *Sadko*, *Carnaval*, and had followed Nijinsky in *Schéhérazade*, *Le Pavillon d'Armide*, and *Petrouchka*. In 1916, he had come to America with the troupe, and when the company returned to Europe stayed and took over the Metropolitan Opera Ballet and subsequently the Chicago Opera. He formed his "Ballet Intime" and toured with the Barrère Little Symphony, later making an extensive trip through South America and the States with Ruth Page as his leading dancer. For some years prior to the time I joined him, he had been established in Chicago, teaching and directing. His tour was an annual event.

The one I participated in was his last. He was once a great dancer, but had never been, I believe, a very great choreographer. Age, family responsibilities and the dreadful wear and tear of his profession had raveled him to loose ends. At the time I met him, he seemed incapable of coping with the distracting responsibilities of management. And with all the good will in the world, real kindliness and the reinforcement of his incomparable training, he achieved something always just short of his dreams.

So many of the great Russians have gone through this pathetic cycle. Cradled and reared in the enormous organization of their theater, served by the best minds of their generation, they were dismayed to find, on being set free, how much was achieved by the collaboration of others and how childishly helpless they had suddenly become. After Diaghilev's death, the Russian ballet fell completely to pieces and the performers wasted in scattered confusion for five whole years until Massine reorganized them. The stars' predicament was compounded by a haughtiness bred into them, a complete contempt for any other form of dancing which is the hallmark of the Russian Imperial Ballet School; no, let me be more exact—of any European ballet school whatsoever.

This haughtiness was a shield, I believe, for his dismay and bafflement. He had been given all the golden opportunities the United States had to offer— and here he was, inexplicably, with an ill-assorted group of pupils on a second-string tour. His great heart was breaking a little.

He was a warm, passionate man with a true paternal feeling for his charges. They were devoted to him, but that didn't make them dancers to be proud of.

What a sight he was, standing on the station platform, while the porter assembled the packages and boxes of his mongrel company. And the company, tired and chattering, struggled behind and drew lots for their berths. (The electrician and carpenter did not draw lots; they got lowers, by contract. My salary as solo star was fifteen dollars a week more than the carpenter's. But time has worked readjustments since then. The carpenter now gets considerably more than the soloists.) In Chicago, Des Moines, Louisville, Montgomery, Hollins, Macon, Pittsburgh, Bolm stood on the platform, his neck scarf loose, his shapeless felt hat pushed back from his waving hair, the sweat on his forehead still damp from haste and confusion, urging us to collect and trying to recall what he'd surely himself forgotten. He watched us half with affection, half with disappointment.

This should have been the Diaghilev company and they should be at the Gare du Nord. What dreary sequences and decrescendos had replaced Karsavina, Nijinsky, Pavlova, Rubinstein, Lopokova with Hattie, Tottie, Daisy and Bill? "The King of Spain . . ." he said, as the train started to jog, and the outskirts of some city slid by with its Negro slums, gasworks, and foundries lit up in frightening blue revelations. He dashed his hat on the seat opposite and put his arm in fatherly expansion around a ballet girl who cuddled, munching an oversize chocolate bar. His superb large mouth with the sensitive sensual lips curved in a smile of luxurious reminiscence. "The King of Spain led the cheering. That was in the bull ring in Madrid. There was no theater in the city large enough to house the audience." In Macon, Georgia, forty-five tickets had been sold in an auditorium seating four thousand. "For God's sake," said Bolm to me in the afternoon, "you are a university woman, call up the colleges and music schools and tell them this is art—this is culture—that they should come to see it."

In Paris, the opening night of *Prince Igor*, the audience had stormed right up over the footlights and carried him on their shoulders to his dressing room. He was so overcome by the violence of his performance, the intoxication of their response, that all he could do was lie back on a couch and gasp for breath. "Do you think," he said, turning to Louis Horst, "that the Pittsburgh management will ever pay what they owe?"

"No," said Louis, looking up from his detective story, "I don't."

"It will all come out of my pocket then," said Bolm, "the company salaries."

We had given the Pittsburgh performance in an atmosphere of rage, desperation, disappointment and contempt. He naturally refused to do any solos. His costumes went right back in the trunk unused. He never performed any solos where the audience was not large or responsive, and as his first solo preceded mine and I watched the stage manager repacking his white satin tunic, I knew exactly what to expect from the front. "Save yourself," he said to me, as I did *relevés* in the wings to warm up my feet, "save yourself, don't throw yourself away. They haven't the faintest idea what you're doing."

"I don't suppose one could get a cup of coffee on this train at night? Naturally not," Bolm would continue, rolling his head against the sooty velours of the seat. "We always had such superb suppers after our galas—the Princesse de Polignac, Gabrielle Chanel, the Aga Khan, Lady Cunard. My dear, I will reconsider and have some of your chocolate bar if you don't mind."

He wandered around the car on the long day jumps, talking to this pair of girls and that, talking in Russian to Vera Mirova, the other guest soloist, coming back to where Louis sat trying to reinforce my aesthetics.

As an antidote for this *Cherry Orchard* atmosphere, Louis Horst talked of Duncan, of Mary Wigman in Germany, and of a young dancer, Martha Graham, who he believed would one day be good; he talked for hours and hours.

I had brought on tour a suitcase the size of a small trunk, and Louis helped me with it. Louis also helped me with finding hotels and places to eat. Nobody else did, and I plainly knew none of the ropes. Whatever town we came to Louis knew the best hotel, the best restaurant. He'd been there before. No matter where we went, he'd been there before.

I was not the first person he'd helped, nor the last. In the course of time, he has accompanied Ruth St. Denis (for twelve years), Ted Shawn, Ruth Page, Doris Niles, Martha Graham, Doris Humphrey, Charles Weidman, Harald Kreutzberg, Helen Tamiris and me. He has taught and composed for very nearly every concert dancer in the business. He has given all of us advice. More, reassurance and comfort and when need arose, money. Over the years he has influenced and helped the dancing in this country more than any other nondancer, with the possible exception of John Martin and Lincoln Kirstein. The long talks he had with us worked like yeast in our creative thought.

Louis was a very large man, in appearance a cross between Silenus and a German Micawber. His hair had turned prematurely white which made him look old. He always sought to give the impression of a satyr, but he seemed to me from the first fatherly and kind. I've no doubt he will be outraged by this statement. Louis went traveling in a flat peaked tweed cap rather larger than a tam-o'-shanter. His overcoat was vast; his neck scarf long. He carried a music case and a bag which contained one dress suit, the nightly necessaries and a supply of paperbound detective stories. He read one a day and he seldom read anything else. He had read good books in his youth, he said, and remembered. He never practiced, but an hour and a half before concert time he would try the keyboard and fuss with difficult passages, singing quite loudly to encourage himself. He sang throughout the recital and the alert ear could hear him through the playing. Since he never practiced, it followed he played many wrong notes, but these were of no consequence. Any delicately fingered passage he simply grabbed by the handful and tossed out of his way. He kept the beat and his beat was infallible, his pulse being in fact truer than the performer's.

When his piano constituted the only musical accompaniment, he arranged the instrument in the wings so that he had a clear view of the stage, hanging his coat over the back of his chair and playing in waistcoat and shirt sleeves. When everything was over, he put on his coat for the bow at the end, and then took it right off again and packed it. He turned his own music and gave every curtain cue and light direction. In short, he ran the stage from the keyboard. In between dances, he quietly read the detective story he kept propped on the music rack. On the Bolm tour he found very regretfully he couldn't read because he was on the podium.

When I first saw him sitting with bowed head before a concert, I surmised he was communing with his inner conscience—pulling himself together as I always did. I was very touched at the spectacle of the white-headed man sitting so quietly, meditating, and went up to him and put my hand on his shoulder. He leered at me; there was an Erle Stanley Gardner between the pages of the Scarlatti. (120–125)

La Argentina (1890–1936)
(Excerpt from "The Profession," *Dance to the Piper*)

I managed to procure a seat at the top of Carnegie and saw a lone woman take the stage accompanied by a single female pianist and dance a whole evening. It was a gallant spectacle. And ordinary people, three thousand of them, laughed and clapped and sighed with delight.

Every detail of her program was effective. Callot had done her clothes. The program was beautifully planned and professional all the way. After the experimental, unevenly attended local entertainments, after the tarnished shabbiness of my recent adventures, this was a great comfort to see. It could happen. Beautiful, magnetic and superbly dressed, she danced as a star is supposed to dance, with fervor and excitement. And, oh, the sound of her castanets and the swing of her body! She released us. She carried us through the rhythms and they were enough. The gestures were enough. There was no part of us pent up, unexpressed to be taken home to ferment. Dancing was an honorable profession when it worked, which it so very seldom did. It was worth a lifetime of pain and sacrifice. In the middle of the third dance as I saw and heard the rhythms resolving and changing and merging so satisfactorily, so rich, so altogether lovely, I felt the blood rush back to my breast. How many young artists the world over took heart of grace from this single enchanting figure? She was a sign and a vindication.

What made her supreme?

First, her sense of rhythm, which has never been approached, not only in the castanets, but in the feet and arms and swinging skirts and the relation of all to the music. Second, in her classic, her architectural sense of composition. (Curiously Argentina could not compose for a group—something most choreographers find easier.) But above all, it was the utter womanliness of her presence. Behind her towered a tradition older than ballet dancing and she was schooled in the last etiquette of the tradition. Behind her loomed generation on generation of anonymous lovely women who had lived out their lives in obscurity and died decently and left no trace except in the innuendo of a fan or the turn of a flounce. She was what the northern European has always dreamed about, the Romantic, the Southern, the distant anonymous lady. She never for one moment seemed like a professional. She had the magic of great evocation and summoned up brilliant women, darling and unregenerate. There never was such a parade of ladies. When she lifted an arm, one felt like standing in recognition. And oh—her smile—the flashing of her dazzling teeth, sudden, free and audacious! She was utterly and completely bewitching, as easy as gardens, or wasted time, or skies. And this is a rare quality these days. Female dancers try too hard—their charm has all run to their tendons.

Bear in mind she came to town at a period when women were flattening their bosoms, shaving their heads, sheathing their trunks in tubes to reveal only the insect legs of the overmuscled athlete and you can imagine the effect of those perfumed skirts and antique veils. But the mystery and suavity of her technique, the lordliness of her creations you cannot imagine—and although sound film had been perfected before she dropped dead of a heart attack in 1936, not one foot of film was ever exposed of her dancing. The Rose of Spain! The irreplaceable lovely lady!

I was profoundly impressed and also no little disturbed by her. Here was lyric movement, nondramatic, without story or particularized character, in unbroken flowing design. The design moved the audience, as the design in music moves and compels, the phrasing, the choice and arrangement of gesture. The grave limitations of my own composition became by contrast shockingly apparent. I could not compose thirty-two bars of continuous dance without using character acting to give it interest. Argentina's creations were as intricately formed as a sonnet. All were delightful and several overwhelming. And although, I noted smugly, she was unbearably coy in her comedy, she was nevertheless a master in handling movement, and movement is the stuff of great communication. "We are interested in you," my theater friends used to say, "because you are more than a dancer. You are an actress." But I knew one could not be more than a dancer—being an actress was less. Of the two media of expression, except in the hands of the very great, dancing is the higher, and more evocative and powerful. I do not think this point can be argued. When Argentina crossed the stage, tears filled my eyes. (126–128)

Martha Graham (1894–1991)
("Martha Graham," *Dance to the Piper*)

De Mille's reverence for Martha Graham, recorded in several of de Mille's memoirs, also led her to author a substantial autobiographical biography, *Martha: The Life and Work of Martha Graham* (1991), which was published immediately upon Graham's death. In the essay below, "Tamiris" refers to the choreographer Helen Tamiris (1905–1966), honored for her ensemble choreography and for her early use of jazz and Negro spirituals in her dances. "WPA," an acronym for the Works Progress (or, later in its existence, Projects) Administration, was the largest agency created by F.D.R.'s New Deal. Funded by a vote of Congress, it lasted from 1935 to 1943 and, overseeing public works projects in the areas of infrastructure, social services, and culture, was the nation's largest employer during that period. "Martin" refers to John Martin (1893–1985), whose 1927 appointment as the first full-time dance critic at the *New York Times* made him effectively the leading critical voice for dance in America; he was a fervent champion of modern dancers, Graham, in particular. "Watkins" refers to Mary F. Watkins (d. 1974), a music critic for the *New York Herald Tribune*, who was appointed its full-time dance critic just weeks before John Martin's appointment to the *Times*, making her the first full-time dance critic on a U.S. daily paper. The comment that Graham's company members looked "Villagy" meant that they looked as if they might be bohemians from Greenwich Village, a neighborhood of Manhattan associated with radical Leftist politics and sexual freedom during the early part of the twentieth century. For those readers who aren't dog fanciers, Louis Horst's "dackel" was his dachshund—*dackel* being the German term for that breed. The ellipsis in the text is part of de Mille's original.

I went, as Louis Horst urged, one Sunday night, to see Martha Graham.[1] She performed with the assistance of three of her pupils from the Eastman School. She was impressive, certainly, but I found myself neither charmed nor moved. All of the dance public was arrested, but, at first, very few became enthusiasts. Martha, however, continued giving concerts, and no one of us ever stayed away. Each time I saw her, I saw more.

This was a stirring period in American dance history—a period of revolution and adventure. There were at least ten soloists working in New York, each making experiments. There were a score or more imitators expanding and developing our discoveries. Every Sunday, throughout the winter season, at least two dance concerts were given, frequently more, and the two dance critics, *Times* and *Tribune*, spent the afternoon and evening zigzagging through the forties in an effort to keep up. We all turned out en bloc for every occasion, wrangling and fighting in the lobbies as though at a political meeting.

Louis Horst played for a great portion of the concerts, sometimes accompanying Tamiris in the afternoon, dashing off to Doris Humphrey in the evening and working all night on the score of Martha's new première.

The dance seasons these days are quite different. They are more professional and vastly more expensive, and the elegants show up in full dress, something they never did before, but the atmosphere then was crisp with daring. We risked everything. Every one of us had thrown overboard all our traditions, ballet, Duncan, Denishawn, or what not, and were out to remodel our entire craft. No one helped us, and there were no rules. We worked alone. We struck sparks from one another. It was a kind of gigantic jam session and it lasted nine years, until the end of WPA. There are brilliant young dancer-choreographers today, but no one with the power of Graham or Humphrey, and all of them are derived from and imitative of the styles launched in the thirties or earlier.

I am glad I participated in the period of the originators. There is a force and wonder in first revelation that has no duplicate. Greater dancers may be coming, greater and more subtle choreography, but we worked when there was no interest, no pattern, no precedent, no chance. We made it all as we went along, and every concert was a perilous test for all of us, a perilous, portentous challenge. The whole subsequent flowering of concert dance had its seed in

---

1   All dance concerts except those given at Town or Carnegie Hall took place on Sunday nights. It was strictly against the law to dance in New York State on Sunday, but this was the only day theaters were available for rental. We broke the law until we were threatened, at the instigation of the Sabbath League, with arrest. Then the dancers organized and, headed by Helen Tamiris and me, we went to Albany and changed the law.

this period. But from the first Martha was the most startling inventor, and by all odds the greatest performer that trod our native stage.

In the early days when I first got to know her, there was a good deal of talk about Graham, a lot of it unfriendly. People wondered what she was about. They always rushed like crazy to see at the next concert. Folks resented her unorthodoxy—the cult of her students, her temper, her tyranny, the expression of her face, the cut of her hair and, not least, her success.

The first time I saw her off stage, she was sitting in a New York theater in a melancholy which I had been told was her characteristic public pose. I had not met her, but I could not take my eyes off her. Heads were turning all around. Martha's presence, no matter how passive, cuts through attention, arrests speech, interrupts ideas. At the moment, she was sitting unmoving and silent. Her dark head with its cavernous cheeks and sunken eyes dropped on one shoulder. She held a single rose in her right hand which she sniffed from time to time. Louis Horst, to whom she did not address a word, sat solidly beside her. She looked half-starved, tragic and self-conscious. Two of these things she certainly was not. She ate enough for three. And while she was, from time to time, quite thoroughly unhappy, she was not ever, I learned, self-pitying. But she was unquestionably aloof. The first theatrical tradition she broke was that of being a good egg—one of the gang. She foresaw she had a lot to think out, and she arranged to have the privacy to do it in. This people resented. They said she was queer and arty. She wasn't queer; she just wasn't around.

I got to know her in a quite plain, folksy way because Louis Horst took us to dinner occasionally at Hugo Bergamasco's restaurant. Hugo was our flutist and served Italian dinners cooked in the back room by his mother and wife. Hugo made fine Prohibition red wine and discoursed on modern music as he served the spaghetti. On the dining room walls hung signed photographs of Martha and me, the sexiest ones we could find. I almost always thought of her as a girl friend—almost, but not quite always; one does not domesticate a prophetess.

From the beginning, Graham knew what she wanted to do and did it. She was born in Pittsburgh of Scotch Presbyterian parents, and raised in Santa Barbara, California. Her father was a physician who specialized in mental ailments. So from an early age she grew accustomed to the idea that people move as they do for reasons. Her father, for instance, used to detect lying by the manner in which people held their hands. He did not wish her to dance. She had to wait until he died before she started training.

She entered the Denishawn School in Los Angeles while attending the

Cumnock School and came under the spell of Ruth St. Denis. Thereafter she never took any aspect of dancing flippantly. When she was graduated from high school, she joined the troupe as a student and performed tangos with Ted, Japanese flower arrangements with Miss Ruth, and music visualizations to Doris Humphrey's choreography. I saw her during this period. I remember her hurtling through the room to Schubert, or sitting barelegged on the polished floor with smoldering watchfulness. The mask of her face was like porcelain over red-hot iron. One felt that the gathering force within might suddenly burst the gesture, the chiffon, the studio walls, the pretty groupings of graceful girls. The intensity she brought to bear on each composition was not comfortable to watch. She went with the troupe on a European tour. Ted Shawn built an Aztec ballet around her which gave her the opportunity to vent some of her ebullience. In this she had the chance, for instance, to gnaw on his leg. No one subsequently, they told me, ever did this so well.

It was during this tour that she came under the influence of Louis Horst, then Denishawn musical director. He urged her to try her own wings. So she up and left, and with great courage came to New York and started out on her own. Horst left the home fold shortly thereafter.

Denishawn viewed this double departure poorly. Girls did not rebel this way. Not since Miss Ruth herself dressed up as an Egyptian cigarette ad in 1906 and gave Oriental mysticism a new lease on life by undulating in a roof-garden restaurant had a young woman broken with tradition so flagrantly. For the last two decades dancing had been Russian, which was art; American, which was commercial (tap, acrobatic, ballroom, or musical comedy, the last a vague term applicable to anything successfully cute); Duncan, which while emotionally good for young girls was fast losing favor; or Denishawn, which combined the best features of all. Graham had the audacity to think that there might be still another way, stronger and more indigenous.

Martha put in a couple of seasons in the *Greenwich Village Follies*. Then, with a little money saved, she started serious experimenting. She taught at the Eastman School of Music, entering the project with great diffidence. But Horst believed she had genius. He accepted, however, no easy revelations. He scolded and forced and chivied; the relationship was full of storm and protest.

"You're breaking me," she used to say. "You're destroying me."

"Something greater is coming," he promised, and drove her harder. "Every young artist," he explained once, "needs a wall to grow against like a vine. I am that wall."

Louis chivied me also about many things. He never stopped urging me to leave Mother, to take lovers, to give up comedy pantomime, open my own school, to read Nietzsche, to stop practicing ballet exercises, to get away from my family, to give up all thought of marriage.

Louis had paid the rent and bills of I don't know how many pupils, had paid for their pianos, given his services, held their heads, buried their dead and taught their young. But my indication of normal well-being revolted him—or so he said, particularly in relation to Martha. She, he believed, had been set aside for a special vocation. There was neither time nor opportunity for private life. She had elected the hardest of all professions for women, and she was a pioneer in that profession. She was, I am sure, although she has never said so except indirectly through her work, also convinced in heart that it must be for her either art or life. . . . She could not have a home in the ordinary sense if she wished to serve her talent. Through her a new art form was to be revealed.

Ballet has striven always to conceal effort; she on the contrary thought that effort was important since, in fact, effort was life. And because effort starts with the nerve centers, it follows that a technique developed from percussive impulses that flowed through the body and the length of the arms and legs, as motion is sent through a whip, would have enormous nervous vitality. These impulses she called "contractions." She also evolved suspensions and falls utilizing the thigh and knees as a hinge on which to raise and lower the body to the floor, thus incorporating, for the first time, the ground into the gesture proper. All this differs radically from ballet movement. It is different from Wigman's technique, and it is probably the greatest addition to dance vocabulary made this century, comparable to the rules of perspective in painting or the use of the thumb in keyboard playing. No dancer that I can name has expanded technique to a comparable degree. She has herself alone given us a new system of leverage, balance and dynamics. It has gone into the idiom.

This may not seem much to a nondancer. But compare her findings with the achievements of other single historical figures. Camargo in her lifetime is supposed to have invented the *entrechat quatre*, or jumps with two crossed beatings of the legs, and to have shortened the classic skirt to ankle length. Heinel created the double pirouette. Vestris, the greatest male dancer of the eighteenth century, expanded the leg beatings (batterie) from four to eight and evolved pirouettes of five or six revolutions. The father of Marie Taglioni put her up on full point although others had been making tentative efforts in this line. Legnani exploited the *fouetté* pirouette—not her own invention. None of these altered the basic principles or positions of ballet technique. Anna Pavlova is credited by Svetlov, her biographer, with adding the trill on points. These are each minute advancements for a lifetime of experimenting.

It may be argued that Duncan created a new way of moving. But this is not strictly true. She refused, rather, to accept the old way and evolved a personal expression that was based on simple running, walking and leaping. She worked almost without dance technique. Her influence has been incalculable, but her method was too personal for transference.

In the twenty years prior to the last war in Germany, Rudolf von Laban and, after him, Mary Wigman developed a fresh approach with an enormous code of technique and, being German, correlated a philosophy and psychology to go with it. But they and their schools represent the achievement of an aggregate of workers and their style stems strongly from the Oriental. Strangely enough, Graham's style, for all its Denishawn background, does not. And in evaluating her work it must be remembered that Graham's technique was clarified before ever she saw a dancer from Central Europe. The two great modern schools, German and American, evolved without interaction of any kind. It is bootless to discuss which, if either, is more influential. I am inclined to think Graham's contains more original invention.

It is noteworthy of Graham that in twenty years of composing she is still what she was at the beginning: the most unpredictable, the most searching, the most radical of all choreographers. She is one of the great costume designers of our time, as revolutionary in the use of material as Vionnet. In point of view and subject matter, in choice of music and scenery, she cuts across all tradition. And for each new phase, there was needed a whole new style. Her idiom has shown as great a variety as Picasso's.

In ideas she has always led the field. She was doing dances of revolt and protest to the posh days of 1929. She was searching religious ritual and American folkways when revolution became the young radicals' artistic line in 1931–1933. The Communists then suddenly discovered that they were Americans with grass roots down to the center of Moscow and put every pressure on Graham to make her their American standard-bearer. But she was nobody's tool. She was already through with folkways and making experiments in psychology, and while other concerts were padded with *American Suites* and *Dust Bowl Ballads*, Graham began to turn out her superb satires, *Every Soul Is a Circus* and *Punch and the Judy*, which foreshadowed some of Tudor's work and a very great deal of Robbins and de Mille. The dance world seethed with satire and Martha concerned herself with woman as artist and then woman as woman, inaugurating her poetic tragedies *Letter to the World*, *Deaths and Entrances* and *Salem Shore*, and developing the first use of the spoken word in relation to dance pattern. Everyone else began to do biographies; Graham delved deeper and deeper into anthropology—*Dark Meadow*. She began to search Greek mythology for the key to woman's present discomforts—*Labyrinth, Cave of the*

Heart, Night Journey. Nowadays the doctors sit out front biting their nails and taking sharp note.

Her students plainly worshiped. She was followed by a coterie of idolaters. To the Philistines, and they included all the press except Martin of the *Times* and Watkins of the *Tribune*, she was a figure of mockery, "a dark soul," a freak. The public and critics were in turn outraged, exasperated, stimulated or adoring. No one was ever indifferent. This is the exact status quo today—twenty years later.

The center of all this turmoil one might have supposed was a virago, a wild-eyed harridan. Well, she could be. If she thought her prerogatives were questioned, she was a very bold woman to cross. I was told by her girls that Martha in a rage was like something on a Greek tripod.

Furthermore, she could be formidable when it takes great courage to be. In 1936 the Nazi government invited her to the Olympic Games—the only American artist so honored. This would have meant worldwide publicity and a whacking great sum she badly needed. Let anyone who so much as bought a German boat passage between 1931 and 1939 dare to look down his nose at the offer. Martha received the representatives courteously and replied, "But you see half my group is Jewish."

The Germans rose screaming in protest. Not one of them would be treated with incivility. Their status as American citizens and as her pupils would ensure their protection.

"But," said Martha, "I also am an American citizen and their friend and sponsor. And do you think I would enter a country where you treat your citizens and their people in such a manner?"

"It would be too bad," said the Germans, "if America were represented by any but the best."

"It would be too bad for you," said Martha, "because everybody would know exactly why."

Martha told me this herself and added cheerfully that she knew she was listed at the German consulate in New York for immediate attention when opportunity offered. No dancer from the United States went to Germany that year.

I saw her only in one of her alerted moods. It was during the time she was working under the direction of Massine in his *Sacre du Printemps*. They achieved a really splendid clashing of wills. He accused her of stubbornly refusing to do anything he asked; she claimed he asked her to do what was outside her technical abilities. She had never in her life done anything she didn't believe in. He, on the other hand, was a king in the theater and used to instantaneous and terrified obedience. Stokowski rode herd. She had resigned twice before they got the curtain up. I saw her sitting on her bed in Philadelphia with a cup of cocoa in her hands.

"I wouldn't have got out for anything in the world," she said pleasantly, her eyes bright as a vixen's in the brush. "There is no power that could have made me give up. I think he hoped I would. But I won't. But of course I've had to resign repeatedly. Oh, but I was angry today. I strode up and down and lashed my tail."

Strangely enough, the impression she has always made is essentially feminine. She is small—five feet three inches. On the stage, she seems tall, gaunt and powerful. She looks starved, but her body is deceptively sturdy. She has probably the strongest back and thighs in the world. She has an instep under which you could run water, a clublike square-toed foot with a heel and arch of such flexibility and strength that she seems to use it like a pogo stick. Her feet have an animal-like strength and suppleness that makes you feel she could, if she chose, bend her knees and clear the traffic. She is able actually to do things with her feet in an inching snakelike undulation that no one else has even approximated. She has a split kick, straight up, 180 degrees.

She is well-turned-out, almost to the degree of being crotch-sprung. (I am not now speaking sartorially. She is that as well.) It was on her own body that she built her technique.

Her arms are long and inclined to be both brawny and scrawny; the hands are heartbreaking, contorted, work-worn, the hands of a washerwoman. All the drudgery and bitterness of her life have gone into her hands. These are the extremities, roped with veins and knotted in the joints, that seem to stream light when she lifts them in dance.

But all of this is statistical chatter. It is the face one sees first and last, the eyes and voice that hold one. I mentioned the other characteristics because once she starts talking, there is no time for remarking them. The shape of the face is Mongoloid with skin drawn taut over the bones. The cheeks are hollows. In the eye sockets, the great doelike orbs glow and blaze and darken as she speaks. Her eyes are golden yellow flecked with brown and on occasion of high emotional tension seem slightly to project from the lids while the iris glows like a cat's. The little nose is straight and delicate. The mouth is mobile, large, and generally half-opened in a kind of dreamy receptivity. The skin of her glistening teeth, the skin of her lips, the skin of her cheeks and nose is all exposed and waiting with sensitive delight like the skin of an animal's face, or the surface of a plant as it bends toward light; every bit of surface breathing, listening, experiencing. The posture is just this, a delighted forward thrust that exposes the mouth. In more than one way she resembles Nefertiti, the long passionate neck, the queenly head, the bending, accepting, listening posture.

Her laughter is girlish and light—quite frequently a giggle. She has a sly wit that reminds one in its incisive perception of Jane Austen, or of Emily Dickinson whom she so greatly reveres. She loves pretty female things although she lives stripped to the wheels, and she manages to dress with great chic on an imperceptible budget, having the happy faculty of always appearing right for any occasion. Her hair is black and straight as a horse's tail. Her voice is low, dark and rusky, clear and bodiless like most dancers'. Her speech—who shall describe Martha's speech? The breathless, halting search for the releasing word as she instructs a student, the miracle word she has always found. The gentle "you see it should be like this," as her body contracts with lightning, plummets to the earth and strikes stars out of the floor. "Now you try it. *You* can do it." Thus Diana to the rat catchers.

No one can remember exactly what she says, the words escape because they are elliptical. She talks beyond logic. She leaps from one flame point to another. People leave her dazed, bewitched. Young men fall in love with her after every lunch date. Young women become votive vestals, and this can get tedious. They tend to clutter up the hallways clamoring for Martha's wisdom like sparrows for crumbs.

Everyone who could has always gone to her for advice. God knows how many she has heartened through the years. She has talked vocation problems with anyone—even nondancers. She has laid a steadying hand on the back of all young men starting on the black and uncharted path of the male dancer. Having something of the quality of a nun or a nurse, she has always given one the sense of boundless strength, the reassurance that although circumstances might be tragic or dismaying, they were not outside nature. No one could say she was the healthy out-of-doors type. On the contrary, she was a thoroughly neurotic woman leading a most unusual life, but she had faith, faith in the integrity of work and in the rightness of spirit. This she has always been able to communicate. To every boy and girl who entered her studio she has said something that has illumined the theater, so that it could never grow shabby or lusterless again.

I very soon took to going to her for advice, for reaffirmation and for critical help. Although she never admitted to the role, although we worked in alien styles, she became a kind of mentor. After every concert I rushed to her for analyses. Three times she said the word that has picked me up, dusted me off and sent me marching, the word that has kept me from quitting.

Why could one believe her? Was it the sense of obsession in the face, or the sheer integrity of her life? One faced a woman who for better or worse never compromised, who, although she had known prolonged and bitter poverty, could not be bought or pushed or cajoled into toying with her principles. She was a brave and gallant creature. There are few such in the world, almost none in the theater. One stood abashed, and listened. If her words sounded arbitrary, there was the seal of her life upon them and the weight of her enormous achievement. One could not turn aside lightly. In the most evanescent of all professions she is now regarded, and I believe rightly, as an immortal. Dancers for untold generations will dance differently because of her labors. The individual creations may be lost but the body of her discoveries is impressed into the vocabulary of inherited movement. Boys and girls who have never seen her will use and borrow, decades hence, her scale of movement. Technically speaking, hers is the single largest contribution in the history of Western dancing.

In 1931 she produced *Primitive Mysteries* based on the Catholic Amerindian concept of the Virgin, and with this composition our native dance theater reached a new level. Thenceforth Martha was recognized as a notable in the field of American creative art. For a new work she was granted half a Guggenheim fellowship. (Being a dancer, although the greatest, she was naturally not entitled to the usual grant awarded a painter, or writer, or scientist.) She went to Mexico.

The following winter I had occasion to visit her in her studio on 9th Street. She said to come late, see the end of rehearsal—about eleven o'clock. (She had to work at night. Most of her girls had jobs during the day.) I came late. This was the first time I had actually seen her in the throes. At the conclusion of rehearsal, the girls were dismissed and Martha went into her little sleeping cell and didn't come out. Louis Horst said I was to wait, that Martha was out of sorts. I waited the better part of an hour. Then Louis suggested, in a dispirited way, that I might as well go in as not.

Martha's room was about five feet broad as I recall it, and it contained a bed, a chest of drawers and an armchair. Louis more than filled the armchair. I took a box. In the center of the bed was a tiny huddle buried in a dressing gown. The only visible piece of Martha was a snake of black hair. Every so often the bundle shivered. Otherwise there was no sound from that quarter.

Louis droned on through his nose, "Now, Martha, you've got to pull yourself together."

There was a great deal of wheezing and huffing as he spoke. That was because he had four chests and all his mechanics seemed to get muffled down. "You can't do this. I've seen you do this before every concert. You're a big enough artist to indulge yourself this way, to fall apart the week before and still deliver on the night. But the girls are not experienced enough. You destroy their morale. You tear them down. They're not fit to perform."

He was right. She not only rehearsed the girls and herself to the point of utter exhaustion, changing and re-creating whole sections until the very eve of performance, she always ripped up her costumes and spent the entire night before and all day when she was not lighting in the theater in a fever of sewing. Incidentally, she cut and stitched her costumes herself with the aid of a sewing woman. Apparently she had to do this as a nervous catharsis. Contrary to all rules governing athletes she never slept for two nights before an appearance.

The girls worked for nothing, of course. The box office barely paid the advertising and rental, never any of the rehearsal costs. Martha taught the year around to pay these and her living. To meet their expenses, some of her pupils waited on table. None of them were adequately fed or housed.

These girls are not to be thought of as the usual illiterate dance student who fills the ballet schools. They were all adults; many held degrees of one sort or another and had deliberately chosen this form of dancing as opposed to the traditional for serious and lasting reasons. Among their ranks they have numbered great soloists, Jane Dudley, Sophie Maslow, May O'Donnell, Dorothy Bird, Anita Alvarez, Anna Sokolow, Yuriko, Pearl Lang. No other choreographer has had a concert group of superior caliber.

These girls had a style of appearance which became widely known long before their work was understood. We always said then they looked Villagy—but the term is misleading. They may have been unorthodox in many ways, but they embraced every possible sacrifice in order to serve their work, and lived like ascetics. They took the stage with the ardor of novitiates and the group performance was incandescent.

Their leader worked them without mercy and I am told used to grow almost desperate. She worked them until midnight every night except Sundays and holidays, when she worked them all day as well. The abandoned husbands formed a club, "The Husbands of Martha Graham's Group," to amuse one another while they waited. One New Year's Eve the men turned ugly and things eased up a bit after that.

"You cannot work your girls this hard and then depress them. They will not be able to perform," said Louis to Martha on the sad night.

Without showing her face or moving, Martha whimpered. "The winter is lost. The whole winter's work is lost. I've destroyed my year. This work is no good."

"It is good, Martha," said Louis persuasively.

"It is not good. I know whether it's good or not. It is not good."

"It may not be so successful as *Mysteries*"—whimpers and thrashings—"but it has its own merits."

"I've lost the year. I've thrown away my Guggenheim Fellowship."

"One cannot always create on the same level. The Sixth Symphony followed the Fifth, but without the Sixth we could not have had the Seventh." (This was sound thinking and I stored it away in my own breast for future comfort.) "One cannot know what one is leading into. Transitions are as important as achievements."

"Oh, please, please, leave me alone," begged the little voice. I ventured a very timid ministration. I felt like Elizabeth Arden approaching the Cross.

"Martha, dear. Dearest Martha, I thought it was beautiful." There was the sound of a ladylike gorge rising.

Louis got stern. He rose; he loomed, not over—that was impossible because of bulk—but near her. "Martha, now you listen to me. You haven't eaten all day. Get your clothes on and come out for some food."

Martha tossed the blanket a bit. The snake whisked from one side to the other.

Louis got his ulster. Louis got his cap, a flat one with a visor which sat on the top of his white hair. Louis put the coat on Max, his dackel, and leaned to pat Martha's Maedel. Louis progressed down the street displacing the winter before him. Low in the Horst umbrage cast by street lamps the dachshund wagged on the end of a string. Louis wheezed out his disapproval in a cloud of warm breath. "It's not worth it. Every concert the same. It's not worth it. She's put us all through the wringer. She destroys us."

"But, Louis," I said, pattering after and peering up and around his coat, "she is a genius." He snorted. "Would you consider working with anyone else?"

At this he stopped. He slumped down layers of himself to a thickened halt. "That's the trouble. When you get down to it, there is no other dancer."

The date of this conversation was 1932. Up till 1949 he still played for her classes, conducted her orchestra, comforted her girls. He still stood beside her, hand in hand, to take the bows at those times more frequent in her life than in most when the power and the glory are present and spectators and performers are wrapped in mantles of bright communication.

I begged Martha to let me study with her but this she refused. I had genuine need of her help. I had need of her encouragement. Doubt, like a mold, had begun to film over my hopes. It wasn't just that I was afraid I wouldn't suc-ceed. There was also the growing belief that whatever I did, however expert I became, I would never be more than a glorified parlor entertainer, could not be for the very nature of the medium I had chosen. Martha moved; I grimaced. One gesture of true dance opened doors that were to be for me forever closed. I had therefore obviously to learn to move. I was not a good dancer and no choreographer whatever, but following the promptings of a persistent instinct, I turned my back on all I had done and faced the dark.

During the next five years I taught myself to choreograph, and I took a hostile press right in the teeth for that period of time. Five years is a long period in any girl's life; in a dancer's, it is usually one third of her career.

I was trying to learn to compose dances, not pantomimes, nor dramatic stories, nor character studies, but planned sequences of sustained movement which would be original and compelling. I did not know how to begin. Everything I attempted seemed to develop either into trite balletic derivations or misconceptions of Graham. I tried to learn form and style through studies of English and American folk dances and through reconstructions (necessarily largely guessed) of preclassic (1450–1700) European court patterns. It was slow work and it was bloodless. One does not think out movement. One moves. One thinks out pattern. One moves well if one is used to moving and originally if one has developed through exercise a spontaneous idiom of expression. But I had nowhere to dance, and no company to work with.

Out of the top of my head, from fined-down nerve points, I tried by friction of will to generate ideas. Creation is not teased this way. Creation is an opening up, a submission to the dear, unwilled forces of human life. But how was I to know this, or knowing it to respond, I who was shut away from all the good, natural happiness of the world?

I used to try not to wake in the morning, and when awake, wonder what I could do all day. When I left a rumpled room for class, I was late. My exhaustion in class prevented any progress. I ate alone. I struggled with undancing all afternoon. I resisted the temptation to run to Mother for dinner. I ate dinner alone at a restaurant. The evenings were dreadful. I couldn't work. I couldn't play. I withered, unwillingly, inch by inch, with mounting terror, and the lifeblood grew black in my heart, and I could think of no good dances.

Every creative worker goes through bad periods, but today he usually manages to keep performing. If one can but just keep moving, the creative log jam breaks. Through muscles, through the racing of the blood, the running of feet, rhythms are set up that generate below fear and one is away on a new pace before one has given it a thought. But if one does not keep dancing or if there is no reason for dancing . . . I would stand in my studio two or three hours and not know whether to start north or south, whether to lift an arm or let it alone.

Mother didn't understand what I was doing, and she didn't like it. But she never withheld her savings or refused any possible effort to help. She followed in blind loyalty, although her heart was oppressed.

Why all this fancy experimentation when I could be funny, genuinely funny? Friends expostulated. My family wailed. And I fought the mists.

These were the days when Martha Graham moved like an angel in the night. Just to know she was there finding paths where my feet trod vapor, with the strength in her spirit to leap out where I stood dumb, was companionship. "We all go through this," said Martha. "You are being tempered. You are a sword in the fire. Be glad. There is achievement ahead."

"But, practically, Martha, what do I do tomorrow between waking and sleeping?"

"You make yourself a program of activity, and you do not stop once for five minutes to consider what you are doing. You do not permit yourself to reflect or to sit down. You keep going. That is your only responsibility."

"But if someone would only give me a job."

"That is beside the point. Whether they do or they don't, we keep going."

"Martha, let me work with you."

"Certainly not. Find your own way. I won't let you lean on me."

"Martha, you have genius. You know where you're going."

"I don't know where I'm going. None of us knows that. And someday I'm going to give you a good smack."

"Martha," I said one day, beating my breast over a sundae, "I have no technique and I have no time or energy to acquire any—that is, not sufficient."

"Technique!" Her voice rang with scorn. "Technique! I can see technique at Radio City. From you I ask something greater than that. From you I ask what cannot be learned in any class. Reaffirmation. Your '49, your American studies, have given me courage."

Martha Graham said this to me. (144–160)

Antony Tudor (1908–1987) and Frederick Ashton (1904–1988)
(Excerpt from *Speak to Me, Dance with Me*)

Tudor and Ashton, Britain's greatest choreographers, were both guided early in their careers by Marie Rambert (1888–1982), at whose studio, in the early 1930s, de Mille met them. Her description of Tudor's odd jobs relates to that period. The Bengali modern dance pioneer, Uday Shankar (1900–1977), who inspired Tudor during the 1920s, was in London to study art when, still in his early 20s, he met Anna Pavlova, who encouraged him to become a dancer and commissioned two ballets from him for her company, one of which he performed with her. Again encouraged by Pavlova to create his own Indian ballet, Shankar spent several years in India and Europe to find collaborators and patrons and, by 1930, founded his own company, the Uday Shankar Company of Hindu Dancers and Musicians, which toured widely in Europe and, sponsored by Sol Hurok, the United States, between 1931 and 1938. In 1938, he disbanded the company and returned to India.

"Hugh" was the British dancer Hugh Laing (1911–1988), Tudor's longtime partner and creative sounding board. Constant Lambert (1905–1961) and Sir Thomas Beecham (1879–1971) were conductors. (Lambert, also a composer, became the musical director of Sadler's Wells.) Lord Berners (Gerald Hugh Tyrwhitt-Wilson, 14th Baron Berners, 1883–1950) and Sir Arthur Bliss (1891–1975) were composers; Lord Berners was also a writer and Bliss was also a conductor. Rex Whistler (1905–1944) was a painter who also designed for the ballet. The economist John Maynard Keynes (1883–1946), husband of the Diaghilev ballerina Lydia Lopokova (1892–1981), supported the ballet. The dancer Pearl Argyle (1910–1947), known for her personal beauty, danced with both Rambert's Mercury Theatre and Ninette de Valois's Sadler's Wells. Arnold Haskell (1903–1980) was a leading British historian and critic. Kirk Askew (R. Kirk Askew, 1903–1974), who paid for the lunch that de Mille and Ashton enjoyed in London's high-toned Mayfair neighborhood, was a leading New York art dealer.

It would seem that de Mille confused here the names of Diaghilev's régisseur Sergei Grigoriev (1883–1968)—who, with his wife, the Diaghilev ballerina Lubov Tchernicheva (1890–1976), staged some Fokine ballets for Sadler's Wells in the 1950s and '60s—and of Nicholas Sergeyev (1876–1951), ballet master for Marius Petipa's ballets at the Imperial Theatre in St. Petersburg, who emigrated from Russia with detailed notations of choreography for many of the theater's classic ballets. During the 1930s period that de Mille is discussing, Sergeyev used those notations to stage for Sadler's Wells *The Sleeping Beauty*, *Giselle*, *Coppélia*, and *The Nutcracker*. His Stepanov notations of the classics reside in the Harvard Theatre Collection, where they are frequently consulted by contemporary ballet masters as well as by historians.

Antony struggled, experimented, and missed; taught stupid children, janitored, stage-managed, wandered around London (I seem to remember a cane) looking at things he couldn't afford, but Antony was finding a style. Two years later, he produced *Jardin aux Lilas* and the first totally new balletic voice of our time was heard.

Antony derived from Fokine, but between Fokine and Tudor, Proust had happened, Verlaine and Rimbaud, the Freudian school, and the new cacophony of music. Tudor tells stories about men and women dramatically, and therein he departs from Petipa and is linked to Fokine. His ballets, like the master's works, are succinct, compact and brief. Antony's ballets are all of a piece and cannot be broken into set dances, and the style is not interchangeable but particular to its own drama. Most of the Petipa ballets are in four acts and play in as many hours. They follow the same formula of separate *divertissement* and narrative mime. The Petipa pattern was discarded by Fokine, as well as the Petipa deportment, the eighteenth-century balletic stance and decorum. Fokine adopted the broken knee, the asymmetrical posture of classic statues, the free use of arm and back. As an inheritor of Freud, Tudor went the whole range of emotional impulse and susceptibility. He had at this point never seen Graham nor any of her pupils, but in his *Planets* he closely approached her technique and her psychological attitudes.

Just before I arrived in London, he had seen Uday Shankar and been enormously impressed. He was to go through his Indian period that summer in a matter of six weeks, but the sense that the arms and hands are an extra voice and not merely appendages to the spine remained a hallmark of his style; the visual effect is watery and permeating. Embraces and filigrees of arm movements, faint rubbings-out, like little sighings or half-heard exclamations, seemingly whispered in the air, are never mere decorations but evocations and echoes. In the same sense that Proust's digressions are the aura of his story, just so are Tudor's gestures overtone extensions. Each physical statement sets up a rippling of contrary suggestions, and each step is wreathed with doubts, regrets, aspirations, until the dancers seem literally to be moving through the human mind. He uses accompanying figures to expand or comment on the soloist's statements, producing through an accumulation of subtle choreographic devices a climax at once emotional and decorative. In effect, Tudor has translated emotion in all its contradictions and suggestibility to the terms of visual movement. This is magic and this is unique.

His ballets remain through the decades without any dimming; and even though the great shock of his idiom has disappeared, the delight and the strength remain. Tudor has been enormously influential and greatly copied.

His disciples must, however, content themselves with producing vagaries and a few of his pretty devices. They cannot approach his impact; a brain cannot be copied.

Tudor has never stopped working, but he has produced in thirty-five years only nine lasting successes. Why after nine straight masterpieces did creative energy wither? It is a strange life pattern. One can only compare it to Rossini who, at thirty, just stopped, gave himself up to a lazy social life, with spaghetti parties for the gilded elite. But Antony has never been very rich; Antony has had to support himself with the drudgery of daily teaching. Lately, companies have hesitated to commission new works because they had no guarantee they would get a vintage Tudor. The later Tudor was flawed. Why?

I think the answer is simple. Hugh was Antony's friend, housemate, and artistic instrument; all the male lead roles were created on him. He was a limited dancer, but a good actor, a sensitive comedian, and a theater artist of unblemished taste. And he was crucially influential in the forming of Antony's style. (Indeed, I believe Antony's special use of music derives largely from the fact that Hugh had absolutely no rhythmic beat and could move only in long, vague melodic phrases.)

But he was more than this—in my opinion—he was a choreographic collaborator, with structural ideas, dramatic solutions, and merciless criticism. He helped. No one who had ever been in rehearsal with them could doubt how much. All good dancers assist through their bodies, but Hugh made decisions, Hugh balked, yelling at what he did not like, denounced openly in the rehearsal hall to everyone's acute embarrassment, and went home with the choreographer to find the correct and satisfying answers. This is collaboration.

When in 1948 Hugh got married and separated his artistic life from Tudor's, performing only in the old roles, participating merely as a casual critic in the new works, the tone of Antony's work changed. His beautiful movement remained, the form blurred. In September 1963, in Stockholm, he found himself again with *Echoing of Trumpets*. He was alone, but so strong was his antiwar conviction that the passion carried him through to a new and splendid work.

Frederick Ashton made the more immediate success, although not of a financial kind. His brilliant invention had been immediately apparent and he had had the blessed good fortune of three extraordinary women as tutors: his teacher, Marie Rambert; his designer, Sophie Fedorovitch; and presently he had Ninette de Valois as his patron and boss. As soon as she was able, Ninette enticed him away from Mim and set him up as chief choreographer for the Vic-Wells Ballet, and there he had the added advantage of association with an ex-Diaghilev soloist, de Valois herself, and the superb men she surrounded herself with: Constant Lambert, Lord Berners, Thomas Beecham, Arthur Bliss, Rex Whistler, and Maynard Keynes. The quality of these minds had, unquestionably, a beneficial and shaping effect on the young hero of Notting Hill. Mim let him go, although she minded to the point of desperation, because she knew he deserved wider opportunities than she could provide. With him went Alicia Markova, Pearl Argyle and alas, Arnold Haskell, who had been so useful, and who now switched, if not loyalties, at least focus and burning hope on the rival theater.

Freddy was to be the champion for English choreography. And he prepared himself with brisk British attention; there was no muddling here. Now he was able to study the classics because they were being revived with the help of Grigoriev in Ashton's own theater. Ashton became a disciple of Petipa. He learned how the master brought dancers onstage, got them off, developed a *pas de deux*, and Ninette was able to advise him, because although lacking the daring and perception of Mim, she had actually danced in big repertory and was a very respectable choreographer herself. She knew the craft, and it is above all his great craft that distinguishes Ashton. In his case one must use the word with reverence. This word, this idea, has a special importance today when people accept accident and happenstance as part of their working technique; he does not, nor has he ever. His is the kind of technique that develops the instruments which steer vessels, that grinds microscopes and telescopes, that balances watches. Even in his ornamental pieces, in the pure decoration that he puts so lavishly on the stage, one finds a craft like Cellini's, like Fabergé's. Each dancer and each phrase is set as a master goldsmith sets a gem.

There is, in addition, the masterly skill of apportioning the formal pieces and the storytelling pieces—I, who have failed often, know how brilliant is his expertise in this. He has given to the formal *pas de deux* a new stature, and this is, perhaps, his best signature. He cannot achieve the unfathomable mystery that Tudor sometimes attains nor the majestic impersonality of Balanchine. But in Ashton's duets there is a kind of human love, and he has used the word himself in describing his own work.

His range is unmatched. For in contrast to the story ballets is the abstraction of the César Franck *Variations*, absolutely without peer in its kind, and the beautiful decorative frivolities: *The Birthday Offering* and the dances in *Midsummer Night's Dream*, where sheer prettiness is raised to such a pitch of finesse as to approach the celestial. His humor is entirely his own, as I suppose all humor must be, it being the one absolutely individual trait in human character never shared like the other universals, anger, fear, or hate. Ashton's *Façade*, *Mme. Chrysanthème*, and *Wedding Bouquet* could have been done by no one else. The last is silly; it is frightening; it is hugely funny. It reminds us that one of the strongest and most important books of the nineteenth century was written by an English mathematician who thought he was composing a comic nursery tale for a little girl.

Ashton's invention seems to be endless—like a mountain spring. Over the years many people, including international names, have helped themselves shamelessly to his goodies. Indeed, recognizing the thefts becomes a connoisseur's sport. It is unlikely Ashton cares. He promptly invents something new. In this nonchalant resourcefulness, he suggests Rossini, as lazy as prolific, who when composing in bed, his knees serving as music desk, let fall occasionally an aria to the floor and promptly wrote out a new one rather than put himself to the effort of getting up and retrieving the dropped pages. Ashton troubles about nothing, theft, imitation, piracy. He simply works on ballet after ballet after ballet.

That season I had lunch with Freddy in Mayfair. (Kirk Askew was paying for it. Naturally neither Freddy nor I could afford a Mayfair lunch.) Just before we came to the sweet, which I greedily wanted, he said, "Well, goodbye. I have to go." And I said, "That's too bad. When will you be back? You're coming back to finish your sweet?" And he said, "No, I think not. I'll be back in two or three months." "Where are you going?" I asked. And he said, "Oh, out to New York. Virgil Thomson has sent for me." And over he promptly went to choreograph *Four Saints in Three Acts* to enormous acclaim. Between that abrupt departure and today stand one hundred and fifteen finished Ashton ballets. ("Oh," he said, "I should think so, easily, easily, and several moving pictures and operas.") Of this, probably twenty to twenty-five are authentic, enduring masterpieces. Fokine left only eight and two solos.

Freddy may seem to work with facility and speed but there is nothing complacent about his efforts. He still, after all his enormous success, spends the day before beginning a new work in the Brompton Oratory on his knees. He is not a Catholic, but he does not wish to pass up any chance for available help. He "vomits his way to the first rehearsal." After one *pas de deux* is outlined he begins to believe he can make it. At least, this time. (196–202)

Katherine Dunham (1909–2006)
("Katherine Dunham," *Portrait Gallery*)

> De Mille's last book, the 1990 *Portrait Gallery*, consists of fifteen essays, each devoted to an artist, an impresario, members of her family, or, with characteristic generosity, individuals in her em-

ploy. This word-portrait of dance star Katherine Dunham gives a cutting sense of the racism that even a spectacular performer of African American heritage had to negotiate in both New York and Hollywood during the twentieth century: as daunting as life was for de Mille and Martha Graham as they made the arduous climb toward acceptance of their art during the 1930s, what Dunham faced was harsher. This literary laurel wreath by one grande dame of the theater to another is tightly focused, sensitive to the individual as well as to the career, and, of course, beautifully written. The phrase "the needle trades theater," in New York, refers to the auditorium of the Central High School of Needle Trades, founded in 1941 by the New York City Board of Education and now called the High School of Fashion Industries. Located in a Manhattan building with landmarked murals by Ernest Fiene, at 24th Street near Eighth Avenue, close to the Fashion Institute of Technology, the school opened its doors to dancers during the 1940s, including de Mille and the fledgling Ballet Society.

De Mille uses the names "Ballet Theatre" and "American Ballet Theatre" interchangeably, although the company, founded in 1940 as Ballet Theatre, did not add "American" to its name until the mid-1950s. The Spanish singer and actress Raquel Meller (b. Francisca Marques Lopez, 1888–1962) was an international star during the 1920s and '30s.

When Katherine Dunham started her career in the early thirties, there were only a half dozen black dancers in New York. There were tap dancers, it is true, there were eccentric dancers, and there were the lively members of the Cotton Club line, but there were no dancers outside the commercial media, and the commercial dancers did not include any moderns, any ballet, any ethnic or folk—not one. There were no black students of dance, for the good reason that there were absolutely no opportunities for them to perform. There was accordingly no hope and little pride.

The first Broadway show to mix races was the Howard Dietz-Arthur Schwartz 1932 musical *Flying Colors*, which I co-choreographed with Warren Leonard and which had a serious ballet called "Smokin' Reefers." When I say the races were mixed, I mean they were housed simultaneously in the same theater, but they were prophylactically separated, quite segregated, the one group moving onstage as the other left it; they never mingled in view of the audience. The same, of course, was true of the dressing room and backstage arrangements.

The black girls, in those days called "colored," were a heterogeneous bunch —physical education teachers, tap dancers from the Cotton Club, gymnasts, honky-tonk girls, and just plain flotsam and jetsam having nothing to qualify them except their color. A few were highly gifted; some were disciplined. Some were savages, literally. In those ugly days the black girls were not permitted to use the white girls' toilet, and the conveniences permitted them were generally unspeakably filthy. They were shut up twelve hours in the theater. They made do as they could. They were forced to. They were all or nearly all on the verge of hysteria, and the hysteria was not without cause. The show's designer, Norman Bel Geddes, did not let a concern for safety restrain his fantasy. The girls were asked to dance (not by me) in costumes that blocked their vision and bound their arms tightly to their bodies, so they were unable to get their hands free, even when they had to pass close to lights of such intensity that any contact could have set them aflame. They had to walk out on platforms thirty feet above the heads of the actors below and dance without a guard rail of any sort.

There were, as a matter of fact, dreadful accidents. One time they were all seated on tall ladders, the white girls on the bottom rungs, which were safe, and the black girls on the top rungs, which were unsafe. During the performance one ladder tipped and fell over against a second, and so they toppled like dominoes right around the stage. The black girls at the top of the last ladder, knowing for a full six seconds that they were going to fall before they actually did, were helpless to save themselves, and waited in frozen horror. By the time the last one was lifted off her prone ladder, her hands had become hysterically fixed in rigor to the wooden rungs; she had to be taken to the hospital.

There was another reason for emotion. One night at a dress rehearsal the black girls began screaming in the dressing room, twenty of them shrieking and out of control. We all worked on them—stars, chorus boys, chorus girls, members of the staff—with pitchers of cold water, wet towels, and slapping hands. Then I said, in a moment of vision, "Are you hungry?" I gave them, I remember, $10 of my own money to buy steak. (You could buy quite a lot of steak for $10 in 1932. The weekly rehearsal fee that year was $20.) They came back happy as lambs and danced beautifully.

I was fired from that show, and Albertina Rasch put her name on my work, but that is not this story. When I was given a chance to do a ballet for the Ballet Theatre, in its opening season (1940) at the New York [City] Center

Theater, I premiered my first work, *Black Ritual*, a voodoo ceremony with an entirely black cast to the music of Darius Milhaud's *La Création du Monde*. This was not an authentic ritual, but my idea of what a voodoo celebration might likely be. I chose to do a Negro ballet not because I knew anything about the black heritage or black roots, but because I was shy of rehearsing my first work in the studios uptown, where the regular company worked out side by side with Michel Fokine, Anton Dolin, Adolph Bolm, Antony Tudor, and Eugene Loring.

I was given a studio down on Fifth Avenue near 14th Street, and we began gathering girls together again in the same haphazard way as we had for *Flying Colors*—the same sorts of girls—and the rehearsal conditions were, as before, chaotic. We met at night after our regular jobs were over. It was very hard to hold the dancers together. They were late. They were absent. They went to funerals. They went to christenings. Any excuse would do. I never had the same group three nights running.

Finally one evening I gathered them together and confessed, "I can't go on. This is my first chance to do a ballet for a big company, but it's also your first chance as black girls"—"as colored girls," I said—"to appear in a major opera house with a major ballet company. The chance has never existed before. You must do yourselves proud and I hope you'll do me proud, because it's my chance." Then I dismissed rehearsal.

The next night when I went back, there on the piano was a bouquet of flowers from these starving girls. I said to them, "I'm touched to the heart, but you must keep regular hours and you must come or we can't get the work done. Now we will take half an hour off and have some hot soup, which has been prepared for us by a friend." Another dancer, white, had made marvelous mutton soup, and we all had a big bowlful and hot rolls, and then they were ready to work. We kept the dancers fed thereafter, and they turned in a beautiful job. Their main deficiency, it seemed, had not been race or poverty or lack of training; it was, in plain English, hunger.

At this point I was looking around for a leading lady. The girl I had chosen, Luane Kennard, although extraordinarily beautiful, proved to have no magnetism. My friend Mary Hunter suggested that I take into my group Katherine Dunham, who had just come east from Chicago. Dunham had made a success in her hometown and had built a good name for herself, chiefly at the University of Chicago, but she was still unknown in the East. She had recently been brought to New York by the head of the needle trades theater for her debut. So three times she sat in the anteroom of my rehearsals, waiting for me to interview and audition her—waiting long stretches of time with a sweetness and humility most extraordinary to remember.

In the end I chose not to use her. In a way this was a historic blunder, but in another I followed a very real instinct for self-protection: my work for the blacks, although quite sincere, was false. Dunham could not possibly have fitted in with the design I was fashioning, nor the technique. Whether or not she would have wished to is also questionable. I had a strong hunch that maybe she would evince more talent than I could absorb, and some apprehension prompted me not to expose myself to humiliation.

Indeed, she would have been difficult to assimilate, because shortly after the Ballet Theatre season (in which *Black Ritual* failed), she had her own opening and was an uproarious success. Her dancing—stimulating and effective, vigorous, full of life, immediately and adorably communicative—was perfectly irresistible. She was thereupon invited to give a series of Sunday nights. New York took her to its heart and made her a very big reputation. It is amusing to think of that near encounter and how patiently and sweetly Katherine submitted to my whims and nervous terrors. Forty days after the experience—literally about forty days—she was as well known as I was, if not better known.

She needed girls, and so she selected whom she liked from my group, now unemployed: Luane Kennard, whom she chose quite rightly to put into a minor chorus role, and Lavinia Williams (the mother of Sara Yarborough, later a star with Alvin Ailey), and some few others. It was out of very rough material, misfits mostly, that Dunham made her first group, with patient, antlike industry, day by day by day. It is hard enough for the rest of us to compose dances with trained students. Katherine had to do all the training herself, and she produced results that were astonishing. She asked of her group nothing they could not physically do, and do right away, without months of study (although she did set them to practicing very hard daily). She was able to produce with the simplest and most direct means a sense of spontaneity and exuberance, something that requires the highest skill, so that her dancers seemed right and comfortable in all they did. She simply set them dancing, and they seemed just to be having a good time. They were thus able to enjoy immediate results, and this was probably the main reason she was able to hold these tatterdemalion gypsies together.

Katherine always seemed natural, and her large scenes with many people always seemed spontaneous—totally deceptive impressions, both. Her large scenes were works of art and were organized with deft skill. It was her tragedy that she was the first of her kind. At the time her concerts were introduced to the American public, blacks had not been indoctrinated to concert work and did not buy tickets; their own theater was entirely given over to tap dancing and nightclub routines. Katherine's sophisticated studies of folk materials were new to them, and the experience of going to the downtown Broadway theaters and mixing with white audiences was unfamiliar. Change in this has come about very, very slowly. There has been by both races a great reluctance to mingle and share, not only in the cities of the South but in the cities of the North as well. Katherine had to plow ahead with largely white audiences, which it is true, she conquered completely, as was her wont. But there were disadvantages.

She herself had a very simple technique: a rudiment of ballet, I suppose some small aspects of modern—Duncan perhaps—but no tap, none of the big virtuoso black forms. She never attempted what she could not do, and whatever she did was accomplished with great finish and deftness. The treasure she gave was her personality, and that was nothing short of magic, for she had the unusual combination of seductiveness—very real, compelling, and strong—and humor. There have been many great comic women dancers, but few who have been sexually alluring. Among these few (Raquel Meller, Renée Jeanmaire, Gwen Verdon), the combination of both talents signifies, of course, a really first-class mind. Katherine combined all of these qualities with the viewpoint of a scholar and a scientist. In this I think she was unique.

A good part of her success was due to the unfailing and delicious wit of John Pratt, her husband and collaborator, who had been a painter of promise in his young days in Chicago but had given it up to design costumes and scenery for Katherine. These had to be paid for entirely out of company funds, which Katherine for the most part earned. To keep costs down, Pratt employed an ingenuity that has rarely been matched, using all kinds of material, new designs, new fabrics, new devices. His problem was to create folk costumes that could be made, for the most part, by extremely poor people possessing a minimum of craft. He made use of all the good cotton prints he could find, from Japan, from Africa, from the West Indies (these were probably manufactured in Birmingham, England, but they were intended for the island trade), as well as straw from Cuba and South America and artificial flowers and hats from all over. Wherever the company traveled, it purchased whatever the troupe could lug along.

Pratt's daring and joyousness, his unexpected combinations, and the humor and the piquancy of his ideas as displayed on beautiful young black bodies were an unexpected delight. He made his wife one of the most attractive sirens in the western world. Her hats were outsized, her skirts had more flounces than seemed possible, the roses she put on were manifold, and the fake jewelry was extraordinary, but it all worked together. Pratt used rags and working materials like denim and corduroy, or the most wonderful hand-dyed goods, like the Haitian "Gros Blue" and "Carabella" and cheap Martinique prints, and the effect was merry and persuasive and humorous, while never, ever condescending. Blacks often have a flair for dress, which he indulged and accentuated.

Pratt worked for very few artists other than his wife, but that does not lessen in any way the impact of his style. Some of the notables for whom he did work were Alicia Markova, Harry Belafonte, Miriam Makeba, Jerome Robbins in *Look Ma, I'm Dancing*, and Hermione Gingold. In Chicago, he dressed the Balaban and Katz Chorus Line. He died on March 26, 1986, of cancer of the mouth. An inveterate smoker, he refused to curb his habit until it was too late to save his life. His death was a great loss to the theater, as there are few finer costume designers.

Katherine Dunham was a pioneer, very truly. She had to train her company, as a good many others have. But she also had to take care of them, shield them, protect them, and in a real sense maintain them. She had no money, but she had to see that these people were housed and fed despite every possible prejudice and barrier. It amounts to a historic achievement.

People forget. Now people can go anywhere, stay anywhere, but in the thirties and early forties it was terrible for blacks, particularly on tour. In 1930 I gave a midnight performance for managers and agents; I rented the tiny Little Theater for the purpose, closing off the balcony and filling only the orchestra seats. I wanted our beloved cook-housekeeper, Mildred, who was black, to see the show, and sent word that she must be admitted. The management would not seat her downstairs with the white audience. They opened the dark, empty balcony and ushered her in, absolutely alone, and she sat there, solitary, throughout the evening. I heard about this from the management, and she was very embarrassed that I had heard, because she knew the news would pain me. Mind you, this was not in the Deep South; this was in New York.

In 1944, fourteen years later, I met up with Katherine in Hollywood. She had gone from success to success, and quite wonderful things had happened to me. I was in the West with American Ballet Theatre rehearsing *Tally-Ho*. She was there with her troupe, rehearsing and performing. Every city she went to posed the same problem: How should she house and protect her girls and boys? She solved the Hollywood situation by renting an unfurnished house that had once belonged to Wallace Reid, the great silent film star, and by laying pallets side by side on the floor. There were cooking utensils and plastic or paper plates and cups, but I don't think they had anything else. She and John kept a room for themselves and a closet for her beautiful costumes, and John set up his sewing machine among the mattresses. There he stitched on the costumes that made theatrical history, and there the girls helped him sew. In this way Katherine was able to keep her dancers out of the dreadful rooming houses and filthy hotels to which they would otherwise have been relegated. The dimensions of this persistent problem and the amount of trouble it caused her have never been discussed, but they were significant.

While I was in Hollywood I wanted to take Katherine out to lunch—but where? This was 1944. I went to Chasen's and asked for an upstairs banquet room, which they opened up for me. There Katherine could eat a simple restaurant lunch as my guest. She came with her elegant husband; Katherine, draped in stone martens, looked rather better than a movie star—say, Merle Oberon. We had a good lunch with some friends I thought Katherine would like to meet. I looked all around the room at the stacked tables and chairs, and I bowed my head before this young woman who was one of our major artists and who was leading her people and mine, my colleagues, to great things. Downstairs the restaurant was fairly full, but there were plenty of empty tables.

About a dozen years later I met her in Kingston, Jamaica. I had heard that she was dancing there, and my husband, who was her manager, had to talk about business. She was very dispirited. She had just concluded a triumphant tour of South America in which she had been quite literally the toast of every big city and had made a very great deal of money. Alas, her business manager had absconded with the lot; she had been plucked clean. She was as penniless as before she had begun the trip. Dear Katherine! It was careless of her. She should have safeguarded herself. She didn't. We sat in the garden of a broken-down Jamaican mansion, and she gave me a beautiful little basket that she had found in some Latin American country, to carry my powder compact and handkerchief in. "It's all I have at the moment," she said. She also gave me a very, very small emerald to take to Mae Frohman, Sol Hurok's assistant and her particular sponsor, explaining, "This has been a bad year, or the emerald would be a much bigger one." She and John Pratt then sat glumly in their tropical garden. The Jamaicans had not yet learned how to go to the theater and how to respond; anything as sophisticated as Katherine was quite beyond them.

Many years have passed, a lifetime of achievement, and Katherine has been through many experiences, glories and disasters. She has been a star in Broadway musicals, a *grande vedette* in Paris, a star in London. For the past twenty years she has spent a good part of the time in Port-au-Prince, Haiti, where she has a sizable property with a beautiful villa, in large part designed and built by John Pratt. The house centers on a swimming pool fed by rock springs and contains a big kitchen and enough bedrooms to rent out to paying guests. Katherine has her own wing, with a master bedroom containing a bed of some acreage—the largest I have ever seen—and a sunken bathtub. Since she has grown somewhat portly and arthritic (for years her knees have given her wicked trouble), she has been forced to resort to a wheelchair and always the arm of an assistant. I wondered about the sunken bath. "How does Katherine use her gorgeous Roman bath?" I asked. "With difficulty," replied her assistant.

Across the road from Katherine's living quarters lies her enormous estate, which once belonged to Pauline Bonaparte, Napoleon's sister, and her husband, General Leclerc. Only a few columns of the original mansion still stand, but many stone buildings have grown up since, as have formal gardens, and around and through all stands the great primeval jungle: mahogany trees, rubber trees, frangipani, every kind of tropical nut and fruit, dark, mysterious, superb, and unfamiliar. These trees themselves, let alone the historic remains, are of considerable worth. I think Katherine wishes to make a museum of the place, and the Haitian government would do well to listen to her.

Her present position on the island is extraordinary. She is a ranking personage in voodoo, having gone through the complete initiation. She is a known writer of delightful and beautifully composed books. She is a recognized anthropologist, and of course she is the best-known dancer the Haitians have ever sheltered. She is also a hostess with an international, interracial, world-famous circle of friends. She is Madame Dunham, decorated by the government and treated like royalty. Her position and property have remained undisturbed even through the recent political unrest.

There she is so treated, but not here. Part of every year she teaches at the University of Illinois in East St. Louis, a bleak spot with not a friendly tree nor a friendly bush, a neighborhood of decaying houses and obsolete businesses and cracked pavement, a neighborhood of sinister, eerie aspect like a dream: sinister to enter, dangerous to stay in. Indeed, Katherine's leading dancer was murdered there for the few dollars he had withdrawn from a bank in order to visit his mother. The place seems friendless and hopeless. But there Katherine is established, with her drums and her tape equipment and her many assistants. There she teaches, and the children, the young men and women, come to her by the dozens.

Nominally these students attend the University of Illinois, but in reality they come to Katherine, and they sit in the room while she beats drums and her assistants beat drums and she establishes the ancient rhythms. She talks to them about the way the Latins walk and the Indians walk and the Negroes walk and the mixtures of these, and then she says, in her little-girl, ever-fresh voice, "You see how it is." Then she shows them. Because of her weight, one would think she would waddle, but Katherine Dunham does not waddle. She walks like a princess, a lovely girl, still magic. "You see how it is. Now do it."

Of course they can't do it. She can't explain how she does it. This is living art; this is the thing that cannot be explained. But the compelling and imaginative alternatives she offers these troubled young people have persuaded several away from lives of crime and drugs and have even, according to police records, broken up gangs. She does it easily, as a matter of course. They cannot—but someone will. Someone will take fire. There will be a follower. The young keep coming.

Katherine Dunham's honors and medals are in many respects history-making. She has of course received the usual American tokens of esteem, culminating in the Kennedy Center Award and the recent President's National Award for the Arts. Very unusually, she has been given the Albert Schweitzer Award for her humanitarian work in fostering intercultural rapprochement. Through Brazil, she received the Gold Medal for the Dance from UNESCO's International Committee on Dance. In Brazil also she broke the color line, receiving the country's highest civilian distinction, the Order of the Southern Cross, and helping to win passage of laws forbidding discrimination on the basis of color, religion, or origin. In Haiti she holds (among many other distinctions) the Grand Cross of the Legion of Merit, that country's highest civilian award, and in France she is an Officer in the National Legion of Honor and Merit. These medals and ribbons are all very beautiful, and whenever Katherine is on display she wears them across her breast.

Dunham's contribution is like no other, and oddly enough, it is the one true historical contribution of her people to American dance. Alvin Ailey produced a vigorous and remarkable group, but the technique is entirely modern dancing and ballet, and the treatment of all the subjects is, from the dance point of view, totally modern. Arthur Mitchell's Dance Theatre of Harlem is splendid, but that company's technique is classic ballet, and in particular Balanchine's, and it performs only ballet works. Dunham alone has tried to reconstruct the dances of black people: American, African, Caribbean, South American, Latin American, all of them. She has done this with a remarkable eye for exactitude, not pedantically, but with deep feeling. For these reasons she has given us a panorama of black dancing in the West which is historically important and aesthetically beautiful and moving.

Dunham belongs in the great folk tradition of Uday Shankar and Igor Moiseyev, but she is less formal in design, less spectacular in technique, and infinitely more personalized. Her works consist of a series of genre studies, employing popular, that is, common or traditional, steps. Her use of the body and hands is always particular to a time and a people. It is not in any way generalized, and in that sense it is not classic. Dunham tells about the people that interest her, the people she has known. It is from the aggregate of their individualities that the truth emerges gradually, not as old worn-out formulas but as the old familiar, *ours*.

We owe much to the black theater, and whether we know it or not, we owe a great part of our individuality in the dance to the black theater. Jerome Robbins is in debt, as I am and as are Eliot Feld, certainly Twyla Tharp, and yes, even Balanchine. It is essential that the work of Katherine Dunham be preserved and continued. It is our link with black history. She alone has dealt with indigenous material and indigenous expression. We need it. In truth, we cannot develop without it. (38–50)

Alicia Markova (1910–2004)
("Alicia Markova," *Portrait Gallery*)

> In this word portrait, several names may be unfamiliar to contem-
> porary readers. "Princess Astafieva," with whom Alicia Markova
> studied as a child in London, was Serafina Astafieva (1876–1934), a
> graduate of the Imperial Ballet School in St. Petersburg and a for-
> mer dancer with the Imperial Ballet and Diaghilev's Ballets Russes;
> she opened her London studio in 1916. Charlotte M. Yonge (1823–
> 1901) was an educator and author of both nonfiction and fiction,
> notably *The Heir of Redclyffe*, her 1853 novel marked by themes of
> Christian self-sacrifice and repentance. Elsa Maxwell (1883–1963)
> was a gossip columnist famous for her parties for celebrities and
> royalty; she was an intimidating figure, both physically and socially.
> De Mille's phrase "Rachel on her death couch" refers to the leg-
> endary French tragedienne, known as Rachel (née Elizabeth Félix,
> c. 1821–1858). Markova's later coach, Vincenzo Celli (1900–1988),
> was an American actor who studied ballet at La Scala, in Milan,
> with Enrico Cecchetti for a six-year period, beginning shortly af-

ter the end of World War I. Celli became a principal dancer and choreographer at La Scala for some dozen years. However, in the early 1940s he returned to New York and taught ballet there for the next four decades. In addition to Markova, his students included Jerome Robbins and Agnes de Mille.

Because of its evanescence, a characteristic that has been impossible to correct in thousands of years, the dancing art is classed as a minor one. Now, however, we have films and can preserve the beauties of its chief works and its finest performances. Unfortunately, films cost money, and the people with the money have not until recently been persuaded to spend it for anything so commercially unrewarding, with the tragic result that fine works have been lost and the memory of performances of legendary beauty have dimmed into obscurity. Fifty years ago Alicia Markova was acclaimed the greatest of her kind, but who remembers her vividly? Who can recall why she was so outstanding?

I can. I saw her repeatedly. I worked beside her—not with her, but beside her in the same studios, at the same barre, on the same stage. I can testify that she was indeed the stuff of immortality.

Why was she so extraordinary? First of all, her appearance. She had inordinately long arms and legs and a small head. Her body line therefore had the pure luxury of ease and melting continuity that made for delicious phrasing. Her arabesque (a ballet position in which one leg is raised against a strongly arched spine and the supporting leg is straight) was more fragile, aerial, and brilliant than anyone else's, possibly because of the almost double-jointedness of her hip and back. It invariably brought the shock of delight one experiences from the high E of a great coloratura. One old gentleman sitting beside me gasped, "It is not possible, but I see it with my eyes, so she must be doing it."

Her foot was long for her height, but very slender, strongly arched, and as delicate as a bird's claw. On the end of this delicate parenthesis she alighted and hung poised like the crescent moon, a stillness in the movement of time.

She was tiny, dark, compact, and as fragile as Venetian glass. Her legs and ankles seemed so remarkably slender, her hands so tapering, one felt they would snap off with the first jar; actually, a tennis champion's wrist, or a surgeon's, was probably a weaker instrument. In those delicate leg bones she had the kick of a stallion, and although she appeared not to have the virtuosity or durability of, say, a Baronova or a Toumanova, she could in fact do anything (except brilliant turns). Her technique was prodigious; her technique was bolts of lightning and steel. However, it took a professional eye to recognize this.

She seemed to laymen to float in a mist, and they remained wonderstruck—even people who professed to hate dancing and who had been dragged to their initial evening of the experience.

In keeping with her unworldly effect, her expression was demure. The dark lashes rested tranquilly against the wax-pale cheek, a Mona Lisa smile was fixed on the noncommittal lips, until she suddenly glanced up in child-like wickedness and chuckled with a tiny sound like something very valuable breaking.

Always about her there was an aroma of sadness, a hint of death in the moment of consummated effort. This was her Jewish heritage, as it was Anna Pavlova's, who made her worldwide reputation with a dance of death, the "Dying Swan."

On reflection, I realize that Markova seemed, for all her delicate beauty, unphysical, even unsexed. Admittedly, no great ballet dancer is physically sensual—preferably, she is the instrument of sensuous release—but she, more than anyone else (with the possible exception of Margot Fonteyn), suggested romance while preserving always the chaste austerity of classic discipline. It could almost be said that the passion of her discipline, like all great restraints, was in itself a kind of sensuality.

Although English (born Lilian Alicia Marks), she was in face and body astonishingly like the Russian Pavlova—the same black-and-white beauty, the same serene brow, the dark, burning eyes, the precise, patient mouth, the swanlike neck. Indeed, Markova was well aware of the likeness and was often accused of modeling her style closely on her great predecessor's. She did not have Pavlova's gift of outright hypnotism, but she did have the same quality of dancing in an aura.

For quite a period she even claimed that the spirit of the Russian inhab-ited her body. Jerome Robbins, when a very young performer, invariably used to station himself in the wings to watch Markova's *Giselle*, which he felt, as we all did, was history-making and worth attention. But he was impious. As she came offstage with slightly heightened breathing, demanding powder and a towel, he asked pertly, "How's the spirit doing, Alicia? Are you in tune tonight?"

"Not bad, ducky, really not bad." She twinkled. "That last bit was pretty good." Then she was off on a *pas de bourrée* too rapid for the naked eye to fol-low. She minded his joking and his mocking not a bit. She simply disregarded it and rushed back onstage to rejoin her "spirit."

Markova's story is straightforward, even simple, a tale of chilling discipline and fanatic acceptance of the proofs, trials, mortifications, and final glories of perfection.

Hers might be the history of a nun or a saint, as she was dedicated from youth by her parents to a calling, much in the style of a maiden given to temple service.

She was born in London in 1910, the daughter of a prosperous Jewish engineer named Marks and an Irishwoman who adopted Judaism in its most rigid and orthodox form, marrying in a synagogue. "Think of the strength of mind of that woman—think of the character," said Alicia soberly, fixing her great dark eyes on me as she spoke. "An Irish Catholic, yet she abandoned her entire background and family and accepted, for love of her husband, a way of living so strange and overwhelming."

There was no grand plan in the choice of Alicia's vocation; it came about almost by accident. The little girl was set to dancing simply because she seemed to have an aptitude for it and because her mother had been impressed by Adeline Genée and Anna Pavlova. Alicia herself at the beginning had no overwhelming desire to dance, nor ever expressed one, and correspondingly her family felt strongly neither one way nor the other. But they did all things meticulously in that household, so she applied herself to the job with cool precision, learning to move nicely just as she learned to keep her clothes neat and to speak politely when addressed. She remained always the excellently brought-up middle-class British child, dancing throughout her youth hard and correctly, if without expression of any sort.

Other ballerinas may have been more emotionally infectious, more adorable or communicative. Alicia's art, through sheer concentration and focusing of impulse, became transfigured gradually to the beauty and cold endurance of the star's. A young student, Sydney Francis Patrick Chippendall Healey-Kay, first saw her dancing at the Kensington Theatre in South London on December 27, 1920, and he was so struck with amazement that, in a gesture flashy enough for any Hollywood musical, he rushed out and bought a bunch of white chrysanthemums with the last of his allowance and sent them to her anonymously. Alicia at this point was ten years old and was performing the leading dance in a Christmas pantomime. Her solo, unusual for a child, was an Oriental slave number that ended with a stunning shriek and a stiff-backed fall onto her skull. Alicia remarked with characteristic slyness that she was gratified every night, as she lay panting on the floorboards, to hear gasps of concern and horror.

Her father had wanted a son, but he loved Alicia and shared with his first-born all the interests he had longed to develop in a boy. For many years the future Giselle, the epitome of fragile vulnerability, rushed off in spare moments to rugger matches and ice hockey.

Mr. Marks died when Alicia was thirteen, and Alicia took over the role of head of the family, including the male role at the weekly Sabbath ritual. At this young age she shouldered the support of her mother and three sisters.

Her early dance lessons, her first performances, and even her imminent seasons with the Diaghilev company (with which she danced from age fourteen to nineteen—there didn't seem to be any law about child performers) were policed by a governess-dragon named Guggy, who kept her from all easy contact with other children and colleagues and from all daily effort that was not included in the barre regimen. Alicia could do nothing for herself around the house. She had been appearing with the Ballets Russes for a year before she was forced by Guggy's illness to tie on her own slippers, apply her own makeup, and take her costume off a hanger. As for making a cup of tea, washing her stockings, or sewing on a button, she was helpless! Whenever Guggy had to go out shopping, she locked Alicia into her room with no playmates, not even her younger sisters. Alicia learned to love cats and talked only to them. "After removing my ballet slippers at each performance," she later wrote, "[Guggy] would take them to the strong electric light of the make-up mirror. If she found so much as a spot or a streak on the pink satin, I lost my chocolates, not only for that day, but for the entire week, and, in addition, our visit to the cinema was cancelled."

After the Guggy treatment, becoming first dancer in any company must have seemed a simple task. Is it any wonder this child grew up bewitched by ambition? From the time she was eight she was treated as someone apart, a conditioning usually reserved for young lamas or queen bees. Not even royalty is reared in this wise. It explains much in what dancers have come to recognize as Markova's aloofness. It explains much of the mystery and unworldliness of her art. It explains further her lack of creativity. The girl who did exactly as she was told for over twenty years, who remained as passive as a baby, as cherished, as self-absorbed, grew to be the perfect instrument for more aggressive forces—but herself initiated nothing. Choreographers always agreed that she was a delight to rehearse, as she did precisely what was asked and nothing else. But she knew what would suit her, and her suggestions were valuable. Her memory was legendary: she could remember not only everything she had done, but—much more unusual—what she had merely seen. She could compose nothing, not even a schoolroom series of steps. She had to see and to copy.

This passivity explains her life history, which constitutes an awful and impressive story that she told with the propriety of a Victorian children's tale. Reading her autobiography, one forgets that the chief characters were the mad and rascally bohemians who comprised the Ballets Russes. Diaghilev, the demon-genius who drove them to world renown, became in her version "Sergeypop," the "one whom Alicia considered the greatest man on earth," while the tainted and inflamed group he ruled with such sadistic vigor appeared as kindly folk suitable for any Charlotte M. Yonge novel. One might be reading about nursery teas and how little brother broke his cricket bat. But one is not.

Diaghilev first saw Alicia in the ballet classes conducted by Princess Astafieva in Chelsea and invited her to join his company at Monte Carlo. She was at this point a slight, thin fourteen-year-old with black hair cut in a Dutch bob; she wore white socks and middy blouses. Guggy took her to rehearsals and brought her back to her hotel room. On nights she did not perform she was in bed by seven-thirty.

She was given the lead role in *Le Chant du Rossignol*, Balanchine's first choreography for Diaghilev, in 1925. She made a notable première at the Lyrique in Paris, with Stravinsky conducting. Her success earned her the promise of better roles. I saw her in 1929, when she was eighteen or nineteen, dancing the "Blue Bird" variation and Papillon in Schumann's *Carnaval* at the Coliseum in London. She seemed like any string-bean adolescent in a diamante bandeau, like a little girl dressed up in her mother's party clothes. I think she must have weighed sixty pounds. She had all the voluptuousness of a grasshopper, but she hit the stage like a veteran. For all her youth, she *was* a veteran.

Unfortunately, Diaghilev died in that year. The immediate disbanding of his company brought Alicia's career to an abrupt stop. At that point the young choreographer Frederick Ashton introduced her to Marie Rambert's tiny Ballet Club theater in Notting Hill Gate in London, and there he devised ballets for her. The little auditorium seated only 125, but its stage was the only place where she was invited to perform. Her salary was ten shillings and sixpence—roughly $2.50—a performance, a sum worked out to cover the exact cost of new slippers and taxi fare. Rambert thought that Alicia could very well use buses and dance like the others for eight shillings, but the Number 52 bus did not run after 11:00 P.M., and Alicia won out. This was a good thing from a prestige point of view, because it ensured her and Ashton (who also got ten and six) the highest salaries at the Ballet Club.

Ashton was her artistic mentor and coach, but there was also another, a protégé of Diaghilev's who had danced leads with the greatest and who believed in Alicia's fabulous promise. He was her first admirer, Sydney Francis

Patrick Chippendall Healey-Kay, an Irish boy, now transformed into Anton Dolin. He had studied beside her in Astafieva's classes and watched her progress in the Diaghilev troupe, where he himself had starred, and he now became her partner and constant companion.

Dolin was internationally known but by no means in Alicia's class as an artist. He was athletic, flamboyant, and unbridled, and produced narcissistic displays of egotism matched by only a few. With her, however, he curbed his more aggressive instincts, and he served her truly and well. They made a remarkable couple, the unleashed vulgarity of the one offsetting the purity of the other. When she joined him he was busy making a commercial career in the music halls; he took her on as partner, and she obediently did the two and three performances a day with surprising zest. From time to time they made forays to the Continent with a more legitimate concert group. Alicia always returned to the Ballet Club in between trips.

In 1934 she was invited to join the newly founded Blum-de Basil Ballet Russe as a soloist, which promised international exposure, but she decided instead to throw in her lot with Ninette de Valois and the budding Sadler's Wells company, on the promise that they would mount all the great classics for her on a normal-size stage. This decision plunged her advisers into acute consternation; they implored her not to bury herself in a group of students in the suburbs. She followed her instincts, however, and in January 1934 starred in the first full-length English *Giselle*.

Marie Rambert took me to the première. People were very proud of Alicia. She was a hometown girl and doing nicely, but of course, they thought, was not to be compared to the Russians—to Toumanova, Baronova, or Danilova. Ninette de Valois and Rambert thought otherwise, de Valois for patriotic reasons and Rambert because she based her opinions not on current comment but on exactly what was before her eyes, and her eyes were among the sharpest in England. I was present when she took Alicia's head gently in her hands and kissed her. "You have come of age," she whispered.

Giselle was followed by *The Nutcracker* and the complete *Swan Lake*. Alicia now had the three great classic roles under her belt, something she never could have achieved in twelve months with any other company. She left the Wells to help form the Markova-Dolin Company (1935–38), with Bronislava Nijinska as chief choreographer. Then, in 1938, she joined Massine and the Ballet Russe [de Monte Carlo] and started touring the world, wishing to give herself serious competition and wider challenge. In the Russian company she was just one of an incredible group of soloists, which included Danilova, Toumanova, Youskevitch, Slavenska, Riabouchinska.

Markova's name was at this point practically unknown in America. She could not possibly consider herself a star until she danced *Giselle* in New York. That night everything she did provoked an ovation, an eventuality that her partner, Serge Lifar, had not foreseen. He became upset, and somehow, as Alicia was being set down from a high lift, her foot became broken. "However," Alicia told me later, "I continued the whole solo variation, little hops on pointe and all. Think of it: right across the stage on one toe on a fractured foot. In the mad scene I began to feel something was wrong, and it seems at the end I passed out cold."

"When finally Alicia stepped out in front of the curtain alone"—this was Lifar's rival, Pat Dolin, speaking straight from the heart—"she was greeted by a roar of applause that was almost terrifying. Just behind the curtain Lifar was being held back by two male dancers."

New York had witnessed enough to know what moved before its dazzled eyes, and the city and all its press were at Markova's feet, broken or sound. Backstage there was a good deal of explanation in Russian about what had happened, and some plain monosyllabic English.

When the Ballet Russe split into two sections after phenomenal quarrels, threats, and lawsuits, Markova joined the Massine faction and toured with them for some years. Then she moved to the American Ballet Theatre, in one of those swift coups that proceed so naturally and spontaneously from lunch at the Russian Tea Room.

Dolin had been a choreographer and star in the American Ballet Theatre since its inception in 1940, and had been anxious to install his great colleague and partner in the new fold. For her part, Markova was nothing loath to rejoin him, for he had proved over a long period more understanding than anyone else in setting dances for her. He was, moreover, a remarkable theatrical figure in his own right and was acknowledged generally as an unmatched partner for classic work. Markova was annexed as top star. Gollner, Baronova, and Stroganova, their noses just a touch out of joint, stepped obediently aside.

Madame Marks, as she used to be called at Ballet Club, knew her own wishes. She never shared her dressing room with another woman. She insisted that every costume be cleaned each time she wore it. (Costumes almost invariably belong to the company, not, as in opera, to the star performers, and two or three ballet stars have to share the same dresses.) Nora Kaye came offstage one night during *Romeo and Juliet* and held out her arms for the next costume, a cloth-of-gold robe. She was informed that Markova had visited the theater that afternoon and that on her instructions the overeager dresser had sent the costumes to the cleaners; there would be no further changes during the current performance. On hearing this news, Miss Kaye's face was, as they say, a study.

At the time Markova lived sparsely in unmodified hotel rooms, without a personal maid. She had instead a kind of acolyte—neither dresser nor maid, but a humble young professional who ran errands, stood by, listened, sympathized, handed things, and worshipped. This person was always present and silent. Besides her recompense she received instruction and coaching in ballet technique and the daily opportunity of watching genius. Markova always talked in front of her as though she were not there, with regal imperviousness to human criticism; two or three intimate attendants constituted for her complete privacy.

It goes without saying that her discipline about sleep, food, and drink was rigid, continuous, and lifelong. She did not smoke. Her only real expenditure was on ravishing clothes by name designers, but these did not include furs or jewels. She held herself to a severe budget, permitting herself a first mink coat only after the South African tour in 1949. About twenty-five years of dancing paid for this. She always supplied all her own tutus (to ensure their freshness), her own headpieces and accessories, and, of course, all slippers and tights—a very sizable expense. She rarely entertained.

Dolin seemed to live high and fancy, but he was doing public relations for both of them, and Markova paid for half. It was always Dolin who held court in his dressing room for columnists, civic functionaries, movie stars, and fans, talking his way through cold cream and towels. His dressing room had the air of a levee, but he usually remembered to point out the quiet little figure, already cleaned up and dressed impeccably, sitting in attentive silence.

He was very grand at these séances, lounging about in his expensive dressing gown. He was ducal, even royal, languidly receiving homage and never rising. At one interview I stood in his dressing room for ten minutes discussing problems about the current production (he was appearing in my *Tally-Ho*, and there was much about his performance that distressed me). Elsa Maxwell was in the other chair, but he didn't bother to introduce us. He also didn't bother to offer me a seat. At the end of the interview I said quietly, "You must excuse me for not removing my hat," and I left the room.

When the royal couple went out socially, it was Pat with his Irish wit who talked; Alicia, looking exquisite, sat in a nimbus of attention and chirped. She was not seen too often without him. Two of Pat's jobs as big brother and partner were to escort her to dinner and to see that she amused herself in her scarce leisure moments. I have known him, with this in mind, to take her out to watch him play bridge. Alicia did not play bridge. If by any maneuver you could sneak her away, get her feet up, her hair down (metaphorically, of course; not a hairpin was ever loosened, even by her speedy daily activities), a very small drink in her hands, you would find her reminiscences worth the effort. The fact that she rarely took time out to comment does not mean that such passed her unmarked.

Her fame grew. She received all the prizes, all the medals, the OBE being her crowning achievement. Alicia is a dame of the British Empire and can quite correctly be addressed as Dame Alicia, although I think she prefers her old Ballet Club sobriquet, Madame Marks.

In the summer of 1941, Dolin organized a school and concert series at Jacob's Pillow, Ted Shawn's farm near Lee, Massachusetts, using the personnel of American Ballet Theatre spiced with visiting guest soloists. I was to be a weekend spice. I arrived on a rainy night to find matters in considerable turmoil. There were tales of Markova hurrying from several classes in tears. Baronova was crying down the road in a neighboring farmhouse. Everyone rushed around, very busy with housekeeping and rehearsal chores, stopping only to snarl at one another. I was assigned to a dormitory with Lucia Chase, who wasn't crying that summer; Nina Stroganova, who was; and Nana Gollner, who moved through all with good-natured untidiness.

When I arrived at Jacob's Pillow, Markova had been closeted upstairs for two days and showed no signs of coming down, although the weekend performances were imminent. Passing across the upper hall, I peeped unkindly through the half-open door. She lay in Ted Shawn's great double bed, stretched like Rachel on her death couch, the dark silken locks unmoving against the waxen shoulders. The eyes, neither open nor shut, stared in sealed misery.

Few changes had been made in the room. Beyond replacing photographs of Shawn and his young men naked in the wind with more maidenly symbols— the ballerina's tutus suspended as always inside out, a satin ribbon tossed on the dressing table and a silk robe over a chair—the great star had done nothing to transform any of her rooms. She was a transient everywhere except in the theater dressing room. In that room only was she at home, and half an hour after she took possession, all the implements of her trade and her working comforts were in place.

In the farm bedroom the little head remained unmoving against its pillow. I watched for some time in fascinated shame. Tears trickled down her cheeks in an unending stream. In an adjacent room another lady devotee of Dolin's lay ill and weeping. (Most great male dance stars, I have noticed, seem to have one or more of these dedicated followers trailing after them, asking, and getting absolutely nothing except the privilege of attending to mail, shopping a little, keeping a list of the star's social engagements, and waiting hand and foot on the brilliant center of their attention. Sometimes they are paid as secretaries and sometimes they foot their own bills.)

Downstairs the new master of Jacob's Pillow sat at dinner. The hoi polloi—the corps de ballet and friends—ate in a kind of barracks, but I, as guest artist, was entitled to a place on the host's right.

"Rooms full of weeping women," he said, spooning up his soup vigorously. "I wish they'd either get well or . . ."

"Or what, Pat?" I asked.

"Or—well, now look here, ducky, the house is getting positively soppy with tears. What good does it do them to go on like this? I must say I think they enjoy it, I really do, but *I* certainly don't. For one thing, the weather's too damp."

"I think Alicia is not enjoying herself."

"Then why doesn't she stop? Women are too preposterously silly." He called to the cook, "Send a tray up to Madame Markova."

This was promptly returned untouched.

"Pat, what is the matter with her?"

Parenthetically, I wish to remark that for all his naughtiness, capriciousness, and flamboyance, Anton Dolin was one of the kindest-hearted men in the dance world. When there was genuine trouble he was the first to help. He labored for years to get the insane Nijinsky asylum in America. He succored Olga Spessivtzeva in her lamentable madness. He helped innumerable young artists with money. In the case of Markova, he shared an alliance of friendship and ambition. He was devoted to her, even dependent on her, but he could never resist wicked Irish mockery.

Alicia continued crying until it was nearly performance time and active measures had to be taken. An old friend and balletomane, a father and head of a household and thus someone used to family tantrums, advanced into her chamber of melancholy, pulled her from the bed, and shook her until her teeth rattled. "Alicia," he said, "if you don't start getting ready for this afternoon's performance, I'm going to turn you over my knee."

She whimpered and started to pick at her makeup. He left her to the care of assistants, who, scared to death and speechless, rushed to propel her through the preparations. She was supported across the yard to the theater. The porches still dripped with summer rain. There was the smell all about of wet pine and the green glitter that promised a brilliant sunset.

Alicia leaned in her dressing gown against a dank post. Her acolyte waited round-eyed beside her with the tray of powder, hairpins, and mirror. I was about to do a comedy dance and stopped to say that I hoped Alicia felt better. She gave me a graveyard smile and looked west to the Berkshires. Paddy Barker, her student assistant, shook her head with air of a nurse who knows that the end is inevitable but hopes it will be quick.

When I left the stage, Alicia was in her skirt and trying out the points of her slippers. Her breath still came unevenly from crying. Below stairs, while I changed, I listened to the music of the prelude from *Les Sylphides* and felt the slight jarring of the floor overhead from her great soft descents. At the conclusion, there was a full six seconds of silence and then tumult.

Several girls drifted below and stood dazed. "What happened?" I asked. They sat, unable to continue with their changes. It seemed Markova had never before approached the beauty of her performance that afternoon.

I hastened to offer my congratulations. Alicia was bouncing around upstairs in the farmhouse, clad in a darling dressing gown and as happy as Christmas morning, purged, delivered, vindicated. She had tied a bow in her hair. "It was rather good, you know," she said to me with brilliant eyes. "I can't say I was too displeased."

"The girls said it was transcendent."

She put her head on one side and considered. "It was all right," she said. Then she scampered off down the hall to visit the other invalid's room, whence presently came peals of girlish giggles. They sent down for enormous trays of food.

I do not know why she carried on this way. I do know that she had only one concern in life: to dance better and better and better. This was all she did. She did not interest herself in one other thing. She never married—never, as far as I know, was even engaged. She was given over from early childhood to a dedicated and exacting vocation. Outraged nature must have backed up on her from time to time and taken blackmail payments. The sacrifice she made was enormous. Whether or not it was necessary is a question she probably asked herself from time to time at lonely moments.

Alicia came to the theater as a rule before anyone else. For a gala she was in and out of the place all day, but for each routine appearance she was on hand at least three hours ahead of time. Her room seemed as businesslike and as prophylactic as a surgery. The dressing table had pristine, dainty skirts and spotless cloths laid over the makeup. On a white-covered table lay her shoes, pair by pair, long and exceedingly narrow (triple A). Markova's feet were flawless—white, supple, and unmarked. Most dancers' feet look like the ace of clubs: gnarled, jointed, skinned, bruised, and blackened, with horny nails and rubbings and scars that have bitten into the tissue. The feet of dancers who dance barefoot cannot be imagined; they are hoofs. But Markova gave her feet solicitous, almost medical, care, and they were dreams.

She took ten minutes to put on her shoes. She cleaned everything she owned every day. She puttered and fussed and mended, the acolyte sometimes helping her clean, sometimes watching her. But often Alicia was alone and wanted it so. She was like a young mother assembling her first layette, cutting off connections with the world. She was already beginning to connect with the audience. They did not know this. It was afternoon still; many of them were at their offices. It would be an hour yet before they got ready for dinner.

After some while of this meandering, Alicia put on practice clothes and her makeup base and went onstage for a lesson from her coach, Vincenzo Celli. Celli put her through an hour or two of everything he could think of. In lieu of a barre, she hung on to the wardrobe trunks or the tormentors. Other members of the company appeared and started practicing, but apart from her. When she left the stage to go to her dressing room, she was dripping. Her acolyte waited with a towel, for from now on she had to keep in a light sweat. (Her audience was probably now having cocktails.) She sponged off and finished her makeup. She gave half an hour to her hair.

Twenty minutes before curtain she stripped and got into her all-silk tights. I have seen Alicia stripped. She had no body at all. She had no bust, no stomach, no hips, no buttocks; she had two long supple arms and two long strong legs, joined by a device that contained in the most compact manner possible enough viscera to keep her locomotive. She was utterly feminine but as incorporeal as a dryad. Her slenderness, her lack of unneeded flesh, was a rebuke to everything gross in the world.

The tights were held taut by elastics and tapes that wrapped around her twenty-one-inch waist (this was long before the time of elasticized stockings and tights). Her toes were swathed very exactly in lamb's wool to prevent shoe friction, and the priceless little mummies were then inserted into the flawlessly clean satin boxes, which were glued to her heel. (Pavlova used spit in the heel of her shoes, in the old tradition; Alicia used LePage's glue—it is stronger.) Then the ribbons were sewn; she had to be cut out of her shoes after a performance. Five minutes before curtain she stepped into the tutu. As the orchestra started she walked onto the stage. It always took four men to help her with the flowers on the return journey.

Classification is silly. Many stars are flabbergasting artists, quite different and mostly blessedly contemporary. When performers reach this standard of excellence, choosing between them becomes a matter of personal taste. But John Martin of the *New York Times* dared to risk his very considerable reputation by writing, "[Markova] is not only the greatest ballet dancer in the world today, but very possibly the greatest that ever lived"—a claim impossible to substantiate, but eye-catching.

I happened to be backstage the day after Martin's incredible pronouncement was printed. In my minor way, I was going through the process of warming up, quieting down, and cutting off from daily life. I passed Alicia's room. She was standing alone, rubbing the toe of a slipper with a piece of gauze soaked in benzene.

"Alicia," I said, slipping onto her sofa, "tell me something. As one woman to another, how does it feel to read in a newspaper a statement like Martin's—'the greatest ballet dancer of all time'?"

"That's very well and good," said Alicia, placing the slipper precisely beside its fellow, drawing her silk dressing gown up neatly, and sitting down with crossed ankles. "It's easy to write something like that, but it's I who have to live up to it. What am I to do the next day, I ask you? I said to Celli, I must work all the harder. I mean, ducky, the audience is going to expect something after reading that bit. It will be hard lines if I let them down. There's always the next performance to think of. That's what I said to Celli."

Alicia had at the time reached the age (not a great one) when in the days of Russia's Imperial Ballet the stars were forcibly retired and pensioned, but she was dancing better than ever, with virtuosity and an enormous brilliance of dynamics and power. Instead of slacking off with the years, she seemed to be attaining greater and greater physical and emotional strength and achieving subtler and more exquisite refinements of style.

Building her reputation had been hard; maintaining it was harder. When Pavlova danced, she was the only great ballet star most of us had seen, and she brought with her the excitement of revelation. The theaters of Markova's day bulged with dandy technicians, and the beady eyes out front were knowledgeable and blasé, while in the wings stood those ready and able to crowd the star off center spot. If Markova seemed at times mettlesome to the girls and boys who worked with her, she was only fighting for her position and her future. One mistaken step from an assistant, one hand on a wrong light lever, undid a hundred hours of practicing. Markova might have had the proverbial nervous temper of a ballerina; she also had the responsibility. She might have seemed fragile, childish, and gentle, but cross her will, or turn on the wrong light, or make a damaging mistake in tempo, and you would know why Britain had withstood the blitz and held Gibraltar and girdled the world, and lasted as long as any other country in recorded history.

After an ovation, this airy, fairy, feathery little thing was known to place an armful of white orchids deliberately on the floor, pass silently and exquisitely over to where the head electrician waited uncomfortably, and break him.

She was acclaimed the greatest ballet dancer for just one reason: she intended to be. (19–37)

Carmelita Maracci (1908–1987)
(Excerpt from "Hooray for What," *Dance to the Piper*)

> A choreographer, a dancer of almost unbelievable virtuosity, and one of the great ballet teachers in twentieth-century America over some fifty years, Carmelita Maracci taught established and prospective stars of the ballet and the movies. Among her most well-known students were Carmen de Lavallade, Janet Collins, Donald Saddler, Paul Godkin, Jerome Robbins, Tommy Rall, Janice Rule, Julie Newmar, and Geraldine and Josephine Chaplin (children's classes). Among the dancers who could be found in her classes were Cynthia Gregory, Erik Bruhn, Leslie Caron, Cyd Charisse, Herbert Ross, Bella Lewitzky, Teo Morca (Flamenco), Christine Sarry, Gerald Arpino, and William Carter. The ballerina Allegra Kent, a devoted pupil, has also written about Maracci's classes in her memoir *Once a Dancer* . . . Although de Mille, a friend as well as a student of Maracci's, published a fuller chronicle of the dancer's tumultuous career in *Portrait Gallery*, this excerpt from *Dance to the Piper* is de Mille's most exquisite writing about her teacher and friend. The "Warren" reference is to de Mille's early dancing partner and lover, Warren Leonard.

While waiting for something or other to happen I lived at Margaret's house and took classes from Theodore Kosloff and Carmelita Maracci.

I had heard about Maracci from many sources, but the first time I saw her was when I went to class at the Perry studio on Highland Avenue. She was dressed in a little knitted bathing suit and she sat upright on the edge of her chair, her insteps, the most beautiful feet in the ballet world, crossed precisely before her. She was smoking. She had tiny hands with long, quick fingers, the nails extravagantly long for castanet playing. She was very small, doll-like, and compact. Her black hair was nailed, Spanish style, in a knot at the back of her head. I have said she was doll-like, but there was no hint of prettiness in the face. She had rather the head of a precocious monkey or a wicked marionette. Under the bald, hard, round forehead, the eyes opened large and were flecked with yellow lights reminiscent of Graham's. The large mouth, peeled back from strong teeth, was aggressive and mobile. It was an angry little head, proud, taut and passionate—the head of a Spanish gypsy. She always held it curbed in as though there were a bit in the mouth, the cords of her neck jutting out in strong, vertical lines. She looked under flickering lids as though she were about to bolt. Her voice rang out in flat Southwestern speech. (She had been born in Montevideo of Italian-German parentage, but she talked like a housewife in Bakersfield.) "Oh my goodness," she said, in washday Bakersfield impatience, "show some gumption! You look like limp lettuce leaves. What do you think you're doing?" And with this she threw her cigarette down and ground it out on the studio floor under the toe of her pink satin slipper. "Now, let's get going!" Up came the chest, the spine tautened. Her neck and head assumed the tension of accumulated force which is a dancer's preparation. The long arms moved to fourth position, her knees galvanized, and she was off on cold legs, without a *plié* or an excuse-me, in a series of the most astonishing *chaîné* pirouettes one could ask for, revolving as fast as the eye could follow, as smooth as silk unwinding from a spool. Her lungs were filled with smoke, her thighs relaxed from sitting down. She stopped in arabesque, erect like a T-square, the straight supporting leg planted on its delicate point, the structure of her body balanced and counterbalanced, sinew against bone against height against sinew hung in the air, tension counterbalanced on tension. And the lovely, tense foot was adequate to all, attaching itself to the bare floor and permitting the body to branch and flower above. She posed there on one point, in defiance of gravity, until her knee got tired, and then, and only then, she allowed her heel to touch ground. She had remained immobile, in full flight, for about twelve seconds.

"Glory be to God," I said.

"Well!" said Carmelita, with a throaty chuckle. "That was pretty good. I think I'll have another smoke on that one. Now, how about some of you trying?"

One day Anton Dolin, the English star, visited her class. Carmelita rose from her cigarette, winked at her girls and unleashed a series of *entrechats-six*, interspersed with *entrechats-huit*. She sat down, breathing a trifle hard, her nostrils flaring, and asked Dolin for a light. I dare say his hand shook a trifle as he tended it.

"Stretch your feet," she would yell suddenly, sitting on the floor at our ankles and taking the offending member in her strong, surgical fingers. "Isn't that a good pain? I like to feel pain like that. That kind of pain is accomplishment."

As we left at the end of an hour and a half, not too tired (her classes were built for exhilaration, and she had the great pedagogic faculty of helping us each day to do one single thing we had not done before), she would change her slippers and re-enter the empty studio to practice herself, alone—something very few ballet dancers will force themselves to. She also practiced two hours of castanet and heel work daily, all of this in addition to her composing.

She lived and worked in a cottage that had been built out of one of the schoolrooms in the Hollywood School for Girls. It was strange to walk up the familiar path with dancing clothes under my arm instead of Caesar. She and her husband invited Warren to make his home with them, and I tagged along whenever I could arrange to. She never had doubts about her work. I found out shortly why.

Up to this point, I had not seen her dance. I had heard rumors, but these were so extravagant that I gave them little attention. The night before she entrained for a San Francisco concert, she asked me to watch a rehearsal. I sat in a studio where I had done a daily practice for six months and where we had had our parties. The place smelled of wood and floor wax; the trumpet vines tapped at the windows. Carmelita walked on incredibly high heels to the center of the room and sat down on a kitchen chair. She said to the pianist in her plain dancing-class voice, "I'm ready, I guess." And it began.

The dance she showed me was her *Cante Jondo* or *Deep Song*. It was one of the greatest solos I ever saw in my life. This girl worked with thunder. At the end I walked to her quietly and put my arms around her.

"I'm glad you like it," she said, matter-of-factly. "I think it's good myself."

It is no ordinary experience to discover one evening that an intimate, a known, well-loved, daily companion has something close to genius and stands outside of the standards we set for ourselves. The person speaks with the usual voice, laughs with the ordinary expression and then, without transition or warning, becomes a figure of magic. I have known this experience three times, with Carmelita, Antony Tudor and Sybil Shearer. It is a very humbling experience. It involves some of the fastest reorientation a person can be asked to make, and strong discretion because one is brought up sharp against the knowledge that the other fellow has known the score all along.

Carmi has remained a staunch friend and a great teacher. I have never seen her dance in concert that I was not deeply moved. She is brilliant, passionate and strong. She can also be delicate and impish. At once satirist and tragedienne, there are few of like caliber. (227–230)

Trude Rittmann (1908–2005)
(Excerpt from "Trude," *And Promenade Home*)

> The events of this excerpt took place in 1943, during rehearsals of
> the Broadway show *One Touch of Venus*, for which de Mille served
> as choreographer and her frequent colleague Trude Rittmann
> served as musical arranger. A comic presentation of the Pygmalion
> theme, the show, directed by Elia Kazan, had a score by Kurt Weill,
> lyrics by Ogden Nash, and a book by Nash and S. J. Perelman,
> based on the novel *The Tinted Venus* by Thomas Anstey Guthrie.
> As Mel Gussow reported in a 1987 story in the *New York Times*,
> Marlene Dietrich, originally cast in the title role, had withdrawn
> with the critique that the musical was "too sexy and profane,"
> thereby opening the way for the casting of Mary Martin in the
> part, a performance that propelled her to Broadway stardom. In
> one of the many bittersweet coincidences that marked de Mille's
> life, she entered rehearsals for *One Touch of Venus* immediately fol-
> lowing a forcible separation, owing both to her work and the War,
> from her new husband, serviceman Walter Prude, stationed in
> Hobbs, New Mexico.

The heat that August in New York was oppressive. Indeed, it has been every
August and I have spent most of them right there and similarly employed. It
is hard on the dancers, for, although they move more easily in warm weather,
they have to eat salt tablets to fend off prostration. Their clothes soak through
in an hour and they must devote every evening to enormous laundries. Hands
drip and slip, making lifts dangerous as the girls slide like fish through the
boys' insecure clutch. Feet blister. But the dancers work without complaining.
At least they work for pay, however small. At this point in my story, rehearsal
pay was twenty dollars per week, and after decades of no work and no pay,
they were delighted to slip and blister in their beloved vocation, and when I
sent out the call for auditions, they came flocking in the hundreds. After preliminary script study, a Broadway musical begins for the choreographer with
dance auditions. All auditions are held on an empty stage lit by the one overhead third-degree light permitted by the electricians' union, a 500-watt bulb
which makes the actor or dancer look like something in a badly kept morgue.
It matters little. The management is in any case half blinded by the bulb. {Not
until 1957 did Actors' Equity finally force the theaters, through their contract,
to install a strip light of three bulbs.}

This light persists for the duration of rehearsals and may not be altered. Sometimes the house curtain is lowered below the light to protect the eyes of those in the auditorium. To lower the curtain, the house carpenter must be called for a four-hour minimum at $5.20 per hour. He charges as much to raise the curtain later. If any additional light is used, the house electrician must be called on the same terms, that is, $41.60 to put the lights on and off for rehearsal, allowing a four-hour interim for work. It is understood, on pain of union blackball, that the carpenter will not touch a button nor the electrician set his hand to a rope. The actors generally, therefore, arrange to make do with the single 500-watt bulb. Most directors and actors, who pass their entire working hours for the five or six weeks of rehearsal time under these conditions, attempt to protect their eyes with shades and dark glasses. Six weeks in this glaring tomb without any sunlight at all has a noticeably debilitating effect.

Whenever I call the dance auditions, every single member of the staff is on hand, invited or not. In particular, all the men are present. The dancing girls, like the singing girls, are required to run a gantlet that is nothing short of formidable; they must be under twenty-five; they must be pretty, fresh-looking and bright. So far all would agree, but beyond this there is a margin for differing personal taste. The choreographer has requirements of his own; but these are considered academic by the rest of the staff. There exists, for instance, a widespread belief in the Broadway theater that I don't know a pretty girl from a three-legged stool, so the boss men gather to instruct me. They fear that I will lean in the direction of ability as against charm, nor believe, as I do, that lack of ability cannot be pleasing no matter how presented. Apparently they do think I know the difference between a good-looking boy and three-legged stool, because they leave the theater in a body when I start to audition the men; among these I am allowed to pick and choose as I like. This is not always happy or easy. During the war, for instance, the choice was paltry; the U.S. Army and I saw eye to eye and they got first pick. But I am not ashamed of my record with either young women or young men. Diana Adams, Virginia Bosler, Nelle Fisher, Lidija Franklin, Pearl Lang, Gemze de Lappe, Bambi Linn, Betty Low, Annabelle Lyon, Joan McCracken, Allyn McLerie, Raimonda Orselli, Sono Osato, Katharine Sergava, Emy St. Just, Evelyn Taylor, Jenny Workman all entered the Broadway theater in my shows. Also, Peter Birch, John Butler, Ray Harrison, James Jamieson, Kasimir Kokic, Scott Merrill, James Mitchell, Marc Platt.

Whatever ideals the staff has in mind, there are certain physical characteristics peculiar and constant to dancers. Dancers are nearly all smaller and more tautly knit than other people. They appear always so much smaller than the singers or the actors on any stage, the difference in height is so marked as to make them seem like another species. Their chief and most appealing characteristics are their slenderness and their posture, a soldierly spine and a sense of supple readiness that no other people acquire, not even great athletes. They are as relaxed as cats, alert for any demands even while resting. Their walk can be recognized by any professional, but it is not particularly attractive. Ballet dancers walk splayed out and flatfooted, very nearly a shuffle. The moderns stride with what amounts to a spring or lope. They all walk from the hips like Indians. They put the heel down hard because the ground is their ally; they trust their feet. The dancer's face is intelligent, quiet—unlike the actor, who feels called upon to practice his faculties of response every minute in every conversation. Dancers who are comedians are more alert in expression than lyric dancers. The dancer waits and watches, trained to keep the countenance clean of grimace, to express only what must be expressed with an effort of total will.

At all auditions a brisk horse trading goes on in the front row where the staff sits, a high jump for a redhead, the promise of passion in a face for a model's thighs. We agree upon a balanced group at last while the poor wretches stand half naked in line in front of us, swaying with embarrassment, hope, despair, fatigue and anger. The union permits us three chances in which to weed out twelve or fourteen from, roughly, four hundred applicants. We make mistakes. It will become clear in rehearsal later, and only in rehearsal, who can act, who can follow direction, who can play comedy, who can phrase music, and which beauties can do none of these things. Every replacement costs delay and confusion—several hours of wasted effort. At the time of our new show, *One Touch of Venus*, choreographers were permitted by Chorus Equity to hire extra recruits and given three days in which to make a final choice. This practice, although prolonging the suspense for the doubtful few, made the final decision fairer and saved the choreographer and group the terrifying waste of work thrown away on a casualty. For it must be remembered that there is no dance script, and accordingly, every individual body that leaves the rehearsal hall takes away in head and muscles part of the actual texture of the composition. In deference to the performer's feelings, the rules have been altered; we may start work now only with the exact number we require, or fewer. We may not, for any reason, diminish the number once rehearsals start. But since no studies of any kind are permitted before rehearsals, since every step must be demonstrated by the choreographer and learned by rote in rehearsal, the situation becomes almost insurmountable.

And as all steps are developed on live bodies, hired by the hour, and as each dancer's body is a unique instrument with individual modifications, the composition must be achieved in rehearsal; any departure from formalized class technique necessitates experimentation. The choreographer, for reasons of sex, strength, or virtuosity, cannot always work out problems beforehand on his own body. That is why even the most skilled and experienced craftsmen plan, before rehearsal, little beyond sketches and are usually unaware of the exact types or even the exact numbers of people needed. No musician would be required to hire orchestra players before his piece had been composed and scored. But composing, scoring and rehearsing occur simultaneously in dance composition.

I had projected the *Venus* dances in a light lyric mood full of what I hoped would be irony. I immediately got to work with favorites sweating through hours in the studio all day. Such preparation is now forbidden by union ruling—but in those days a choreographer was permitted to find out what he wanted to do before getting into full rehearsal. At night I plotted steps and patterns on paper close to the telephone. A call from Hobbs might come through at any time.

Few Broadway composers are responsible for any of their own orchestrations. Most of them furnish only the song melodies, while the overtures, the incidental action accompaniments, the transition pieces, the ballet and vocal variations, the musical reinforcement and "glue" of the show will be arranged by someone else. There are, for this purpose, a handful of experts who function as musical amplifiers and arrangers. The most notable of these and the most helpful to me over the years has been my former concert accompanist, Trude Rittmann.

Trude sat knitting and whistling between her teeth while I pushed people around the room. When an amount was blocked out she would go to the keyboard.

"Jean," she would say, picking the most musical girl in the room, and Trude always knew within minutes who was musical, "count for me in eights at this rhythm."

Then she improvised melodic variations on the song tunes as we went along, playing full out, changing keys, modulating, developing a musical climax where the choreographic climax was shaping.

"How would it be if we were to have two fives right here? And if I play three-four against your four-four? Don't change a count. You keep going. We come out together, you see. It gives a brilliance, a shimmer, no?"

"Gee whiz," said the dancers, "that's wonderful."

"It is not," said Trude. "I work it over tonight." And that's what she would do, taking her glyphics and scrawls home—she worked—how late?—how early?—in her impeccable little German flat with the window corner full of potted green plants. And in the morning she would return with a new arrangement—but every count exactly as rehearsed. We proved it with excitement and joy. The blueprints of this musical arithmetic were to be handed to the composer, Kurt Weill, to translate into his own style.

"Now I'm tired," said Trude, stretching out full length on the floor of the studio, her music case under her head, her glasses off at her side, her slender ankles crossed. "You go on."

The dancers mopped up on their towels, changed shirts and started in again. After a time, we would be aware that our musician was sitting up on the floor. Her glasses were back on.

"Now just where is all that going?"

"I thought at the beginning."

"And just what am I supposed to play for that?"

"I thought the verse—"

"Impossible! Impos—maybe not! Wait a minute." And on she tried, changing, inverting, shifting keys and rhythms. "What's happened?"

"Nelle's fainted. It's her hay fever again."

"Ah, poor child!" And Trude was back on the floor, Nelle's head in her lap. "Give her air. Don't crowd. Lift up her feet. There, dear, lie quiet. Keep fanning. Some water—not too cold—wouldn't hurt—at the back of her neck. I think I'll faint myself. Lie quiet, Nelle. There's no rush. What a life!"

It was always Trude who raised the dead, comforted the sick, counseled the forlorn, and who found out and informed me of what I should know in order to help. She was big sister, mother, schoolmistress and scoutmaster.

Oh, the tears she had wiped away on our long transcontinental concert trips! "*Liebchen*, dear heart, sisterle, don't. It's not worth it. Pull yourself together. Your work is getting clearer now. Be grateful for that."

"Oh, Trude," I said at the end of these long hot August afternoons as we picked up the mess in the emptying studio. Trude policed a studio like any sergeant—she couldn't bear mess. "Oh, Trude—what you have watched me through!—to have waited so long in such confusion and loneliness." I looked to the west where was the sunset and, farther along, Hobbs, New Mexico. "And now to abandon him and come back to the rat race in this hot stinking city."

"Dear heart," said Trude, "you have to do your work. Later you can stop."

"Later! Will there be a later?"

"*Ach, ya!*" said Trude. "One hopes." Trude had had precious small reason for hoping. Trude at the beginning, at the first flush of her success, had had to abandon everything and come out of Germany, leaving so much she loved behind.

"If I could choose," I continued, pacing up and down, "if I could live one way or another, cut my pattern clean—be like other women, simply a wife or mother, or like great artists, sure and undivided. But all parts of me are set against each other."

"Do not question how you are, Agschen. This mixture may be a strength. Use it. You may have something to say for women that the others will not know. But in any case, that's how it is. We live with ourselves. And you have decided this way for now. Has he written?"

"Oh, yes—and phoned. But it's hardly the same."

"I should think not," Trude laughed. "However, the time will pass—it always does."

"You think so, Trude?"

"Absolutely—but, Agnes, watch the new girl, Lizzie. There's trouble there. I think she will not last rehearsals. Maybe if you could praise her a little—just once—no matter how it goes on your nerves. I know you think she's disgusting, but one word would do miracles."

"Lizzie is dreadful and stupid and off beat."

"Agnes, have some pity!"

"No."

"Well, then, have some tea with me. We talk about Walter. It will settle you. You say he likes music?"

Trude is a small brown-haired woman with a dry piercing laugh and thick glasses. Her body is that of an adolescent European schoolgirl, neat and plain and very young in appearance, but as she lives slumped over the keyboard, one hardly notices this charming fact. Her hands are small, with the square spatulate fingers of the professional pianist. She was, when I first knew her, victimized by constant migraines that nearly knocked her flat and her Empirin bottle was a fixture beside the erasers and five-lined paper.

Before every concert performance, she used to go on the stage, complain about the piano, arbitrarily readjust the lighting Joseph Anthony had spent four hours setting, and while her headache mounted, start in on forty minutes of five-finger exercises that had obviously been arranged by the Gestapo. She played the performance excellently, although her nerves were tense. We quarreled afterwards about tempi; this is traditional with all dancers after every performance.

I grew very fond of her. She never gave way, but she developed in compassion, understanding and tolerance and I like to hope I did also, but I rather doubt it.

At the time of our *Venus* rehearsals, Trude had not only headaches but backaches. This condition in no way improved when a few years later Mary Martin, while rehearsing *South Pacific*, cartwheeled exuberantly right off the stage and into the orchestra pit where Trude sat playing. Martin, who was appalled, was picked up shaken but intact. It was Oscar Hammerstein who noticed minutes later that Trude was lying on the keys and had not moved at all. She was out cold.

Trude always arrives for rehearsal promptly, neat as a dressmaker and full of solicitude, inquires about family news, bodily ailments, or any musical revolution that may have occurred since the night before. The dancers stand around ready in practice clothes. They have been warming up for fifteen minutes. Trude carefully folds her coat, polishes her glasses, deplores the state of the piano and, sitting back and taking a deep breath, sounds the opening theme of the rehearsal—*andante sostenuto*.

"You know how I admire you, my dear. You know what a sympathy I have for your work. Yet in all sincerity I must say I don't see where we're going. It is my impression we are smack bang up against a blank wall."

The dancers quietly, without one further word, sit down and open coffee cartons. Some light cigarettes.

I lean over the piano. I am too rehearsed in this to be dismayed.

"Why do you think so?"

"Last night," said Trude, shaking her head dolefully, "I worked for four hours. Four hours is quite a time. One can try much. I tried everything. It simply won't go. It is not unwillingness. You know I work myself to the bone for you. I tried everything."

"Some of it may be good." This is the contra-, or second, voice, usually taken by me, but occasionally by one of the soloists.

"It was not good. I threw it away."

"Oh, you didn't!" *Doloroso*. Someone brings me some coffee. Coffee is slipped between Trude's square worn fingers.

Repeat *da capo*—second ending.

"Perhaps you can remember some of what you didn't like."

Sotto voce, cantabile, poco a poco accelerando. "Please, Trude, please."

"No, what's the use? It was no good." She walks to the window and stares down at the city in ruins. "Perhaps another arranger . . ."

"Trude, I implore you. Let me despise your music too."

Trude emits an unwilling yelp. Dancers *tutti chorale*, "Oh, Trude, what were you working on?"

"Oh, well, that's all very well and good—no—" She plays sixteen bars grimly.

"I think it's lovely."

"*Ach!*" Trude makes the sound a good *Hausfrau* utters when she finds rats in the larder.

"Play it again, Trude. The rhythm in the base [*sic*]. Please, I implore you. Look."

Trude looks. "Why do you put the accent on the third count? Here, do it again for me. Wait, let me mark that."

Her pencil is on the music paper. She whistles between her teeth. I rush about the room. The dancers have risen and are following. Coffee is kicked into corners. *Allegro con brio al fine.*

These are Trude's warming-up barre exercises and she must go through them full out at least once every three days. This opera can be varied—as, for instance, *lento*, when Trude looks through me and says morbidly, "Do you believe in what you're doing? Can you honestly say you do? From the heart? We know, we have to make compromises in this field, but there is a level beneath which—" Or it can be the scherzo attack, *giocoso*.

"I have something quite nice. It's a surprise. Hold on to your heads—same counts—"

The cast yells. The leading male dancer kisses her. I kiss her.

"Now you think of something good for a change," she says, very smug, picking up the morning paper and reading as though she were on a train going far away, into the mountains.

"What a girl!" the dancers sigh.

This gift for arranging and developing popular songs into dances and for underscoring scenes, dialogue and business is unique. Her unparalleled help in infusing variety and dramatic effectiveness into shows as well as into accompaniments is common knowledge on Broadway. She has worked with me on seven shows since *Venus*—*Bloomer Girl, Carousel, Brigadoon, Allegro, Paint Your Wagon, Gentlemen Prefer Blondes, Girl in Pink Tights*—every one I have done, in fact, after *Oklahoma!* She has worked on others I have had nothing to do with: *Finian's Rainbow; South Pacific; The King and I; Fanny; Wish You Were Here; Look, Ma, I'm Dancing; Billion Dollar Baby*; the two *Peter Pans*—Jean Arthur's and Mary Martin's—and *My Fair Lady*. She has composed on her own original melodies [for] the ballets in *Look, Ma, I'm Dancing; The Girl in Pink Tights*; and the Uncle Tom ballet in *The King and I*. She is more than an arranger. I rely on her taste as on no one else's and in all departments of my work. I herewith make her my deepest reverence, and there are other choreographers, and the very best, bowing beside me. Several thousand dancers and all orchestrators and conductors rise to testify to the taste, good sense, musicality and creative force Trude Rittmann brings to every show she touches, and the cheer and decorum she maintains in rehearsal.

"She is indispensable," say Alan Lerner and Frederick Loewe.

If in the tart and rather lugubrious exchanges which I have quoted I have given any indication that Trude was depressing, this is not accurate. She was stern and demanding, but the hope and solace and patience that woman could summon when everyone else had stamped out disappointed was why some of us were able to weather the jobs. I cannot number the times she has cleared the hall, brought me tea, or taken me to dinner and then returned to work quietly all night, if need be. The sane musicianly counsel she supplies, the expert eye, the humor and the large background experience which reaches into the best Europe could teach and embraces all forms and styles—these are at the disposal of every colleague who will listen—as well as her courage. And let no one underestimate what courage it takes to make an innovation in the commercial theater. But Trude, like all good artists, proceeds by instinct and not by rule.

Trude says quietly, "I had tonight in the theater a feeling about this work—"
And Trude's feelings are like the needle on a ship's compass. (58–69)

Richard Rodgers (1902–1979) and Oscar Hammerstein II (1895–1960)
("R. and H.," *And Promenade Home*)

> Toward the end of this essay, de Mille mentions a 1944 novel by Frederic Wakeman, *Shore Leave*. Long out of print, it was a best seller during World War II, owing largely to its themes of casual sex and adultery but also to its underlying critique of the glorification of war.

In March 1945 Rodgers and Hammerstein once more collaborated with the Theatre Guild management, Therese Helburn and Lawrence Langner, on a musical version of Molnar's *Liliom*, to be called *Carousel*. The staff that had produced *Oklahoma!* reassembled, Rouben Mamoulian, Miles White and myself. The only addition to our group was Jo Mielziner, replacing Lemuel Ayers as scene designer.

I had had the barest acquaintance with Dick and Oscar when I signed up for *Oklahoma!* but during the rehearsals and afterwards our friendship deepened. By the winter of 1944–1945 I was going to Oscar not only for professional advice but personal reaffirmation. Since every man in my life was far away and unavailable for comfort or council, I began to turn to him as big brother on many nontheatric occasions. The relationship grew to be one of the joys of my life. He had talked for over a year about his plans for *Liliom* and I looked forward to the opportunity of working on a second R. and H. production as the happy reward for being a good girl.

Plans ripened that spring. While the snow fell softly outside his Pennsylvania farmhouse, Oscar talked as only he can, transforming the material of our common craft into hopeful and lyric enchantment.

There have been few lasting collaborations in the history of the theater, even though the theater is, in essence, collaboration. The difficulties involved in sharing responsibility and effort, the trial of work conditions, the apportioning of recognition and rewards have proved more than most friendships could encompass. Preservation of equilibrium implies a restraint rather more subtle than that required, for instance, in marriage. Such a relationship obviously presupposes mutual respect and absolute loyalty, consideration, and steadiness of nerve. Rodgers and Hammerstein have worked together in a team that has lasted longer in friendship (if not yet in business association) than Gilbert and Sullivan. They have been able to do this because they recognize their need of one another and because they practice discipline. I had a ringside seat at their first joint effort and witnessed their great, their unprecedented triumph. I saw them at work in three productions; I was privileged to work beside them.

In a union like theirs, bound tight by creative collaboration, business involvements, administration and public exposure, they are locked closer than most families. Their interdependence suggests royal dynasty. And although the two households live apart with summer homes in different states, they present a common front to the public. R. and H. appear publicly together, they refer to one another in all interviews, they make decisions jointly, their joint word is pledged on all deals, they receive joint and equal honors. One might think that a double opinion on all questions would cause delay; it does not. They act with dispatch.

They always hold their first conferences privately, and come to staff meetings united and in perfect agreement. They decide quickly and they stand by their decisions. In the field of art this is not easy, the artist's birthright being to reconsider and alter. But in the theater hesitation is not always practical, especially in matters of casting and staff. And therefore R. and H. examine all newcomers personally, even the totally unknown. They can see, no one better, talent or lack of it in a face, they can hear it in a voice. Whatever I had that was good, either professional or personal, held their instant attention and no intermediary was needed to tip them off. For years anyone could appear for an audition and be heard and everyone, even the well known, had to—a precaution, although seemingly arrogant, designed to guarantee high caliber of production. They were like doctors who refused to diagnose until they had personally taken the pulse. From the time of *Oklahoma!*'s opening, every Thursday has been audition day. They saw and heard literally thousands, took note, and when the opportunity came in their great international enterprises, sent for the applicants and placed them.

This attention to detail has always governed their activity. Every audition, every rehearsal was watched by one or the other. They had final word on every set, prop, hat, light, inflection or musical key. Absolutely nothing was overlooked, not even after the openings, when Dick policed his theaters with a zest and concern extraordinary for someone who had seen so very many shows through long runs. During rehearsals, Oscar usually stayed with the actors, absenting himself only for rewrites, while Dick guarded the dancing and singing. Even with a management as experienced as the Theatre Guild and with directors as distinguished as Rouben Mamoulian, Joshua Logan, John van Druten, Harold Clurman, and Fred Zinnemann, they never slacked their vigilance from the first day of rehearsal. What has made them uniquely effective (beside their talent) is their professional watchfulness. They check every aspect of their productions like mechanics going over an engine prior to transoceanic flight.

The impression on first meeting them was that here at last were the aristocrats of the business. They spoke softly, intelligently and politely. They knew about theater prior to 1919 and outside of Broadway and Hollywood. They were courteous and charming. Their interests were manifold.

In appearance they are dissimilar. Dick is moderately short and squarish, with a strong compact torso, the developed hands and forearms of a pianist, a strong short neck on which sets and turns a head almost archaic in its concentrated power. When considering, he becomes fixed and monolithic like a primitive. His piercing black eyes grow as opaque as an Aztec's, his face expressionless. The rest of us wait and hold heartbeat because the decision will be Star Chamber and final. "Well," he will say, throwing down his cigarette and smiling so suddenly and graciously that every subsequent remark becomes illuminated by the unexpected release, "I'll tell you what we'll do," and then he outlines a practical course of action, which may not be what you had in mind at all, but while he talks you will be convinced, or at least you will wish very much to be.

"I want you at the end of the dance," he will say, "to get a big hand—not a cheap hand. I want you in your way, in your own style, to stop the show—without, of course, sacrificing any of the delicacy or tenderness you value. I know you can do this without compromise; you have that kind of technique." The challenge has been thrown by Rodgers, S.J. And under the spell of his hypnotic persuasion you rush to meet it.

He kids and jokes companionably at all rehearsals, but he is a figure of some terror, through sheer nervous tension, high voltage, and the unforgettable overtones of his world power. His diction and tonality are straight New York, a flat, crisp, didactic voice, something like an instructor. He is the reverse of talky. He does not converse; he pronounces with judgment frequently unexpected and sharp, like summer lightning. Most of his comments are *coups de grâce*.

But at moments of direct personal approach he can be gentle. I suspect he feels in some ways cut off, even yearning; the banter is too constant, the quips too quick and sharp to betoken anything but vulnerability. He moves behind verbal machine guns. But just as the greatest quality in his music is a lilting delicious scherzo with overtones of hovering sweetness, so in his manner and in his eyes (when he is off guard) there is a brooding quiet, a kind of unappeased hunger, a woe.

Oscar seems solider, more the country gentleman, the paterfamilias, the benevolent, genial eighteenth-century man of letters. He looks too neighborly, too understanding, too philosophic for our gypsy and disreputable trade. Oscar is somewhat older, but his respect for Dick's judgment amounts to veneration. He is a tall, broad, heavy and gentle-faced man with a soft voice, a Yankee twang when excited, and a chuckle that is one of the most auspicious sounds our theater ever housed. He has, for all his size, the quietness and discipline of an athlete. He smokes little, drinks almost nothing at all, and practices daily exercise and massage. Like Dick, he is always immaculately dressed. He wears beautiful custom-made shoes of glove leather that fit over his insteps without laces. He walks quietly; he waits quietly, he watches with attention genial and silent and can enter and leave a rehearsal without being observed or interrupting work in progress; but he will have learned a great deal.

Dick is considerate and quiet, too, but always noticed. He takes a chair by the director, or by the piano, or he sits chatting in the auditorium with a member of the cast, or he dictates his entire morning mail. But he misses nothing, not an inflection, not a turn of the wrist or a grace note. And none of us ever misses the fact that he is there watching. In music rehearsals he is, of course, an active participant; he plays well and frequently takes the piano to give pace and dynamics.

When I started rehearsals for *Oklahoma!* I asked for an interview with him about the ballet music and handed him a detailed scenario broken down into seconds as I had done for Aaron Copland. He nodded and stuffed it into his pocket, then proceeded without slackening step into his song rehearsal. "Aren't you going to read this?" I asked. "You have all the songs, haven't you?" he answered. And, smiling, he hurried on.

No further word coming from him, the dance pianist and I began piecing his song tunes together in a kind of sequence—purely as a makeshift—and without warning, suddenly Dick materialized like a chef standing over the piano with pepper and salt, accenting, changing keys, shaping phrases, organizing both pace and music. But when at last we came to the final death struggle at the end of the ballet, we found that the score contained no melody suitable for breaking a man's back. I sent bulletin after bulletin upstairs to Rodgers, but he was coaching songs and too busy to come down. Finally in desperation we set the fight in silence to counts, and showed it this way at the first run-through. At conclusion Dick came tearing up the aisle and grabbed my hands. "It's wonderful and I like the silence. We'll put some tympani underneath to cue the dancers." And that is how it remained. I was startled by this seeming casualness, but Dick knew it would be all right. He added a coda and the whole piece worked out well. If he had found the effect weak, he would have given prompt orders.

The most noticeable differences between the men are in their habits and methods of work. All matters except the writing and reading of lines are dominated somewhat, I should say, by Dick, but it is Hammerstein who composes first. His incomparable ear and flair for metrical form establish rhythms that are later translated into melody. Oscar works at his farm in Pennsylvania or in his superb Georgian study in New York, slowly and painstakingly, beginning at dawn every morning, writing at his stand-up eighteenth-century desk and pacing the floor, muttering. Dick works anywhere—his home, backstage, the orchestra pit, frequently in a cubicle in Carnegie Hall—rapidly and easily. (The eight-minute aria of Billy Bigelow in *Carousel*, which had taken Oscar many weeks to conceive and complete, was set by Dick in two hours, as fast, in fact, as he could indicate melody and key changes on paper.) Dick seldom revises or alters. His work is virtually complete when we go into rehearsal. Oscar, on the other hand, does considerable editing; the job for the rest of us just begins. So Dick sits watching. Oscar is more relaxed perhaps, because busier, and not so constantly present. Both are available with ideas and time when needed.

Oscar, who has the reputation of being folksy, down-to-earth and more or less cracker-barrel in his style, is actually prone to considerable daring in his search for new forms. He has attempted startling and lovely experiments. His first version of God in *Carousel* as a New England minister and his wife was extraordinarily imagined but shocked Calvinistic New Haven and was immediately and entirely deleted, the two characters becoming one, the star-tender, the keeper of the heavenly back doors, "The Mother-of-Pearly Gates," but the first version had a dry toughness that the second lacked and a quality that Oscar has frequently had to yield before audience hesitation or surprise. This occurred in one third of the scenes in *Allegro*.

Dick is more conventional, classic, if you will. He is not so interested in experimenting as in reaching the audience emotionally and he prefers the direct and proven methods for doing this. He thinks the words of a song should be heard and understood, and the best place for the singer is, therefore, standing on the footlights and facing front, all but motionless, surrounded and framed by perfect quiet. To this end, the lights are as a rule lowered and the singer picked out by a special spot. This treatment rather handicaps the director and gives small scope to movement invention. It can become monotonous. But monotony to Rodgers is of no concern beside clarity. If the song is good enough there will be no talk about monotony. And under his care the song is generally good enough.

Neither man has an eye for color. And this is strange considering Dick's great love for modern painting. On the other hand, he can grasp the form and idiom of dance movement with the skill of a choreographer and has always been creatively helpful in placing and cutting dances. Oscar has no true visual appreciation; he admits he does not know how to look at painting. Pure gesture communicates nothing to him. But if he recognizes only dramatic content, how sensitive he is with this! My feeling for character, for intimate comedy, for the pattern dictated by situation and mood, even my willingness to forgo the effects that would ensure a final hand were treated by him with gentle and appreciative intelligence.

In setting stage business for their songs I strove, without contradiction of text or character, to broaden the author's original intent by adding my own comment. Sometimes quite sly and expressive jokes could be contrived by playing off one medium against another. But they always were keyed to scene and mood. In this way the dances are rooted into the score and dialogue and have become part of the flesh; that is why they are always reproduced no matter who stages the revivals.

The authors were appreciative. Dick's enthusiasm for any subtle rhythmic device or a gay "button" at the end of a piece (the trick that drives the point home sharp and clear), Oscar's joyous and tender excitement when I did something revealing of character, when I added speech to the dances in *Carousel*, for instance (Oscar is in love with language and likes to see it get on), were the rewards of working with them. They were equally vocal when dissatisfied, insisting on eighteen tries and my heart's blood, insisting and persisting until the curtain was up. Then time stopped and they cut. I have seen Dick yank out ten minutes of his own music without an attempt to save it. He has also yanked ten minutes of my dancing, but he put the scalpel into my hand.

In spite of their great skill, the tryout periods for their shows have always been quite as hard as any others; but there were little diversions and encouragements peculiar to association with them. There were the quatrains and parodies Oscar improvised under his breath apropos of rehearsal occurrences. Many a lunch ended with a completed song quite as brilliant as any published. There were Oscar's outrageous and superb puns murmured half apologetically as though not expecting the corroboration of a giggle or even the turning of a head, like his designation of a delicate caress on a cancan girl's bustle as a "gosling," or his wordless comment as when at a particularly stringent moment, having ordered a cut against my bitter opposition, "and don't come out of rehearsal hall until it's done," he sent a tray of twenty cartons of coffee where I sat alone brooding (this was, of course, after coffee rationing had ended), or when he had discussed for days the cutting of another number, the *Carousel* clambake dance, he said, sitting down quietly, "Convince me," and sometime later, "You argue well, but I don't agree."

"I don't agree too," I replied patly.

"That makes us even. But I have the choice."

I answered, "That's candid. I can accept that."

"My dear," he chuckled, "you'd better. You have to."

Or again, when hearing me express extreme dissatisfaction with my own work, he put his arms around me and murmured, "You be careful what you say about de Mille; you're talking about the woman I love."

Both men, wise in this difficult business, are generous with advice. Oscar takes time off to read and consider lengthy manuscripts and gives [counsel] and help. But one can talk to Oscar about anything at all. For Oscar one clips items from newspapers and magazines, marks passages in books, reports conversations overheard, remembers specially, finds drolleries, thinks more lucidly and perceptively. Oscar is never under any circumstances bored; everything is new and provocative, even the conversation of adolescents. I have seen him set aside work and spend half an afternoon teaching chess to an eight-year-old. Oscar has given away a dozen young professionals in marriage and stood godfather at a score of christenings. Dick fascinates and amuses, but it is Oscar whose hand they ask to take at solemn moments.

And at moments of need. I went to him once on behalf of Ballet Theatre. It was the first time I had ever approached anyone in his position for money. I had not warned him about what I came for. I sat down in great disquiet in the beautiful Georgian chair, surrounded by the fabulous porcelain and books, and faced him over the mahogany desk with the silver accouterments. He smiled and waited. I squirmed and moistened my lips. He didn't speak.

"It's just this—" I stuttered.

"All right, yes," he cut me short.

"Yes what?"

"Yes a thousand dollars. Never mind the pitch. Do you want Scotch or bourbon?"

Oscar and Dick take on together not only the regulation charities expected of men in their position, but their own foundation and causes, political issues and social reforms. They work hard at them, writing pamphlets and sketches and songs. Oscar devotes a real measure of his time and resources to this.

Both are businessmen in the historic American tradition and combine the drive and power of nineteenth-century empire builders with eighteenth-century politesse and philosophy, living in ducal splendor and maintaining a suite of offices outside of the law firm they all but endow. Seldom in the history of the theater has anyone approached their business success. Their four great plays have been running very nearly continuously in at least three countries for from ten to fifteen years. They each separately have a dozen or so permanent successes that bring in constant royalties. In addition, they have functioned as producers for others' work with enormous return (*Annie Get Your Gun*, "Happy Birthday"). They publish their own music and print their own books. They are now currently producing their own movies.

Far from exhausting them, these manifold interests and diversions are like catnip; they revel in the multifarious responsibilities and incomes. In this huge zest for affairs and returns they share equally.

Whenever we boarded a train together, Oscar would stop me and, placing a hand on my shoulder, say in his gentle, even voice, "Now, Agnes, what have you forgot this time?" (This was not a frivolous question. I had been known to forget or leave behind suitcases, briefcases, reading glasses, single shoes, music and, once, myself, when the Oklahoma City fire department was dispatched to find me and fetch me to the train.)

What have I forgot? Oh, so much. It is hard in a few pages to sketch these complex, contradictory, fascinating, passionate and gifted men who played such an overwhelming role in my life and of whom I grew so fond, so grateful to for so much, with whom, in fact, I fell in love, yet who, for all the rich and fruitful hours spent together, the miles traveled, the honors and horrors shared, were bent on preserving what in the end could not be shared. For over the years they became more and more concerned with what tragically and inevitably must raise barriers between their ambition and all collaborators.

Carousel was a tough show for the choreographer because it was based on a strong and well-written play and there seemed small need for dances. The ballet in Act II, therefore, represented probably the hardest challenge I'd ever met. It entailed a real job of dramatic invention, close to playwrighting. I struggled and strained, but at last the bosses avowed themselves pleased.

The opening night in New Haven was a real surprise. This was, as Jo Mielziner remarked, the best musical-comedy script he'd ever read and it had been beautifully directed, but almost none of it came off as we had expected. The staff repaired to a hotel room where sacrifice and a cold supper awaited. There followed the kind of conference that professionals seldom see: in two hours we made a plan, throwing out or drastically altering the better part of Act II, half my ballet, five complete scenes (and with one the services and hopes of an elderly actress who had come out of retirement for the first real chance of her life), a couple of good songs and several verses in the remaining ones.

At the end of two hours we were all well exercised.

Although neither of the authors could have foreseen the audience reaction that night, they must have been to some degree prepared, because they set to rewriting with an alacrity and organization that bespoke foresight.

One of the assistants said as we left the room after that dreadful first *Carousel* conference, "Now I see why these people have hits. I never witnessed anything so brisk and brave in my life." And indeed, not three minutes had been wasted pleading for something cherished. Nor was there any idle joking as at the *Venus* conferences. We cut and cut and cut and then we went to bed.

Oscar went earliest, as soon as he could get away, because he would be up at six, working. And he had a list of required lyrics, scenes and liaison bits that would have daunted any lesser theater craftsman. For the next two weeks he was due to put in five or six hours of creative writing every day from dawn on.

Oscar would be alone and quiet in his room with his wits about him. But I was scheduled to begin in public. And into the room with me would drag the slightly soiled and shopworn brutes known as my dance company. They had to pull it out of their backs. I thought I had better be ready to help. Therefore I was also due up at six.

One might with time, one would think, build up a toleration for the try-out period, but working with Rodgers and Hammerstein always seemed more significant than working with others. Their united force was greater, their passions channeled deeper, their intent more noticeably implemented. One could no more think of their failing than of the war effort failing. One always felt that Posterity sat in on all staff meetings and had a good deal to say. Also our old colleague, Box Office, but this time dressed in a silk hat and carrying a gold-headed cane, and this time with voice mellifluous and venerable. There were elements of Patriotism and Mother Love and Honor in what they expected, and what you were privileged to give. Dick had never had a failure, he kept saying. And were you going to be the one to help him to this unprecedented, humbling experience? Oscar had had several, long before, and at the height of his great fame took a full page in *Variety* and advertised his worst notices with the endearing caption, "It happened before; it can happen again." This public penance, this propitiation to Fortune made him the more worthy of serving. It was only human for others to watch with jealous eyes for the misstep in the splendid parade. But we who marched alongside were very proud and minded the music and the step carefully.

All night I minded and counted and planned. All day I rehearsed. Between times I walked the streets alone in the twilight and thought of how someday I would not have to work like this. I would sleep and waste time and think of frivolities. Someday I would look forward to the evenings.

In Boston the spring freshened and flickered, the young green leaves dancing in the air like insects, and everywhere women lifted their heads and wondered how their men would find them. For the waiting had dimmed and blurred all of us. This had been a time of wrestling to hold vigorously to hope. And like any strong experience it had shadowed our faces. But we believed still that childhood would one day come back to the earth, and not a hat was bought that Easter without a personal prayer behind the act, not a daisy, not a yard of ribbon. In every house throughout the land cupboards were being opened and dresses shaken out and somehow the feminine rustling and stirring was a surer omen than the changing map. It was time for the war to be over. It was the earth season for a new way.

Meantime I was living in a hotel room. And he was in a place designated by a number. And I walked alone, back and forth across the common and up and down streets where families were sitting down to dinner, and men entered doorways and were greeted.

If there is a limit set to dreadful times they become bearable, but if none is known they are unbearable. And yet, they are to be lived through, and whether the end will come today or tomorrow, six years, never . . . they are to be lived through. My friend Arthur Davison Ficke, the poet, dying, said to me at this point, "The European war will be over in five years, but the war in Asia—this is a secret, don't breathe it—the war in Asia will be a thousand-year war." Ideas like this had to be listened to and endured. One leaned into anguish as a dancer leans against space, and the living balance within sustained. And one day passed and one day and one day and that year was done.

We were now getting into the second spring of separation. Nothing seemed to change. Europe was being recovered mile by mile, but the Pacific and its hundreds of islands stretched across our lives. One could not think beyond this geography. One dared not look at maps or reports. If one read a book, it might possibly be something like *Shore Leave*, that dandy sabotaging of women's morale which, in an agony, I discussed with Walter, suggesting that if all husbands and lovers were unfaithful all the time, it were just as well not to advertise the fact to their women. He reassured me after his own fashion: that he was terribly surprised at my concern about anything so badly written.

Walter's news was broken and sparse. He didn't like the English weather. He had arrived in November at Liverpool, had not been piped off the boat as I had hoped, but had disembarked in a grim clanking, marched down streets without a light in black pouring rain, and had been shut immediately into a transport train for Stone, Staffordshire, where it was still raining. "Out of the frying pan into the mire." In August he had written, "Yesterday, a Monday, we had summer." Elizabeth Bowen had been extremely kind. Lise Harland had invited him to dinner. She had lost the child she was carrying in a recent bombing. He had given her nylons. He had visited a neighbor, the Countess of ——, and here, there was a hole in the paper. But she wrote to me herself directly, so I found out who *she* was. He was camped, I learned much too late, in the paddock adjacent to Rebecca West's farm at High Wycombe, but because I couldn't notify her, she never leaned over the garden wall and asked him in. It was raining a good bit. I was not to buy any more furniture. Couldn't I arrange to rest a little? He saw no end to the war. London was infrequent, but quite fun. He visited a friend of mine, a quartermaster in Westminster, who had a flat. There was, however, fog in London. And rain.

In all this boredom and complaining, I was now and then drawn up sharp to the realization that he was in the middle of it, in daily mortal peril. There was the simple reference to a toy factory that had got a direct hit in the town nearby; most of the casualties were old women and very young girls. His battalion had devoted New Year's Eve to cleaning it up. There was the casual remark about a job of detonating leftover land mines along the beaches—routine work, he said—they all had to do it. The point was to try to guess correctly in which direction the chain reaction of the explosives would proceed. Sometimes they guessed wrong; they found this wry. I stared at that letter a long time as it sat on my breakfast tray. But he never spoke of active combat or any of the plasterings on his air base—never a word.

We had stopped making plans in our letters. We talked vaguely of Afterward. But Afterward seemed hardly possible and in the meantime we were spending all our time among people neither of us knew. Every episode that had occurred between us in our brief communion had been worn bare with the retelling. I searched the headlines and maps for some name on which to fasten an intimate fragment of gossip or a personal reminiscence, but history was between us, and whisperings and turnings of the head and liftings of the hand were blotted out by world events which everyone shared. There was nothing for us alone. We kept trying to imagine how the circumstances seemed under the other set of conditions; but of course we could not. About this time I realized I had forgotten how his voice sounded.

But once in a while the public sharing was so awful as to destroy space. There was the night in the Ritz elevator I saw the tragic terminal headline "ROOSEVELT DEAD!" In the great gold cloakroom of the Colonial Theatre, to which I had, as a matter of duty, to go, with the paper spread on the marble-topped gilt table, I read the details. The coat woman complacently knitted. Tears of horror and grief fell through my fingers as I read and I was oppressed with terror for the reconstruction without the man whom so many and so disparate people had come to trust.

"Well, it was about time for a change," said the cloakroom woman, "and thank God we are spared That Man." That Man, in this case, was Wallace. "And soon I hope we can have someone sensible and have a change from all this idiotic spending." I continued to weep without answering. On the other side of the wall, June Busted Out again. It was 9:04. I went back in the auditorium and saw Pearl Lang get her hand and retire to the wings, where the cast stood appalled, round-eyed, not speaking.

The same night, in Germany, Walter was smoking at mess with the French officers when, hearing a commotion in the road outside, they all ran out to find the sentries with some Russian D.P.'s. The Russians were distraught and making a terrible noise, begging, apparently, to see the commander. It was hard to understand them, but one name came through, and their persuasive and apparent grief. The D.P.'s had a radio, and they knew the American officers had none, and so they had come hurrying up the road to bring the news. And there, under the moon and the blossoming branches of a Bavarian spring, these two groups of men confronted each other and several wept.

I knew of this only much later. We were in Boston with a show to ready and our minds were fly-specked with our tiny troubles and hurts. Finally one day Dick watched with grim lips the revised ballet and that night the new ending was tried out. "Well," he said in relief as it finished, "I wouldn't have given you a nickel for it this afternoon."

"I know," I said.

He hugged me. "It's all right now, kid. The changes work. You've got a hit."

Opening night in New York my protégée, Bambi Linn, stopped the show cold. This is a phrase often used, but seldom actually witnessed. The first time I ever saw it was when a debutante named Ethel Merman sang "I Got Rhythm" in a Gershwin musical, *Girl Crazy*. At the conclusion of the *Carousel* ballet, the actors four times tried to resume dialogue before they were permitted to be heard, and when minutes later Bambi, having changed costume, made her next appearance, she was greeted with such a roar that she had to step forward and bow. Her face burned with excitement and two little girls in the wings burst into tears. The audience continued to yell. This happens frequently in opera houses but almost never in the commercial theater. The sound in the opera houses is lyric and ecstatic. The sound on Broadway is sharp, instantaneous and important. Behind this clapping is the noise of thousands and thousands and thousands of dollars, of telegraph wires humming, radio stations broadcasting, recording machines turning over, agents telephoning, reporters typing. The roar from a Broadway audience opens every door in the theater world. Immediately. That night.

Bambi woke up to find herself famous. (232)

Alicia Alonso (b. 1920)
("Alicia Alonso," *Portrait Gallery*)

> The ballerina Alicia Alonso studied with several influential teachers in New York, as mentioned here, and her astonishing technique and memory are tributes to all of them. Alexandra Fedorova (1884–1972), a 1902 graduate of the Imperial Ballet School in St. Petersburg, was a soloist with the Maryinsky Ballet, a member (briefly, in 1909) of Diaghilev's Ballets Russes, and a principal

dancer and choreographer with the Riga Opera Ballet, among other companies. The sister-in-law of the choreographer Michel Fokine, she settled in New York in 1937 and became a popular teacher there. In the December 2002 issue of *Dance Magazine*, Wendy Perron wrote of her "side extension almost up to her ear (still in evidence in her 70s)" and of her "tiny, strong feet that could go up on pointe in soft shoes." Fedorova's students included Robert Joffrey, Nora Kaye, Gower Champion, and Eugene Loring. Enrico Zanfretta (1863–1946) was the son of a ballet teacher in Italy, many of whose students emigrated to New York. As Ann Barzel wrote of the son in the April-May-June 1944 issue of *Dance Index*, "the Zanfretta who taught in New York advertised as . . . teacher of 'ballet, character, toe—deportment and pantomime,' taught without musical accompaniment and was scornful of the 'quicky methods' of the new simplified schools. His style was archaic and included much fluttering of the wrists and deep curtsies." Husband and wife Anatole Vilzak (1896–1998) and Ludmila Shollar (1888–1978) were both graduates of the Imperial Ballet School in St. Petersburg and both performed with many companies, among them the Maryinsky and Diaghilev's Ballets Russes. In the United States, they taught at the School of American Ballet, the Ballet Theatre school, their own Vilzak-Shollar school (where Alonso studied), and, in the case of Vilzak, the schools of the Washington Ballet and the San Francisco Ballet.

Cuba has three chief exports: cigars, sugar, and Alicia Alonso. Everyone in the world knows about Cuban cigars and sugar. Everyone in Cuba knows Alicia. She is hailed with "Viva Alicia!" on sight, and bands accompany her arrivals and departures. Her name is not a household word outside of Cuba only because her traveling is politically restricted. The knowledgeable, however, are aware of her, and her place in history is assured.

She is a dancer, one of the finest classic ballerinas living today. What makes her unique, what makes her different from all predecessors, all rivals, is one simple fact: Alicia is blind. It is highly unusual for any athlete to have impaired vision, but for an active dancer to continue working with such a disability has never before occurred. Alicia is famous, however, not because of her blindness but in her own right, compared to the sighted. As Richard Philp, the editor of *Dance Magazine*, says, "She makes illusion. She is illusion."

She has other distinctions. Unlike most stars, who are notoriously and by definition self-centered, she is public-spirited. As a matter of fact, she is a militant revolutionary and has contributed to the social history of her country. Finally, she has built a ballet company that is a national institution and has world prestige.

Alicia is a small woman, and very attractive. Her two outstanding characteristics are her enormous smile and her eyes—her great eyes, black and piercing, blind yet piercing, apprehending accurately what they cannot perceive, judging, choosing, dismissing, masking in their impenetrable depths the inflexible will. Barbara Barker, assistant to Igor Youskevitch, the classic star and former head of the dance department at the University of Texas, says, "I think what happens when she talks to you is that she stares as though she were trying to see you, or, more particularly, as if she didn't want you to know that she can't see you. She looks very intently at where she hears your voice coming from. The intensity of that look is startling, and very hard not to flinch from."

Reinforcing the eagerness of Alicia's eyes is her smile. Her wide, slightly undershot mouth is like a child's, voracious for experience, determined to taste all, to know all. It is quick to smile, quick to speak. Her soft, voluble tongue, waiting to taste, flicks between the half-parted lips, which roll out the lightning Spanish. Alicia seems like a lady lizard that one longs to tame but cannot.

Her nose is straight and large, with the sensitive, quivering nostrils of a doe, alert to any signal. Her neck is long and supple, bearing the elegant little head like a tropical flower on its tender stalk. Her body is small, beautifully formed, with small breasts and hips, long arms and legs, the feet and arches of a great dancer. They were not hers early in her career; she had to create them. Her fingers taper. Her nails are extravagantly long, protruding three quarters of an inch beyond her fingertips and rendering them useless, one would think, for anything beyond ornamentation. But Alicia sews and makes all her own headdresses. She also paints.

Alicia Ernestina de la Caridad del Cobre Martínez y del Hoyo was born with perfect vision and saw quite clearly and normally until she was nineteen years old. She was the youngest of the four children of Antonio and Ernestina Martínez, and was brought up in the fashionable Vedado section of Havana. Her father was an army veterinary surgeon, and fondly hoped to give Alicia the confined, proper, comfortable life of a nicely raised middle-class girl. She went to Spain when she was eight and learned the flamenco dances, but only in order to perform them for her grandfather, a Spaniard living in Havana. That was to be all the dancing she was ever to know, her father supposed, except what she needed for ballroom purposes. As she puts it, "He no want me to dance. He not like the frivolity of stage, especially dancing."

But Alicia did not have the personality of a confined middle-class girl. She was an exotic, and she expected to do strange things. Her nickname was Unga, "the Hungarian." A neighborhood playmate, Fernando Alonso, and his brother, Alberto, were the sons of Señora Laura Rayneri Alonso, who managed the Pro Arte concert series and school; they introduced Alicia at the school, and there, unknown to her father but with her mother's connivance, Alicia started dance classes. Fernando helped her, with increasing enthusiasm. When she was a teenager Alicia saw no reason to continue formal academic training and stopped. She could read and write, but she has had to pick up other knowledge as needed—not too difficult for her, as she has an avidly curious mind and a totally retentive memory.

Fortunately, the Pro Arte school of ballet boasted a real Russian ballet teacher, Nikolai Yavorsky. However, there was not a pair of pointe shoes anywhere in Havana. Many of the pupils were forced to work in sneakers or bare feet.

It soon became apparent that Alicia was remarkably gifted for ballet dancing. It was equally clear that Fernando was falling in love with her, and his family, growing alarmed, hastily sent him to continue his studies in Florida, to put a safe amount of saltwater between him and temptation. However, Fernando persuaded Alicia to follow, which she did enthusiastically. He seduced her in quick order, and they lived happily and precariously together, dancing all day. She was possessed of an ambition that he had never before seen. Indeed, I believe it has never been surpassed in the theatrical world in this century. She also became pregnant. She was now a mature fifteen years old.

The couple proceeded to Spanish Harlem, where relatives took Alicia in. In a month, after giving birth, she was back on the dance floor, struggling to perfect her technique. Fernando now acted as her coach. Her baby, Laura, was turned over to whoever could be arranged for in the way of a nurse. Everyone helped, even Alicia's contemporaries. She spent all day practicing, taking time off only to feed the baby, to marry, and to cook for Fernando. Eventually it seemed practical to send Laura back to Havana, so she did.

Alicia got a job with Lincoln Kirstein's Ballet Caravan, where she followed Marie-Jeanne in the role of the sweetheart in Eugene Loring's *Billy the Kid*—a role in which she has never been surpassed. After the Ballet Caravan tour, Fernando and Alicia attended the School of American Ballet and the Vilzak-Shollar School and danced in the chorus lines of two musicals, *Great*

Lady and *Stars in Your Eyes*, the latter choreographed by Balanchine. Jerome Robbins, Muriel Bentley, and Nora Kaye were also in that chorus. In 1941 all five joined the newly formed Ballet Theatre as corps de ballet dancers. Alicia performed in everything she could, attending daily classes given by Alexandra Fedorova and Enrico Zanfretta, the Italian ballet master who also trained Carmelita Maracci. It was Zanfretta who gave both Alicia and Carmelita their first knowledge of Enrico Cecchetti's style.

In short, Alicia's schedule consisted of unbroken training. At eleven o'clock every morning she did the company class. That was an hour and a half of really hard work. Then she would take class at another school, another hour and a half to two hours of exhausting exercise. Every night before the performance, in full makeup, she would do a warm-up coached by her husband, and then, dripping with sweat, she would go to her dressing room, dry off, get into her costume, and conclude with a full evening's performance. I never heard of any other dancer putting herself through such a regimen.

I said to her one night, "Alicia, you will be exhausted."

"I must do this, Ahnes (no Cuban can pronounce the *g* in my name), or I won't get strong," she replied. "I must get strong."

Alicia got strong. Gradually, she was given solos to do—not important ones, but noticeable ones. She always distinguished herself. When Mrs. Martínez in Cuba first read the notices of these appearances, she burst into tears, not because the reviews were bad but because they were very good. Alicia also appeared in a double-page spread of pictures in *Life* magazine. When her mother hesitantly showed them to her father, the long-suffering lieutenant, he shrugged, then smiled broadly; he later displayed them proudly to his fellow officers. Alicia believes that he bought out the entire Cuban allotment of the magazine for that week.

Alicia's energy was inexhaustible. After the long and punishing hours of practice and rehearsal, she would give up her dinnertime to costume fittings, arguing over each seam, each tuck, the color and weight of the material, as though she were a pilot readying a new airplane. She knew her reputation would be modified by those seams.

Her feet began to change. They were not beautiful; "more like spoons," said a contemporary. She made them beautiful. They became remarkable even among great dancers. They grew strong, of course, as well as flexible, agile, correctly schooled. But those qualities do not begin to describe the flashing, flickering dazzle of Alicia's footwork—what dancers call brio, which means bravura technique. I think her feet moved more rapidly than anyone else's, and always correctly in line. They were strong as steel but seemed soft and caressing. She stroked and touched the floor as a musician touches his instrument. She melted into the floor or she ricocheted from it like hail bouncing. At times she seemed not to have anything to do with the floor but simply to pass above it. "Her feet were not just doing a required step, they were expressions on their own," said her favorite partner, Igor Youskevitch.

Alicia was nineteen and succeeding splendidly when she began to notice that she was bumping into furniture, that she could not see her partner when he was at her side but only when he was slightly in front of her. Instead of seeing in a semicircle, as most people do, she seemed to see only in a triangle. Nor could she focus in a straight line; she had to turn and run in a little circle, which made lifting harder for the boys. In short, she had no peripheral vision.

She and Fernando played games to test the exact limits of her sight. In March 1941, Lucia Chase, the head of Ballet Theatre, arranged for her to go to New York Hospital to have her vision tested definitively. "Detachment of the retina" was the verdict, and she was ordered to have an operation. She lay in bed with her eyes bandaged for three months. Fernando stayed right beside her—"the inspiration of my life," she called him. She became the mascot of the hospital ward, where everyone referred to her as "our girl."

Leon Danielian, a fellow student at the Mordkin Ballet, went to see her at what is now the Columbia Presbyterian Medical Center. Although her eyes were bandaged and she lay motionless, her feet were moving under the coverlet. She was doing *battements tendues*, pointing and stretching her toes without moving her body. According to Danielian, "I said, 'Don't move,' but she said, 'I have to keep my feet alive.' It was extraordinary to see her. She was heroic about it."

At length the bandages were removed. Alicia could see better, but certain troubles persisted. A second operation, a very serious one, was recommended. It too was only partially successful. The third operation was in Havana. Her doctor told her she had only one chance to see: she would have to lie completely still for a year with her eyes in bandages.

The orders were brutal. She could not move her head one sixth of an inch for twelve months, nor laugh, nor cry, nor chew hard, nor play with her child or her dog. Every day and every evening Fernando sat with her and helped her learn the great roles with her fingers—*Giselle*, *Swan Lake*, Aurora. She would show him the dance she was practicing and he would correct her. "It was torture for me to lie still, feeling my body gain weight and become flabby," she recalled. "I saw all the steps I had done and how often I had done them wrong.

I danced in my mind. Blinded, motionless, lying flat on my back, I taught myself to dance *Giselle*."

After a year of bed rest she was allowed to lead a modified life, but not to dance. She took walks with the Martínezes' Great Dane, and stealthily visited the ballet studio two blocks from her home, where she practiced every day. No one told on her. Then a sudden tornado visited the island. Alicia went outdoors to help her dog, who had just given birth, and the glass door of the porch shattered, showering all over her head and face. She fell. Her screams brought Fernando rushing; he picked her up, but found her miraculously unhurt except for minor cuts.

After the hurricane accident, the doctor told Alicia she could dance again, if she did so discreetly. He probably reasoned that if she could come unscathed through flying glass, torrential downpour, mud, and a bad fall, she could weather the exigencies of an ordinary ballet performance. She notified Ballet Theatre immediately by cable and returned to the United States, leaving Laura and Fernando in Cuba. When she arrived in New York, her head was still in bandages from the broken glass. Suddenly she was asked to go on in place of Markova, who was ill, in *Giselle*. Anton Dolin, who had always believed in Alicia, was her partner and régisseur and shepherded her through this extraordinary and terrifying comeback. She was instantly acclaimed. We now had a new ballerina.

That was gratifying, but Alicia faced a great challenge. She had partial sight in one eye but no peripheral vision. Her first task was to learn how to move independently on an open stage. She arranged to have two very strong spotlights in different colors focused on the front of the stage, a safe distance from the edge. These she could sense. She was aware that if she stepped in front of their glow, she was in danger, for beyond the lights she was in immediate peril of plunging into the orchestra pit. Of course, any fall would have been broken by the wire that is always stretched at waist height across her footlights, but I don't think the wire could have prevented Alicia from hurling herself full force into the danger zone.

For the most part, she danced within the cage of her partner's arms. Her partners were very carefully trained in how to guide, how to lead, without seeming to do so. As long as she was encircled and supported, she had their protection, as though by a trained nurse. All the time she was onstage with a partner, his voice guided her: "Come back," or "You have room to move forward," or "Go more to the side." Sometimes Youskevitch clicked his tongue. But when no partner was there, when she was alone, what guided her? There were always flashlights in the wings, but this does not explain the miracle of a blind girl rushing, racing, leaping, throwing herself rapidly in dazzling light against a wall of black emptiness—without falling.

Reader, try this experiment. Tape your eyes closed. Now walk around your bedroom, with which you are familiar, without using your hands. Walk beautifully, proudly, grandly. Now imagine that the fourth wall has been removed and in its place is a yawning pit, ten feet deep. Now run the course. Take to the air. There is no help, no safety. There is freedom to fly in beauty or to plunge to destruction. Alicia's stage was a minefield, and this was her nightly testing. She has been quoted as saying, "The dancer enters a bullring at every performance. At every performance he faces death."

Alicia was known for her balance, her rapid dancing, and her turns. Her balance was so exaggeratedly good that sometimes her partner confessed to pushing her off balance in order to force her to follow the musical phrase. As for her speed, she had the fastest feet in the business. They flashed and folded into the boxlike fifth position, and opened and arched out and shut like knives, with the rapidity of someone flicking a wrist. Her *pas de bourrée*, a tiny traveling step on full pointes, was of a gossamer, shimmering perfection unapproached by anyone within my memory. (I especially remember the *pas de bourrée* in the final waltz in Fokine's *Les Sylphides*).

Her turns were unmatched. The secret of the balletic turn is the use of the head and the eyes: by snapping around as your body revolves, you maintain your focus on one fixed spot so it never deviates, except for the merest fraction of a second. This is called spotting, and it is indispensable to preventing vertigo. When a dancer does the turns and pirouettes in one place, the head motion is easily discernible, for she moves her head to focus each time she makes a revolution. When she does the turns in a chain or line (*chaîné* pirouettes) across or around the stage, her vision is fixed on the corner toward which she progresses. On reaching the corner, she spots the next corner, until the circle is completed. But what if her vision is obscured, so she cannot find a point to fix on? How then does she make the revolutions? What keeps her from losing direction? Alicia Alonso could see only points of light, but she did the turns serenely, beautifully, and rapidly and ended just where she intended to end, with her arms out to the audience and a slow smile spreading on her wide, mobile lips.

Alicia was saved by artificial arrangements and also by a sixth sense, an extrasensory instinct. I was helping her along a passageway once. There were stairs ahead leading down. Suddenly she stopped, six feet in advance of the well: "There is a change of level ahead, a descent. I feel it." She anticipated my warning.

One time she did not anticipate danger, however. During a rehearsal of my *Fall River Legend* she was completing a ferocious pirouette, one foot held straight out in front of her, waist high, cutting the air like a scythe. My two-year-old son suddenly left my side and ran toward her. She stopped with a scream, her hands to her head. "Was he there? Was he there all the time? I can't see." I quickly reassured her: "He wasn't there, Alicia. He ran out suddenly. He was naughty." We were completely undone. The baby thought it all extremely funny. If her foot had caught him on the side of the head, she would probably have killed him.

Alicia's condition has fluctuated over the years, but she has never regained clear sight. She has had three operations on her retina and two for cataracts. "I had cataracts in both eyes," she explains, "like a veil covering my eyes all the time, and each time thicker." The morning after one operation, in Barcelona, she almost saw clearly for a moment: "I was so happy I could see again, I said without thinking, 'Oh doctor, you didn't shave this morning.'" When she reads, watches TV, or attends auditions, she uses high-powered binoculars like a naval commander's.

Having solved the problems peculiar to her own agonizing condition, Alicia must tackle the problem all star dancers face: maintaining the great and fragile technique. The discipline for this must continue until she ceases to dance. Now an acknowledged ballerina of world renown and the most famous woman in her own country, she must still walk into class, place her hands on the barre, and sweat.

Whenever Alicia takes class, she is driven to the school. "Are we there?" she must ask, turning her unseeing eyes to the building before which the car has stopped. "We are there," answers whoever has brought her, opening the car door and lending her a supporting hand to guide her up the front steps. In the classroom, however, she walks unhesitatingly and authoritatively right across the open floor to her place at the barre, where she executes her moves on order and on count. When she leaves the barre, she is surrounded by an unhelpful and unsupportive space in which other bodies approach and recede. Naturally the other dancers are careful of her, but she asks no favors. She can hold her own.

For an hour and a half daily she goes through the full routine, under the discipline of Fernando or, often today, of their daughter, Laura. Why does one of the ranking dancers of history submit to this? Nay, demand it? The pianist can hear what he does. The singer too can hear. But the dancer lives within the instrument and cannot see, so there must be an outside caretaker. The work for any star, as for any beginner, is unremitting and painfully hard, so there must be a disciplinarian to goad her on to the effort. The spirit and the flesh flag and droop, even with the indomitable Alicia.

Triumph by triumph Alicia mastered all the great roles. She became known as a phenomenally quick study. She learned Antony Tudor's *Lilac Garden* with three hours' preparation; she opened the bill with a Balanchine work, as programmed, then proceeded directly upstairs to the rehearsal hall during the following ballet. Four hours after the first frantic phone call she stepped out in the Tudor role and completed it without fault.

When Nora Kaye fell ill and was unable to open *Fall River Legend*, Alicia learned the ballet, a fifty-minute work, in two weeks. It was in a dramatic style that she had never before attempted and to a modern score of a kind quite unfamiliar to her.

In 1947 Balanchine created her signature piece, Tchaikovsky's *Theme and Variations*, which she and Igor Youskevitch performed for years. It was instantly recognizable that theirs was a union made in heaven. When Igor first danced with Alicia, he didn't know the partnership would be the smoothest of his career, and the most rewarding; as he later put it, "When we danced, we'd flow together." He was a great Old World cavalier, the star of the Ballet Russe de Monte Carlo, and she was a magic girl from a southern island: it was a collaboration that became a legend.

Most ballerinas have a coolness and an impersonality, a disembodied effect that comes from total intent and total concentration. Alicia adds to this the warmth of an extremely passionate woman. She is a Latin, and even her stage relationship with her partner is that of a woman who favors and is excited by the man. Whoever he may be, she does him the homage of recognizing him as a man. When there is also real personal feeling, as in the case of Youskevitch, the union becomes electric. They were both tender, caring, and proud. As Youskevitch said, "We felt pretty together. It was the best partnership I ever shared. We felt we were important."

Other dancers go through the schooled positions and transitions with varying degrees of expertise. Alicia murmurs, sighs, seems to be talking. There are no positions, no transitions, only yieldings, bestowings, yearnings, gestures that are serenely loving and of a continuing, living breath. She moves in life. Her feet, her torso, her arms, neck, and eyes, are one continuing action, taking their dynamics from her meaning. She talks. Her heart is open. Here is the essence of a dancer. It is her core she gives us; it is our core.

It goes without saying that her partner must be sensitive in order to further these inclinations. Of Jorge Esquivel, her pupil-partner, she says, "He responds at any movement what I do. He's like an echo, like a conversation." And he says, "With every position, every balance, she transmits to me all her expertise." And Youskevitch says, "We felt pretty together."

Oh, and they were! They danced in an aura of enchantment. Everyone believed they were in love. It was the common understanding for years. James Mitchell, the former dancer and film actor who is now a star of the TV show *All My Children*, tells about it: "I remember when she and Igor would do *Black Swan*. The entire company lined up in the wings on one another's shoulders to see her do her balances, her turns. The excitement . . . they were in love, and you could sure tell it. . . . The interplay between them, always without interference to the context or style, was absolutely breathtaking. She had that gigantic smile, and her tongue was just slightly extended. We all enjoyed watching." He goes on to say, "I partnered her in *Fall River*. I remember her being very soft and light, not like the others, who were solid. She was like gauze."

Barbara Barker, Youskevitch's assistant, says, "What I sensed in her—and I'm sure that a lot of other people have sensed it in her too—was the passion for her partner. She is just such an enormous flirt, and an enormously intent performer. But Youskevitch was always the important one. Their emotional bond was obvious."

"Why doesn't she marry him?" I once asked Lucia Chase.

"She is going back to Cuba later. She wants Fernando for her old age," Chase replied.

Alonso and Youskevitch danced together until 1959.

James Mitchell continued:

> When Alicia was programmed to do a pas de deux, Nora Kaye might follow it with *Fall River* or *Pillar of Fire*. Alicia would finish to screams, flowers, applause, and repeated curtain calls. The stagehands then would set up whatever ballet was due to follow Alicia, and the new cast would assemble. But Alicia would not go to her dressing room; she would stay right on stage and rehearse anything she had missed—a few pirouettes, balances that did not last all of ten seconds. Nora might be on that same stage trying to get herself into the proper kind of emotional state for her own performance, and she would literally have to kick Alicia out of her way, because Alicia just wouldn't leave. It was her stage.

Every individual who achieves prominence must have iron in his soul. Iron? Glue, rather.

Every other person, every situation, is twisted, bent, used toward the one purpose of the one will. The supreme artist or statesman may seem on occasion harsh, and invariably oblivious and selfish. What matter, as long as the unique quality is achieved? That is the sublime goal.

Walter Terry wrote in the *Saturday Review*: "Alicia Alonso is that rarest of dancing creatures, a prima ballerina assoluta. The vast public sees only a great artist, a remarkable virtuoso who can do multiple pirouettes. As an American ballerina she brought us international luster for more than three decades, a vision of enduring dance beauty."

Alicia went back to Cuba in 1948, at the height of her popularity and fame in the United States—"Because," she now explains, "I am a revolutionary. Because to me, the most important thing is the human being. Human beings are more important than my own art, than my own life. My life, my art, would have little value if human beings did not have the right to go to the theater, to have an education, to have a high standard of living, and other fundamental rights. The human being is worth more than any dollar bills that you could place in front of me. I want to feel I have given my life knowledge back to the people. I want to feel I have a little place permanently in life itself."

In fact Alicia returned to Cuba because at that time both Ballet Theatre and Ballet Russe de Monte Carlo had stopped functioning, for financial reasons. She suddenly found she had no American stage to dance on. It suits her now, however, to believe in the greater humanitarian and patriotic reason—which was present also.

Alicia Alonso began dancing in Havana without capital or backers. The Pro Arte lent her costumes, and she bought transportation with money from the advance sale of seats. Eventually Fernando, president of her new ballet company, and his brother Alberto, the artistic director, won subsidies from the Cuban Ministry of Education. They didn't receive much. This company had to be built out of their own unceasing labor. There were no trained dancers, no choreographers, no composers, and no designers. All of these had to be found. Furthermore, initially there was no audience.

The will that kept Alicia dancing in spite of sightlessness worked all the time in her behalf. She had been known in the Ballet Russe de Monte Carlo as the "Black Cobra" because of her relentless drive toward what she wanted. What she wanted always was preeminence. Today her heart bleeds for the woes of others, for the poor of her country, for the hungry and the miserable, she says. It is very true that she feels deeply about these things, and she says she thought about them for years. She used to talk at great length of doing something to help the deprived people of the world, in particular the Cuban people. While she talked, Fernando did something: he joined the Communist party. He and Alberto were active in all the Communist agitation, even under Fulgencio Batista, before the advent of Fidel Castro. When Castro finally entered Havana as a young militant, taking up the course of injustice and righting the popular wrongs, there were the two Alonsos in the front rows of meetings, plainly visible in all the old newsreels. They threw their entire enthusiasm into the cause of the new hero. This was unusual, because on the whole dancers are too egocentric to be interested in anything except their own careers.

In a few years, Alicia followed suit and became one of the most vocal advocates of the new order. In Cuba there was now only one way of thinking—Castro's—and this pertained to everything everywhere on the island, out to the ten-mile fishing limit. Castro is a Stalinist. He does not hold truck with any newfangled, pantywaist, democracy-spoiled Russians. Alicia falls right into step. She can address any group at any time, and is eager to do so. In all Iron Curtain countries, Alicia is considered a dear little rabble-rouser. She flows like an uncorked bottle.

She repeatedly tours South America, Russia, China, the eastern bloc countries—never England, seldom Germany or France, and only occasionally the United States. In Washington she once held a committee of senators and representatives spellbound for thirty-five minutes while she addressed them (not about Castro). Her English is faulty but forceful. She loves holding crowds in abeyance and then stirring them to enthusiasm with pyrotechnics of exhortation, just as she loves holding them in silent awe with her exquisite dancing. Alicia does not persuade, she performs, and she is no more democratic than the czarina. One thing is certain, though: she is one of Cuba's best advertisements.

These days Alicia seldom comes to her old stomping grounds. The relationship between the United States and Cuba is so ticklish and her presence in this country is achieved with such difficulty as to enjoin caution. When she does come, it is as a model of discretion. Her friends and close intimates understand that she will talk about anything except politics.

Alicia has received every high honor the profession can bestow, as well as many national medals, particularly from Eastern European countries. Perhaps her most noteworthy awards are the Cuban Carlos Manuel de Céspedes and the Gold Medal of the Gran Teatro Liceo de Barcelona. She was voted a National Hero of Labor by the Cuban Workers Union and holds membership in the advisory council to the Ministry of Culture and in the national committee of the Writers and Artists Union of Cuba.

On a return visit to Washington, D.C., with Ballet Theatre, her old friends flocked to pay homage, particularly the members of the company who had known and loved her. Enrique Martínez, a fellow Cuban, came from seeing her awestruck. "She is beyond time. There is no time for her. She has no age," he said to me. "And Ahnes, she has a new husband, much younger, very nice—a writer." It was true. Alicia, who had been away from home a great deal, found that Fernando had been incautious. Of course fidelity was not required of anyone in Havana, but decorum was. Fernando had been rather too public, particularly considering that his wife was a national idol. He was sent away, and Alicia divorced him and married the editor of a dance publication.

In the spring of 1977, after an absence of seventeen years, Alicia Alonso came back to American Ballet Theatre for an unforgettable *Giselle*. There was muttering among the Cuban refugees, who did not like to see Castro's darling returning. But a great many other people did, and every seat in the Metropolitan Opera House was sold out, to an audience in full evening dress. The crowd assembled in good time and found the auditorium doors locked. The police were busy searching for bombs. For an hour and a quarter the audience waited, standing in the lobby. Then the all-clear sounded, the doors opened, and the people streamed in.

But what of Alicia, waiting backstage, preparing to make a comeback after seventeen years before the most exacting audience in the world? She was preparing to dance the most demanding role in all of dance repertory, and she had to keep trigger-ready for a full hour and a quarter and at the same time face the threat of death! Well, her nerve held. She kept her muscles warm and prepared, and when she jumped lightly from Giselle's doorsill, she was greeted with a roar such as I have heard only in a football stadium. It was topped by the continuing clamor that broke over her at the close of the work. Alicia was back. Never mind bombs.

Alicia came to Austin, Texas, during the week of March 22, 1982, for the jubilee organized in honor of Igor Youskevitch's farewell. For some time Youskevitch had been head of the dance department at the University of Texas. Now having reached the age of seventy, he was retiring, leaving Texas, and going back to New York to live. Dancers from all the world over gathered to do him honor, and the university managed to get permission from our State Department and the Cuban government to have Alicia come. She arrived from Havana with her new husband and four hefty bodyguards, who were dressed in ordinary suits that bulged with what looked like very effective hardware and who followed her closely everywhere.

She had promised to do a pas de deux with her present partner, Jorge

Esquivel, and if she liked the looks of Youskevitch, a pas de deux with him. When they had danced together in the 1940s, she had proclaimed that he was the best partner she had ever had. But that was forty years previously, and they had not danced together in all that while. Time works cruel changes: loss of balance, loss of elevation, loss of muscle tone, loss of breath control; all of these can eat away a great technique. But Igor's old *Giselle* costume was brought by his former costume mistress, and he stepped into it as if it had been fitted for him the night before. He was still the most beautiful man in the business, and he was still a danseur noble, a true one.

Alicia came to the rehearsal studio with her bodyguards to judge him. Barbara Barker peeped through the door, and later reported:

> She was in there with Igor, giving herself a barre, and Igor was doing what he always seemed to be doing, which was smoking a cigarette and looking out the window while waiting for her to finish. Just watching her give herself a truly killer barre was an amazing experience, because she has ear-high *grands battements* and effortless balances. Then I watched Igor try some supported pirouettes, some lifts. I don't know whose judgment she was relying on, because Jorge Esquivel and the bodyguards and Anatole Vilzak, her old teacher, and Walter Terry, the dance critic, were with them. She couldn't see what Igor was doing, but she decided that she would perform with him. On the day of performance the stagehands were finally notified what was going to happen.

Walter Terry devised their appearance. It was Alicia's second appearance of the evening. First she performed with Jorge Esquivel in *White Swan*. At the end of the program Terry announced that there would be a surprise. The whole proscenium of the theater was then filled with a giant movie screen, on which was projected a home film that Tina, Igor's wife, had shot of *Giselle* at the Hollywood Bowl in 1945, with Igor and Alicia doing the pas de deux from the second act. It was a silent film, and the orchestra accompanied it softly in the background. At a given moment the image on the screen was frozen and all the lights came up slowly on Alicia and Igor, standing in the identical pose in the same costumes. As they were revealed you could hear an enormous gasp, as four thousand people caught their breath simultaneously. This woman and this man on stage! The audience's beloveds, the immortals, the legendary lovers, now grown old and honored, Igor with silver hair and Alicia very nearly transparent. His gallantry, tenderness, and care, her kindness and gratitude to him, were beyond wonder. Their lifts were like mist, like caresses.

At the end, as Igor led Alicia forward for bows, carefully avoiding the flowers at her feet, Alicia clung to his hand and turned her sightless eyes up and around the balconies. Then she stepped back and apart from him and made a royal obeisance to the floor, laying her head in the dust at his feet. There followed absolute silence. People were heard to sob. The silence was shattered and pandemonium broke as Igor gathered her up.

Barbara Barker shared in the wonder of that evening, but she was also responsible for all the housekeeping details surrounding the performance. She reported:

> During the whole series of events prior to this—classes, lectures, seminars—Alicia had come in and out with her bodyguards. On Saturday, the day before the performance, she came to me with her honorarium check, which was for $6,000, and she said, "Cash, please." So I called the president of the university, and he called the president of a local bank, and the local banker opened up the vaults and cashed her check. All day Sunday she and her bodyguards shopped, and when they boarded their flight to Cuba on Monday, they were loaded down with VCRs, tape-recording equipment, slide projectors, and every conceivable thing you could imagine for filmmaking. It was all for her school and company.

Alicia's life is now dedicated to her school, which has become a national ballet school subsidized by the Cuban government. This institution, which holds auditions around the island, furnishes complete academic schooling as well as dance training. "In the last few years," says Alicia, "our prima ballerinas have won numerous prizes, in the Soviet Union, in Bulgaria, and in France. Of course, since the revolution we have been able to train men from an early age, and now also men are recognized. We have developed the Cuban Ballet School according to our own physical characteristics, our own taste, within the boundaries imposed by international techniques and standards. We are doing a great deal of work with children, and at the same time we give educational talks in widespread centers."

Jorge Esquivel is one of the school's stars. He was a foundling in the Casa de Beneficencia Maternidad de Habana, an institution for children whose parents had no means of support. Alicia and the Cuban revolution gave him opportunities he would never otherwise have had.

Alicia continues: "We also have another company, the Ballet of Camagüey, and also the Folkloric Ballet, and a third company that dances at the opera, and a fourth that dances for television. All dancers say they have broken down the prejudices against dancing as a homosexual activity. We have always kept in contact with the working masses—always. We are members of the military work brigades, because we are also working, not a separate class of artists who consider themselves superior to the working class. We have our own mass organization, like the Communist Youth Union and our labor union. We are totally politically integrated and we do voluntary work. Often we harvest tomatoes, grapefruit, coffee, and oranges. We used to harvest sugarcane, but that was too strenuous, and after studying the situation the government agreed to assign us work more in line with our profession."

Jorge Esquivel adds: "Whenever there is a mobilization, all our people go; there is a high level of revolutionary consciousness. We work together in labor unions. We keep in touch with the managers in order to plan political and ideological work for our fellow workers. We have cultural activities such as museum visits, expositions, book discussions, and movie debates. There are weekly group meetings about administration and governance. Staff, stars, and pupils eat, dress, and play communally."

Cuba is a small country, and in a sense Alicia is a prisoner of its political position. She uses the island as a springboard, however, a jumping-off place for repeated trips to South America and all the Communist countries. Further, she is happy there. In Cuba she is treated like a queen, and she deeply loves the land. "I can only stay away from Havana three, four months at the most," she says. "I need come back. I need how blue the sky. And most of all I need the sea." Above all, the building of a company is a fascinating necessity to her. Hers is a good company, worthy to be a national company. Unfortunately, it is not quite of that stature, because it has only one central figure, one star, one set of capabilities and achievements. It is the vehicle for a single woman. There have been several people in the history of dancing who have made their own troupes their tools, but those troupes have not endured beyond the performing of the central figure, and they cannot possibly grow or perpetuate themselves.

Alicia says repeatedly that she believes in the people and the people's rights and the people's expression, but in translation it is her rights and her best interests that she serves. The marked limitations of her disability are ever present. No dancer is allowed to surpass these limits or to outdance her, and the choreography must adapt to this peculiar Olympian restraint. She keeps younger dancers straitjacketed beside her, refusing to let them advance to bigger roles, which could allow them to rival her or replace her. To possible rivals she can be deadly. She believes in equal sharing, but not in the theater and not truly in political situations. Does any Communist? She invites great men to dance with her, but never great women. Maya Plisetskaya's brother, Agary Plisetsky, has been her partner for years, but Maya, a very great Russian star, has not been asked to stand on the same stage. No great choreographers have been developed by Alicia's company; Alberto did the chore for many years, and now there are others, who don't rank because they have to serve Alicia's purposes and also because this theater has the quaint habit of not paying choreographers. This rather dampens the enthusiasm of visiting creators.

Now, at sixty-nine [1990], an unheard-of age for a classical ballet dancer (in the mid-nineteenth century, ballet stars retired willingly when they reached the age of forty), Alicia still practices every day and still performs. Occasionally her grandsons partner her. She performs excerpts from *Swan Lake* and *Giselle*—seldom the long, body-wringing roles, but she performs. The excerpts she chooses are those bits requiring the most rapid and brilliant footwork. "When will be my last performance?" she says. "Just do not miss any of my performances, because you don't know exact if that's going to be the last performance."

Alicia has accomplished many great things. She has served dancing beautifully and she has served her country. Will she have the nobility of spirit to accept the fact that she is mortal? Will she be able to make the enormous gesture of yielding to history and bowing aside so that the Ballet de Cuba can develop and progress? She has done so much in her life, this fragile, nervous girl. Can she do this? To step aside requires the creative vision of a prophet, the humility of a saint. This may prove to be a crueler, more insupportable challenge than her blindness. (70–91)

Three Soviet Ballerinas:
Eleonora Vlasova (b. 1931), Galina Ulanova (1910–1998),
and Maya Plisetskaya (b. 1925)
(Excerpts from "Russian Journals," *Dance Perspectives* 44, 1970)

> In June 1966, as the second half of a cultural exchange with the USSR that opened in 1961, with the Bolshoi Ballet's visit to the United States, American Ballet Theatre performed in the Soviet Union. De Mille was one of the choreographers whom ABT director Lucia Chase took along, and she kept meticulous journals of the trip, from which the first word portrait, below, is derived. The dancer described is the ballerina Eleonora Vlasova, who took on the title role in the Stanislavsky's production of *Esmeralda*, a part she had performed often in this ballet based on Victor Hugo's novel *The Hunchback of Notre Dame*. The occasion of the following two portraits was a second trip that de Mille made to the USSR,

in 1969, to represent the United States at the first International Ballet Competition, held at the Bolshoi Theater. "Toya" was the interpreter assigned to de Mille during her second visit.

The performance took place at eleven in the morning, and the theater was more than half empty. Eleven is a dreadful hour for dancing. It means the performers have to be up and at breakfast at six-thirty and have to begin warming up by nine. It's early in the day for that kind of effort. The audiences dislike it also and so they don't come. So why does anyone continue to program shows at this hour? It's a decision of the cultural bureau and it doesn't matter if no one comes; the state pays the deficit.

The Stanislavsky may have been a secondary company but they were given at least seven full stage sets that included the entire façade of Notre Dame, and the costumes, although old-fashioned, were sumptuous. The production would have cost $250,000 in the United States. It wasn't very attractive and the cast was uneven, but the staging was opulent, and the star role was danced by one of the loveliest performers I've seen in my life, Eleonora Vlasova, whose limpid lyricism and winsomeness, whose beauty of phrasing made her numbers stand out sharply from the general unmusicality of the others. One began to question whether or not Frederick Ashton or Roland Petit had lent a hand—or whether possibly the little miss herself had choreographic gifts and transformed her solos and pas de deux from commonplace to magic. Her *pas de bourrée* exceeds in beauty anyone's— Ulanova's, Markova's, Plisetskaya's, Pavlova's. With her this basic ordinary step became a kind of sighing, a shivering of the ankles, as though she were blown weightless.

The audience responded apathetically, except for a hard core of teenagers, who threw wild orchids. I longed to throw something, too, but I had come unprepared and had nothing. I lay this text, which she will never read, at her lovely feet.

But the choreography, oh Lord! Every dance, every phrase (except hers), began with the same split jump and backbend in mid-air, followed by a *tour de sauté* and pose in arabesque, like a clearing of the throat before speaking. I had seen this in the Bolshoi and Kirov choreography. It seems to be universal to all Russian companies except, of course, the Moiseyev dancers. Rage, hate, terror, supreme joy, exuberance, maidenly anticipation or bliss are all expressed by the same leap, turn in the air, and pose, invariable and unchanging, the difference lying only in the degree of backbend. The step rarely has anything to do with the music, as the music has rarely anything to do with the theme.

Most of the pantomime is overdone except when occasionally illuminated by the genius of some talented performer. The dances are "numbers," some designed with considerable craft and with an eye always to gymnastic climax. Climax which is dramatic, lyric or the fruition of design is unknown here. Igor Moiseyev alone practices these consummately. He, however, no longer works (through his own choice, I'm sure) for the ballet companies.

Esmeralda was premiered in 1844 and could not be considered an unfamiliar or avant-garde work. Nevertheless there were eight pages of notes, which were carefully studied by all during intermission.

We have nothing in our culture like Ulanova. She is treated by the Soviets like an amalgam of Eleanor Roosevelt, Mother Cabrini, and Sandy Koufax. She does not get the screaming accorded the Beatles; she gets the decorous, respectful deference given heads of state. Ringed with cameras wherever she goes, she receives flowers from strangers on the street, gifts, salutations, applause. She is everywhere recognized, even as she walks about informally. Postage stamps have been struck in her honor, statues cast, porcelain figurines fired and boxes enameled; and even after retirement her picture is more in the papers than that of any other living stage personality. She is considered an immortal.

When she first danced outside of Russia, her exposure to Western eyes was arranged with concern for national prestige. She is a small woman; she was given a partner, Konstantin Sergeyev, brawny, stalwart, virile, with the shoulders and back of an Atlas and the stage manners of a Louis XIV courtier. She did not have to fight for this presentation, nor did her management, the Kirov Theater. Her government did it for her. She was a national treasure and was presented in just this way, with patriotic protocol.

I remember when I was told she had change of life. The news did seem awfully public somehow. But her health was of concern to the people of Russia.

"Why, she is treated like royalty!" I said to Toya.

"Indeed she is not," Toya replied briskly. "Royalty can be replaced. There is only one Ulanova in all time."

Ulanova has not the aspect of anyone who has appeared publicly. There is none of that energy, that responding force, none of the mobility in her face that marks the actor. She suggests a highly intelligent, retiring librarian from—because of her Slavic features—the Middle West. It's a quiet, disciplined and thinking face turned in upon itself—not outgoing. She is concerned with what she thinks of you, not the reverse, which, of course, is not the actor's way. What you think of her is now established history and she can relax.

She has a slender, trim figure and the upright resilience all dancers command. Like most Russian women, she wears no make-up. Her clothes are simple, in lovely soft colors, her jewels choice but subdued (beautiful jade in gold and one large diamond). Her feet are small and her legs girlish and straight. There is not a hint of the musculature that drove those legs through the greatest leaps since Taglioni's or those feet through flights like birds.' I notice legs with very nearly medical interest. Of Ulanova's, were I ignorant of their identity I would say, "Pretty, but quite untrained—in no way professional." Of the prodigious mechanisms that made their feats possible, of the driving motor, there is not a trace to the casual eye. She walks about tinily and neatly, a middle-aged woman in good condition, with fading ash-blond hair and a cold eye. The steel in Ulanova's Jane Austenish deportment made itself known, I am told, in arguments that she always won and in performance. I have seen her in incredible rippling runs on pointe, her feather-like jumps and gambols, her bracing of back and leg in the overhead lifts where she moved like a branch or a banner, defying all gravitational risks. . . .

She has retired from performing and now works hard coaching the young stars, organizing, judging and advising. She proceeds through her responsibilities for the most part unsmiling, receiving tributes—they come every day, everywhere—with quiet aplomb.

Maya Plisetskaya, also a judge, stepped into the awesome spot vacated on retirement by Ulanova. She is altogether different. There is nothing gentle or reserved about this girl. She is wild, magic, Amazonian, a lady unicorn. Hers is possibly the most beautiful neck in the world, supple, and forward thrust with the tilt of eager exposure and yearning. Her neck precedes her. The jutting chin, the long throat, the long face and the enormous eyes give her the expression of a doe, but a fierce doe. Her mouth is large and either held shut in decision or open widely in that flashing smile which lights up theaters. It would seem masculine because of its vigor were it not Plisetskaya's and altogether feminine. It is the kind of smile that helped make Argentina famous. On the left corner of her mouth, near the beautiful lip, a mole is placed with 18th-century coquetry. Her hair is bronze and tied at the nape to fall in a rope down her back. Her body is straight and lean and she wears miniskirts, an affectation almost unique among Russian women, who are generally conservative. Plisetskaya dares to follow Western mode in foreign-bought clothes, and she dares wear make-up. She dares anything she wishes. She favors large rings; a gigantic topaz adorns her long beautiful finger. Beneath the minis her strong legs flash like knives. (27–28, 48–49)

The Stricken Body: Picture from the Inside
(Excerpt from *Reprieve*)

> In her 1981 memoir, *Reprieve*, de Mille recounts her battle to fight
> her way back to life and art from a massive stroke, a physical devas-
> tation that coincided with the suffering, from cancer, of her beloved
> younger sister, Margaret. In the excerpt that follows, de Mille calls
> on her sensitivity to bodily sensation, heightened by her decades as
> a dancer, to analyze, meticulously and suspensefully, the effects of
> the onslaught to her brain.

My primal concern was, of course, food and water, and next the faces of help-
ers. And then, as I began to get basic hourly needs straightened out, the extent
of the damage to my body and brain, and its manifold symptoms, became
evident, unexpected and shocking; there seemed to be so many areas in which
I had been besieged and overthrown.

My eyes were affected, not just the right eye, in the terribly hurt side of my
face, but my left eye, too. I couldn't see clearly anywhere in the room. I couldn't
see people. I kept track of how much I could see by a watercolor on the opposite wall, an autumnal New England landscape. I said to my unfireable doctor
one day, quite brightly, "I'm going to be able to see that picture within a week."
And he laughed at me and said, "Not a chance." And, quite abashed, I asked,
"How long do you think?" And he said, "Maybe with luck in six weeks." It
was dreadfully depressing, dreadfully. I couldn't even look at TV at that point.
Well, I didn't care. In fact, I cared about very little. I slept.

What worried me agonizingly was that I could not get my touch back.
Sometimes I lost track of my right hand completely and had to hunt through
the bedclothes to find it. I couldn't feel how long my arm was, or where my
hand was in relation to my forearm. I had to feel along the inside of the arm
with the left hand until I reached the member. I sensed that I *had* a hand, but
it always seemed to be in the middle of the forearm. I actually felt along the
bone and into the fingers with astonishment at its length and distance until I
came to it, quite surprisingly, a long way off and way down there. I kept being
surprised by how long my leg was, how long and far away my foot was. I would
feel where my foot ought to be, and where I thought it was, and it was inches,
oh, a foot longer, which was startling. And when I raised an arm, I didn't know
where it was—before, behind, to the left, to the right. And if I closed my eyes,
I didn't know whether it was still up or had moved somewhere else. If I ex-

tended an arm, I strained the muscles and tensed them. But the hand always fell to my coverlets and I never knew because I was still making the effort. This is an astonishing experience.

We always know, in normal life, where our hands and feet are. We don't think about them consciously, but we know because there is an unceasing radar playback from every part of the body telling us, "This is there," "This is near," "This is not within reach," "This is painful," "This is comfortable," "This is hot!" "This is soft." We don't have to look and we don't have to be aware, we just know. Now I was without those signals, and I didn't know.

I could feel motor impulses, and in a couple of weeks I learned how to know when I was opening and shutting my hand because I could differentiate the effort and I was generally right in my surmises. But if somebody took my hand and moved it for me and my eyes were shut, I had no idea where it was or if it had been touched at all.

The loss of the sense of touch is not just curious and teasing, something to be remarked upon like a Novocained jaw during a tooth operation. It is, as a matter of fact, dangerous and limiting. Touch is with us for a reason, namely, survival, safety and usefulness. And without it we are perhaps more greatly damaged than if we lost our sight or hearing.

Half of me was imprisoned in the other half. The dead side seemed unaccountably heavy, gigantically heavy and restrained with bonds. Cement. Wood. When I rolled in bed and tried to get onto my right, or dead, side, I rolled against a dyke of unfeeling matter which I lacked the strength to go over or rise against. If I rolled to the left, I could not lift the right, not possibly. I lay on my back, unmoving at night for about five months. There were mercifully no bedsores and this is a tribute to the nurses. But I seemed to be incarcerated in a carapace of iron, like a medieval torture suit. It didn't hurt, but I could not get out. Inside were all my viscera pumping, living, moving, contracting, expanding. But if I tried to move or bend or turn my head, there I was, locked in, trapped.

I used to lie awake at night and move my foot. Could I feel my toes? Could I feel *any* toe? Was my foot going up and down and sideways as I thought it was and as I wished and directed? Sometimes I thought I felt, but it might have been the faint, almost imperceptible sound of my nail on the sheet. It might have been, somehow, a brush against the sentient leg and a transfer of signals. Could I feel my hand? What could I do to make my hand feel, to know what it felt? It turned out after hours and hours of experimentation that I could not feel and there was nothing I could do.

Because of the confusion in the sensation centers of my brain, because all of the nerves had become tangled (as though they were ripped like wires out of a telephone exchange and left lying loose and matted, as one doctor explained), I felt lots of strange things that had nothing to do with fact. In a paralyzed arm or leg there is no feeling at all. It is absolutely dead, cut off as though it were no longer a part of my body. Time stops for that limb. Events stop. But I was desensitized, and in what I was experiencing there was a constant tingling in my face and in my arm and leg. This is the classic symptom. Shakespeare speaks of it:

"This apoplexy is, as I take it, a kind of lethargy . . . a kind of sleeping in the blood, a whoreson tingling." [*King Henry IV—Part 2, I, ii*] I felt tinglings, vibrations, numbness or inaccurate awareness; great heat when there was no heat at all, great heat all of the time, so that I looked to see if my body had broken into sweat and found it hadn't, and pain for no adequate reason. For instance, one night I upset a glass of water on my bed tray and in due course the sheets soaked through and the sensation was transferred to my body, but I cried out, frightening my husband half to death, because what had reached me was not the feel of a wet sheet, which everyone, beginning with very little babies, knows about, but pain. I could feel hot water, but not immediately, only after a count of about four and a half, too late to prevent scalding. I felt no cold, and when my hand or the arm was left outside of the covers and I finally happened to retrieve it, it would come in all but frostbitten. I didn't know.

When my foot bumped into something, I felt it in my groin.

There were, in addition, irrational and insane jerkings which I was not aware of. My hand would fly out and encounter, well, whatever there was to encounter. And as for putting a finger out and pointing it at an object . . . out of the question! Nor could I dial the telephone. Of course, holding a pen or the shuttle of a loom was impossible. And training that right hand to do the most primitive bidding was like training a wild animal. Of all the years that I had had it and disciplined it and cared for it and accepted its service there was not a trace, and although I am strongly right-handed and thought right, it was not my hand. It was not anybody's hand. It could have been the hind leg of a donkey.

Inside my mummy of unfeeling insulation, inside my corset, I had to keep alive and intelligent and eager. There was absolutely no other point, no other reason. Make the effort. Don't think. But, of course, there was a seepage of disheartenment from the various unrelenting blocks. It sapped my strength. "Oh," I thought on wakening, "if only I could have two hours of my right hand! Two hours! I could go back." Two hours were not to be given me. I had to go on without the respite. And what I did not realize—and perhaps no one does who has not experienced this, or the doctors who attend them—is the exhaustion that comes from just doing *anything*. Doing any practical chore, any puny, trivial thing costs six times the effort it costs in normal living: sitting up, lifting a fork, riffling through the pages of a magazine. Enormous. One is tired. One sleeps. (55–60)

$\mathcal{E}ssays$

"The Contribution"
(*Dance to the Piper*)

> De Mille discusses her own and her colleagues' rehearsal practices. Much of her essay rings true for today's choreographers, although in two passages de Mille's insight—happily—failed her. The early group works of Martha Graham (such as *Heretic* and *Celebration*), which de Mille surmised in the early 1950s were lost forever, in fact were reconstructed in burnished editions during the 1980s and 1990s by Yuriko (Kikuchi)—usually in collaboration with dancers from the original casts or with Graham herself—for the Martha Graham Dance Ensemble, which Yuriko founded and directed. Too, when de Mille published this essay nearly sixty years ago she couldn't foresee the advent of video technology, which would make it possible and affordable to record choreography, at least in part, by way of individual performances.

We had breached the bulwarks, Tudor above all, then Ashton, de Valois, Eugene Loring, and I lastly. Two years later Jerome Robbins with *Fancy Free* was to confirm the new tradition. (George Balanchine, whom many consider the greatest living ballet choreographer, was no revolutionist. He worked in the direct line of development from a classic premise.) How did we differ? Beyond the individual works and the personal style, had we really made a new tradition?

Ballet gesture up to now had always been based on the classic technique and whatever deviated from this occurred only in comedy caricatures. The style throughout, the body stance, the walk, the run, the dynamic attack, the tensions and controls, were balletic even when national folk dances were incorporated into the choreography.

We were trying to diversify the root impulse and just as Gershwin impressed on the main line of musical development characteristics natural to his own unclassical environment, we were adding gestures and rhythms we had grown up with, using them seriously and without condescension for the first time. This is not a triviality; it is the seed and base of the whole choreographic organization. If dance gesture means anything, it means the life behind the movement.

The younger choreographers believed that every gesture must be proper to a particular character under particular circumstances. (In the classic ballets the great solos could be interchanged with no confusion from one ballet to another.) Tudor developed the storytelling quality of his choreography to such a degree that each gesture, formed out of the emotional components of the moment, is almost as explicit as though the dancers spoke. The new choreographer does not arrange old steps into new patterns; the emotion evolves steps, gestures, and rhythms.

And for this reason, the line between dancing and acting is no longer clearly marked—though by acting I do not mean realistic imitation. Consider the role of Hagar in *Pillar of Fire* (created by Nora Kaye)—a frustrated woman who gives herself to a man she does not love through fear of spinsterhood. Her turns are an agony of spirit, her repeated balances and falls a bewilderment and frustration, her leaps a striving for release. A sailor beside me, seeing her throw herself into the arms of a man she did not love, groaned aloud. He had, as it happened, just witnessed a passage of technical virtuosity very nearly beyond the scope of any other living dancer. But he was not aware of this and did not clap. He did not cheer. He groaned and said, "Oh, my God!" He could recognize trouble when he saw it.

Hagar's gestures were chosen with prayer and fasting. Antony Tudor worked with his dancers like research students shut away for months. He traveled with them, danced with them, practiced beside them day and night. Nora Kaye was rehearsed for a year, exploring with the choreographer every possible psychological overtone. He brooded over her, informed her so clearly with his idea that it is impossible to say where composition ends and performance begins. The fluttering of her eyelids, the smoothing of a dress, the pause and turn of head, the drawing in of breath, were as firmly set and as inviolate as a series of sixty-four pirouettes.

Contrast this with Massine's method, where the human bodies are used merely as units of design, grouped, lumped, and directed into predetermined masses. But as performers the dancers were called upon to go it blind and fell back on their own resources. And their resources were the classic technique and the Petipa and Fokine repertoire. The young man, for instance, who played the wolf in *St. Francis* was at work on the role for two weeks before he discovered that he was portraying a carnivorous animal and not an Italian adolescent. Frequently, the cast was not even clear about the plot of the ballet they were spending a summer in creating. And when Massine left the [Ballet Russe de Monte Carlo] company and his enormous vitalizing influence was removed the gestures wore down through sheer unthinking repetition to the point where the performers could not have themselves explained what they were doing. Anything was permitted as long as toes were pointed and arms kept moving.

Between Fokine and Tudor stand Proust and Freud as well as Graham, the Ballets Jooss, and Mary Wigman. And lastly, it must never be forgotten that the new generation of choreographers is almost entirely English or American and our cultural heritage is different from the Slavic or Germanic folklore that influenced our forebears. We dance what we know about. The sailor watching Hagar recognized his own kind of misery. He does not particularly recognize himself in *Swan Lake*. Mind you, the sailor likes *Swan Lake*. But *Fancy Free*, *Pillar of Fire*, and, I think, *Rodeo* talk to him. Animals, birds, magicians, FATE, LOVE, BEAUTY, DEATH, and, above all, MAN, have largely disappeared. I, for one, had grown weary of MAN.

By the time I composed *Rodeo* I had crystallized a technique of composing. It was in essentials the same method I had fumbled with in my early pantomimes, but it has routined itself with the subsequent Broadway practice into a true discipline.

To make up a dance, I still need, as I needed then, a pot of tea, walking space, privacy and an idea. Although every piece I have done so far for a ballet company is a *ballet d'action* or story ballet, I have no preference for this type—quite the contrary—I think the lyric or abstract ballets more pleasing and much more enduring, but my knack has been for dramatics.

When I first visualize the dance, I see the characters moving in color and costume. Before I go into rehearsal, I know what costumes the people wear and generally what color and texture. I also, to a large extent, hear the orchestral effects. Since I can have ideas only under the stress of emotion, I must create artificially an atmosphere which will induce this excitement. I shut myself in a studio and play gramophone music, Bach, Mozart, Smetana, or almost any folk music in interesting arrangements. At this point I avoid using the score because it could easily become threadbare.

I start sitting with my feet up and drinking pots of strong tea, but as I am taken into the subject I begin to move and before I know it I am walking the length of the studio and acting full out the gestures and scenes. The key dramatic scenes come this way. I never forget a single nuance of them afterwards; I do usually forget dance sequences.

The next step is to find the style of gesture. This is done standing and moving, again behind locked doors and again with a gramophone. Before I find how a character dances, I must know how he walks and stands. If I can discover the basic rhythms of his natural gesture, I will know how to expand them into dance movement.

It takes hours daily of blind instinctive moving and fumbling to find the revealing gesture, and the process goes on for weeks before I am ready to start composing. Nor can I think any of this out sitting down. My body does it for me. It happens. That is why the choreographic process is exhausting. It happens on one's feet after hours of work, and the energy required is roughly the equivalent of writing a novel and winning a tennis match simultaneously. This is the kernel, the nucleus of the dance. All the design develops from this.

Having established a scenario and discovered the style and key steps, I then sit down at my desk and work out the pattern of the dances. If the score is already composed, the dance pattern is naturally suggested by and derived from the pattern of the music. If it remains to be composed as it does in all musical comedies, the choreographer goes it alone. This, of course, is harder. Music has an enormous suggestive power and the design of the composer offers a helpful blueprint.

All I know about dance composition I learned from folk dances. These are trustworthy models because they are the residuum of what has worked; there is no folk dance extant that did not work. I had first become aware of the importance of folk dancing when Dr. Lily Campbell asked me to reconstruct medieval singing games for her class in English Drama. I have studied folk forms since where possible. It must be remembered that outside of Louis Horst's classes in preclassic dance forms, choreography is taught nowhere and there are no texts on the subject. I learned by trial and error as did all my colleagues.

Through practice I have learned to project a whole composition in rough outline mentally and to know exactly how the dancers will look at any given moment moving in counterpoint in as many as five groups. As an aid in concentration, I make detailed diagrams and notes of my own arbitrary invention, intelligible only to me and only for about a week, but they are not comparable in exactness to music notation.

At this point, I am ready, God help me, to enter the rehearsal hall.

I don't believe any choreographer ever overcomes his terror of the waiting company. Imagine a composer facing the New York Philharmonic with his score projected in his head, not a note on paper, and the task before him of teaching the symphony by rote to the waiting men. He could start by whistling the main theme of the first violins.

Well, there they stand, the material of your craft, patient, disciplined, neat and hopeful in their black woolens. They will offer you their bodies for the next several weeks to milk the stuff of your ideas out of their muscles. They will submit to endless experimentation. They will find technique that has never been tried before; they will submerge their personalities and minds to the blindest, feeblest flutterings of yours. They will remember what you forget. They are pinning all the hopes of their past practices and future performings on the state of your brains. There they stand and consider you as you walk into the room. If they know you and are fond of you, it's easier. But at best, it's a soul-challenging moment.

The choreographer is apt to be short-tempered and jumpy at these times; he has not only to face the psychological problems of mastering and guiding a group of human beings, but all the problems of composition simultaneously. I take comfort in hot coffee. With the friendly warmth of a carton between my hands and the steaming rim to hide my face in, and the piping hot reassurance in my stomach, I can just manage to step out on the floor and make a suggestion. Dancers very quickly learn to hand me coffee before they ask a taxing question such as "What do we do next over here?" I find a ring of cartons waiting around my chair in the morning.

It's a good idea to give the company for a beginning something definite and technically difficult to get their feet down on. The minute they start to sweat they feel busy and useful. Like Tudor, I always try to start with two or three dancers I know who are sympathetic to my suggestion, and I have learned to have the rehearsal planned through to the end, preferably on a piece of paper in case I dry up mentally. Standing and scratching one's head while the dancers cool off in their tights, and then put on extra sweaters, and then sit down on the floor, and then light cigarettes and start to talk, is what one wishes to avoid. No group of workers in the world is slower to lose faith or interest, but they are human. While you are struggling to find the exact phrasing they get tired in the back of their knees. And when you ask them to get off the floor and try the jump in the eighteenth variation they rise creaking. Then you grow hot with anger that you cannot solve the problem and punish their bodies for your own stupidity, forcing them to do it again and again and again, pretending that it is their lack of performance quality that invalidates the idea. But no one is fooled. Neither you nor they. You scold them. And your company quietly grows to hate you. They are now more or less useless for your purposes. If you were working with marble you could hack at it for a year without any deterioration of material. If you were writing a book you could lay down your pen, take a walk, take a nap, have some coffee and come back to find your manuscript just as you left it. But dancers stand with patient drawn faces waiting for your brains to click.

One could simply terminate a rehearsal and wait for a more fruitful moment. But after all, the dancers are there to work, the hall is rented, the pianist hired and attentive.

There are, however, the times when one scrapes absolute bottom. The matter in which he deals with these moments is the exact measure of a choreographer's experience. Balanchine dismisses a rehearsal without any ado at all and goes home. If, on the other hand, he likes what he is doing, hell can break loose around him and he pays not the slightest mind. Short of hell he nearly always is surrounded by a roomful of chattering, knitting, practicing dancers and visitors. Massine holds the entire company in the room. They sit for hours sometimes while he wrestles with one or two soloists. If he gets stuck he keeps it to himself as he never explains a single thing he is doing to anyone he is working with. Martha Graham sends her group from the room and has it out with God. I cannot endure the sight of one person sitting down waiting. A sense of guilt and tedium oppresses me exactly as though I were failing a guest. I, therefore, allow in the room with me only the people I am working with, never any visitors, and inside the rehearsal room no one may sit down or chew gum or smoke. I have to keep myself geared to such a pitch that if I relax or allow the dancers to relax the rehearsal for all effective purposes is over. Outside in the waiting room or hall they may do as they like—drink, chew, eat, gossip, play cards. This pertains to the beginning weeks. When the composition stands by itself on the floor and is no longer a matter of hypnotism between me and the group, everything is easier.

But with all the good planning possible, there comes sooner or later the inevitable point of agony when the clock dictates and one must just set one's teeth and get on with it. Then one wrings the ultimate out of one's marrow. The astonishing fact is that it is there to be wrung.

The dancers themselves frequently help. For the very reason they are human and have wills and imaginations and styles of their own, their manner of moving will suggest an infinite number of ideas to the choreographer. They can evoke where clay and canvas cannot. The minute the choreographer moves a tentative hand or places a foot forward, they are behind him imitating. The stimulus of their interest will excite him. He will improvise beyond his expectations. He may not know exactly what he has done. But bright-eyes has seen; the gesture is immediately reproduced. The choreographer can then turn around and watch his idea on someone else's body. This he can correct and edit. A sensitive performer needs only a hint, a breath, and he is off, the rhythms generated in his body helping to push the design ahead.

When I have verified certain ideas on my test dancers (if I get two or three good gestures in two hours I consider the morning well spent. Half a dozen pages of notes can boil down to three jumps filling in all about five seconds of time), I call in the group and teach them together, using the first performers as models.

Sometimes the solo figures are developed first and the group patterns blocked in behind like the orchestration to a melody. Sometimes when the soloist has simple dramatic or storytelling movement the group is set first and the soloist added. In these cases I go to the back of the theater where I can get a perspective of the stage and add on the soloist by shouted direction. Bambi Linn is so responsive to group movement that she can interpret instructions invented on the moment and screamed out while the dance is in full progress.

Big designs are largely headwork and must be visualized in advance. Obviously a large group is too disparate an instrument on which to improvise—until it is aroused.

Such times are memorable. They usually occur when the group is exhausted after hours of work, late in a studio at the dinner hour or at night in the theater when everyone else has gone home. There, in absolute privacy and with no impatience to be gone to other concerns, working together in perfect community of understanding, the moment comes. And quite simply every single performer knows what to do as though he were inside the composer's head. In this art, the interpreters are present at the actual moment of creation and if they share the labor they also know some of the glory. They are grateful for this and stand abashed and wondering. And so, by God, does the choreographer.

Choreographers have notoriously poor memories. And for a group that has no documentation of their work this is unfortunate. Possibly they keep in mind as I do the variants to each step. This tends to be confusing. Certainly most dancers remember through their muscles and as a consequence can remember only what they have themselves performed. Music is an enormous memory aid. But where the original dancers cannot be brought together for purposes of revival much of the original detail is always lost. Some works disappear entirely with each change of personnel. All of Martha Graham's early group compositions, for instance. There was nothing like these great works in all of dance literature. Nor will she ever compose in this vein again. We have suffered an irreparable loss.

Even in the more durable ballet companies when the choreographer is absent personal idiosyncrasies of style gradually work alterations that in a few years make the dance unrecognizable. In a repertoire of twenty-five or thirty ballets every role is remembered by heart. All the choreography of the old classic ballets is handed down from generation to generation entirely through tradition. But in this case the task is not too difficult. As they were composed in the exact idiom that is taught daily in every ballet class and as the steps and positions are rigidly prescribed there is less chance for variation.

Without the aid of a camera, however, it is almost impossible to preserve the more experimental modern choreography. Very few choreographers have used moving pictures to record their work, largely, I suppose, because of the cost.

Given a fair chance, the dancer will remember, and fairly accurately, the documentation of the work. Learning everything by rote, retaining the entire repertoire in his head, he is probably the quickest learner and the most retentive in all the performing arts.

In the spring of 1948, on the opening day of Ballet Theatre's season at the Metropolitan Opera House, Nora Kaye, one of the company's two ballerinas, was taken without warning to the hospital with virus pneumonia, three hours before the curtain rose. She had no understudy in *Lilac Garden*. Alicia Alonso had performed it twice six years previously and not at all in the interim. She used the supper hour to refresh her memory under Tudor's coaching, opened the bill with a Balanchine piece, went back upstairs to the rehearsal hall during *Tally-Ho* and then four hours after the first frantic phone call performed the work in question, a role of real intricacy and twenty minutes' duration, without a single mistake. Bear in mind, there was no score for her to study. This prodigy of memory is in a class with the Toscanini legend; but he has all his needed scores on his library shelves.

A more spectacular example occurred this spring (1951). In the first movement of William Dollar's *Chopin Concerto*, Norma Vance, first soloist, hurt her foot and was unable to continue. Paula Lloyd, working in the corps, who had merely watched the solo rehearsals, stepped in a few bars later and finished the ballet to the end without rehearsal of any kind. What's more she maintained her place in the ranks simultaneously stepping in and out of the solo role as need arose. It was this extraordinary act of professionalism that prompted Virgil Thomson to remark beside me, "These are the most highly trained people in the theater, far, far better disciplined than opera singers."

The circumstances which governed the creation of *Rodeo* were not unusual; nearly all ballets are composed just this way—with the company in full motion. If there were difficulties there were also enormous advantages not to be found in other forms of the musical theater. In the first place, the company was a unit and had worked together for years. Furthermore, they were all dancers with a uniform training and discipline. The cast of a musical play on the other hand I knew would be made up of a heterogeneous group, dancers from various schools, actors, singers, acrobats, all ages and sizes. If I did the new Rodgers-Hammerstein show I was going to have to face this situation. And there would be other problems as well. In a ballet company choreography is the essential element and the choreographer complete, total boss toward whom all artists bend their will in the interest of a common success. The drawbacks, not enough money, not enough rehearsal time, and always exhaustion, do not overbalance the advantages of scope and power.

In a musical play all would be different: the dances would have to suit the book; they would have to build the author's line and develop his action, adding an element not obtainable through acting or singing and necessary if for no other reason than their dynamic effect. The problem of preserving character, period atmosphere and style would be a tough one since the bulk of the play would be performed realistically in a style as divorced from dance gesture as speaking is divorced from singing. Transition was accordingly going to have to become a fine art, for if the audience could not be swung from dramatic dialogue through song into dance and back again without hitch, the dance would be destroyed. The choreographer was going to have to learn surgery, to graft and splice.

Furthermore, in this medium the dance director was no longer boss or anything like. By tradition the composer was a tyrant although Oscar Hammerstein was to prove shortly that the author of the book might be equally important. The director had some say and also the producer, but the dance director not much. The designers were never charged to protect the dancing. They were told only to fill the stage with color, to see that the girls looked lovely whether they could move or not, to favor the star and to do something sufficiently splashy to get more shows to design. If the dancing was hobbled or overweighted, it never reflected on anyone but the choreographer. The duration of numbers would be strictly limited—because of course for every minute of dancing there would be one less minute of singing or acting, something the composer, author and director never forgot. Besides it had been established long since, had it not, that the general public was less interested in dancing than in anything else?

Compared to a ballet schedule, the rehearsal time, five weeks, seemed unlimited, but I knew from past heartbreaking experience better. I would get the dancers, it is true, for seven hours a day (the Equity maximum) for one week, and they would not be rehearsing any other ballets or performing at night. But the second week they would be called for the staging of songs and crowd scenes, and the third week they would be taken constantly for costume fittings. The fourth week would be cut up with run-throughs of the whole play and the fifth devoted entirely to traveling to the out-of-town theaters and dress rehearsals. If the dances weren't largely completed by the end of the second week, I would be sunk. This was a harsh time sheet.

But every aspect was challenging. If I had to fit dances to the story, the story itself might suggest much. If the score were good and the songs witty, they might help further and the music would be composed to the dancing right in the rehearsal hall and orchestrated only after the dance was completed. I could order exactly what I wanted at the moment on the spot. The other members of the creative staff might be more powerful but they were not ungifted. One did not have to take full responsibility alone. One had great collaborators. And there was money for anything reasonable one needed, and one could pick one's cast at will. And last and most wonderfully, the curtain would not go up in New York until all had been brought to shining, lustrous perfection. Not a single risk would be tolerated. Not one.

I'd broken my neck in the musical theater several times before but I'd learned quite a lot in the process. I had had to learn to adapt myself to emergency, time and human frailty, and to accept men in the theater—in particular, managers. I had had to discipline myself to avoid risk, to stop providing myself with an alibi for (or means to) failure. I had had to learn the difference between the bearable fatigue and the unbearable, the fatigue of fear. The first can be cured by a night's sleep; the second kills. I had had to find the strength to fail and fail and keep thinking, to come up at last with the idea that works. This is what men pay salaries for—more even than for good taste and vision. I felt quite confident. I did not, in fact, have a qualm, which, considering my history, is inexplicable. Richard Rodgers, who did not know my history, had qualms. He recognized clearly the crucial difference between the two media. Hammerstein hoped for the best, and Lawrence Langner, who had seen a good deal of my work, thought I might bring something fresh to the production.

But even after the success of *Rodeo*, I just barely succeeded in getting the new Rodgers-Hammerstein-Theatre Guild show. Indeed I had heard nothing official until I met Oscar Hammerstein, by chance, in a New York drugstore and knocked a plate off the counter in my haste to speak to him. Dick had qualms, he said. I continued pressing until Dick capitulated.

When I started my tour with the Ballet Russe I had the promise of the dances for the musical version of Lynn Riggs's play *Green Grow the Lilacs*. For I was to tour with the Ballet Russe de Monte Carlo as guest star.

On the first night I had received $27.50, a combination royalty and performance salary. Libidins gave it to me in cash in a dark corner of the stage, knowing that I needed the money badly and that the Ballet Russe checks were slow in coming. He whispered to me that they wanted me to travel with the company right across the continent and dance in all the big cities, and for this I was to get something like a salary.

So, on the tour in my suitcase went a blank copybook labeled *Lilacs* with pages entitled "Ballet"—"Many a New Day," "Cowmen and the Farmer," "Kansas City," "Jud's Postcards," and as I sat happily in hotel bedrooms, I made notes—

"Laurie sits under a tree thinking. She is worried. Downstage left she appears to herself dressed in her own dress, but with a wreath on her head. The music changes to 'Beautiful Morning.' She is moving about in her morning and taking possession of her world. She is to be a bride." (307–319)

"Rhythm in My Blood"
(And Promenade Home)

This survey of individual patterns in the timing and pacing of dances among a select group of choreographers, including the author, is debatably de Mille's most profound statement on the element that is the foundation of the choreographic process. An early reference here is to de Mille's ballet *Tally-Ho, or the Frail Quarry*, set to a score by Christoph Willibald Gluck, arranged by Paul Nordoff. The work was given its world première by Ballet Theatre in 1944, and the names of the characters convey something of the libretto's milieu. De Mille, herself, performed the leading role of "Wife"; Hugh Laing was "Her Husband, a genius"; Anton Dolin was "Prince"; Maria Karnilova was "A Lady, no better than she should be"; Muriel Bentley and Miriam Golden were "Two Others, somewhat worse"; and Lucia Chase was "The Innocent." The company revived it in 1965 as *The Frail Quarry*, with Carmen de Lavallade as "Wife" and uncredited scenery "after Fragonard."

Trude Rittmann, the outstanding musical arranger for Broadway shows, whom de Mille mentions below, is also the subject of an entire profile elsewhere in this collection.

The ending of *Tally-Ho*, or the lack of it, haunted me then as it still does; I intend one day to put it right.

I find it hard to make up my mind about endings; beginnings are, for me, somehow easier come by, as they are for everybody. Fokine, I believe, began frequently at the end and worked backward. Doris Humphrey always composes the end long before she gets to it, about the middle of the work or shortly thereafter. An ending has to be a summing up, the logical total of all that precedes, the final statement; in other words, the point of view. And this was seemingly so difficult for me to achieve I thought it wise to pause at this moment and consider why. And so I set about reviewing my work, its characteristics, patterns and methods, as another choreographer might.

Every worker recognizes his own devices. I can name mine easily. I cannot always control them, but I can name them: I have an affinity for diagonal movements on the stage, with figures entering at one corner and leaving at the opposite, and unless I watch myself, this pattern recurs tiresomely. Why in one corner and out the other? I am not such a fool that I don't recognize the tendency, nor so starved for invention that I cannot think of other geometric directions. But this particular arrangement moves me and releases ideas. Could it be because the first fine choreographic design I ever saw was the *Sylphides* mazurka danced by Lydia Sokolova with the Diaghilev ballet? And when I think of her great leap and the lines of still and waiting women leaning in a kind of architectural wonder for the next cross flight, I understand. That was the path of the first comet and it blazed a mark on my brain. That track spells ecstasy. But behind this reason, there must be more.

I use a still figure, usually female, waiting on the stage, side or center, with modifying groups revolving about, always somehow suggesting the passing of time and life experience. Why does the woman waiting seem to me so emotionally pregnant? One woman standing alone on the stage while people pass until a man enters upstage behind her. Why upstage and why always behind and why the long wait? I cannot be sure, but I remember waiting for years, seemingly, shut away in my mother's garden. My father was absent most of that time and I longed for him to come home to release me from the spell. Possibly the answer is somewhere here.

Why is my use of circles, open or closed, a constant? The avoidance of symmetrical design, with the exception of the circle, my acute difficulty with all symmetrical design, even including square-dance pattern, which one might think was my native language? My repeated use of three female figures, a trilogy which because of plurality takes on symbolic force? And the falling patterns—the falling to earth, the swooning back, the resurrection, the running away always to return to a focal point—seem also to be insistent; and more important, more gross and unbearable, the breaking of all lyric line with a joke, as though I could not trust emotional development but must escape with a wisecrack.

It must be obvious even to people not familiar with dancing that these relations are individual, that they are to some degree sexual, and that they reflect a special personality pattern. I speak of my own work because I have a right to, but these observations apply to everyone. Consider, for instance, some of the recurring idioms of Balanchine: the single male figure embroiled with two to six females, one of whom either blinds or strangles him; the entanglement of either male or female bodies in endless ropes or chains (the lines are seldom made up of both men and women); the repetitive use of the grand reverence, or imperial court bow, as part of the texture of movement; the immaculate discipline of traditional gesture; the metrical, machinelike arrangement of school positions as unadorned as the use of unmodified scales in a musical composition; the insistence on two-dimensional symmetrical design; the superb but classic relation to music. One might build an interesting picture of Balanchine, the man, from these points of style. They are as natural to him as his sniff.

The characteristics of Jerome Robbins are very different. There is above all his free-limbed and virile use of the body, a complete spontaneous release as in sports, an exuberance, a total employment of all energies. Whether the gesture is gay or anguished, all resources are put into play and the strength and vigor of the movement communicates with the gusto of an athlete's. This in part may explain his enormous popularity with all audiences. The gesture is manly, it is keen and bold, and it is complete. Briefly, it is exhilarating, and it brings to the spirit the satisfaction that a yawn or a stretch brings to the muscles. Women choreographers are less released, their movement often blocked or broken, or modified by reticences, not shyness of content but carefulness in physical effort. The difference is equivalent to that between a man and a woman throwing or jumping. Her gesture may be exact and serviceable; his will be total. Robbins enhances this quality by quoting literally from acrobatics and stunts.

His skill in rhythmic invention is the greatest in the business, according to Trude Rittmann, who has worked with all of us. Robbins is besot by rhythm, visual and bodily rhythms as well as auditory, and when he gets hold of a gesture he continues inventing out of the core of the matter until he has built an entire design and must wait for the composer to catch up. His rhythms will then work in counterpoint to the musical pattern. It is thought that if he had turned his attention to music, he might have been a first-class composer. Whereas Balanchine's rhythmic sense is spatial and linked to the music, Robbins's is independent. I, on the other hand, am totally derivative and lean and grow on melody. I cannot move without melody. May there not here be revealed a subtle sexual distinction? The men work free and on their own; the woman must wait for the lead.

But Robbins's most easily recognized trait is, praise heaven, his humor. In its grossest aspects, it takes the form of straight gags—very good ones, but bald and outrageous. In its more sophisticated manifestations, he introduces surprising and impertinent conclusions into his pattern, deliberately leading one on to expect a certain resolution and then insolently offering another, untraditional and slightly rude, though always logical because he is never foolish. He jokes with rhythms, with space, with relations of bodies, with light, with silence, with sound. These are all elements of style.

The grosser emotional fixtures of theme and content are plainly manifest—fixtures such as, in the case of Robbins, a preoccupation with childhood and games, with the bewilderment of growing up, with the anguish of choice. The unexpected, the joke, in this field seems to turn back on the choreographer and sit hard; each love story splits into three or more people; each romance spells destruction or transience; all repeats over and over. There is no resolution. In short, life turns out not be a joke.

For my part, I seem to be obsessed by an almost Henry Jamesian inability for hero and heroine to come together happily, and by that other bedeviling theme, the woman as hunter. These are easily read. But the impregnation of abstract pattern with personality adjustments is, I find, far more subtle and more interesting. A great deal has been written about the kinesthetic transference between audience and dancer in the actual muscular technique; the field of spatial aesthetics remains, however, almost unexplored.

We know much about emotional symbols. They have a history and a science, iconography. Those used by the medieval and Renaissance painters were understood by the scholars and artists of the time—but, more wonderful, they mean to us today spontaneously just what they meant then; they seem to be permanent. We dream, Jung tells us, in the terms and symbols of classic mythology. Moreover, primitives shut away from classic learning dream in the same terms. Is it not also likely, then, that certain space relations, rhythms and stresses have psychological significance, that some of these patterns are universal and the key to emotional response, that their deviations and modifications can be meaningful to the artist in terms of his own life experience and that these overtones are grasped by the spectator without conscious analysis?

Doctors are aware of this and utilize the knowledge in diagnosis. The significance of children's manipulation of space in writing and drawing is carefully studied, and the insane are observed for their relation to and use of walls, floor, doorways, heights, and so forth. Obviously these matters are basic to our well-being as land and air [are to] animals. And as plants will turn to sunlight or rocks or moisture according to their nature, so we bend toward or escape from spatial arrangements according to our emotional needs. In the diseased mind, the reactions are overwhelmingly overt. But look around any restaurant and see how few sane people will sit at a center table unless the sides are filled up. Yet formerly the king always dined dead center and many times in public.

The individual as a personality, then, has his own code in space and rhythm. It is evolved from his life history and from his race memory or, as Jung calls it, the collective unconscious. It is just the manipulation of these suggestions through time-space that is the material of choreography.

Take, for example, a simple daily gesture like walking forward and shaking hands. There are in this, first, the use of a separate limb common to most vertebrates, the upright position of the spine and head characteristic of man, the instinctively recognized expression of friendliness shared by all species as opposed to the instinctive expressions of fear and distrust. With animals, when approaching a friend, the hair lies flat, the ears are relaxed though alert, and all enlargements and ferocious distentions subside; breathing is normal. So with man. Heart, pulse and lungs are easy, the eyes alert but neither distended to see danger nor contracted to pinpoint a target; the mouth is closed or smiling because no unusual demands will be made on hearing (to hear extraordinarily in times of acute danger, the mouth is opened and breathing suspends). And since no unusual effort will be necessary, the muscles neither brace nor tremble. The sum total of all this will be spelled out in the rhythm and position of the reaching hand.

But let there occur the slightest rebuff and see now what happens; hackles rise, hair bristles, lips curl to bare incisors, hearts pound, lungs fill, and on the instant all muscles prepare for attack. In ordinary intercourse, this naturally is not visible on full scale. But it needs only the slight widening of the pupil or nostril, the barest flicker of fingertip, to give the signal; the enemy has been recognized and addressed. Further subtle and meaningful modifications take over when the passage alters by the tension of a specific situation—when, for instance, someone who is often frightened of encounter meets a friend, or one who is never frightened meets someone not to be trusted, or two trusting friends meet under dreadful conditions, and so ad infinitum. Within each of these circumstances the body becomes a totally different chemical organization and yet retains the stamp of its own life habits. {A primary school teacher told me that she knew that children were beginning to trust her when they touched her with the palms of their hands; at first they only poked. It is only at moments of intimacy, possession or pity that an adult will touch with his palms.}

It is the actor's art to mimic exactly with a full awareness of all the overtones and significances. The dancer, on the other hand, explodes the gesture to its components and reassembles them into a symbol that has connotations of what lies around and behind the fact, while the implications of rhythm and spatial design add further comment. Of course the choreographer is no more troubled by all this than is the businessman by the enormous anthropological heritage he puts into play every time he casually tips his hat.

Coleridge says of portraiture: "A good artist must imitate that which is within the thing, that which is active through form and figure, and discourses to us by symbols ... the universal in the individual or the individuality itself—the glance and the exponent of the indwelling power.... Hence a good portrait is the abstract of the personal; it is not the likeness for actual comparison, but for recollection." Every gesture is a portrait. Behind it lie the histories of the race and the individual as well as the comment of the artist.

When I, as an artist, am moved, I must respond in my own instinctive way; and because I am a choreographer, I respond through my instinctive gestures. I may come into the pattern with conviction and the excitement of fresh experience, but this must also reflect a personality habit. It cannot be otherwise. Somehow, as in the grooves in a gramophone record, the cutting edge of my emotion follows a track played deep into the subconscious.

There is a further personal identification in choreography because most choreographers compose on their own bodies. Certain recurring steps can be explained simply by the fact that the choreographer performs these steps well and has a tendency to use them when demonstrating. Martha Graham has a kick and a particular skip that have stood her in good stead for twenty years. The explanation is simply that her left leg kicks straight up in a split, 180 degrees—a very spectacular feat. The right does not; hence the single-legged pattern. (It has been very interesting to observe over the years that Graham pupils who began by imitating her mannerisms have gradually eliminated the personal idiosyncrasies and maintained the great style unblemished. In *Diversion of Angels* and *Canticle for Innocent Comedians*, Graham's gesture has been purified of all subjective tricks and stands in the keeping of her disciples as abstract as the ballet code. It is overwhelmingly beautiful.) I am right-legged and right-footed, and most of the sustaining and balancing work in my choreography is done on the left leg; many of my dancers have complained bitterly. A dancer with short legs jumps in one manner, whereas a dancer with longer ones performs the same jump in quite another. So with composing. And identical pattern problems take on the modification of the composer's physique as well as his character adjustment, for it is always the choreographer who has to start the moving, and naturally he does it his way. If there were no instrument on which a song writer could work except his own voice, unquestionably his vocal restrictions would shape the melodic line.

The choreographer is also influenced by his performers. If I were to work, let us say, with a soloist whose arms and back were the strongest in the dance world and whose phrasing of legato lifts the most beautiful, but whose footwork, on the other hand, and allegro were weaker, quite obviously my composing style would adjust to his needs. Were I to compose with a man of enormous elevation and brilliant *batterie* but less dramatic force, my approach would then be necessarily different. And it must be noted that one works with the dancers at hand. One cannot summon from outer space a dream body capable of anything—or even exactly what one wishes. In the matter of one's own body one has obviously even less choice and must make do.

Furthermore, all artists, including choreographers, are influenced by their peers as by their antecedents. This is the way of organic development. Late Beethoven and early Schubert, for instance, are almost indistinguishable; while Brahms took certain themes, note for note, from Beethoven; and Shakespeare stole nearly all his plots—all the good ones certainly. Had they worked as contemporaries in the same studio, as do choreographers, with the same performers, the tie would have been closer yet. Furthermore, most choreographers, like the apprentice painters of the Renaissance, get their initial experience studying under the personal influence of a master, taking part in the actual creation of his works, and spending years—the formative years—under constant artistic domination. The wonder is that any individual expression develops at all.

But it does develop, and with it the deviations and mannerisms we call personal style. Usually the artist is unaware of the process, as he is unaware of his other spontaneous modes of expression. Few willingly believe the insistent repetition, the catch phrases, the special idioms we use in conversation. Who among us has recognized a first recording of his own voice? We prefer to think of ourselves in terms of universals shared by all mankind—by all the ways, in short, in which we resemble or possibly surpass others. Our neighbors, on the contrary, distinguish us by our oddities and crotchets, and it is just for this reason that a cartoon when effective strikes everyone but the subject as revealing.

If idiosyncrasies of expression constitute a key to others' understanding, they serve the artist in much the same way, as a means of self-revelation and a technique for reaching his emotional reservoir. They determine his work habits and of course the character of his expression. But whereas each worker will develop his own combination, his own formula, so to speak, he will have virtually nothing to do with its choosing and can use his critical faculties only to shape and correct. The emotional key, the kindling spark, lies beyond the reach of his mind deep in instinct. When we find these habitual patterns pleasing, we say the artist has developed style; when they appeal to our taste less, we say that he is repeating himself.

But the great repeated constantly. How do we, for instance, recognize Bach in any two measures of his music? Obviously because it sounds precisely like him and no one else. It is a question, I believe, of what is basically present and not how often the devices and tricks are employed. Indeed, if variety were all, one could compose with a slide rule. There is great style and lesser style, and style altogether to be condemned; but none of it has to do either with repetition or derivation.

It is difficult for the individual to evaluate his own strengths and characteristics, and the theater is strewn with lives ruined by unwarranted determinations to sing, or write, or act. No guarantee goes with desire, and there is unhappily just enough genuine talent neglected to confuse the issue. Nevertheless, granting a modicum of true ability, one must not be afraid to fail now and then. It all depends on the reason why.

One may, of course, fail because one has chosen the wrong kind of work.

One may fail because one has no discipline either in work or the handling of emotional problems.

One may fail because one wishes to fail—a hard tendency to detect, but a history of avoidable catastrophe indicates a need for medical help.

One may fail temporarily because of grief, harassment, or exhaustion and, in the theater, from lack of time.

And then one may fail in trying new and unknown ways of expression. A creative life without failure is unthinkable. All physical growth and emotional change involve discomfort and a good bit of highly unattractive transition. Consider any adolescent, for example, taken at face value and with no thought of what is to come.

This fear of defeat haunts the creative worker uncomfortably, and there are fat days when all of us long to be left alone. But the first moment we permit ourselves to feel safe, the first moment we save ourselves from exposure, we are in danger of retreating from the outposts. We can be quite sure that this particular job need not be done, for, in all probability, it will have been done before.

"One must risk one's career every six months," says Elia Kazan, "in order to stay alive and [be] effective in one's work."

But although work will never be safe, it may happily sometimes be easy and quick. Very frequently the best work is the easiest. But the rhapsodic release comes only infrequently and the professional must learn to compose at will— to employ aesthetic aphrodisiacs. For a young artist, this is perhaps the hardest task. Each person must learn his own path through the labyrinth of escape and idleness. Anne Lindbergh speaks of a technique of "acquiring grace": "Most people are aware of periods in their lives when they seem to be 'in grace' and other periods when they feel 'out of grace.' . . . In the first happy condition, one seems to carry all one's tasks before one lightly as if borne along on a great tide; and in the opposite state one can hardly tie a shoestring. It is true that a large part of life consists of tying the shoestring, whether one is in grace or not."

To translate this into terms of the working artist, the state of "grace," or inspiration, occurs when an idea is both clearly perceived and deeply felt, when circumstances do not block realization, and when technique waits ready and almost unconsciously available. The last is the controllable factor, a technique ready and available at the needed moment. Behind this lies a life's ordering.

For three weeks preceding any big job Jerome Robbins works himself into a lather of excitement on studies, all of which, he explains, may very well be discarded once the dancers are assembled, but without which he cannot begin. These preliminary exercises furnish him with momentum and conviction. They are a warming-up process. Hanya Holm, on the other hand, never prepares this way. She studies and thinks, but when she walks into the studio, no plan has been determined on. It is between her and the dancers and God, she says. But God, I have found, cannot be held to a schedule, and any kind of composition that involves a finishing time—and this is the essence of all theater—makes definite demands on inspiration. Inspiration has to be on tap as long as the components of design are living bodies paid by the hour.

But we may be grateful that very seldom are circumstances propitious and that the work fights through hard and slow. The moment one knows how, one begins to die a little. Living is a form of not being sure, of not knowing what next or how. And the artist before all others never entirely knows. He guesses. And he may be wrong. But then how does one know whom to befriend or, for that matter, to marry? One can't go through life on hands and knees. One leaps in the dark. For this reason creative technique reduces itself basically to a recognition and befriending of one's self. "Who am I?" the artist asks, and he devotes his entire career to answering.

There is one clue: what moves him is his. What amuses or frightens or pleases him becomes by virtue of his emotional participation a part of his personality and history; conversely what neither moves nor involves him, what brings him no joy, can be reckoned as spurious. An artist begins to go wrong exactly at the point where he begins to pretend. But it is difficult sometimes to accept the truth. He has to learn who he in fact is, not who he would like to be, nor even who it would be expedient or profitable to be.

He may think he cannot afford this risk, but it is equally evident he cannot afford hackneyed success. For this is no success. And everyone instantly recognizes what has happened. The breath of life has gone; the workshop has become a morgue.

The real failing, the killing off, is not in taking risks but in choosing some work beneath his capacities and in doing it in a slick and routine fashion purely for recompense. This hurts the whole field of work, dirties and dulls down the audience, and destroys the individual. In the disreputable suburbs of each art form flourish great fortunes made just this way. I do not for one moment wish to imply that first-class work does not also bring in money. God is good, and it frequently does. But let us be sure in our hearts, no first-class job was ever achieved without a good deal in view besides the check.

The folks who think only of money may cynically pretend they do not care, but their stomach ulcers and their alcoholism prove they do most dreadfully. It is not so much a matter of what work is done but how it is done. It is vital to everyone to know that work is necessary and done to the best of ability whether making soap operas or washing floors, and it is only when the dust is swept under the rug that the process of disintegration sets in.

Far better than succeeding regularly is a good tough falling-short of a challenge. All work—one's own and everyone else's—benefits from this effort, successful or not, just as all science benefits from each difficult experiment—even the ones that seem not directly to bring results.

Louis Horst said recently at a testimonial banquet tendered him by the dancers of New York that he wished to thank all the dedicated and devoted artists with whom he had had the privilege of achievement; and he wished also to thank those who had tried and failed, because without them, the great could not have gone so far.

It is not for the individual to demand a certificate of quality before starting. He cannot and he may not. He has to work on faith. And he must listen only to his conscience, which will be stern enough in truth. He must listen to no other voices. For to listen is to be lost—to listen to critic, or friend, or business interest. He can pray only that his tastes and passions will be common to many. But he must suit himself first, himself before everyone else. He must, in other words, marry the girl of his heart despite the family or he will bed down for life with a wench not of his choosing.

I know now how the *Frail Quarry* should end, as I know that this should be its rightful title, but it has taken a deal of living and shaking down to come to terms with my instincts. The ballet was essentially a wry piece and not at all the romantic comedy I had hoped. It had, however, an honorable enough life; poor maimed pretty little thing, it had six years of performing. But today it lies in limbo waiting for a great comedian and waiting for the finish that burns in my brain. (179–192)

"The Milk of Paradise"
(*And Promenade Home*)

In this essay, de Mille revisits some of the themes of "Ballet and Sex"—an essay in her previous book, *Dance to the Piper*—beginning with her condemnation of organized religions, for their treatment of women, and of the "Christian Church," in particular, for its treatment of dancing as well. Her throughline, which might be called proto-feminist, concerns the importance of work to a woman's identity. De Mille, a cum laude graduate in English from UCLA (1926) and a lifelong reader, was highly educated; but she was not a trained historian, and her gift for the puissant declarative sentence could be balanced on questionable evidence, such as her assertion that the ancient poet Sappho was a heterosexual who was the target of a male whispering campaign. One may also be surprised to find that the author recognizes no woman of the eighteenth through the mid-twentieth century, not even Emily Dickinson, as a first-class lyric poet. (In the 1950s, of course, English translations of Anna Akhmatova and Marina Tzvetayeva would not have been readily available.) And it is puzzling that de Mille would exclude Martha Graham from her list of the greatest choreographers alive at the time of this essay's composition, much less that she would rank all choreographers, including Balanchine, as inferior to Michelangelo and Goethe. Still, over a half century after its publication, "The Milk of Paradise"—the title refers to a phrase in Samuel Taylor Coleridge's unfinished poem "Kubla Khan"—remains an impressive as well as passionate defense of dancing as a serious profession and of satisfying careers outside the home as a spiritual necessity for women and, ultimately, for society at large. It both evokes Virginia Woolf's *A Room of One's Own* and anticipates art historian Linda Nochlin's field-changing essay, "Why Are There No Great Women Artists?"

The "separation" to which de Mille alludes at the beginning is that effected by Walter Prude's military deployment and her own professional obligations on Broadway during World War II.

All during this separation I told myself as I wrote my husband that later when he returned I wanted to quit the theater and rest. But deep in my heart

I knew I wanted nothing of the sort. Was it likely that under the stimulus and joy of his return I would suddenly bank my fires? Men have always been able to experience family and work together. It has been assumed that because of the greater emotional demands made on women, they could not have both, and they have hitherto been constrained to choose. But I was in a new century and I was greedy. I wanted wifehood, motherhood and work. I wanted all.

There were two thousand years of domestic history dead against me and against me were the race memories and traditions I had myself inherited. But there was in my blood something else, another need, as deep and as old, and this urged without respite or peace. This would not let me be.

I had drunk the Milk of Paradise and known power. I could not think to give this up. I could forfeit my life, and my comfort, riches and convenience, for love—but not the magic release of work! This was my identity.

The fact that for millennia all such desires have been arbitrarily suppressed in women proves nothing but the brutality of convention. In primitive and ancient cultures women were thought, because they were women and because they gave birth, to have special powers and were the preferred celebrants vital to certain life and death occasions.

Mastery in any field is attained by practicing what is valued at times of recognized importance. No genius, no matter what the field, is an unprecedented accident. There must be a need, an expectation and trust. Behind Sappho was a long line of honored female poet-composers, the last supremely great female composers in the history of music. She was the culmination of a tradition {There were similar priestess-musicians in Egypt, Assyria, Babylonia and India.} and it is instructive to note that Sappho was not only by contemporary accounts (which is all we have of her, since the music has been lost) the greatest of her profession but that she was a good wife and mother and that her social reputation within her community and during her lifetime was exemplary. It was a century later that the boys in Athens started a whispering campaign of personal defamation which reinforced a growing legend: that any woman who dedicated herself to art must be a freak, that artistic creativity was compensation for lack of creativity in more natural and suitable functions. This myth was not based on fact, or on any larger understanding of women's capacities or happiness, but directly on men's convenience. Women have at last, to their terrible cost, come to accept this view. It suited their men. And they understandably wanted to suit their men.

As the conviction took hold, and woman began to think of herself as not only different but inferior, she gradually lost her function of a necessary ritual voice in the community. Where is she, for instance, in the Christian Church? In the Hebraic? The Moslem, Hindu, or Shinto? On her knees with her head covered up and her mouth shut, removed at a prophylactic distance from the high altar and all sacred vessels. In our church women have been considered from Old Testament times unclean, a moral and ritualistic hazard. The very functions and powers that primitive religions cherished here betray her. Women from the end of the first century A.D. have not been allowed to officiate in the church, build or design the church, compose or write for the church, perform in the church {Women have been admitted to Protestant choirs only within the last three hundred years.}, nor even for some hundreds of years sing as lay members of the congregation. "Woman was represented {by the early Church Fathers}," writes Lecky, "as the door of hell, as the mother of all human ills. She should be ashamed at the very thought that she is a woman. She should live in continual penance, on account of the curses she had brought upon the world." {*History of European Morals*, Vol. II, pp. 357–358}

Consecrated women, that is, women whose every female function had been exorcized, neutralized and spayed, were permitted certain holy or clerical offices but always secretly, and behind bars. At one period the unsterilized were forbidden by papal edict to sing anywhere at all, even over their slop pails and washboards. But this restriction could not long prevail. Women's natural rejoicing while scrubbing floors and cleaning out the garbage was not to be restrained and they gave tongue to their enthusiasm. But only domestically. The church doors remained shut except at a most terrible price: the dedication of her entire life, private floor-washing and all.

And many thought the cost slight. For among other attractions the church provided the only art experience the average person, male or female, could know. During the Dark Ages its vast projects exploited all the talents available in any community. Throughout eight hundred years of endowed scholarship it developed the many arts it could use. But the arts it could not use—chiefly dancing—withered. No ecclesiastical or ritual choreography was composed nor was any method of dance notation evolved, as unquestionably would have been done had the holy fathers wished to preserve any visual ceremonial. The artists the church was permitted to use, that is, men, achieved great works. The artists it was not—what became of them? Barred up. Barred out. Wasted. Lost.

Stimulated by religious sanctions, the average husband and father placed even harder and more cruel blocks in the path of women's imaginative expression. By persuading themselves and their wives that no woman could devote time to anything but her husband and household without moral treason, they managed to discourage undomestic yearnings. Men wanted their wives womanly; by that was meant, we gather, they wanted them steadfast, attentive, enthusiastic, enduring—most certainly enduring—and serene; and by serene was meant that the women were to have no doubts about men's judgments and no disturbing inclinations of their own, a concept successfully implemented by a child a year—usually a convincer. Sixteen children without benefit of pediatrician, nursery school, or corner drugstore guaranteed attentiveness.

The women who were at the head of a great household were in a position of considerable influence: they administered battalions of servants; they supervised the many domestic industries which supplied virtually everything used in daily life, and which had to be made on the premises; they ran dispensaries for whatever medicine was needed; they arbitrated and organized and instructed. They did not, therefore, have much leisure and any free time there was they devoted to husband and children and not to idle flights of fancy.

The women had no doubt great satisfaction in being necessary and effective and may well have been both serene and content; we have not heard otherwise. The important point is that we have not heard. They were speechless. The experience of rearing up families, which was the universal lot of all lay women, did not find in seventeen centuries a single authentic female statement.

Nor did any of the men speak up. Men have sung about acres of pearly breasts, snowy throats and bee-bruised lips, but about the service, companionship and character of his helpmeet, not one word. Until the Victorian era the sharer of bed and bosom remained "my wife, poor wretch!" Consciously or unconsciously, women have lived for hundreds, for thousands of years with the belief that their happiness lay in serving god wholly or in serving husband and children wholly. Thus by religious sanction and matrimonial reinforcement the great taboo was fixed in our mores.

For over a thousand years woman's chief creative expression was restricted to the statements of saints and visionaries locked behind walls, special in nature, in no way representative of ordinary woman, her passions or fate.

Outside the safety of the church most transgressors against the social code paid dearly for their defiance with loss of caste and with cruel personal restrictions. Only lower-class women were permitted to embroider or paint, the two being considered of an equally artisan nature. Certain pretty outcasts were permitted to sing or act, although there were long periods of interdiction against even depraved women doing either. But within and without the cloister the usual price of self-expression for intellectual or well-born women was the forfeit of sexuality.

As late as the eighteenth and nineteenth centuries, when gentlewomen began to have what we would consider professional careers, the majority remained spinsters. The married few took husbands late when the pattern of their minds had been firmly set, like Elizabeth Barrett and George Eliot. The exception that leaps to mind is, of course, George Sand, but it must be remembered that if she had many lovers, she found by her own admission lasting happiness with no one; she remained ill-mated and lonely throughout.

And as one considers the great names of the last two centuries certain facts become apparent: many worked semisecretly under male pseudonyms; few married, fewer still bore children; very nearly all were sick, flat on their backs as often as not.

And what kind of art did these rebellious lonely people produce? Except in two fields, not the best. There were among them a few lyric poets not comparable to the greatest men, a few second-class painters, no architect, until very recently no sculptors, not one single first-rate composer excepting the nuns Kassia, Mechtild, and Hildegarde, whose work their church did not think fit to preserve but who left a tremendous contemporary reputation.

This is a fairly frightening history. It matters not a whit how you educate a girl, what techniques or attitudes you teach her. If she knows that her men will not welcome her talents she is going to proceed timidly. Put any gifted child at the keyboard, train her, exhort her six hours a day, but let it be borne in on her that there never has been in recorded music a first-rate female composer, that no man will consider her work without condescension, and, worst of all, that within herself she may provoke conflicts that she cannot hope to surmount, and you may get results, but they won't be Beethoven. {It is interesting in this connection to consider what educators have found in regard to the schooling of Negro children: that they show no inferiority of endowment or application until about the eighth year, when the full realization of their social status and lack of opportunity becomes clear to them. Trauma frequently cripples further development.}

This has been wasteful for art, cruel for the women, and unhelpful to the men because they have been persuaded to build up their pride of manhood on assumptions that were bound to give way the moment women found the restraints served no good purpose and need not be endured.

Today women know almost as much freedom as in pagan antiquity and turn eagerly to the arts, but to only three with promise of supreme success:

First, now as before, and always, to the performing careers, where in spite of long periods of interdiction and censor they have managed consistently to excel. Second, to creative storytelling and prose, in which they hold their own with the best. And third, to choreography. In this field they have practiced without restriction. No man ever barred the way here because no man thought highly enough of the business to keep women out, as he had done from so many august, holy, or honorable occupations.

The Christian Church had proscribed dancing and it was utterly without dignity, cut off from all serious motivation, the sources of ancient meaning and glory. The Christian Church was the first great church to do this. So strongly had dancing been involved in all previous worship that it took more than one thousand years to root it out of the Catholic service (a good deal longer than it took to root women out). But it was at last eradicated and there remain now only vestigial remnants in the Mass. The church is poorer for the loss; the effect on dancing has been disastrous. For two thousand years dancing and dancers have struggled under religious and social censure more formidable than that placed on any activity, except sin itself—and sex.

Dancing nevertheless remains the germinal art, the mother of theater and all other arts, in an anthropological sense the mother of the church. And it is in this ancient medium that those members of the community debased from proper participation in more honored practices have served a quickening purpose. The rejected art and the rejected artist meet here in apt congress. Here woman is despised for her trade and not for her sex, and there is all the margin between success and failure in this differentiation. It has been the women who have transfigured not only the art, but the point of view and purpose of its practitioners, its status and relation to other arts and to the community. Dancing is the only art where women have functioned to such crucial purpose, but it is the only art where they have not worked in the teeth of universal doubt.

There have been great male choreographers—Noverre, Bournonville, Petipa, Fokine, Massine, Balanchine, Ashton, Tudor. I think one must truthfully report that the greatest have been men. But there has been no artist in a class with Michelangelo, Shakespeare, Goethe, or Bach. Indeed, to rank any choreographer with these seems like impertinent hyperbole. Nor have there been any male figures comparable in dynamism and originality to Isadora Duncan, Martha Graham, or Mary Wigman.

The very handicaps and limitations which have frightened away gifted men work to woman's advantage. Here her training and habits stand her in good stead. Here even her body is helpful. Anonymity has been her history. She is at home in an art without literature, without past or future. She has never hoped beyond today and tomorrow—or much beyond the door of her house. Are not her daily efforts spent on evanescence? Cooking, washing, watching, caring, each day erasing the labors of the day before as each gesture erases from the air its precedent? And as every day's work must start afresh in endless repetition, so each dance begins clean with no record. The dancer enters space without a guiding mark and the pattern is rehearsed and leaves no sign—no sign except the exchange between living people, the relationship established, if only once and never again. The patience for this is woman's special endowment. She is aware that there is no substitute for the breath of life; that it is unique and personal; that the unduplicated action, the unrepeated speech, the gesture or word thrown away or heard by few or only once may be as important as any public message. She remembers that the source is inexhaustible; that it is the moment of life that counts, the rebirth, that again and again and again the dancer jumps and runs, and when he falls, another, by vital invitation, leaps out. This, woman understands. This is the stuff of her life.

Women today comprise nearly one third of our total working force—many thousands of them in the arts—but the ones that turn to dancing do so still for the antique reasons—power and Dionysian release on their own terms.

Dancing ranks with women's oldest professional careers, religious dedication and prostitution. It is inextricably related to both. First as priestess, then as prostitute, then as theater performer the dancer found a way of winning fortune, an excuse from household slavery and enforced seclusion.

Dancing has always been fruitful in its effects of direct fulfillment and satisfaction, and today the appeal is, as before, spellbinding through the body. It is not the concomitants of theatrical success that draw young girls so much as the vision of becoming generically DANCER in the permitted dress, exposed legs, free and floating arms, aerial skirt. I think they want this because it produces effects of transformation as recompense for all they find insupportable in woman's traditional lot.

Dancing inflames and exercises the sense of the viewer (hence its long connection with prostitution) and of the performer (hence its long connection with religion). It is a physical release as no other performing art can be, because it is practiced on the whole body; the body is the instrument, the medium itself, and the exposure is total and voluptuous. Therein lies the clue to its compulsive lifelong hold. It can become more frequently than not a substitute for physical sex and it has all too often been chosen as a vocation because woman's life, sexually speaking, has become in our civilization unsatisfactory, uncertain and expensive to the individual.

In what way, then, is dancing a solution? Briefly, it guarantees satisfaction and control to people who are afraid they will not otherwise know them. A dancer can do more than pray or hope; she takes matters into her own hands.

Every girl has known from time immemorial that she had better have a dowry or looks, and if she possessed neither, there was usually nothing for her but to be family drudge or enter the church, where God could be counted on to overlook what husbands would not. On her appearance still depends in large measure her chance for a good marriage and children, for a continuing sex life, for a high income. Numbers of ill-favored women have succeeded to the physical rewards of life, it is true, but it is in spite of handicap and by exercising faculties not demanded of the more handsomely endowed. Age and appearance, therefore, are important, particularly in any situation where women outnumber men.

Doctors assure us that any feeling of inferiority induced by physical appearance, short of mutilation, is in reality a symptom of a deeper conflict, and that the truly beautiful are as capable of self-doubt as the plain. This may be so, but it is not the prevailing popular understanding.

A woman's age has always been important because her value has been reckoned chiefly as a breeding animal and fecundity determined her economic status. This is happily no longer so.

Youth and physical beauty, nevertheless, are still held up before us as a promise, and have been in legend, story and song. We are told, and we believe, women more than men, that to win love, but, more imperatively, to retain love, we must be beautiful. It is a terrifying threat. And it faces us on every billboard, magazine page, screen, stage, shop window and, yes, even on the pages of every nursery picture book, because the princess was always beautiful or became so. And as we grew up, we accepted the idea more and more. Mother's friends always spoke of "the fine little boy" or "the son," but it was "the pretty little girl," and if that adjective was omitted and the word "dear" substituted, we became sensible of something hurt or slightly damaged and needing special tenderness.

Woman's best approach to happiness, we learn on all sides, is the quick rousing of men's erotic interest, and the advertisements are explicit as to what rouses men. It can be bought in a bottle—and it is quite expensive but well worth the price. Five of the largest businesses in the United States—cosmetics, ladies' clothing and accessories, furs, jewelry, both real and false, women's magazines—have sprung from the premise that romance follows beauty and that beauty can be purchased. The young woman is advised to make herself lovely and then lie around like a kind of bait, and she is warned that only after the trap has successfully sprung can she satisfy her own inclinations.

Now, for many young people this is a dismaying proposition. A girl may very well feel she cannot make the grade; she may also feel fundamentally outraged in having her life controlled by someone else's tastes, implying, as it does, a passivity which she may interpret as helplessness.

The fact is many women do not favor being passive, are downright frightened by it, having witnessed centuries of results. Young girls see quite a lot of women, particularly mothers, and often they are not enchanted. They see mothers tied to housework who would prefer not to spend their days sweeping and cooking. They see mothers and older sisters doing jobs and chores which are considered more menial and less important than fathers' jobs and that bring in no money. It is father who has the cash for his freedom; mother must ask. Indeed, mother has almost no freedom at all to speak of. Mothers are always at the call of other people's needs and desires. Their daughters find little charm in the pattern. They would like to be free to please themselves, forever children, unless they might grow up to some of the freedom of father. But growing up for a woman, as they observe, seems to mean less freedom, and no guarantee of happiness. And so some of them, the dancers, never grow up.

Very few dancers develop the bodies of mature women; they keep lean in the hips and flat-breasted, a phenomenon remarked on by all costume designers. It is also a fact that the greatest performers, the women best capable of communicating sensuous satisfaction, are in their bodies least sensual. In effect they have sacrificed all organs of personal fulfillment and maintain and cherish only the means for public satisfaction, the system of bones and sinews for levitation and propulsion. The ballet foot and leg, which when used to its full capacity can evoke an almost physical response, is in repose as tight and straight as the leg of a mule. Certain great soloists have been lacking in even primary sexual functions and are known to have menstruated rarely in their lives. For the rest, very many, possibly a majority, are partially frigid and do most tend to be, in spite of legend, more chaste than otherwise. I do not mean to imply that they are not passionate and gallant, but that certain deep rejections and fears prevent easy sexual release. The majority of American women are, it is claimed by medical statistics, partially frigid, and perhaps dancers no more than others. In any case, the dancers have evolved a substitute expression and do not mind the state so bitterly. This, of course, is no good answer to the fear of life. But it is an instinctive and practical one.

Even Isadora Duncan, who clamored the loudest for love, was no exception. She was a true sensualist and she seems to belie in the richness of her experience all I have argued about women's substitution of dancing for life. But consider her point of view repeatedly expressed: she vowed when very young never to submit to woman's usual fate, never to marry, that is, never to put herself or her fortune into any man's keeping, to bear children if and when she pleased, to leave them or look after them at whim, to be absolutely free and to remain so. She wished to have the freedom of a pagan as she imagined it, for she recognized love as a transient ecstasy. The communion on which marriage is built she never, I believe, envisaged, nor constancy, security, fruition, these being the rewards of the female life she scorned. She followed a dream, power without responsibility, release without cost. And her way of attainment was the cultivation of her body. The littlest ballet pupil in first position before the mirror is starting on the same historic path. {I would like to interject that very few daughters of contented mothers have become ballerinas. I cannot name a father who urged a dancing career on his girl unless he was himself a dancer and looked upon the matter as one of natural succession.}

For in dancing the face matters least and the body is beautiful if it functions beautifully. It is not the shape of the leg, but the use of the leg that tells. Furthermore, and most felicitously, the beautiful use changes the flesh and corrects all manner of imperfections. Contrary to maxims, one can by taking thought add a cubit to stature. When a dancer stands before a mirror, she no longer sees what her big brothers see, but a promise. If her nose turns up or down, no matter: men will gasp at the carriage of her head. If she is fat, she will get thin. If she is thin, the muscles of her back and thighs will enable her to move like a voluptuary. And who is to say or who cares what she is, whether this or that, if she stands in the center of a stage in the revealing and beautiful uniform of her trade, escorted by the best cavalier in the business, who has forfeited the right to refuse her and must take her if she is the best, not the prettiest, mind you, but the best and the most skillful. And there for all to see, in public, she will perform with him the ritual of romantic courtship. More than in any other art, there are enormous rewards as regards direct attention, admiration, emotional release, and they remain always under the performer's command. She never surrenders her will. She gets her rewards directly by her own effort. There need be no intermediary— and for any female who doubts her powers this is a temptation of frightening persuasiveness.

Dancing represents sex in its least costly form, free from imprisonment and free to a great extent from emotional responsibility, and, above all, as a sure thing, independent of someone else's pleasure. In other words, it means freedom *from* sex. The forces which impelled women to the austerity of the church operate to form the great dancer. In a strange transmutation dancing is a form of asceticism—almost a form of celibacy.

Is, then, the aesthetic impulse rooted in neurosis and unable to develop except under the compulsion of pain? Are these brutal disciplines and forfeits necessary to creative effort? The ancients did not rely on any such goads and, notwithstanding, their art flourished. The restraints we place on women creators could well be accidental to our culture, of no great profit to the individual or the work, but, rather, destructive to both. I believe this to be the case and that the genius with which certain women write or paint or compose or choreograph derives from faculties and needs beyond any mere act of compensation. I believe that talent is compounded of the entire personality and is as much a sign of exuberant health as of sickness. But the bewitchment of hundreds of thousands, of millions of girls by the dream, by even the discipline of dancing cannot be called creativity, nor even vocation. It is escape, it is protest, and it is, in large part, hysterical protest.

For a time it serves the art form well, but only for a time. In the working conditions of our world and theater the dedicated ones are forced under emotional whips to greater and greater effort. But there is a limit. The personality ceases to expand, ceases to breathe, in certain aspects it withers and this is reflected in a stunting of the art. The audience is always aware.

An act of suppression that cancels out emotional or imaginative life, the one at the cost of the other, is obviously wasteful. With either choice a major section of the personality is wrecked and all human relations, in marriage and out, must suffer.

A dancer's release, like most magic, is transient and won each time by renewed and arduous effort. Dancing has become consequently a kind of sexual limbo whose inhabitants identify their own flesh with their purpose, a confusion not equally true for women artists whose bodies are not their lifework. Dancing is, in a deep sense, the only physical union many of these women know, a sort of automarriage. And as with all such narcissistic unions, there develops an aura of melancholy and the promise of death. Many a young dancer has drowned in the mirrors before which she spends her life. The others live only when the reflection from the audience fans breath back into their emptying spirits.

Whatever rewards the dancer knows in place of the usual emotional and sexual associations, she is frequently assailed by doubts in her late twenties or early thirties. Even the very great know these morbid spells. The needs of the heart cannot be cheated forever. The dancer grows frightened. The dancer realizes suddenly she is a spinster and aging, no matter how fast she gets around the room. The life of merciless effort, the dimming chances of permanent fame, exhaustion and the growing comprehension of what old age means to a fading athlete without family or home suddenly terrify even the staunchest. The conviction grows that the sacrifice has been too much and perhaps not necessary. There is many a *volte-face* at this point and a marriage with at least one child in a frantic effort to put life back on balance.

But our theater is not set up for family life; dancing in particular is conditioned by worldwide touring, uncertain irregular seasons and precarious pay. Dancers today do not inherit the career dynastically as they used to, like the Vestris, the Taglioni (five distinguished members and three generations in this family), the Grisi, Elssler, Karsavin clans. Our dancers are not protected wards of the state with guaranteed salaries and pensions. The married dancer is called upon to relinquish jobs that would further her career and settle for domesticity against professional interest. Many do this serenely and good-naturedly; this is nothing more than the problem of reconciling life and art, which is present with all workers, but in a dancer's case, particularly for women, it is final. She may consider the exchange worth the price either way. She may not and live in perpetual conflict.

It is astonishing under the circumstances that none of these factors deters young girls one whit. Five million of them in this country alone [in the mid-1950s] are studying to be professional dancers.

Perhaps this is so because women today, even dancers, cannot bring themselves to accept these conditions as permanent. They see no reason why they should not have both work and family, what with Deepfreeze, Waring mix and diaper service. They believe also with all their hearts and hopes— because it suits them so to believe—that sweet reasonableness and a sense of fair play will dissolve the major block to the double life: their husbands' attitude.

Marriage is difficult with any artist. "A man does not love a woman for her genius; he loves her in spite of her genius," writes Maurice Goudeket, the husband of Colette. Marriage is perhaps hardest of all with a theater personality because the work is not wholly under the control of the individual. Dancers above all do not make easy wives. The union has to run a gamut of conflicting loyalties. A dancer's husband has to share his wife's discipline. His life is as curtailed as hers and quite literally by hers. Most men, particularly men outside of the profession, find such conditions onerous.

But the unrest is general and pertains to all careers and all classes of society. Preachers, doctors and teachers warn; magazine and newspaper editorialize. The women's magazines are particularly explicit: if the wife has to work outside the home she must never let it impinge on her husband's schedule, and if inside the home she must see that it is finished and put away before he comes back from his own work and she must never for one moment let him think that hers is important compared with his, or his interests and hobbies and needs. And for this reason and because it will be construed as a direct reflection on his virility, she must not earn more money. He will develop ulcers, sinuses, abscesses, tuberculosis. He will borrow the classic symptom of women's frustration, the bitter, black headache, and although women's magazines do not care to name this, he will add one of his own, partial or total impotence, which is a form of suicide and just as unanswerable. He may in the end leave her.

If the women do not depend on their men as their grandmothers did, the men similarly manage to do without them. It has become a game of mutual attrition played out on a level where both are pitifully defenseless. Medical statistics and divorce courts list the ruin. The suicide rate among men, the alcoholism, the excesses of sedation and narcotics, the growing overt homosexuality, the juvenile neuroticism and delinquency attest to the monumental cost of the emotional adjustment. This is the "furious and lamentable region" that Conrad speaks of, "the dwelling place of unveiled hearts" where there is neither right nor wrong but only human suffering.

Woman has always accepted with grace, with pride and satisfaction, her husband's interests and achievements, taking joy, taking not in any way a sense of diminution and shame. Can the husband endure to learn this? Does he wish to? Will he not rather attempt to put things back as they were, stuffing all hopes, ambitions and zests not centered on himself into the family cupboard and setting his back to the door? Indeed, indeed, things cannot go back. Pandora's box is opened. The girls are earning money.

It is of no consequence who works better—men or women; it is important that each work differently and that each be allowed to try without penalties. "Never destroy any aspect of personality," said my grandmother George, who had no career except caring for her family, "for what you think is the wild branch may be the heart of the tree." Not all women want a double life. But those who do should not be denied on the grounds of sex. It is not easy to be a devoted wife and mother and a first-class artist; it is equally hard to be an artist with no root experience in life. It is impossible to be a good wife or a wise mother, embittered, balked and devoured by inner energies. Creative exercise can be disciplined to a household schedule—not easily, but women everywhere prove it can be done. For when all faculties are exercised the enormous releases of strength and satisfaction more than make up for the extra attention demanded. Extra attention? No, rather, elimination of waste and repining. The alternation of diaper washing and composing spell one another in mutual refreshment. Ask any responsible working mother. And the children will reflect the zest and energy of the parent's life—and as to the work, how it flourishes! How it flowers and expands! Even under discipline, perhaps particularly under discipline, because it is voluntary and joyful, because the sources of life are fulfilled and replenished and because, as in all things, the greater the range of accomplishment, the greater the capacity for more.

I think this is what Isadora Duncan meant when she spoke of founding a new religion: the total release of women's hearts, the total use of their gifts.

Women have bent to the yoke and the scars of their durance are upon their children. But with the lessening of all social and religious restrictions, with widening economic opportunities, with practical invention bringing ease and leisure, there stands between woman and whatever life she yearns for only one barrier: her husband's good will. Failing this, she fails all. She must have his blessing, his pride in her achievement. Let him dower her with this and there will come the great works for which we have waited so long. But beyond and beneath there will come happiness.

It is an act of recognition that is needed, an act of love. (213–231)

"Old New York"
(*Portrait Gallery*)

> Since the publication of "Old New York" in de Mille's 1990 col-
> lection, *Portrait Gallery*, a few of her conclusions have become an-
> tiquated. As of 2009, parts of Harlem have been gentrified, and
> some real estate there has become valuable. Governmental support
> for scientific study of the universe has been stalled by a decrease in
> resources and by the decrease of popular enthusiasm for it. The im-
> provements that de Mille describes in the lives of domestic servants
> have been called into question by the plight of illegal immigrants
> in domestic service, some of whom have been subject to widely
> publicized abuse by their employers. Even so, this essay chronicles
> a vanished New York that many readers of Edith Wharton and
> Henry James will fondly appreciate. And the Cathedral of St. John
> the Divine is *still* under construction.

My greatest gift, I believe, is my memory, which is obviously long, but also
accurate and highly visual. I learned to remember in color, and, what is much
rarer, I learned to remember in sequence. The fact that I fitted words to my
memories, that my parents were both highly verbal and my father memorable
in his remarks, acted as a kind of preservative for very much of what happened,
so that the New York of the early part of this century is quite real and vivid to
me. The world of women in which I grew up, having a younger sister, female
cousins, and many aunts and later being sent to a girls' school, was impressed
on me in all its aspects. I shared in the exhilaration and the suffering and the
risk of the century's tide.

I was born in 1905 in New York City, on 118th Street in Harlem, at that time
a quiet middle-class white neighborhood. All our neighbors were white, different kinds of white. There were no specific black communities anywhere in
New York then. Indeed, there were few blacks. The recent Jewish immigrants
lived mostly on the East Side in the Bowery district, the Chinese nearby,
strictly close to the Bowery, the Italians in the West Village, Germans and
Hungarians on East 86th Street, and Irish Catholics everywhere. The Irish
were servants or policemen, or, when affluent, ran bars or city government.
There were lots of them, but there were few Latinos. Harlem was "pure"
middle-class American, and our flat was close to Morningside Park, where we
went walking in the mornings with our nurses and learned to hopscotch and

roller-skate and where street boys played games in the dirt with extravagant multicolored marbles called aggies.

Above to the west jutted the rock on which stretched Morningside Heights and the Cathedral of St. John the Divine, not yet finished but well begun, with truncated towers and interrupted transept waiting. On the roof of the completed Lady Chapel an angel triumphantly blew her horn against the New York sky. She was high above us, and she was the last thing we saw against the darkening west and the first thing we saw each day as the morning sun gilded her wings and her raised trumpet. That angel was our guardian and our promise.

We lived in a railroad flat, rather dark, very long, and extremely ugly, but with conveniences—some quite surprising, some we don't have today: the dumbwaiter in the kitchen, for instance, which brought us milk, fresh milk, in nice glass bottles every morning, right up to the icebox, and all our meat and groceries right up to the stove and kitchen worktable. All deliveries were free, of course. The icebox was wood, with a zinc-lined chest at the top into which the ice man dumped, every other day, a large block which he carried, balanced and dripping, on a shoulderpad of a folded burlap bag. He wrestled this with large iron tongs into our box, chipped it down to size, and wedged it there.

We had three bathrooms, two very nice ones and the smallest for the maids. This was scarcely more than a sunless closet that contained the barest raison d'être and a tiny window giving onto a brick wall, admitting little air and no sun. At that, it was more luxury than the maids had ever known in the Home Country. Each room boasted electricity from a bulb hanging in the center of the ceiling—an execution light. There were additional globes, wired down to the sides by my mother for more kindly illumination. Every room also contained a gas jet, which we never used but which was there just in case, because about electricity you never could tell.

Just as you never could tell about the telephone. We had one, cumbersome and not always reliable. But we could call anywhere in New York City easily; Orange, New Jersey, after a little wait; Philadelphia after a longer wait. The western cities were out of the question, but to anywhere out of town it was more expeditious to send a telegram, which would be delivered within two hours—a neatly folded brown paper in an envelope, written in a florid but legible hand at a cost, I believe, of ten cents. Transcontinental telegrams cost a quarter. These telegrams were delivered by small boys in special Western Union or Postal Telegraph caps, caps that entitled the wearers to free subway rides and free entry into baseball games (the bleacher section of a ballgame cost fifty cents, the subway ride five cents). The owners of the caps may have earned only pennies, but they were members of the elite.

Mail was delivered two times daily; a letter cost two cents, a postcard one cent. A letter addressed within New York City usually arrived at its destination the same day, but without fail the following morning. In London a letter posted before noon always arrived the same day, and frequently the reply was delivered that very night. Of course there was no expediting machinery or computers to help in the delivery, and of course the postman's sons did not go to Harvard or Oxford.

Because my father was a playwright, young and unseasoned although quite successful, he was a man of limited means and precarious income. We were a family of four and could afford to employ only what was considered a very modest staff: a full-time live-in cook and a full-time nurse, a weekly cleaning woman, and a weekly laundress. (The washing was done in great tubs in the kitchen, taken to the apartment roof in fine weather, and hung there on lines. As a result, all the roofs of the apartment houses of New York were ablow with sheets and petticoats. In bad weather the laundry was strung out on lines in blind back airways and manipulated by pulleys from the kitchen window.) Mother helped all the time in cooking, household mending, marketing, family shopping, supervising, and minding the children. Mother kept very busy.

My father could easily afford all the necessary salaries, because the laundress received fifty cents an hour, the cleaning woman twenty-five cents, and the Irish cook and the Irish nurse $10 a week each for their full-time services. They were given their means and their beds, and they had half a day off every week and a full day off every two weeks. As I recall, there was no summer vacation. I do not know about sick leave or sick pay. I do not remember their ever being sick. No doubt Mother ministered to them if they were. They were there and busy, and we always had hot meals, home cooked, and we children were taken out twice a day for walks and play, in hot or cold weather. We were given cold baths every morning and castor oil when indicated, in great tablespoons, with orange juice or root beer as a disguise (no help). We also got cod liver oil once a day, in a tablespoon, without cause, no matter what. And we had fresh air, fresh air, fresh air. My mother was insane about it. One could have fresh air then, even in the city. One came home all blown and healthy to the comfort of Service.

And one had fun. New York then was lively and picturesque and colorful. It is more practical now, as well as more astonishing and frightening, but it was more varied then. All the street noises were fun and more diverting then, not ear-splitting or mind-deadening. The fire engines, which now stop conversation or thought, then invited participation; they were drawn by live horses. These remarkable animals were trained at the first alarm to leave their comfortable stalls unaided and stand waiting in the traces of the engines until buckled into harness, as was explained to us when the Horace Mann School third-graders visited the fire station. The firemen slept upstairs, in the firehouse, we were told, and when the alarm sounded they dressed in a matter of seconds, because their pants stood ready in their boots. Then they slid down a brass pole to the ground floor, clapping their firehats on their heads and shouldering their big coats as they rushed to the engine. In less than a minute they were out and away. A little French boy in our class interrupted to ask, "But what if they were in the toilet?" We looked at him with wonder. He had dared to ask the unmentionable. We were all dying to know, but he had actually voiced it, I suppose because he was French. The fire chief smiled. "We have arranged for those situations," he said, and explained nothing.

But the glory of those engines and the accompanying pumper, which had to be manned by hand! I often saw the engines in action. Under the wheels of the engine and under the hoofs of the galloping horses ran a black-and-white Dalmatian, a "plum pudding" dog. The dogs were also housed in the fire stations and had a soothing effect on the horses, I was told, and very possibly on the firemen. Beside the driver, who had to be unusually expert, sat a fireman with the rope of the bell in his hand, which he pulled rhythmically, sounding an alarm that superseded every other noise in New York. It was the sound of this tocsin that maddened the horses into a frenzy of superequine effort. They snorted and pawed the earth, and good Lord, how they galloped, insane to get to the smoke! There was a ladder truck, with the firemen standing on the running board and hanging onto leather straps, and a hose and pump truck, with firemen standing in back and hanging onto whatever they could. They went hell for leather, to find on arrival, very often, insufficient pressure at the fire hydrants, and in winter no pressure at all because the pipes iced over. I forget what they did then, besides curse and pray. The engines get places more quickly now, and buildings are seldom found on arrival to be in ashes, which is undeniably a good thing, but the process of saving them was certainly more entertaining then: four to six galloping horses and an engine shooting sparks! Wow!

The white wings, street cleaners, went down the streets twice every day in their white suits and with their little carts of rakes, brushes, brooms, and horse manure. They did not have a call or a bell; the horses could be relied on to provide them with work without notification. They were our city house cleaners, and they were as comforting to have around as any good domestics.

There were a great many street vendors of fruit and flowers and candy and drinks, and their calls and cries filled the air. And the knife-grinder! There were street organs, mostly turned by Italians, and their sound too could be heard. Sometimes the organ-grinders had monkeys dressed up with perky little hats, begging donations.

Occasionally came the sound of a piano through an open window, and this was a delight, because many people played well in those days, there being no mechanical music except now and then a player piano—but that was too vulgar for consideration. There was always something nostalgic and dulcet about personally made tunes, good or bad, heard at a distance and filtered through the sounds of busy street life.

There were other things to hear: trolley cars, with their bells ringing (on Broadway, Sixth Avenue, Eighth Avenue, Ninth Avenue); the rumble of buses, the fine two-deckers, and on Fifth Avenue the top decker, which was open to the sights and to the weather; the racket and banging of overhead railways on Third Avenue, Sixth Avenue, Ninth Avenue, and Amsterdam Avenue. These structures cut the light from all the adjacent buildings and, with their numerous iron supports, complicated the street traffic. But they did permit one to get downtown quickly.

And boys calling "Extra!" at times of crisis—they could be heard, always at the end of the streets, as windows flew up and heads appeared. "What happened?" "Who?" "Read all abaht it."

Fairly frequently from alleyways there came the unmistakable clang of a blacksmith's anvil and the clatter of a newly shod horse proudly stamping back into the streets. These sounds have completely gone from our life.

One could hear all this in the New York streets, to the end of a block, and although everybody complained, of course, about the din of the city, compared to today it was country silence. In addition, one came in from whatever noise there was to peace, absolute silence. There was no noise in the homes, none at all, there being no vacuum cleaners or Waring mixers or air conditioners or, Lord be praised, radio or TV. Indoors was quiet and restful, unless one made a rumpus oneself.

The stores then were different from the stores today, especially the food shops. To begin with, the shops were small and cozy—meat on one side, fresh and canned vegetables on the other. There were only a very few large stores of many departments, and these were situated way downtown at Herald Square, where Macy's and Gimbel's were, and they were truly marvelous. They had everything. They were Big Business.

That was where the *New York Daily Herald* was printed, in a beautiful two-story building, a kind of pavilion, designed by Stanford White, with ground-floor and basement windows of plate glass through which one could watch the late edition coming off the presses and being folded, gathered in piles, and stacked. Outside, two bronze workmen hammered a great bronze bell every hour, with reverberating and resonant clangs, deep and full-throated. All the busy pedestrians stopped to watch, and the bronze men never missed a stroke. They are still now, and this fine bell never speaks, but stands opposite a silent Horace Greeley, who, a perch for pigeons and hoary with their droppings, looks disconsolately at his dirtied shoes.

As to the uptown shops, the shops in our neighborhood, fruit and vegetables were not nearly so plentiful, certainly, nor so varied, nor by any means so exotic as we know now. Fruit was within season and it was limited geographically, and vegetables, except for potatoes, were limited by the season. All the summer vegetables disappeared with the autumn and were gone for months. Of course there was no frozen food. Look at the shelves of any supermarket and visualize just what this loss would mean. We used tins or home preserves, but preserved food was supposed to be not so nutritious, not even quite safe.

There was no nonsense about keeping merchandise out of reach. It was supposed to be poked, smelled, patted, even tasted, and to this end it lay invitingly open, uncellophaned and accessible to all, including small boys who thieved. And to flies. The shopkeepers took care of the children; long strips of sticky yellow paper hanging from above made a show of warding off the flies. The paper was soon as thick with black lumps as currant cake, but fresh ones were always zooming in.

The shops were redolent with the smell of freshly ground coffee beans (no tins) and tea, spicy and fragrant, in large japanned chests from the Far East (no dinky teabags). Standing around were great glass jars of candies and sugardrops (unwrapped).

Bakeries were good and plentiful, particularly the small shops known as home bakeries. Some of the big chains, however, had been established. Cushman's was worth the walk up to 125th Street for its charlotte russe, which I relished to the point of ecstasy (pale pink preferred). It was reserved as a reward for exceptional behavior.

Delicatessens flourished.

Butcher shops were forthright, the meat being hacked up in full view of passersby by fat-fingered men with bloody hands and bloody aprons. We were not so squeamish about the fact of butchery in those innocent but robust days. We ate flesh; we faced the fact. There was sawdust all over the floor and a great bloodied chopping block conspicuously displayed, on which the meat was cut according to individual specification and weighed carefully in front of each customer. For five cents extra one could get a large bunch of soup greens, and bones, including marrow bones, were free. There was no refrigeration anywhere, except in the stalls where meat was hung, and also occasionally for oysters. In the storage bins the meat was cold and preserved in good order, but once brought into view, it was on its own.

Mysterious and awe-inspiring drugstores displayed bottles and tins of unmentionables and castor oil, and enormous glass jars of colored liquid, in the windows outside, but few cosmetics beyond eau de cologne. They were beginning to have soda fountains, with little marble-topped tables and chairs with curly wire legs like musical signatures. Poisons were displayed quite brazenly on the counters. Arsenic, for instance, was used for cleaning furs. It was accountable for taking off quite a few curious juveniles.

Every block had one or more notion stores—shops selling ribbons, hooks and eyes, sewing thread, tape measures. This was because nearly every woman sewed, and most of the clothes were made at home. There were very few cleaning establishments; one had to walk quite a distance to find one. One did one's own cleaning.

And the dime stores! The five-and-tens, Woolworth's, were in fact five-and-tens; hardly anything in them cost as much as a quarter. What one could buy for an ordinary dime! I remember little bunches of red roses perfectly made, about five inches across. There must have been two dozen buds in each, all fashioned in New York sweatshops by starving tubercular girls, made beautifully, and sold to me for my grubby dime.

Just then, at that time, there was an influx of new Japanese stores. The market was flooded with cheap Oriental ware. For ten cents one could buy a spray of paper cherry blossoms, well made, and for fifty cents an entire branch. For a dollar one could obtain a small Japanese garden, with real moss growing for grass, ferns for bushes, dwarf trees bending over tiny pools, little bridges, miniature stone lanterns, and pagodas (these were Chinese, but who could tell the difference?). There were besides all kinds of paper fans and paper lanterns, even pretty paper umbrellas. The salesmen spoke hardly any English, but they knew how to sell.

A great many poor people, bums and vagabonds, crowded the streets, a good percentage of them with pockmarks—smallpox scars. Policemen in high hats and carrying billy clubs—the police never carried pistols—beat them up regularly and told them to get a move on. Street urchins built little bonfires in the gutters and were soundly thrashed by the officers' billy clubs, and the officers' boots stamped out the sparks of their fires. ("But Father, those boys are cold," I would say. "I think the police are mean." They were, too. "Get a move on," they yelled as they swung.) Not infrequently people fell down, dropping onto the pavement, and ambulances were slow in collecting them. The dray horses that pulled the great delivery wagons slipped on the icy streetcar tracks and fell too, dragging the carts over on top of themselves. Sometimes they had to be destroyed where they lay; sometimes they were goaded to their stumbling hooves with enormous trouble, curses, yelling, and lashings of whips and cries and the horrid scraping of iron shoes on the iron tracks. These sights burned themselves into memory.

The focus of any neighborhood was the church, whatever kind, and the spire of the church was always the tallest edifice in the neighborhood. One looked up to the cross or the spire or to the trumpeting angel. The skyline then consisted of blowing wash atop buildings, endless little smokes blowing out, and church spires—many, many spires. (In 1911 the roofs were black with people, as the population took to the top of the six-story buildings to watch the first airplane circle Manhattan.)

Has the weather changed much? It seems to me the seasons were more violent then. The winters were shrewd and hard to endure for all of us, rich as well as poor. Every day my mother dressed herself in her shirt; drawers; corset, which had to be pulled up tight, sometimes by one of the servants while Mother held on to the bedpost; on top her camisole, at least two petticoats, and the big dress; and when she went out there was superimposed a coat or cape, hat, veil, gloves, bag, furpiece, muff. We, the small children, were bundled up into a tremendous number of undergarments held together with buttons everywhere, smocks and sweaters and coats and hats and earmuffs and tippets, mufflers and mittens and gaiters, and then, all but immobilized, we were dispatched for a rollicking romp.

In their way, the summers too were fearful. In the summer all the nice apartments suspended green striped awnings on the outside of every window, which helped a little, but not very much. They were pretty, though. But oh, the heat! So many people collapsed from prostration. Every theater, every kind of public auditorium, was closed from Decoration Day to Labor Day. The theaters shut down totally, leaving the actors to rehearse in the dark, empty, fetid houses. Those actors who could took to the seashore or the

Catskills. The others looked for jobs in department stores and similar menial positions.

The poor went out on the fire escapes and carried their bedding with them in order to live through the nights. Those who were domiciled close to the elevated tracks stayed indoors and raised the windows and endured the closed and used air, which became very nearly insupportable. Many succumbed. The ice wagons rolled constantly down each street, followed by a crowd of boys begging for slivers. On every block the police opened fire hydrants to allow the children to play in the water, while the wading pools and the reflecting pools in Central Park, not designed for swimming, were black with waders and splashers. The police did little to stop them, it being a question of survival.

Through it all the women buckled up in their corsets and petticoats and camisoles and long stockings. Why did they do this? There was no law saying they must. The doctors advised against it. The reformers fulminated. The corset manufacturers said they ought to in order to be modish—that is, attractive to men—but even the corset manufacturers were becoming cautious; whales were being decimated, and there was a marked shortage of baleen. The first result, as could be expected, was that corsets were becoming very expensive. Nevertheless, every woman had at least one or two pairs and endured the constrictions. The practice of compelling a woman to wear a corset on all occasions from the time she was fifteen was inhuman, but it persisted. Every woman also wore a petticoat, or two or three—even women who washed the floors, women who did the laundry and ironing, and these were backbreaking chores in those days of no detergents and heavy flatirons that had to be heated on the gas range.

And another thing: no woman had money she could keep. Even the floor washer and the laundress, who slaved for a pittance, could not call their meager quarter dollars their own. Their money became the property of their husbands. Their houses were not theirs, nor their clothes (not even their corsets), nor their children. My father used to call out to my mother, "Ann, come and blow your child's nose." This remark was considered very funny, and everybody laughed. Mother thought it unfeeling and unpaternal, but no one realized the full irony of the exchange. I in fact did not belong to my mother; I belonged to my father. I was my father's property.

Our lovely streets in Harlem are now neglected and festering. Morningside Park is today one of the most dangerous spots in this city, and after dark no sane person would venture into it, or even pass close by. The neighboring houses are broken and filthy. On occasion there have been tales of rats attacking the children. And of course the neighborhood is no longer middle-class. There is not a white face to be seen from one month's end to the next. The present inhabitants don't like the environs any more than we would. But they have to stay.

Street boys no longer play marbles or build innocent bonfires in the gutters; they mug old ladies and trade crack. All the police carry guns and use them.

The streets don't look the same, but this we expect. The fire horses are gone, together with the parlor maids, the white wings, and the ambulatory street vendors, who couldn't be heard even if they were here and still trying. Gone are all the newsboys, the trolley lines, the double-decker buses, the els (they were torn down beginning in 1938, and the scrap iron was sold to Japan, which returned it to us in the bodies of our soldiers).

The church spire in any Manhattan neighborhood is barely visible, dwarfed and belittled as it is by business enterprises. These days one looks up to office buildings, and the towers of New York have nothing to do with intellectual or religious ideas. In fact, the entire island has become a remarkable conglomeration of stone monoliths, gravestones dedicated to greed.

Nothing is so picturesque, as pleasant-sounding, as personal, or as friendly as it was. We know we must expect changes; architecture and customs change with time. Always have. Must do.

On the other hand:

St. John the Divine is nearly finished. Because the church stands on a steep, rocky abutment, topography helps this holy edifice maintain superiority; its angelic trumpet can still aim at God's heaven and not into an office window. The angel still blows her challenge in triumph against clear sky. But in this St. John's is unique.

There are no laboring children on the streets, no delivery or mail boys. They are in school, learning it's hard to say what. People are older now, and healthier. The present generation has probably never seen a pockmarked face, for smallpox has been wiped out; tuberculosis, syphilis, meningitis, and infantile paralysis have diminished. Childhood disease is no longer rife nor fatal; the majority of children live. Although cancer, heart disease, and now AIDS seem virtually untouched, we have taken giant steps toward health. There are fewer one-armed or one-legged cripples. Most people, even elderly ones, have all their own teeth, something that was unheard-of in my youth. And there is no glint of gold when a person smiles. Only the indigent and the homeless smell. Most people can bathe. Even the poor have running water, generally hot.

The enlargement in the number of available drugs is spectacular, but active irritant poisons have been taken off the open drugstore counters, where they used to stand readily within the grasp of children.

As to enlargement of the variety of foods and nourishment: on the shelves of our supermarkets all the produce of the entire globe is displayed handily at the same time, year-round, despite the season. Most of the food is wrapped in plastic and is untouchable and sterile, and although the goodies seem devoid of attraction, there are no flies and no contamination. The fact of butchery is screened away as in an operating theater, and only the results are displayed, composed and laid out in their transparent shrouds. One does not now have to wait to choose and supervise the cutting and wrapping. This saves sensibilities and time. It also saves lives. Everything we buy is sealed up, protected, prophylactic. It's dull and frequently a nuisance. But we stay alive.

We have reached the moon, have broken the atom and harnessed atomic power. We have preserved the sound of dead voices and the look of dead people and their actions. Space no longer exists, nor time lapse. There is really no such thing as foreign or far-flung people. We see and hear instantly. Yet we have not succeeded in settling the basic, immemorial problem: our daily bread.

There are as many beggars on the street, as many indigent, hopeless, and insane people, as when I was a child. The need and the terror are the same. None of that has changed one bit. The drugged criminals frequenting Morningside Park are desperate people. I do not think they care particularly about the adventure on the moon.

"The poor ye have always with you." Was Jesus Christ, our savior, a profound economist or a hopeless pessimist?

But one group is better off, and the history of this century is distinguished chiefly not by mechanical or scientific advancement in medical research and the attendant blessings but by the emergence of one half of the human race from bondage. Women have come out of the closet—all women, poor as well as rich.

There are today only very few professions women cannot enter. They share in medicine, law, academics, government, building construction, weight-lifting, policing, firefighting, garbage slinging. I do not know about cattle slaughtering.

Women own their own wages. They have first claim to their children and an equal voice in divorce.

Domestic service has been greatly reduced. In fact it has all but disappeared, discommoding the housewife, certainly, but eliminating the slave class. Servants today make a decent wage—better than that, a good wage. Devices for saving the mistress's knees and back have been invented (and notice that they were not invented until it was the back and knees of the mistress that were involved), so ladies can still have sufficient leisure. But so can their servants. This is new.

As a symbol of the great evolution, women have discarded their corsets, for the first time in three hundred and fifty years. For the first time in two thousand years they are choosing their garments for reasons of practicality—all women, not just day laborers. They have gone into pants. Considerations of comfort have won out over sex, which is as drastic a choice, as basic, and as difficult to achieve as though women had altered their skeletons—which as a matter of fact they have also done, finding slim hips more suitable to trousers than the wide pelvis of their grandmothers.

These astonishing changes have occurred in an unprecedentedly short period, historically speaking, and within my lifetime. Who made the revolution? Not wayward, militant, or flamboyant spirits, although they were present, calling attention to themselves and their triumphs. No, the revolution was made by those unknowns, with effort and patience, patience and endurance, with trying and with tears, by our aunts and our cousins, our nurses and teachers, our cooks, our mothers.

And by us, unceasingly, endlessly trying. (290–304)

Art Is
(Excerpt from *The Book of the Dance*)

Works of art are the symbols through which men communicate what lies beyond ordinary speech. Many people think of art as something special and apart from their daily lives, as a luxury, an occupation or hobby for impractical individuals. This is a mistake. Men cannot live without art. It is a necessity, as religion is. If men cannot communicate they die of loneliness. Art is communication on the deepest and most lasting level.

All of us need to tell what is in our hearts, but most of us manage to say what we really mean only at three or four high moments in our lifetime, and perhaps then only to intimates. The artist tries to reach anyone who will listen; but to do this he must talk through symbols.

The ability to convey or reproduce emotion gives great power; it is a tremendous gift, mysterious and precious. Men value emotion; it is one of the chief well-springs of human activity, but it is perishable. It lasts only a brief time and it can affect people only while it is strong. So artists try to fix it in forms that will endure and that will arouse a response in many people at widely different times. (7)

Curtains Up

Prodigal Son (George Balanchine)
("Acrobatics in the New Choreography,"
Theatre Guild Magazine, January 1930)

The larger part of this essay, which reviews the 1929 London première of Balanchine's last ballet for Diaghilev's Ballets Russes, has
been republished several times. However, the entire essay, to this
editor's knowledge, has not been seen since its original publication.
When it appeared, de Mille was twenty-five years old. It is her only
surviving publication in which, for her byline, she used her full
given name, Agnes George de Mille, with its embedded honoring
of her mother's father, the theorist of economics Henry George.

Among its references is the name of Germaine Mitty—famed
for her acrobatic dancing on pointe at the Folies Bergère—who was
brought to New York with her partner, Eugene Tillio, by Florenz
Ziegfeld for a featured number (the "Algerian Dance," in the
"Passion's Altar" section) of his *Ziegfeld Follies of 1921*. "Kreutzberg"
refers to the German-born, Mary Wigman-trained choreographer
and soloist Harald Kreutzberg (1902–1968), whose performances
during tours of the United States in 1928 and 1929 had a profound
effect on many American dancers. The German illustrator Hans
Henning Voight (1887–1969), who went by the name "Alastair," was
a self-taught artist whose black-and-white drawings in books of
the late 1920s remind commentators of the art of Aubrey Beardsley.

Felia Doubrovska (1896–1981), *Prodigal Son*'s original Siren, trained with Enrico Cecchetti and at the Imperial Theater School in St. Petersburg and, after a performing career in Europe and America, joined the faculty of the School of American Ballet, where she was cherished by many students who went on to become stars of the New York City Ballet. With Diaghilev's Ballets Russes, she also created roles in Bronislava Nijinska's *Les Noces* (The Bride), in Balanchine's *Apollon Musagète* (Calliope), and in Léonide Massine's *Ode*. Serge Lifar (1905–1986), the original executant of *Prodigal Son*'s title role, went on to become a choreographer for and the director of the Paris Opéra Ballet. De Mille does make one factual error that has not been corrected: the ballet has a male corps of only twelve young men, not the twenty-four whom the author remembered.

De Mille can use language idiosyncratically sometimes. One such usage occurs in this essay: the French word *première* to mean "first dancer" or "principal dancer," rather than, as is customary in dance writing, the first performance of a dance or a show.

The American acrobatic dancers playing moving-picture presentations, revues and vaudeville are pioneering in a new era of stage history. The acrobatic teams know nothing of this. They go about their own business breaking each other's necks, earning what money they can. It is the concert dancers, the ballet technicians, the actors, and directors who, realizing the prodigious skill wasted in these stupid exhibitions, have begun to borrow one or two tricks for use in connection with their own work. The results of the experiment are important.

Adagio, as acrobatic dancing is professionally termed, derives its name from the type of music it employs. It developed from the classic *pas de deux* and is, like its predecessor, an arrangement of technical virtuosity without marked continuous rhythm or formal design, accompanied by slow music. Instead of the charm and lyric beauty of the classic variation the modern adagio substitutes raw energy and sensationalism. But for all its roughness and distortion it is fundamentally romantic. Performed by a male and a female (except in these days of multiplication, when it is sometimes performed by as many as four males and a female), it constitutes even in its most gymnastic version a kind of love dance. For while it makes no pretense to mood or story it does produce in essence the ideals of strength on the part of the male and of buoyancy and grace on the part of the female. With the man as a basic pattern, the girl floats, hovers, descends, balances, flings herself into space, turns and returns in her falls, skims the earth, is lost in her partner's embrace, frees herself and mounts again to be carried offstage transcendent between heaven and earth.

Due to the fact that adagio performers are not dancers but acrobats, their work is seldom if ever such as I have described. Knotted thighs, stretched and pulsing ribs, whitened skin, the dangerous manipulation of a shockingly thin girl by a husky boy in a tinsel loin cloth are generally the most one can look for. The audience's attention lags. It demands entertainment. It is given an unvarying display of exercises that appeal neither to intellect nor emotion. Excitement and suspense, breathtaking risks, feats of superhuman endurance, higher and higher falls, ruder and ruder whirls, backbends that seem to crack the spine with every twitch of muscle, balancings and liftings that strain heart and pulses to the bursting point are the frenzied answer to the public's growing indifference. Interest in the entire matter would have died out long ago were it not for the fascination of knowing that at any moment of the performance one of the girls might very well be dropped and killed.

The pity of it is that this vulgarity has exploited for years the materials of great dancing. It remained for Diaghilev, canny impresario, who barred from his stage nothing, however grotesque, until he had tried it, to see in adagio technique the elements of new dance expression. Patterned on the relation of bodies to one another and not on the relation of bodies to rhythm and space, it presented the means for intense emotional symbolism. The first step, of course, was to accentuate the romantic aspect. Hitherto the female part of the design had been treated as a ninety-five-pound weight handy for displaying the combined skill of the dancers or, in the case of the classic *pas de deux*, a disembodied spirit, the ideal of femininity, rather than a physical being subject to restrictions of gravity and human weakness. Now, for the first time, the ballet dancer finds herself a vertebrate. She has come to have substance, contour, emotions, and the customary means of expressing them. She lies in the man's arms as a woman. No classic *première* would have touched her partner, except to hold his hand while she did something difficult on one toe, to sit on his chest prettily with her silk ankles crossed, or lean against his arm as she bent way over backwards. The ballerinas now clamber up and down their partners with unhesitating technique. Conventions are shattered. By the neck, by the waist, by the knees, by a wrist and ankle, they support one another—roughly, sturdily—with no regard for what is seemly, with regard only for what will best express their idea.

One of the roughest of these dances, and by far the most effective, is the love duet performed by Doubrovska and Lifar in *The Prodigal Son*, a ballet produced by Diaghilev for the first time in London last July. Doubrovska as an ancient Biblical courtesan full of splendor and wickedness hangs against the Prodigal's body, her arms locked over his bent elbows, her wrists dangling, her long slender legs bent so that her toes trail in the air, her knees moving slowly in rhythm with his steps. He crosses the stage languorously under this sensuous burden. She sits before him and with frenzied strength jumps to her toes. He wraps her about his waist like a belt (a variation of the trick made famous years ago by Mitty and Tillio), and with feet spread apart watches her slide down his body to the ground, where she lies in a coil, hand clutching ankle, spine tense as a sprung trap. He sits beside her, swings toward her, away from her, tries to lift himself from the floor, sinks back, and twists into her arms in an inextricable tangle. This scene constitutes one of the most important seductions to be found on any modern stage.

Aside from the subject matter of the returned wanderer, which has been important for approximately two thousand years, the method of treatment is worth noticing as a useful development of the adagio. For the same reason, less athletic themes and their treatment should be considered. Happily, adagio lends itself to subtleties as well. Imaginative concepts hitherto seldom expressed except with words, the moods and imagery that words connote, can be wrought into visual form by the same hackneyed acrobatic stunts. It is with vigorous wiles that the courtesan lures the Prodigal into her power, as we have seen, and vigorously she makes known her triumph. Her attendants immediately smother him in her crimson train. She mounts to the shoulders of one of them and stands looking down a good ten feet at her subdued lover. In this device, a tumbling trick, Doubrovska opens up an entirely new field for theatric expression. Literally she towers over her prey. No actress by voice or presence could dominate the situation more completely. In another ballet of the Diaghilev repertoire, *Apollon Musagète*, Terpsichore balanced in swan-dive position on the bended back of Apollo transforms herself into pinions. Literally Apollo's song is winged. Fused to his body she swims in air. She floats clear of earth. No leaping *première* ever more definitely achieved flying than this acrobatic dancer. Motionless in space the arched body of the girl transfigures Apollo, and dancers and audience rise in ecstasy to thin heights.

The choreographic designs shift and pyramid and change as the Russians attack all the major passions. Their dances vary only in form. The underlying method remains constant, the reduction of human gesture to bare essentials, heightened and developed into meaningful patterns. This is, of course, the technique used by Kreutzberg in his psychological studies and by Martha Graham in her relentless satires on human nature. It is a technique well suited to just this type of work. For packed with emotion as the theme of the dance may be, the method of treatment is not emotional at all, but psychoanalytic, and carries with it always an intellectual commentary on the subject it deals with. If, then, the treatment is stressed more than the emotional theme a new school of satire results, which is neither burlesque nor humorous imitation but true satire, thoughtful, just, uncompromising.

In the work of the Germans, of Graham, and of the Diaghilev troupe, satire for the first time has found expression in dancing. The new ballets are profound and sinister criticisms of life: The effect produced by exaggerated human gesture and the imitation of animal movements by a chorus of twenty-four [sic] young men in *The Prodigal Son* far outreaches the attacks on modern civilization in any of our expressionistic dramas. With a few silly movements the dancers achieve finally and ultimately the decadence that Noel Coward strove to reveal in his *Dance, Little Lady*, that O'Neill satirized in the conversation between the Hairy Ape and the Fifth Avenue Promenaders who talked and looked exactly alike. Bald as eggs, dressed identically, moving identically, crowded together as closely as possible, the dancers hop over one another's backs, circle around alternately squatting and rising, rear themselves into architectural formations, crawl down each other to the earth again, scramble about sideways in ridiculous positions like crabs. Their movements are those of children at play, their attitude that of sinister, super-sophisticated adults. They are abortions, gargoyles, abnormal, undeveloped creatures found in the drawings of Beardsley and Alastair. They range themselves in serried ranks, and open and shut their mouths, goggle their eyes, stick out their tongues, wiggle their hands in their ears, thumb their noses. They are the epitome of all the gossiping, scandal-mongering neurotics the world has ever bred. They seize the Prodigal, strip and rob him, bind him to a pillar, and hiding behind it so that only their hands can be seen pat him up and down. The humiliation of their touch on his body is almost more than he can suffer. Long after they have gone he remains rigid with arms stiff at his sides and fingers quivering in anguish. Then in an excess of shame and grief he turns to the wall and pulls himself up until his body hangs pilloried, shrunken with loathing, knees drawn taut. In this manner he comes to the earth. In this manner he crawls away. He thrashes in the dust, draws himself into knots, kicks free, turns feverishly over and around and back again. Broken, prostrate at the feet of his father until he receives some sign of welcome he embraces the patriarch's ankles, takes hold of his waist, his shoulders, lifts himself up into the man's arms and clings there safe and comforted, folded like a child in his father's mantle. Those who watch hide their faces from the gentle wonder of the scene.

Lifar's crippled progress away from the city of sins is as realistic an expression of remorse as the most intense acting. In the one case the outward trappings of grief are exactly reproduced, in the other the symbols of the grief itself.

What magnificent possibilities this new point of attack opens to every branch of the theater! Already on our stage the way is prepared. Actors voice aloud unspoken thoughts. Scenery depicts mental and moral conditions. Costumes, props, lighting, and sound aim chiefly to produce a psychological effect. It is inevitable that sooner or later drama resort to imaginative gesture, which is at once the most fundamental and direct means of revealing emotion. And though it is not likely that an actor will ever find himself disqualified for ordinary parts because he cannot boast a handstand or two or a fair to middling neckroll, the technique fostered by Diaghilev's troupe, the technique going to waste on every vaudeville stage, can be used and will be used to achieve effects of imaginative and emotional beauty hitherto only dreamed of. (36–38)

Romeo and Juliet (Film Dances, Agnes de Mille)
(Excerpt from "Hooray for What," *Dance to the Piper*)

During her early years as a choreographer, de Mille experienced many disappointments and injustices on Broadway and in Hollywood. This is one of the more notorious instances. "Carmelita" refers to Carmelita Maracci, the subject of a profile elsewhere in this collection. Richard Pleasant, the young man whose invitation to tea de Mille declined, became one of the co-founders of Ballet Theatre. Meanwhile, another young man was driving de Mille to despair. By the age of twenty-one, the producer Irving Thalberg (1899–1936), a Hollywood wunderkind, was the executive in charge of production at Universal City, the California base of Universal Studios. Although admired by many cineastes for his work at both Universal (*The Hunchback of Notre Dame*) and, eventually, at M-G-M (*The Big Parade, Grand Hotel, Mutiny on the Bounty, A Night at the Opera, The Good Earth*), some critics never forgave him for his ruthless editing of Erich von Stroheim's Universal silent features *Foolish Wives* and, most of all, *Greed*—an epic now generally considered to be one of the greatest movies ever made and permanently damaged by Thalberg's demands that von Stroheim first take down the film from its original running time of ten hours to four and then, on top of that, by Thalberg's own imposed cuts that resulted in a commercially viable running time of just under two and a half hours. At some point in the 1950s, a janitor tossed the cut footage into an incinerator, rendering *Greed*, for its partisans, the greatest *lost* film ever made. (Thalberg, of course, had nothing to do with that loss.) De Mille clearly experienced the producer in his ruthless mode, although it was also the case that Thalberg—who had suffered a major heart attack in 1932—was to die in 1936, the year of *Romeo and Juliet's* production. Norma Shearer, the movie's Juliet, was not only the studio's most popular star but was also married to Thalberg; at the time of his death, from pneumonia, the couple had a small son and an infant daughter.

I continued taking classes with Carmelita through the autumn of '35. I even organized a class of my own and started experimenting with gesture and the teaching of pantomime at the Perry Studio. A lanky youth who answered the phone and kept the studio bookings used to wander in and watch. I forbade visitors, but he seemed so inconsequential that I permitted him to come and go at will. His name was Richard Pleasant, and he remarked once on leaving that he intended sometime in the future to have a big ballet company of his own and planned to give me a chance at real choreography with a proper big group.

I said "Yes, yes," and "Thank you" and no, I wouldn't go out to tea with him.

I was desperate for money. I organized an infant's class for rich moving-picture children. But I found I was not gifted with the young. Twenty minutes of my instruction would reduce the more sensitive ones to hysteria, sometimes with vomiting.

I lived, of course, with and off my sister. I lived presumably in luxury but I lacked the ten dollars' cash a starving friend once asked to borrow. I never had in my purse more than carfare.

The director, George Cukor, phoned one day offering me the dances in the forthcoming Irving Thalberg production of *Romeo and Juliet*. Norma Shearer and Leslie Howard were to be the stars. I accepted with unbusinesslike alacrity.

I made my terms with Thalberg while he stood sipping a glass of milk for stomach ulcers, and the terms were splendid. He was a small and romantic man, as elegant as an Oriental prince. He made his decisions with the conviction and speed of absolute authority.

Terms settled I asked for a clarification of style; did he want a small party of, say, forty people in a realistic room of the period with sixteen dancers or so, or did he want a royal court ballet in the grand manner? He considered. Since the set was to be rather larger than the floor space of the Grand Central

Station, and was to serve as background for five hundred people, ten grey-hounds and a couple of chained leopards, we decided on a full-scale *quat-trocento* entertainment and I planned to dish up something that would do no disparagement to the head of the Holy Roman Empire. My London pianist, Norman Franklin, was cabled to hunt music in the British Museum. Oliver Messel teamed reluctantly with Adrian and designed the fantastic and exqui-site ballet costumes. A thirty-voice choir of small boys bearing golden apple trees and singing *a cappella* a fifteenth-century madrigal accompanied Juliet's entrance. It was a bit above the Capulets, I felt, but so was everything else in the picture. Thalberg was made acquainted with every step of our plans, and Cukor, who was an imaginative and encouraging director, paid daily visits to the rehearsal studio. But I did not actually see Thalberg again until he walked on the set the day of shooting.

Once hired, I was treated like a world-famous director. We had our own unit complete with assistant, prop boy, rehearsal studio, secretary and pianist. The beautiful auburn-haired Mary Meyer was my soloist and assistant. We worked unmolested on pay for four months.

To our surprise we were ready in three weeks, so in order to keep busy for the next thirteen weeks, we gave each other classes and studio performances of the dances for all kinds of guests, for everyone who was interested. Hardened business executives and studio managers grew quite soppy with enthusiasm; the toughest of the lot, the company accountant, dropped in often. It made him feel like a better man, he said. Only Thalberg did not come. He was too occupied. And the camera man—I begged the camera man to come. Every gesture was being carefully devised for a special camera angle. But he did not. He was too busy also.

Thalberg at last appeared four months later when we were on set in full costume. "What in God's name is this?" he said. "Stop the cameras. Shearer has not even made her entrance yet." The forty flaming torches carried by the forty boys were doused by the fifteen firemen and the girls and boys told to go and sit down. Thalberg was apparently taken completely by surprise and voiced his doubts at length to Cukor, but said not one word to me. That was Monday when we were supposed to film the first of the three dances.

Tuesday Thalberg walked on the set and said, "But this looks like a Hollywood spectacle."

"It does, doesn't it?" said Cukor, chuckling. "Let's improvise something different."

Having followed his exact instructions, however, and having achieved what was up to that point the best composition of my life, I refused to improvise. They shot the dance, which I had planned as a fugal arrangement of five groups of girls pivoting around the soloist (Shearer), but they shot it as a series of close-ups of Miss Shearer back-lit, and peeping around her hair. I wrung my hands. I shouted at the master camera man but he was out of hearing up in the air on a boom. "This was not devised for this angle," I called. "All you will get in eight counts is a row of rumps backing towards the lens." But they bade me be still and promised that it would look lovely anyhow, setting up their apparatus behind arches, under balustrades and around Italian youths, down flights of stairs and muttering about composition while they shuffled reproductions of Piero della Francesca, Simone Martini and Ghirlandaio who certainly hadn't figured in my plans. They placed their machinery as fast as possible and got on with the shooting briskly since they didn't intend to use much of the dance anyway. That was Tuesday.

On Wednesday we did the next bit, another series of close-ups with no dancing figures visible. On Thursday, Thalberg had seen the rushes and his assistants told him they looked like Botticelli.

On Friday he was still afraid of the Hollywood connotations.

On Saturday he was undecided.

The following Monday we finished eight full shooting days on one dance sequence. (The balcony scene had taken six days to shoot, the potion speech four—for four days Norma Shearer wept and shrieked from nine in the morning until seven at night.) Thalberg came on set and thanked me gravely for the job I had done, which he said was of great excellence. I am told this praise was without precedent. He then invited me to do the dances in *Marie Antoinette*, which would have been a guarantee of further income and possibly greater opportunity. But three months later he tragically died.

When I saw a cut version of what actually had been filmed I went outside the projection room and lay down in the grass and was very, very sick.

Herbert Stothart, the head of M-G-M's music department, found me wandering around the studio late at night. He ushered me into his study and poured me a stiff drink. "Oh, my dear," he said, "this happens to everyone here. Every single artist that comes to this place. I have only one piece of advice: get it on film, somehow. Fight later."

I tried to get it on film to the point of nuisance. No go.

Stothart had his own troubles shortly. Having settled with Thalberg and Cukor to score the picture entirely in fifteenth- and sixteenth-century modes, he had arranged and orchestrated the major portion of the work and was happily in New York recording carillons and refined counterpoint by the best choirs and madrigal groups when Thalberg, by some unhappy miscalculation, heard a broadcast of Tchaikovsky's *Romeo and Juliet* overture. He was on the transcontinental telephone in ten minutes. "Why did nobody tell me about this?" he roared. Stothart was ordered to add the Russian tunes throughout. This he did, wretched man, counterpointing against the more lush passages fifteenth-century plain song—the whole poured like chocolate over the Elizabethan iambic pentameter.

The picture was a great success. It is still playing in Nicaragua. It was, notwithstanding its involved musical score, very moving—largely due to the acting of Shearer who turned in a superb potion and death scene. Shearer was no comedian, but she could reach tragic heights. She did again in *Marie Antoinette*. She enjoyed playing anguish; it exercised all her faculties. She could perform a scene over and over and over and over—pouring tears, her eyes like faucets. "Doesn't this tire you?" I asked. "Not at all," she replied. "I love it," and she began to pour afresh as she ran back under the hot lights and bathed her face in spouting salt with the vigor of a kill at the tennis net. She brought this athleticism to every activity.

Thirty or forty complete shootings were made of every important scene. But of my first dance—not one, and of the second dance only half of one and that mostly in close-up. The third involved forty people but was played as a love duet between actors.

The dances must have cost close to one hundred thousand dollars. This however, by my reckoning, was not the greatest waste. The dances were good. (230–234)

Rain Dance
(Excerpt from *Speak to Me, Dance with Me*)

When de Mille left England in 1934, after a stay of two years, she carried with her a secret garden of personal memories. Many of them revolved around the young British writer Ramon Reed, author of the libretto for de Mille's ballet *Three Virgins and a Devil*. Perhaps the happiest time they ever spent together was during a U.S. automobile trip, in the mid-1930s, which de Mille, Reed, and his male nurse, Henry Arthur Sharpe, took from the East Coast to the West. During that period, Reed—who, in a wheelchair from a debilitating disease, was making what everyone knew would be his only visit to America—asked to tour California. (Reed died shortly after, while still in his twenties.) The drive continued into Colorado and New Mexico, where the touring party, with almost literary coincidence, ran into Martha Graham and Louis Horst, who led them to an authentic rain dance and an epiphany.

We proceeded south—our object Gallup and the Indian ceremonials. As we drew into town we passed the Santa Fe station. It was one-thirty P.M. and the "Chief" was due—"You've only seen those little toy English jobs. I want you to see a real virile transcontinental snorter."

And it came right in on cue—roaring and puffing, venting steam from every orifice, its pistons and wheels grinding up life and geography. (Oh, what have they done to our trains?) As always, my heart beat until I thought it would burst. "Wow!" said Ramon. The engineer waved to us from his cabin window as he went by.

The engine stopped, panting, down by the water tower and the cars ground and shrieked and clattered to a stop. Out came the porters with their little footstools. "Gall-up," they yelled. And down the steps in princessly decorum came Martha Graham followed by Louis Horst.

"God is with us!" I shrieked. "Ramon, of all the people in the world, it's She Herself!"

I nearly knocked her down in my eagerness. She came right over to the car and leaned over Ramon—she, about whom I had been talking for two years.

We took four cabins in a row at a motel and washed our faces and prepared to go up to Zuni, where Louis had learned five minutes after arrival that there was to be a secret rain dance. How did Louis know? Louis knew everything necessary always.

He said it was there and we never doubted his word, but there seemed to be no sign of it and every stray Indian, mostly young girls, pulled their Czechoslovakian printed shawls over their mouths and stared at us silently with agate eyes. The more loquacious shrugged without speaking. So we parked Ramon and Sharpe under a tree and went exploring.

And suddenly there it was—in the central plaza, which was very small— about twenty men in Stone Age masks of wood and feathers, their bodies painted in symbols, stepping and shifting to the undeviating thump of two sticks on a sack of cloth. One man sat on the ground in the center and beat. For thirty-five minutes he never let up and he never accelerated, on and on, an unvarying unresonant thud. The dancers slowly reorganized the universe through their bowels and continued and continued. There was only one other white man present besides us three—the members of the Pueblo stood about unmoving and attentive.

"They killed their Catholic priest nine years ago," whispered Martha, "and the Church has not replaced him. This is a very fierce place—one does not trifle here, they warned an airline against sending a plane over the reservation—the airline persisted—the first plane fell."

There was no sound except the light rattling of beads and gourds, the sliding and whispering of deer-shod feet—the sound of breathing was muffled in the masks.

The beating went on. No watcher moved. When a girl shifted her shawl back, the freshening rain wind lifted her hair. I pelted down the street to the car. "This is worth the trip to America—get in your chair and follow me." Sharpe never transferred him so fast in his life and then began pushing him up the rutted and rocky alley, Ramon urging him on as though on horseback.

"Good God!" breathed Ramon. "James Frazier! Here we come!" Martha and Louis had disappeared. Sharpe, Ramon and I were at a corner. We didn't move. Suddenly all the dancers, masked, rattled, beaded, and painted, converged toward us, literally on top of us.

Ramon looked up into the great hovering masks. I turned around incredulously. We had done nothing. We had made no sound or move. A young brown Indian laughed with perfect teeth. "He's crippled—he's got to go—we can't have him here."

"But he can't help that!"

The boy just laughed. "Go up to the roof," said my laughing friend.

"He can't climb," I explained compassionately. The boy laughed. "Up!"

Sharpe took firm hold of the chair and began to push it down the alley back towards the car rather faster and more bumpily than was medically wise. Three enormous masks kept right at his heels shaking rattles. But there remained five close around me. They said nothing, but their meaning was quite clear.

My anthropological delight turned to something more primitive. It couldn't happen, but it was happening. We were surrounded by savage displeasure and no means of communication, and we were five and they were nearly two hundred.

I climbed the pole ladder. The boy looked full in my face and said the most educational phrase I'd ever heard before or since: "You're white. Bad for the dance."

Martha and Louis were on the roof with the one other non-Indian and although the view was fine, rain made the adobe move under our feet; the dance below us was achieving the result it wanted. I grew restive—the effects were unvarying and I was concerned about Ramon. "Let's go!" When we left not a head turned. The beat diminished with distance, it didn't accelerate, it didn't retard. The rain accelerated.

We had forty miles to make over bad roads and the storm was now heavy, with lightning, thunder, and rushing streams. But we got through and Ramon came out laughing from under the clothes we had piled on him. We were all soaked, but after hot baths we had dinner and drinks and the kind of talk Ramon had waited all his life to hear and had come across the world to find and that night he had it. (289–292)

Dark Elegies (Antony Tudor)
(Excerpt from "Hooray for What," *Dance to the Piper*)

De Mille's discussion of *Dark Elegies* per se occupies only a small portion of this excerpt, which recounts the author's return to London during the winter of 1936–1937, following her disastrous experiences on the set of *Romeo and Juliet* and in the rehearsals of *Hooray for What!* What has been completely sidestepped here—although it permeates the tone of the passage—is that her young friend and platonic lover Ramon Reed was dying while these events were taking place and that she was also grieving over a broken secret love affair with one of Ramon's friends, the German émigré, Edgar Wind, whose existence she shielded even from her mother, to whom she usually confided everything. (For the full story, one has to consult her later memoir *Speak to Me, Dance with Me.*) Did Tudor, in insisting that de Mille dance the *Dark Elegies* variation, intuit that she would bring to it the intensity of a mourner? Whatever the answer, de Mille here uses her undisclosed experience to energize what she does choose to recount. In the manner of lyric poetry, her omissions give her writing—the ending, especially—the force of a punch without the action of one. A bright spot in this period is that the author seems to have been able to bypass her private turmoil to gain access to her creative energies as a choreographer: it was during this second London stay that she began to lay the foundation in the rehearsal room for what would become her first real hit, the ballet *Rodeo*.

Dark Elegies was made for the Mercury Theatre company of Marie Rambert, the "Mim" in the writing. The handsome and dramatic dancer Hugh Laing (1911–1988) was, at this time, the offstage partner and inspiration for Antony Tudor.

Hollywood had refused to film my group choreography and for various external reasons New York had dropped my dances from the show. So it seemed natural to go back to London where I had friends and where I had scored before, and I was eager to continue studies with a group. A friend in London loaned me his town house which had been closed. I prevailed on twelve girls to give me their time and energies, and for three hours every day we immured ourselves among the sheeted furniture and worked in dust and, since there was no piano, in silence. Six months later when we came out into a proper studio, we had the makings of a suite of American dances, one of which was called *Rodeo*.

This study contained every bit of gesture that was later used in the ballet *Rodeo*, and this is exactly how the movement was developed. The dances were performed publicly in London in April 1938. One year later I saw the first New York performance of Eugene Loring's *Billy the Kid*. There have been several statements in print by misinformed critics that I borrowed my western style from Loring. The exact chronology of performance is herewith stated. But I would like to add my view that the whole argument is bad-natured and specious. All contemporaries influence one another although the thefts are usually unconscious. In the hands of a master, all material, no matter whence derived, becomes a new act of creation; in the hands of a fool, the original is not even approached. It would be odd if contemporaries working as they often do under the same roof did not handle similar problems in a manner reminiscent. The more astonishing fact is that using the same dancers and rubbing elbows one with the other hour after hour they preserve their own styles to such a marked degree.

Peggy van Praagh, who is now director and head of the Sadler's Wells Theatre Company, was my principal dancer. I chose as protégée a girl to whom I paid a small weekly retainer and taught her to act comedy, and I promised her concerts in New York if she would return with me later.

While experimenting with group choreography, I gave a series of solo concerts at the Mercury with Hugh Laing as partner. These were run off in real professional style to sold-out houses. Each concert, as always in England, just broke even; there was perhaps a difference of four or five shillings one way or the other, so I lived on my Hollywood savings. The press was uniformly good.

Tudor was working hard on a new ballet called *Dark Elegies* for Rambert's West End season, to Mahler's *Kindertotenlieder*. He insisted that I dance the fourth solo and in the face of Mim's extreme and expressed doubt forced me into her company for this one work. I refused to let her watch rehearsals which further infuriated her. Antony practiced with me at night and on Sundays, but always shut away. He was kindness itself, and I cost him something in patience. I frequently came late. I was not quick or adroit, and his approach to music proved baffling. He never, for instance, counted.

This was the first time in my life I had ever worked under anyone's direction. We were both nervous. Mim prowled outside the closed door, baffled and furious. Whenever she entered the room I stopped, and we glared at each other like two hostile dogs.

I saw very little of the group rehearsals because I was doing the choreography for the film *I, Claudius* and had to spend all my days in an armory at the other side of London. In this film, I was engaged to do an enormous ballet with music by Arthur Bliss. We had not been in rehearsal more than a week when the star, Merle Oberon, put her face through the glass window of a taxi; the director, Josef von Sternberg, fell ill of an intestinal obstruction; and the film company went bankrupt. The episode was not important. I got most of my money. In remembering it I have, in fact, only one sadness. Merle Oberon phoned me at seven one morning to say she had spent the night deciding to play Messalina as a virgin. I rather regret the loss of that characterization. The important enterprise of the moment for all of us was Antony's ballet.

The first time I saw it assembled, which was the afternoon of the opening, I recognized it plainly as a masterwork but equally clearly as unfinished. I don't mean unpolished—I mean the last five minutes had not been set. The final song was completed at eight o'clock in full make-up and dressing gowns while the curtain was held and Mahler's publisher sat in the wings to see that the ballet met his official approval. The ending Tudor contrived in twenty minutes is very beautiful and a great many of the audience were in tears at the conclusion. Musicians, painters and writers went out of theater raving and sat up at their telephones all next day spreading the news.

The season wound up in the usual battery of quarrels. Rambert was so deprecating about my dancing that the day after the last performance I walked into the Ballet Club, packed my practice clothes and left forever. I never again returned as a pupil. Hugh and Antony also left her theater, something they'd been hankering to do for a long time.

Having by this maneuver left ourselves with precisely nothing at all we decided to pool our wits and make our own ballet company. Hugh contributed his entire patrimony and I borrowed fifty pounds from Romney Brent (paid back with *One Touch of Venus*). We bought scenery and costumes for Tudor's *Descent of Hebe* (Bloch), *Jardin aux Lilas*, *Dark Elegies* and a new work, *Gallant Assembly*, set to music by Tartini. I threw in all my costumes and the best of my repertoire. The Tartini ballet was an unfinished romp containing some splendid movement but on the whole formless and anticlimactic. It did boast, however, superb décor by Hugh Stevenson and a seduction scene for Tudor and me which I believe is the most obscene bit of nonsense in the literature of ballet and one of the funniest. We got ready (the Tartini uncompleted of course) and went up to Oxford where we were to perform a week at the Players' Theatre, only to discover on arrival that the reason for giving us the theater during examination week was the unlikelihood of any audience. And sure enough, as foreseen by the theater owners, we did very badly. In fact, we lost our shirts. The company was excellent and danced beautifully. All the costumes were new. The repertoire consisted of the absolute best of our work—two of Tudor's masterpieces. And in the cradle of British Culture all we could pull in was between two and three pounds a night. But Tudor didn't seem to mind. He delivered a gallant and graceful farewell address from stage on closing night to the handful of spectators, some of whom had come faithfully every performance, and we went out to a party which we gave ourselves.

The week's kitty was divided equally among all members of the company—£3 apiece. We at least owned the scenery although the boys left it lying in their garden in rain all the rest of the summer months.

One of the interested paying customers was Marie Rambert, who came all the way up to Oxford opening night to sit in the middle of the front row. She found, no one was surprised to learn, that Antony and I canceled one another. "A very wasteful clashing of styles," she said. She also found wasteful and extravagant the fact that our tights were of real silk.

No job offered all the next winter. Tudor, who had cut himself off finally from Rambert, made a pittance teaching at his studio in British Grove. What those long months of hopeless idleness and neglect cost a man of his tornado ambitions I hate to think. Hugh held his hands up all this time as also did the devoted girls who believed in him and who gave him everything including their loyalty and time. But there must have been hours of despairing horror; London was for him a city of no opportunity. He simply was not recognized; the people in power in both the commercial and ballet worlds who had seen his work did not particularly like it. So he sat down hard on his strong young bones and sharpened his feelings all through the foggy winter months. There was no help or promise. There was not even regularly enough food. And he had proved to a number of discerning people that he was the greatest lyric choreographer in Europe.

I was without employment also but I could always give concerts and I still had some Thalberg money and a bit left over from *Hooray*. Hugh had his own periods of grave despondency. Antony might not be publicly recognized as yet but those who knew him hoped for a brave future, whereas nobody foretold very much for Hugh. He all but beat his head on the bricks of British Grove. I never blamed him. I wanted to join in. I practiced dully. Hugh alternately raged and consoled. Antony waited.

In time when my group dances were finished I hired a West End theater and gave my last English concert. It was sold out solid and the notices were the best I ever got in England. Hugh as always partnered me and out of this concert came an engagement at the Westminster Theatre, for which I commissioned from Antony *Judgment of Paris*.

That wound up the season—it also wound up our professional union because, although the work had been friendly and good, matters did not stand as before. The forces that were shaping all of us had wrenched us awry. Rival directors have never functioned happily under the same roof without a strong whip to keep them in their proper corners. All cooperative groups rupture for lack of that whip. The ballet troupes are used to a boss and expect their impresario to be imperious and powerful with the manners of the lion tamer. It is generally advisable for him to have control of the money. The creative worker does not exist who can table his passions and give head to the greater need of a rival. I think more important, however, was Antony's deepening conviction that our styles were really incompatible and that the same theater should not house us both. So when he came to me later with the news that he had found a sponsor and was to be presented with his own theater and company, I was not entirely astonished to learn he felt he could dispense with my services.

My protégée and soloist was promised bits by Antony for his new project and was accordingly reluctant to accompany me to New York, although I had trained her and paid her for a year with this precise goal in mind. The choice forced upon her was torturing.

And the Home Office in refusing to extend my working permit made my dim-out official. It was September 1938. England was readying the decks for war; aliens were being sent home that autumn by the thousands.

I packed and closed my lovely flat. I had lived and worked in England for six years, but the two that waved me off in the black November rain from Waterloo Station were new acquaintances, two refugee Germans. It was neither my partner nor my collaborator, nor yet another whom I had thought to marry, but a boy out of a concentration camp who put a bunch of threepenny violets in my hand and wished me Godspeed. (240–245)

Rodeo (Agnes de Mille)
("Rodeo," *Dance to the Piper*)

During the early 1940s, de Mille was invited to make a ballet for the recently founded touring company the Ballet Russe de Monte Carlo, directed by Sergei Denham (1897–1970) and bank-rolled principally by Julius Fleischmann, Jr. (1900–1968). Léonide Massine (1896–1979) was its principal choreographer. David Savelio-vich Libidins (1899–1958) served as company administrator dur-ing the Ballet Russe's early years. Many of the founding dancers were Russian, including the company's prima ballerina Alexandra Danilova (1903–1997); however, some were European, such as the British danseur Frederic Franklin (b. 1914 and, at this writing, still performing mime roles with American Ballet Theatre), and eventu-ally a few, such as Maria Tallchief and Janet Reed, were American. (During the 1950s, those proportions would be reversed.) Maria Bekefi was a prominent ballet teacher in Los Angeles. Massine's 1938 comic ballet, *Gaîté Parisienne,* to an Offenbach score arranged by Manuel Rosenthal, was an enduring hit vehicle for Danilova (as The Glove-Seller) and Franklin (The Baron). Rachel Chapman (1905–1986) was the indispensable rehearsal pianist for the Ballet Russe de Monte Carlo; Franz Allers (1906–1995) was a company conductor; Irving Deakin (1894–1958) was an English-born writer on music and dance who maintained an ongoing association with the company; and Jean Yazvinsky (d. 1973), an erstwhile member of Diaghilev's Ballets Russes, served the Ballet Russe de Monte Carlo as a régisseur. When Michel Fokine (1880–1942) died be-fore completing his ballet *Helen of Troy,* his last choreography, for the Ballet Russe de Monte Carlo, the work was completed by dancer and choreographer David Lichine, with the assistance of George Balanchine (whom de Mille does not mention; she may not have known). German Sevastianov—a nephew of Konstantin Stanislavsky, an erstwhile director of Col. de Basil's company, and, for a time, husband of the ballerina Irina Baronova—was director of Ballet Theatre in its earliest years; it was on his watch that de Mille made her first ballet, the thoughtful yet theatrically unsuc-cessful 1940 *Black Ritual.* (Further discussion of that work can be found in this volume in the essay on Katherine Dunham.)

This is only a small set of the names invoked in de Mille's marvelous account of *Rodeo*'s first night. The writing will carry for a reader unfamiliar with ballet in the twentieth century; and yet, for a dance fan, the names enrich the experience of reading. Every one trails a train of remembrances and a context: "Oliver" was Oliver Smith (1918–1994), the scenic designer and co-founder—with Lucia Chase and Richard Pleasant—of Ballet Theatre, where de Mille, herself, would become an important figure. "Madame Pourmel" was the beloved Sophie Pourmel (1898–1995), who would take such delicate care of costumes for the New York City Ballet. Mia Slavenska (1916–2002)! Nathalie Krassovska (1919–2005)! Great ballerinas, each with her own distinguished career. The passing utterance of "Chaliapin" evokes one of the greatest chapters in the history of the Maryinsky Theater and of the young Diaghilev. When *Dance to the Piper* was published, de Mille could count on her readers' familiarity with most of these artists. In 2009, the story stands, but the general reader's capacity for interaction with it has, inevitably, diminished.

The Russians entrained for the Far West. I went on the same train, but not with them. I had to live on my twenty-five dollars a week and pay my New York rent. I got besides three dollars a day traveling expenses to cover everything—hotels, food, taxis, and so on. Mr. Libidins put into my hands a round-trip transcontinental railroad ticket, first class, which I promptly turned in and rode coach. The difference in fare balanced my budget. I carried my clothes in a light wicker basket to obviate porters' tips. I ate only sandwiches and coffee in cartons. Four and a half days is a long time not to be out of one's clothes, but at the other end was a clean bed waiting at Father's. When we came into stations, I hid behind the luggage until the troupe had cleared the platforms. It would not do for them to see their choreographer coming out of coach; Massine had traveled in a drawing room.

This was July 1942. At every station groups of drawn and pallid young men came aboard leaving women with obliterated faces and whimpering children on the station platforms. We finally reached the Coast.

I lived with Father and his wife during the time the Ballet performed at the Hollywood Bowl and rehearsed the new works. Pop was now head of the dramatic department of the University of Southern California and as Professor de Mille had made a national reputation as lecturer and director. His role in the building of moving picture form and technique had been historic; now in his later years he was devoting himself to writing and passing on his unique knowledge to serious students of the theater. Clara had joined the motion picture department at U.S.C. and gave courses in scenario writing, which she was well qualified to do, having a distinguished career behind her in this medium.

The home they opened to me was quiet, thoughtful, understanding, and very needful to me during the stresses of the time. The days were delivered over to hurly-burly.

The first rehearsal was held in what had been Carmelita's studio, now in the hands of Maria Bekefi. I asked for the men first. If I could break them, I would have the whole company in my hand. As I walked down the flowering drive I heard the music of *Gaîté* and a good deal of stamping and shouting. Shoura (Alexandra) Danilova and Freddie Franklin were standing on chairs yelling the counts and clapping. The men, the great thick-muscled men, and the stringy-muscled girls were stamping and swooping and clenching their fists in a miasma of sweat. It was not a very large room and Shoura and Freddie were up to their waists in Parisian abandon. I glanced in and I went pale; clutching my little dancing bag, I crept up the stairs. Madame Bekefi had taught me in '36. "Madame," said I as I knocked at her apartment, "may I come in? I'm frightened."

"Yez, darling, yez. I have made frezsh coffee."

"Coffee for courage?"

"Coffee for courage! Yez, darling. You have not need to be frightened. You will do good."

I was summoned below. *Gaîté* was finished but the girls hung about, streaming sweat, their shoes and towels under their arms, very curious. Danilova was collecting her slippers.

"You would like this room empty? No?"

"Please." I nodded faintly.

She clapped her jeweled hands and stilled the hubbub. "Madame would like this room empty. Emediately! Get out," she said with dainty succinctness. "Get out. You! All go." Then she turned to me and grasped my hand. "Now I go too because that is more convenient for you. I have great excitement for this. We hope much. *Bonne chance!*" And with a twinkling smile, she walked neatly out on her long silken, fabulous legs and her turned-out feet, leaving a breath of delicious and expensive perfume behind her.

I turned deliberately and faced them. There they were—nineteen of them. Male. Great muscled brutes leaning against the barre and staring with watchful, smoldering eyes. Behind them were Paris, Covent Garden, Monte Carlo and, in three cases, the Maryinski. And behind me? A wall. It occurred to me at this precise moment that with the exception of five soloists I had never worked with men in my life. Never more than one man at a time.

I took a deep breath. "We are going to begin," I said in a scarcely audible treble, "with men riding horses in a rodeo. For instance, if you were riding a bucking horse and were thrown, it would look like this." And I rode a bucking horse and was thrown the length of the room on my head.

"Darling!" said Freddie rushing over to me. "Darling, you'll hurt yourself!"

"Did it look good, Freddie?"

"It looked wonderful! But you'll kill yourself."

"Not me. It's you who are to do it."

The young men, around the room, looked nonplused.

"Well," said Freddie, "no help for it. Come on, boys, let's have a try. Ee—"

The riding movements were neither realistic nor imitative. I had worked for a year in London to make them intrinsically beautiful. When performed correctly they suggested the high vigorous emotions of riding. But they were very difficult because the dancer had always to look as though he were propelled by an unseen animal. He hung off balance in the air. He did not jump, he was thrown or wrenched upwards. His feet never touched earth, it was the horses' feet that clattered in the pebbles. The very essence of the movement was shock, spasm and effort.

Alas, although big boys, they had been trained to move like wind-blown petals. "Raise your arms," I begged them. "you have men's arms, they have striking power, they can control a heavy, moving rope, or the brute furies of an eight-hundred-pound animal."

Up came the delicate wrists and the curled fingers of the eighteenth-century dandy. "Move from the solar plexus and back," I shouted, "not from the armpit. Think of athletes," I entreated. "Think of throwing a ball, from your feet, from your back, from your guts." But it was a long time since they had thrown balls. They had forgotten. They had not used the ground since they were children except to push away from it. Their arms rose up and down but they themselves looked absolutely stationary.

"Don't *plier*. Sit your horse," I implored. "There's a difference." But the strain was too much and they relaxed back into bad second position where they felt eminently at home.

A few Russians lolled on the barre and considered the matter poorly. "It is not dancing," they said. But I had never said it was, and I was delighted to excuse them. They picked up their towels and left in haughty silence. The ranks thinned quickly. I had planned to have eighteen men in the cast. I settled for ten. Those that stayed were ready and able.

For two hours, I rolled on the floor with them, lurched, contorted, jack-knifed, hung suspended and ground my teeth. They groaned and strained. I beat them out in impact, resilience and endurance. I broke them to my handling. I broke them technically, which was where they lived and worshiped.

At the end, I suggested we walk. We what? We walk like cowboys. They looked at me in dumfoundment, their clothes matted to their bodies, their hair all on end and dirty from the floor. They walked. "Not that way," I shouted.

By this time I was feeling pretty frisky. "Crotch-sprung, saddle-sore, with rolled-over high heels and sweat-stained leather, ill at ease and alien to the ground, unhorsed centaurs."

"Look," I said. "The sun in Colorado beats on your eyes like blows. You can't hold up your heads that way in the sun."

"Why, that's right," said a couple nodding in recognition. They began to squint, their gait slowed, they grew hot and dusty and weathered before me. One could almost, as my sister said later, smell them.

Out of this comes folk dancing, and out of nothing less.

I dismissed rehearsal. The survivors, mostly English and American, thanked me.

Next day they couldn't even walk. They sat in the sun and rubbed one another's muscles with oil. And they all had cracking headaches.

I had won.

Two days later I took on the girls. We walked, giggled, whispered, and looked to the far horizon for two hours. They thought this unreasonable. "Oh, Madame, we will be funny when we have costumes. Please do not concern yourself. We will assuredly be funny."

"You be funny right now on count eight." And I set my lips in a merciless line and waited.

We worked for four hours on a boy kissing a girl at a dance. This was the kind of effort they had put into high jumps or turns. They thought I was perverse. They thought I was insupportable. Well, not all of them, perhaps. Lubov Roudenko was breaking her back for me. She had perpetual headaches from the lurching and bucking. Freddie believed. A few of the American boys and girls, although perplexed, began to hope. Even in rehearsal some of it looked good, even to them. And there was always Freddie barking the counts and snapping at their feet. And dancing, dancing until the sweat poured from his back and head. "Oh, darling," he would say gasping, "this is impossible. Well, there's no help for it. Come on boys, let's try. Ee—"

He was the first great male technician I had ever had the chance to work with and I tried everything I thought the human body could accomplish. He was as strong as a mustang, as sudden, as direct, and as inexhaustible. There was no slacking off at the end of a long effort, no dawdling, no marking. He came into the room briskly, dressed and ready at the first minute of the rehearsal, and he worked full out without a second's deviation of attention until rehearsal finished, and the last lift was as precise and as vigorous as the first. With the exception of Massine, he has the most exact sense of timing of any man in the dance world. (He can pick up a difficult tap routine at a single rehearsal—as quickly in fact as he hears it. Only very great tap dancers can do this.) His verve galvanizes an audience as it does a rehearsal. He is the inner motor of the Ballet Russe, the reason they get through the sheer amount of labor involved in each tour.

I shall not forget my surprise when I first placed my hands on his shoulders for a jump and felt the muscles move across his back and arms as I just went up and stayed up. I shall not forget my wonder at the animal force that lifted and carried me. I had danced alone, or with girls or with actors, but with no one of this caliber technically. I came down like a hysterical baby that had been tossed around by a grownup. I couldn't wait to go up again. Naturally, I didn't let him see my delight. I was Madame, the choreographer. He still called me Miss de Mille. We were very formal always.

Luba Roudenko came to me. She was very happy with the role but her friends had told her she had a great technique and might she please, Miss de Mille, might she please do some *fouettés* in the hoe-down? I said no.

Between rehearsals, I sought consolation from Carmelita. "You can't produce work of integrity this way," I moaned. "Not with a company of strangers in two months."

"Of course not," she said. "But you can try," she added gaily. "Something might surprise you. Not integrity, of course." She looked at me hard. "They are paying you, aren't they?"

"Sort of," I mumbled.

In San Francisco we got into the second scene. In Seattle, the third. All along the way I dropped Russians from the cast.

"Dear Agnes," said Sergei Ivanovitch one night in the wings. "I hear you threw Sasha out of rehearsal today. That is unfortunate. To tell truth, I am pained. He is a fine young man, a bit impetuous, wild like all young men, but we must be indulgent. Appeal to his class, dear Agnes, appeal to his class." I gasped in astonishment.

"He is a Count, Agnes, a Count."

At this point I threw back my head rudely and simply hollered. Sasha had been surly, insolent, lazy, slow, untalented, demoralizing, tardy and extremely hung-over.

"Agnes," continued Denham persuasively, "I am the last person not to be democratic. I understand very well your ideals. But he is good material."

I said no.

Nor would I allow the dancers to watch one another. Whenever more than four got in the same room pandemonium developed. Obviously, no choreographer before had explained clearly. After each suggestion there was a United Nations' Assembly at the back of the room. I stamped, screamed and howled for silence. I promised to ask their help when I was stuck. There was a good deal of surprise at this; no choreographer had ever acknowledged the need for help. Again, I criticized my own work sharply. Dumfoundment! All choreographers had hitherto been infallible.

Occasionally I was the one surprised. "Bob! Bob!" I yelled, urging them to dip and curtsy on the beat. The hubbub grew to a roar. "For the love of God, be quiet!" I howled. "And bob!"

"But Madame," said a Russian as spokesman, "we cannot understand who you mean. Which Baub, please?" Four Roberts stepped forward with inquiring faces.

The music gave us trouble; it was difficult.

"No, no, no!" shouted Rachel Chapman, jumping up from the keyboard and beating her fists on the top of the piano. "You are absolutely and entirely wrong. That is not the rhythm the composer vished. I protect the composer. Now listen."

Freddie cocked his head. "She's right, kids. It's syncopated."

Rachel was infallible and exacting. She looked and acted like a Polish lioness. She played terrifically without cease in all rehearsals and in the pit. She and Freddie were the watchdogs of the repertoire. She helped me very much.

Luba Roudenko came to me. She was very happy with the leading role, but her friends had told her she was not showing off her strong technique. Perhaps if she did some batterie and brilliant *chaîné* turns in the hoe-down? I said no.

Rumors drifted up from Mexico. Ballet Theatre was going to have a dazzling repertoire. Fokine himself was down there working hard. My own boys and girls knew they were facing desperate competition and possible bankruptcy. I was to save them. They didn't express this to me in so many words, but it was made quite plain. I was carrying the ball. Somehow I'd become a member of the troupe and when there were no Pullmans to be had and the boys tore the seats apart to make beds for the girls, I bedded down among them three in a row.

Throughout this tour, Danilova, like a princess godmother, threw her arm about me, introducing me to the best restaurants and the most charming hostesses. She had made this trip seven times annually and inasmuch as she and Massine were the biggest box-office names in ballet, she was in a position to introduce me where and as I had never been introduced before. "Our choreographer," she would say, pushing me ahead of her in Margaret's dress into a salon.

We traveled from city to city while the ballet performed its summer tour. Sometimes we stayed a week and sometimes one night. We spent a great deal of time together on the trains.

What does the Russian Ballet look like on tour? Different from what you've been led to believe. Most of the girls and boys are simply, even poorly, dressed. They have no money. In fact, they have borrowed months ahead on next season's contract in order to get through their two months' vacation. They live like indentured servants. The stars are smart. They look like stars. But they travel without maids. Danilova has a faithful follower who maids for her; Slavenska has her mother.

The stars travel in Pullman berths with the company. Denham travels in a compartment, and Massine when he is with them sleeps and eats apart. He is the reverse of chummy even with his lifelong companions. But of course, at this time, he is absent in Mexico building up the Ballet Theatre repertoire.

The girls usually sit mending their tights or sewing the ribbons into their shoes or darning the ends of their blocked point slippers to preserve the satin from floor friction. The care and preparation of tights and slippers as well as the cost of the tights devolve upon each dancer personally.[*1] The girls have to wash their tights at each wearing to make the silk cling, so the washroom is full of pink legs swinging in the train vibration. The girls talk shop, intrigue and knitting patterns. Never anything else. Never, although war, flood, strikes, elections and plague pass over them. Never. They talk technique and what so-and-so's mama said to Mr. Denham last night. The older men play poker in

---

1   The company pays for the slippers five dollars per pair; a pair lasts for about a week. In the last century a ballerina had a new pair for each act of her ballet. These were unblocked silk with a sole like paper. Taglioni threw hers out after a single use as the stage of the Opéra was kept purposely dirty to prevent slipping. The stiffening of the toes introduced the need for a breaking-in process, very tedious to the dancer. Pavlova frequently asked her best girls to break in her shoes, although hers were Italian and relatively soft. She carried literally hundreds of pairs and selected and chose with a kind of nervous obsession. The breaking-in of the hard-blocked American slipper is a real labor and terrible on the knuckles of the feet. The fastening of a slipper requires the same care a surgeon gives his gloves. Markova glues her slippers on her feet around the heel, slips the ankle ribbons through a loop at the back and sews them fast with needle and thread. She has to be cut out of her shoes. (282–306)

three or four languages. The younger men look out of the window and hold hands. Some few read. Not many. They eat five or six meals a day. They are always hungry. They take cat naps, like animals, wherever they drop.

Mia Slavenska sits coiffed and perfumed with a Bruckner score opened on her smart tweed knees. The topaz on her hand is enormous and gives her a sense of reassurance as she leans her exquisitely manicured forefinger against her lovely brow and contemplates choreography. Miss Twysden, Danilova's companion, biographer and helper, knits Danilova's practice tights and discourses on the inferiority of all other companies. The inferiority of all other ballerinas she considers axiomatic. But she is a lady bred and cannot say what she thinks with Slavenska contemplating in the next seat, and with Slavenska's mama staring at her with a hard gaze. Libidins progresses down the car greeting his wards. Slavenska leaves off her intellectual pursuits, smooths the coils of her sun-red hair, straightens the seams on her stalwart smooth legs and corners him. She has been waiting to explain that if she doesn't dance more Giselles she will be distraught and she details what that condition implies in Yugoslavia. David Savielovitch manages to turn the talk into reminiscences of Chaliapin. Mia is distraught. Both voices rise. But no one can compete with his reminiscences. Libidins was once an old-style basso in a provincial Russian opera company.

A great deal has been written about the ballet's glamour. This is an elastic word. In a recent play, *Look, Ma, I'm Dancin'*, and in the film *Red Shoes*, the impression is made that they are a hard-working, healthy group of boys and girls rather like a traveling university. Nothing could be farther from the truth. Hard working they are to the point of slavery, and gay frequently. But healthy? Not very. Raddled with sexual insecurity, financial instability, ambition, jealousy and terror, they are herded from one engagement to another locked within the frenzied confines of their group for ten months at a stretch. They never stop anywhere en route long enough to make outside contacts. Intrigue assumes Renaissance proportions. Romance is a kind of round-robin tournament, and psychosis the hallmark of every experience. Most of the men are homosexual. Most of the women are sex-starved. Occasionally there is a nervous breakdown and a girl is unloaded at some station and left behind in a Midwestern hospital. Occasionally someone has a temper tantrum and beats up his girl friend or his wife, forcing her to seek succor in adjacent bedrooms. Next morning they are all doing *pliés* in a row in perfect decorum.

There are a few gay harlots in the old tradition, very few, for the girls simply haven't the energy. And there are a few happy marriages. These stand like rocks in the currents of emotional chaos.

But it is the bewilderment of exhaustion and transience that clouds most spirits and energies. Janet Reed said to me once, later, when I was traveling with Ballet Theatre, "Last night I came out of the theater and I couldn't remember what city I was in or which way to walk toward my hotel. It turned out to be Cleveland."

So they jog on together locked in the stewing, untidy cars. On arrival everyone frantically stuffs belongings into bags and boxes. Down come Slavenska's furs from the case on the rack. Slavenska's cat is put in a basket by Slavenska's mama. Danilova unpins last night's orchids from the back of her seat. The poker players settle their debts rather loudly. Wet wash is stuffed into hatboxes, knitting into the cosmetics. All, girls and boys, load up and stagger out. There are not arms enough for gallantry and no one can afford a porter; the girls lug their own suitcases. The car looks like an abandoned picnic ground. The porter, untipped, is not charmed.

They pour out of the train chattering, swearing, calling. In the rear or well in advance, Sergei Ivanovitch Denham and David Savielovitch Libidins trundle in dignity down the platform complete with briefcases, porters and neat luggage.

The company mobs the taxi racks, eight to a car, and goes off in search of lodgings. The stars, of course, have hotel reservations, but the *corps de ballet* have to rustle their own rooms. This sometimes takes two or three hours. They sleep always two to a room, sometimes six or eight. One person registers for each group; one person only attempts to pay.

Once settled in they assemble at the theater for replacement rehearsal. The usual breakage necessitates constant last-minute substitution. They snatch a malted milk at six and start warming up for the evening performance. They eat dinner at midnight. They eat in hash houses or drugstores except when they are being fed Champagne and French cuisine by leading hostesses.

The next morning sees them either on a train or taking class with the best local teacher. As there are only six cities in the United States in which ballet can play a week's stand, this procedure is followed two or four times weekly—room hunting and all.

For this they were paid $45 a week, the basic minimum wage for a *corps de ballet* dancer in 1942. Soloists received anything up to $300. Markova and Dolin received the highest fees in the business, $400 and $450 respectively (their salaries have multiplied since then). The basic wage for a scene shifter or grip was $121 and for a pit musician $140.

Every evening I do a barre with the boys and girls hanging on to the costume trunks. I change my practice clothes in the star dressing room shared by the two great ladies of the troupe. They sit at opposite tables, fitted out with their dainties, and they quarrel delicately and precisely over precedence, choice of roles, and the other paraphernalia of their trade. Mia's mama rummages in her trunk. Twysden, the lady helper, knits and practices scorn with unmodified English assurance.

Behind every great star there is usually a sad quiet woman mending or knitting. Some of them are quite horribly young women. Being a ballet mother is a métier in itself and different from any other function in the theater, and they develop occupational symptoms like extreme aggressiveness, extreme nervousness, extreme jealousy, and as regards their own persons, extreme selflessness. They spent their youth sitting in smelly practice studios; they spend their middle age standing in the wings. They are drudges and do all manner of menial and selfless service forever underfoot, in daily oblivion. A few of the ballet boys have mothers too. These are rarer, but I believe more formidable.

The hour before performance is a visiting time in a ballet theater. Outsiders are not welcome, but the girls and boys go back and forth between dressing rooms, gossiping, chatting, relaxing, letting go the outside, integrating more and more closely within their group. They seem to be wasting time. Actually they are undergoing a change. They are warming up, quieting down, cutting off from daily life. None of them will stay away from the theater and miss this hour; it is very important to them.

I visit the corps to go over tomorrow's notes with some of my girls. The corps girls dress in barrack rooms at long trestles. Their tutus hang overhead like large inverted flower corollas. They make up nearly always stripped to the waist, the complicated tapes which pull up their tights dangling loose from their thighs. They are a very pretty sight as they lean forward to apply their enormous false eyelashes or put the markings around their eyes as elaborate and formal as a Japanese actor's mask. Their hair is greased flat and nailed to the head with bobby pins so that they could be shaken like a rat in a terrier's mouth and not a strand would be loosened. With the foliage of tarlatan fluff overhead, the candles for mascara twinkling in front of the glasses, and the naked pearly young bodies stretching and moving, the scene suggests a kind of grotto. They have the most beautiful bodies in the world and they are all pre-adolescent. There is not a hip or a bust among them. But that's all right. It's better for dancing and they all, whenever it suits them, have babies with the greatest aplomb, showing that everyone, but chiefly Mother Nature, is wrong. Between the nymphs move Madame Pourmel and wardrobe women with freshly ironed costumes. They say nothing. Their tired, raw fingers zip and hook and fasten. Their faces are bleached and faded. They are reminders of what lies ahead.

I hang around mostly backstage during performances. I rarely go front for the pertinent reason that from this aspect the spectacle is depressing, and I think it helpful at this moment not to become depressed. If I have spoken of all this with excitement it is because I know toward what the dancers are striving and what lies behind them. And because I have grown enormously attached to them. The plain fact is that from where the audience sits the performances are often poor; they are under-rehearsed, paltry and tired, and rely for their success on the glittering efforts of a few great soloists and the splendid heritage of their name. Is this company just another dingy troupe of acrobats? Does their fascination rest chiefly on nothing but good press agenting? What distinguishes them from any traveling stock company?

Stand backstage at curtain rise and you will see. Their three-hour prepartions are completed. They are ready now in full costume and make-up. They try steps nervously, complaining of the floor, complaining of the new batch of shoes, invocating the Madonna while cracking their tights, scolding the conductor while rosining their slippers, having indigestion from a too cheap dinner behind the electrician's box, having love and heartbreak with finger pirouettes, receiving Denham's benediction center-stage like a lump of sugar. The boxed-in space hums with pandemonium in three Slavic languages, peppered with French. The lights raise the heat to baking point. There is a sudden quiet from the pit and then a roll of drums. The company stops talking and stands. The girls smooth out their tarlatans. The boys run softly in place easing their insteps. The stage manager made up for *Schéhérazade* continues to whisper to the electrician. The national anthem is being played—not their national anthem, a good proportion of them are homeless. They stand this way for "The Marseillaise," "God Save the King," "Maple Leaf Forever," "The Star-Spangled Banner." Nearly every one of them was born in a land whose anthems they will not hear in a hurry. The orchestra starts the overture. They move into place. They spit over one another's shoulders. They do this every night throughout the tour. They say "*Merde*" or "*Ni poukha ni péra*" or whatever three times. They cross themselves three times right shoulder first and touch the wood of the floor. Denham takes up his folding chair and moves to the wings. The lights turn blue. Everyone's mouth goes suddenly purple; their eyes glitter unnaturally. The grease in their hair takes on bright blue reflections. "I beginning," yells Yazvinsky. "Kourrtain!" the curtain moves up. There is a rush of air from the front.

And they are Sylphides, and the music is Chopin. This is their native land.

Every head is bent to the line. Every breath is bated. From toe tip to trembling fingers they are at attention. They move down the stage, these scrapping youngsters, in the oldest living tradition of our theater.

They share all the characteristics and faults of other theater folks with this difference: behind each turn of the head and footfall stand a lifetime of effort and three hundred years of experimentation. There is a glory carried by these poor, dingy, travel-worn waifs. The cost of this effort is isolation and abnormality. It constitutes blood sacrifice; they are dedicated people. They are bound together in common need like blitz victims. They are bound together by training and heritage. They are bound together, poor, deluded fools, by pride. Notwithstanding they are treated like bastard members of a family and are given the disadvantage of every doubt in all practical matters—in dressing-room arrangements, newspaper releases, legal documents, leases, charge accounts, sales agreements, savings and lending, and insurance policies—they are most unnaturally proud. They think they are doing the most difficult and interesting work in the theater.

July moved into August, August into September. The United States lost the Aleutians. Rommel had all but reached the Nile, the Japanese were hard upon New Zealand. We knitted and rehearsed and gossiped back across the continent in cars that were shunted aside to let trainloads of tanks take the right of way, and trainloads of men, some in uniform, but all with intent lost faces. In New York we settled to three weeks of straight rehearsing, six hours a day. At night I prepared the final plans.

All of America was quickening, was affirming itself, was searching its heart. There was high challenge in every face one met. My soldier was far away preparing himself for overseas duty, and I did not know from week to week what he was doing or where he would be next. I used to stand in my studio in the hot summer nights and it seemed to me I could feel the quickening energy around me, the gathering of the force of remembering. If in the face of this enormous self-recognition I could hold up one tiny token of our common life, I felt I was not entirely wasteful of the time.

In some ways this was the happiest period of my adult life. I worked tranquilly between lives. I hoped not greatly; I feared nothing. It was very like the delicious expectant moment when one knows one is about to fall in love but has not yet hazarded the furies and commitments of the enterprise. I was in love with the haunting legends of my land. I was in love also with a soldier. And somehow the one became mysteriously a symbol for the other. I opened the great French windows of my studio to the New York night and walked and walked in the warm dusk lit only by the windows across the way, and played the lovely Texas songs Copland had set and thought of the prairies I had crossed as a child, the prairies where my young man was even then growing up. I thought of the men leaving, leaving everywhere—generation on generation of men leaving and falling and the women remembering. And what was left of any of them but a folk tune and a way of joining hands in a ring? And I searched my heart for the clues to remembering.

In the morning I screamed for three hours at the Russians to shut up and be simple, and in the afternoon I screamed for three more hours to be quiet and be simple. We finished the ballet in ten days.

Luba Roudenko came to me. I said no.

Then came the show rehearsal. Denham, Libidins, Franz Allers, Irving Deakin, Yavinsky, with their wives, and my mother attended. No one had as yet seen any of it. The company assembled in immaculate black tights and white shirts. "Who told them to do this?" I asked delighted. Tradition. They stood quietly. They did not even whisper. They danced without a fault.

There was a cry from the spectators at the end. Libidins roared loudest. "Thanks God, Agnes, Malinki. Thanks God. What a ballet! Ham and eggs! Let me kiss you!"

"What's that?"

"Ham and eggs! *Schéhérazade*, *Gaîté*, *Rodeo*: ham and eggs. Our meal ticket for the next season!" Denham kissed me. Mrs. Denham kissed me. Allers kissed me. Mother kissed me. This was the first time she had seen any of the ballet. She was a trifle giddy.

"Now," I said turning to the dancers, "we will really get to work." But the room was empty. They had left on their vacation.

Since I was to dance the première, I used the time to brush up on my own dancing. I had practiced every night with them before performances and they were considerably alarmed. Before God, I was no technician. I shut myself in a studio and labored on the comedy. But I broke training for three days, borrowed thirty bucks from Mother and dashed out to Nashville, Tennessee—sitting up, of course. There being no seats available, I spent a good part of the trip in the men's washroom. There were two other women there, a crying child and some very disgruntled sailors for company. I went complete with the records Copland had made me. I could not buy or hire a gramophone so for the first time in my entire career I made use of Cecil De Mille's name and borrowed a machine in the local broadcasting studio. In this confined space I danced out solo the entire ballet, rodeo, love scenes, hoe-down and running set for my corporal. He thought it looked promising which was what I wanted to hear.

The company reassembled three weeks later. Massine was about. Because of overlapping contracts he found himself the husband of both groups. Ballet Theatre was housed also in the Metropolitan and their two-week season preceded ours. The two companies of dancers passed one another on stairs, in dressing rooms, rehearsal halls, lavatories, with the chill reserve and un-communicative politeness of enemy officers about to join issue in a contest for survival. The following season they were most of them working for the opposite group and passed their former bedmates with the same hostile con-descension. This behavior is a ballet tradition as old as the five positions and dates from the time when the French despised the Italians and both decried the Russians and Danish. Even within Russia, there has always been ugly feeling between the Moscow and St. Petersburg schools, and considering that the dancers always ended up in the same theater, it made for a liveliness of atmosphere.

Ballet Theatre opened for the first time in the Metropolitan Opera House with the full panoply of Hurok's forces. They produced their *pièce de résistance*, Massine's *Aleko*. Outside of Chagall's superb sets, it had a dubious success. Then followed Massine's *Don Domingo*, which was a real bust. The members of the Ballet Russe were not gallant in their comments. I tried to keep my mouth shut but I couldn't help figuring that none of this hurt me. Then followed *Helen of Troy*, but Fokine had died of pneumonia in mid-rehearsals and his work, later pulled together by Lichine, was at its first performances in bits and pieces. We stood at the back of the theater and watched with grisly gratifica-tion. We rushed to whisper in rehearsal halls and behind costume trunks.

Sevastianov's curt dismissal still smoked in my vitals. He had also, while in Mexico City, sold or destroyed the sets and costumes for *Black Ritual*, some-thing for which I have never to this day forgiven him.

We rehearsed upstairs at night while they went through their repertoire below. Our season began. The same audience returned in the same evening clothes. One noted the same cheering, the same lining-up on the lobby stairs to see who had come, the same promenading of dress and manner and pres-ence, the same greetings, the same wandering, inattentive eyes, the same babbling of technical jargon by would-be initiates, the same drinking away of half the ballets in Sherry's bar by the real initiates, to wit: Mr. Hurok and his weary staff. During the American season one half the group murmured praise, the other half scorn—the parts were reversed the next week. It made no great matter. It all happened between dinner and supper. Differences may have been noted by the people who were there because they loved danc-ing. Their opinion has always been less conspicuously expressed. But the young men prowling at the back of the auditorium, including the youth with spangles in his hair, were undisturbed. From their point of view nothing had changed.

I was spending a great deal of time at Karinska's—the costume executant— watching the fittings. Kermit Love, the designer, practically lived there. He said he stayed the nights too which is possible, though for what purpose I have yet to ascertain. He claimed he had the pants dyed and dried on his own legs so that they would look sun-faded and worn.

On Monday before the opening we showed the ballet to Aaron Copland and I, not Lubov Roudenko, for the first time danced. Massine practiced a barre at the back of the room throughout. He had no more business in that room than Lucia Chase, but bald curiosity compelled him to stay. Deakin came up to me at start and whispered, "I see Bela Lugosi in fourth position back there." I didn't mind. I had so grown in confidence I didn't mind. There were only five guests, but there was a small ovation at the end. Massine came to the front of the room without comment to take charge of the next rehearsal, his *Rouge et Noir*. He sat on a chair with his back to the mirror.

During the hoe-down I had kicked off one of my slippers, and it had shot under the chair on which he was sitting. To retrieve it I had to get down on my hands and knees and fumble long-armed behind his feet. He did not move. He looked down at me with his staring enormous expressionless eyes. "I see you have done a lively ballet!"

"Haven't I?" I said, wiping the dirt off my hands and straightening up. "Yes, I think maybe I have."

We had an orchestra reading. Aaron Copland sat in the front row. I sat beside him until about the twelfth bar; then I shot up and down the aisle. The cleaning women wiping the red velvet seats stood up now and then to listen. Some of the dancers came between the crack of the great gold curtain to hear what their cues sounded like on the instruments.

Then, the afternoon of the opening, we had dress rehearsal. That is, the scenery was up, Oliver's lovely sets. Because of union prices, we only had one hour. There was no time to figure out entrances or exits or spaces. But those surprising ballet dancers figured everything for themselves. This was the moment experience paid off. They solved on the instant every spatial and directional problem. I kept all my entire wits on myself and my own performance. Out in the red velvet auditorium in the endless scallops of empty seats sat Denham and Libidins and apart, very small and alone in a black tricorne, sat Mother.

I believe I didn't eat.

I was in the theater at six. I shared a star dressing room with Nathalie Krassovska. I had my costumes because I had personally gone to Karinska's and taken them away. I check every detail—bow, boots, belt, hat—again and again. Only two costumes this time, not fourteen. I did a careful barre. I put on my make-up. And then who should come into my dressing room and sink into the armchair but Mrs. Massine. She conversed with Krassovska in Russian, but as I stripped and redressed, she cast long appraising looks at my body. And she was a great beauty with the elegance and arrogance of a woman who has known since girlhood that things would come easily to her.

Kermit Love appeared pallidly in the door. "I'm so distressed," he sighed.

"Why?"

He hesitated. "They have made the collar to Milada's dress badly and you know how prettily I designed it."

"Oh, Kermit, for God's sake."

He faded away. Kermit lied like a gentleman. There was not a costume in the house, Milada's or anyone's. It was a tradition of Karinska that her clothes arrive piecemeal in a flotilla of taxis during the evening, some still with bastings and pins, and a half score of seamstresses in attendance to do last-minute sewing on dancers in the wings. The clothes were worn without trial of any sort. It is a tribute to her expertness that no accidents ever resulted. The wear and tear on the cast's nerves was, however, simply dreadful. Karinska has executed three ballets of mine. I have never had anything like complete costumes at the dress rehearsal. Why does anyone hire her a second time? Simply, she is without peer in her field.

Mrs. Massine did not stop talking for a minute. On and on and on she chattered. In Russian, thank God, but noisily. I had only a few minutes to make my peace with heaven. *Rouge et Noir* had been on for a quarter hour. I stepped to the door partly dressed. Danilova beckoned me across the hall. "Agnes, I can help you with your hair. I will show you how to fix so it not come loose. These little secrets I learn through many years." She sat me at her dressing table and got to work with pins in her mouth. On the night of my debut Alexandra Danilova maided me—hairnets, barrettes, bobbies, elastics and ribbons.

Rouge et Noir was over. I went back to my room. Mrs. Massine raised languid amused eyes to my taut face. "Are you nairvous?" she drawled.

"I am," I said. "I am sick at my stomach."

"Good luck! Success!" she said punctiliously.

I turned to her quietly. "I hope we have success. The success or failure of my life depends on the next half hour. And I hope, for the company's sake, there is success. Much depends on this ballet for them, too. If I have failed them they are in a bad way. And they have worked hard, harder than you can imagine."

Under the façade Mrs. Massine like most people has a heart. She was confounded. "As you say," she murmured, "for all—success."

I walked onto the stage. Everyone I knew was out front. Mother had seen to that. She herself was in a box in black lace. Beside her sat Mary Meyer and Edward Johnson and Margaret. The refugee German of the violets and Martha Graham and Mary Hunter were there, and although I didn't know it until later, John Andrews from the Rambert Company, now an officer in His Majesty's Navy with six of the staff of his corvette. They made a fine blue and gold effect in a box complete with a bunch of red roses. And in another box, not by accident, sat Richard Rodgers, Oscar Hammerstein II and Therese Helburn of the Theatre Guild. I had heard they were contemplating a play on Western cowboy life and I thought I could do good dances for them.

Mother alone was not nervous. "This is the first time I have not had to worry about the box office," she said serenely. "And I didn't have to spend the afternoon trying to impress my friends into coming."

The house was sold out.

Behind the gold curtain we stood in our cowboy pants, I among my men, nearly every one of whom has since become an important soloist. Beside Franklin stood Harold Lang, Kasimir Kokic, James Starbuck, Robert Pagent, and David Thimar, and waiting in the wings for a walk-on was Maria Tallchief, and beside her Betty Low, Dorothy Etheridge, Milada Mladova, and Vladimir Kostenko, who was to play Jud in the *Oklahoma!* ballet for six years. We were in our pants because the Karinska cabs had begun to arrive filled with hysterical seamstresses and pins. There was a great rustling of tissue paper in the wings. On one side flowers were being unwrapped, on the other, dresses and hats no one had ever seen. There was also a great deal of whispering as to who was to put on what. Behind every piece of scenery the company in tights and dressing gowns crouched watching, head on head, with painted and elongated eyes like the larvae of insects. On folding chairs behind the tormentor sat Danilova and Slavenska, crossing themselves, spitting, and looking on me with shining eyes. Franz Allers, the conductor, kissed me. "Here we go, Malinki," said Libidins. "Ham and eggs!"

Denham gave his blessing.

"I'm going in," said Allers, and he left to enter the pit.

Freddie spat over my shoulder and bumped his knee against my rump. He didn't say anything. He was tightening his belt and figuring out the spacing within the new set. His eyes darted back and forth. I moistened my lips. This was a terrible moment, but I had company. I was no longer alone. There were men standing all around me—very great dancers. I looked at their thighs and their shoulders and the intensity of their faces, and I knew I would never again be alone.

The large descending octaves sounded from the brass, sharp as sunlight on rocks. We flexed our insteps and breathed deep. The gold folds contracted. The music was suddenly clear under our feet. The naked, living dark yawned.

"This is it, kids," said Freddie, without moving his lips.

If it is possible for a life to change at one given moment, if it is possible for all movement, growth and accumulated power to become apparent at one single point, then my hour struck at 9:40, October 16, 1942. Chewing gum, squinting under a Texas hat, I turned to face what I had been preparing for the whole of my life.

This was not a great performance; we gave better later. Neither was it a great ballet. The style, as I always feared, did break. But it was the first of its kind, and the moment was quick with birth.

There was applause on my first exit. An unexpected bonus. There was applause or response on every phrase. Did the audience laugh on count eight as I had promised in July in California? They laughed, not just female titters, but real laughing with the sound of men's voices, and the laugh turned into handclapping. This happened again and again. The dancers were elated but not surprised. I had promised them laughs. The pantomime was spaced to accommodate them.

There were mishaps. At one point, Kokic grew confused with his new costumes and failed to make an entrance, leaving me to improvise a love scene, without partner, alone, and exposed for sixty-four bars of music on the Met stage. Lines were crooked. Some of the girls clapped off beat. It didn't seem to matter.

The pace of the performance rushed us like a wind. The audience were roused and urging us on. Great exchanges of excitement and force and gaiety were taking place all around. The dancers rushed and whirled, grabbing the right person, because the right person was there, though unrecognizable in an unexpected dress and hair-do. And throughout the pace which was too quick for me, beyond my understanding, faster than could be savored or appreciated, was Freddie's hand, Freddie's arm, Freddie's strong back, propelling, pushing, carrying, and Freddie's feet like bullets on the wood. It was beyond endurance. It was beyond help. It was slipping away too fast, too fast. Also my collar was too tight.

"Freddie," I said at the back of the stage, "I'm fainting. Loosen my collar."

"No time, duckie. Here we go."

And as though we were blown out of the mouth of a gun, he propelled me to the footlights. We separated. Bob, bob. (Which Robert, Madame?) All the trumpets and horns threw their shafts between us. We hung on the brink. The music tore open. We rushed. We clashed. We were lifted. And all the girls had faces like stars with their hair dropping over the boys' shoulders. The great curtain fell. There was dust in my nostrils from the dusty lining of the curtain. It was over. It was done. And I had made so many foolish mistakes. So many hasty things gone wrong. Once more I had been incapable of the perfect effort. "Oh, Freddie," I said gasping, "what a stinking, lousy performance. We must rehearse like demons tomorrow."

I looked at him wistfully but we were walking forward and we were all holding hands and bowing. A large bunch of American corn was put in my arms tied with red, white and blue ribbons. More flowers came, more flowers. The Russians did things this way. They also clapped and called out. Hadn't I stood grinding my teeth at the back of the house for years while they cheered bogus nonsense? We bowed and bowed. At the eighth bow, I looked into the pit. The fiddlers were beating their bows on their instruments. The others were standing up yelling. No one gets the union boys to do this easily. I looked at Freddie in amazement. "Freddie," I said, "this is not a claque. This is not Libidins's contriving."

"Darling, darling," said Freddie, kissing me, "this is an ovation. This is the real thing. Take it." He pushed me forward, and all the company backed away to the edge of the stage and stood there clapping.

We had twenty-two curtain calls.

The grips and members of the company helped me carry my flowers to the dressing room. They filled half the floor space. The doorman could not hold my friends in check.

In the hall between dressing rooms, I met Massine. He bowed formally, and then apparently thought he must say something. He stared at me with his binocular eyes. "You have done a characteristic ballet." I struggled to follow this. "And in Europe I think it will have success." We bowed.

Mary Meyer sat at my dressing table crying and crying. "I can't stop," she said, mopping her nose. "It isn't that this is the most wonderful ballet I've ever seen. I've seen better. It's just that I can't stand you making a success after all these years."

"Aren't you proud of her?" said the friends to Mother. And Annie drew herself up to their shoulders and looking at them steadily with her penetrating blue eyes answered, "I've always been proud of her. Always. When no one hired her. I'll go home now and start the coffee."

And in the lobby Billy Rose was marching up and down shouting, "But where has she been? Why haven't we known about her? How could we have overlooked this talent?"

And Terry Helburn was phoning in a wire to Western Union: WE THINK YOUR WORK IS ENCHANTING. COME TALK TO US MONDAY.

I did some phoning of my own. I called Officer's Candidate School at the Aberdeen Proving Grounds and spoke to a soldier. "It is a success. It has made a furor."

"Oh," he said, "that does not surprise me. I knew it would."

He knew it would! He'd known me six months and seen nothing of my work at all. He took this evening for granted. Well so, miraculously, did my mother. But she had waited fourteen years, had sewn costumes, sold bonds, nagged at her friends to attend her girl's concerts, run errands, done without all luxuries, and hoped, and hoped, and hoped, steadily and without default in the face of reason and proof unlimited that her efforts would meet with no success. She was home now, serving coffee and chocolate cake and salad to all and sundry. This time the doors were wide open. Anyone could walk in.

Oklahoma! (Dances by Agnes de Mille)
("Beautiful Morning," *Dance to the Piper*)

> *Rodeo,* De Mille's 1942 hit with the Ballet Russe de Monte Carlo, led to her engagement by Richard Rodgers and Oscar Hammerstein II as choreographer for their new show about a Western state, which would change the history of musical theater on Broadway. The opening pages of this memoir refer to three of the most important men in de Mille's life outside the theater: Walter Prude, then in Officers Candidate School, whom de Mille would eventually marry; the playwright, screenwriter, and teacher William C. de Mille, Agnes's father; and Henry George, her mother's father, who, with only a seventh-grade education, wrote a widely read book of economic theory, entitled *Progress and Poverty*, which examines the consequences of harsh urban poverty that he saw resulting from the concentration of great wealth in the hands of comparatively few individuals and corporations during the latter part of the nine-

teenth century. (As Agnes put it in a 1979 pamphlet on Henry George's achievement: "He saw degradation forming as he saw the rise of leisure and affluence, and he felt compelled to discover why they arose concurrently.")

Lubov Roudenko was the second-cast lead in *Rodeo* at the Ballet Russe de Monte Carlo, behind de Mille, herself. Warren Leonard had been an early stage (and offstage) partner of de Mille's. The virtuoso dancer and teacher Carmelita Maracci is the subject of a profile elsewhere in this collection. Richard Pleasant was, with Lucia Chase and Oliver Smith, one of the co-founders of Ballet Theatre. "The Guild" refers to the Theater Guild, led by Lawrence Langner and Theresa Helburn, who developed—and finally, on March 31, 1943, saw with satisfaction the New York première of—this landmark musical.

I rejoined the Russians in Chicago and wishing to spend Thanksgiving with my soldier who could procure only sixteen hours away from O.C.S., I had relinquished the première in that city, and took over only after Roudenko had introduced the work. And this was a strange thing: I had spent my life longing to get on the great stages and now that I could at last, I was passing up the opportunities quite carelessly and it seemed to me the only possible course of action.

We traveled west to San Francisco, the city of my mother's birth, the city where *Progress and Poverty* had been planned and written. The great hills sloped down to the water, the hills about which my mother had talked all her life, now green with the first rains, and silky with mists from the wine country. The mists lay on the water where the enormous transports waited, and on the docks alongside the army trains unloaded and unloaded and unloaded. I sat on a cliff and watched the gulls wheel up. "Please God," I said, "let him not be sent to the East." A submarine net stretched across the harbor, the gulls screamed and dipped. There were the clank of machines and chains and the grating of wheels on new tracks. The gulls rose in a scattering whorl from before the War Memorial Opera House (World War I Memorial). The gulls had been my grandfather's favorite bird, Mother always said, the sailor's bird. Gulls meant land ahead. The great late harvest moon lifted and hung, and inside the Opera House we danced for auditoriums of men that were saying good-by. We danced our folk piece, reminding ourselves and them a little of what we had grown up with.

"*Rodeo* is refreshing and as American as Mark Twain," wrote Alfred Frankenstein in the *San Francisco Chronicle.* "It is much the kind of ballet that Mark Twain might have written if his mind had run to ballets. . . ."

By the time we reached Los Angeles, we were in good order. Opening night was for me an unprecedented return. What higher satisfaction could there be than to go back after all the troubles with the most famous ballet company extant, in my own work, a score by our leading composer, brilliant *décor*, and for my partner a great virtuoso?

The Philharmonic Auditorium (where as a child I had heard all my first symphonies, where I had dreamed through musical matinees of doing solos on this very stage) was packed to the roof. The orchestra played splendidly. We danced and acted as never before, and my father sat throughout hearing the laughs turn into hands, hearing the hands turn into calls. I faced about at the end, dripping and breathing and spent, my arms filled with carnations and roses, toward the wings and there, in the exact spot I had stood as a girl waiting to see Anna Pavlova, there under the great column spots stood Pop, smiling and radiant. He was waiting for me. And around about him stood the scouts from the big studios, and the agents, and the musical movie producers. Pop smiled wryly and nodded. Gray and patient, not so tall as before, doubting and trusting with the same smile, his beautiful brown eyes burning black with attention, he nodded and smiled. Haven, fortress, alpha and omega! I dropped the flowers and was gathered home. His suit still smelled of cigar smoke. He still cleared his throat and chuckled as he patted my hair awkwardly.

"My daughter," he said, "you have come a long way. I am so proud." He could not go on. The agents and scouts moved aside and left us. We stood quietly together. My grease paint came off all over his suit lapel.

"There now," said Pop, "this is a good job. You can be well pleased. Go speak to your friends. I'll drive you home."

Pop's adoring university students came loyally in droves and the English department from U.C.L.A., all now devoting their gifts to teaching young officers to write simple declarative sentences with subjects and predicates, and my classmates in uniform, and Warren who got leave from ship welding and was about to be married, and Carmelita, and Richard Pleasant, a captain in the artillery, who kissed my hand and took me dancing.

I waved aside the studio scouts by explaining I had to go East to do a Broadway musical about early life in the West. I talked a little about the new job to Father. He took all my personal episodes very quietly. He trusted in the natural course of events I'd marry and that some instinct would keep me from making a fool of myself. We talked entirely about work. But now I no longer cried; I argued and chivvied with considerable belligerence. When I grew too heated he retired into his beer.

I parted with the ballet in Los Angeles and hurried to New York.

I went for my first interview very firm and determined. Hammerstein seemed understanding but as I had found out, one never could tell. First, I informed him, I must insist that there be no one in the chorus I didn't approve. I sat up quite straight; as I spoke I looked very severe. "Oh pshaw!" he murmured. He was sorry to hear I was going to take that attitude—there was his regular girl, and Lawrence Langner had two, and Dick Rodgers always counted on some. For one beat, I took him literally, there being no trace of anything except earnestness in his face, and then I relaxed on that score for the rest of my life.

I heard the enchanting music. At these auditions, Oscar always read the role of Aunt Eller. Certainly it has never been played so well since. I remember the gasp that went around the room after "Beautiful Morning." Dick looked up from the keyboard and smiled abstractedly. He and his assistant, Margot Hopkins, together at double pianos, always accompanied auditions. They played very many these days. They were having a dreadful time raising money. I advised them to drop from the score "People Will Say We're in Love," a song shortly to become one of the most lucrative hits of the century.

There were conferences and casting. My contract with the Guild called for a meager cash payment and no royalties, and I was to get no further rights of any kind. After all costs were paid off, they promised I should receive an additional five hundred dollars.

A great reservoir of talent had been gathering in the studios for years waiting for some sort of chance, and I had been watching the young dancers mature in daily practice. The *Oklahoma!* line-up was accordingly without parallel. But just for appearance' sake, we took in two chorus girls. They seemed terrified at the vigorous company they found themselves suddenly in and sat or stood locked close together from pure loneliness. The rest were dancers. I obtained the leading role for my good friend, the beautiful Katharine (Katya) Sergava, late of Ballet Theatre. There was a deal of heated argument during the choosing of the chorus. Helburn and Rouben Mamoulian wanted slim legs above all. I wanted talent and personality. Rodgers wanted faces, but was inclined to stand by me on many occasions. His idea and my idea of a face, I found, had frequently to do with the character in it. Oscar wasn't around. Langner was in Washington. We finally chose all but three. Mamoulian rejected my candidates categorically. "They're certainly not pretty. They can't act. Possibly, they can dance. That's your department. They're useless to me."

Two of them were my pupils. I knew they could act. All three could dance. I staged my first tantrum. "If I don't have them, I'll quit the show."

Mamoulian shrugged. "Then just keep them out of my way."

Their names were Joan McCracken, Bambi Linn, and Diana Adams.

The Guild was on the verge of bankruptcy. We worked in their old theater on 52nd Street, which they did not clean for economic reasons. Mamoulian took the stage. I worked below in what had been the foyer and way above in what had been costume and rehearsal rooms, and with the assistance of Marc Platt and Ray Harrison I kept three rehearsals going at once. I was like a pitcher that had been overfilled; the dances simply spilled out of me. I had girls and boys in every spare corner of the theater sliding, riding, tapping, ruffling skirts, kicking. We worked with tremendous excitement, but always under great strain. For the first three days Richard Rodgers never left my side. He sat with fixed surgical attention watching everything. This made the dancers nervous, but it was I who really sweated. He did not relax until the third afternoon, when, smiling and patting me on the shoulder, he gave the first intimation that on this show I would not be fired.

Rodgers is not only a very great song writer, he is one of the most astute theater men in the world. He concerns himself zestfully and relentlessly with every detail of production. Nothing escapes his attention and he takes vigorous and instant action. This might be interfering if he were not sensitive, sensible and greatly experienced. He knows also when to keep his hands off. Mamoulian and the Guild frequently said, "It can't be done." It was always Rodgers who urged, "Let's see."

Our director, Rouben Mamoulian, provided daily challenge. He was used to complete, unquestioned authority and total obedience. As a choreographer in a ballet company, I was used to the same. But here I was no longer Madame the choreographer. I was the dance director in the basement, and although I began work with a respect for him that amounted to hero worship, we immediately ran head on in jurisdictional disputes. I think I can confidently say I would have gone down under the conflicting opinions if Richard Rodgers had not lent me his incomparable knowledge and authority as running interference. Due to his jealous care, my work came shining through for whatever it was worth.

But we all got increasingly nervous. I lost my temper at every thwarting. And when Terry Helburn started interrupting rehearsals to show unfinished work to prospective backers in her frantic efforts to raise money, I blew every fuse I had. Hurling my pocketbook at her head, I shouted and denounced and was dragged off screaming by Marc Platt one day and held under a faucet of cold water until I quieted down.

Once, when my ballet was unnecessarily interrupted, not by Miss Helburn this time, during a run-through, I gave a scream of anguish and hurled myself on Oscar Hammerstein's bosom. He was taken quite unaware and looked down startled at the hysteria on his waistcoat, but it was the comment from the rear rows that really surprised him. "Agnes," said Mother peremptorily, "control yourself."

I snapped up as though a ruler had been applied to my hand. I trust Oscar got over his surprise. I've continued to hurl myself on the same spot for years now. His is the largest and most receptive bosom in the Western Hemisphere.

All the dances in the show were set within two weeks. I set double the amount that was kept. I put the ballet together on the second Sunday when everyone else was home resting and we showed it intact the next night at the first run-through. The cast seemed impressed.

The youngest member of the troupe, Kenneth LeRoy, came down with German measles and retired temporarily from rehearsals, but not before he had infected nine or ten of us. Due to the length of the incubation period, however, we were not made aware of this until we reached Boston. I developed a lethal cough.

We worked feverishly, frantically. I had no other interest, my soldier having gone to Omaha. I wrote him constant bulletins. Of course, he really did not know what I was talking about, not having seen any of my work, nor any ballet at all for that matter. I wrote him anyway.

A. de M. to W. P. N.Y. February 23, 1943

They sent me home in the afternoon, so I've napped and redone one dance, and now I must go to sleep again because I've just got to get well. Besides all the work to do, there's disorganization, demoralization and confusion while I lie at home coughing.

February 24

I'm well again. There was no chance of any rest so nature coped. I blew my lungs in and out of my mouth like a bubble for a week. Now I don't. And I can laugh without paroxysms of the diaphragm, though Libidins asked me last night if I were studying *Traviata*.

Nearly all the important dances are done, only bits and pieces left. I never worked so fast in my life. I've set forty minutes of straight dancing in less than three weeks. The company raves. Rodgers put his head on my shoulder this afternoon and said, "Oh, Aggie, you're such a comfort in my old age." And Marc Platt, my leading dancer, said this evening, "In all soberness, I never worked with anyone I respected more." Katya has made a hit. I've discovered two girls who are going to be sensations, my two leading men *are males* and also the stage manager, so rehearsals are lively and gay. We live in the basement. I see sunlight only twenty minutes each day. The dust from the unvacuumed Guild rugs has made us all sick, and I put away three Thermos bottles of coffee an afternoon. I look awful. Thin, old, and hard.

A rumor came down from upstairs, where the grownups work, that Mamoulian (Mamoo, he is called) did something good at eleven-thirty. Hurok sent for me. He wants two ballets and he wants them this summer.

Libidins sends you greetings. *Rodeo* plays every night to howling success. I asked how the performances were. "In my opinion, pretty lousy, but it seems to make no difference."

Suddenly the five weeks of rehearsal were gone and we had to leave for New Haven. I had coughed and cursed and quarreled. I had run from the stage to the basement and back to the roof. Everyone was worried. At lunch, Celeste Holm held forth on what was wrong with the playing of the comedy scenes. At dinner, I groused about the ensembles. We worried and groused and fretted. I knew the show had possibilities of greatness, but it was being wrecked, wrecked, wrecked. I myself was doing only a hack job. It could be nothing else since I was composing so fast and easily. I wrote my father as much. He said to stop talking and get on with it. There was only one man who rode the froth quietly and failed to turn a hair.

"Do you know what I think is wrong?" said Richard Rodgers as we sat on the stage one midnight. "Almost nothing. Now why don't you all quiet down?" He has learned to worry since, although he has persuaded himself that he never really frets. But that is one of his really endearing vanities. He has become one of the most nervous rehearsers in the business. In 1943, with a great deal at stake, he was blithely sanguine. As for me, I was convinced we were failing, but my deep concern lay elsewhere. Every night at eleven, I turned on the war news, drank one glass of sherry and wrote a long letter west.

So we traveled to New Haven on Tuesday afternoon and now everybody's temper went absolutely to pot. I began to become aware of Oscar Hammerstein, who had stayed up to this point almost exclusively in the book rehearsals. He sat through the endless nights quietly giving off intelligence like a stove. He never got angry or hasty or excited, but when people were beating their heads on the orchestra rail made the one common-sense suggestion that any genius might think of if he was not at the moment consuming himself. Lawrence Langner expounded. Terry Helburn snapped and badgered and barked at our heels, with a housekeeper's insistence on detail. Mamoulian created in spite of the hour and other people's nerves. But Oscar just quietly pointed the way.

To W.P.   *New Haven, March 10th*

We're working around the clock now. Thursday we open. Dick Rodgers took my hand in his yesterday and said, "I want to thank you for doing a distinguished job." There's hell ahead and unless we pull the show up very quick we're sunk. On Fridays, I have hysterics . . .

Kurt Weill and both ballet companies (Ballet Russe and Ballet Theatre) are crawling up and down the back of my neck. I've grown old like a stick but Katya says in Boston she will help me shop and buy a trousseau. I looked at myself in a full-length mirror and received the surprise of my life. I've lived off Italian food (next door to the Guild) and sandwiches for five weeks and done literally nothing but sit on my behind and shout, but miraculously the coughing has shaken off the fat I expected to accumulate. I'm as slim as a boy through the shank. The behind I dreaded simply is not there. Oh jubilation!

When you phone, make it collect. The Guild pays my bills up to $10.00 a day.

New Haven, March 13th

You haven't been getting my letters so you haven't followed what's been going on. All Broadway shows are simply fierce during rehearsals, but this one has been insanity. And only Dick Rodgers has kept me from flouncing out. That and the fact that my life is grounded now and none of this nonsense can touch me . . . Oh yes . . . and the night of the dress rehearsal when I was ordered off the stage for the second time while I was placing dances and then twenty minutes were taken to show boys how to bang pots in a chivaree (something they'd rehearsed steadily for three weeks), I blew a fuse and was dragged out by the stage manager and given coffee and I talked about how I never, never would forgive and suddenly I found myself talking about how I loved you and I talked and talked. And he was smiling at me and I stopped embarrassed and said, "This has nothing to do with the rehearsal." And he said, "But now you can go back to it and run it." And I said, "Now I can run the world." And we skipped back and did. And the next night the first dance stopped the show cold and Dick Rodgers standing beside me threw his arms around me and hugged and hugged.

Half of the audience on opening night was from New York. "The wrecking crew," Ruth Gordon has called them. Agents, backers, theatrical lawyers, first-night hounds, all came up, liked a few things enormously and left early to catch the train and take the news back that it was, on the whole, definitely not a success.

March 14th

Today both Langner and Helburn came to me and thanked me and volunteered the promise of more money than my contract called for. They're going to give me a bonus. [$50 a week augmented later to a small percentage.]

Kurt Weill came to see the show this afternoon. He doesn't think it's good. (It's not but it may succeed.) But he still wants me to do his show, so that's something.

To dinner and back to the God damn theater. Oh for a movie instead! But you'll take me to a movie, won't you?

I hoped to spend the trip to Boston reading a detective story but I reckoned without the Guild. They hired a drawing room on the train. We all crowded into it and in three and one-half hours rewrote the play, chiefly the second act. I was ordered to produce a small three-minute dance in twenty-four hours. I did. But the skin came off the girls' ribs from continuous lifting, and I couldn't seem to stop throwing up. The first night in Boston with the new script was pretty rocky and the press only fair. But funny thing, people went home down the sidewalks singing, and they wanted to come back. No one seemed very excited but suddenly we were sold out.

Lawrence made a list of everything to be done on a yellow pad with a program. The various departments were allotted time on stage exactly like astronomers scheduled for the hundred-inch telescope. Lawrence policed the theater with a large watch in his hand and there was no reprieve possible from his "I'm very sorry, my dear." Every night after the show sharp council was held. I have never seen a group of people work harder and faster except perhaps the same group during the *Carousel* tryout. The entire play was reorganized in two weeks and new long numbers staged—the entire *Oklahoma!* number, for instance.

At this point the play was called *Away We Go!* There were conferences about a change of title. *Oklahoma* was suggested but it didn't seem like a very good title. Lawrence declared himself satisfied if an exclamation point was added. Would people go to see something with a plain, geographical title, we asked. Armina, Lawrence's wife, had been born out there and she thought, with great fervor, they would.

In pure exhaustion, I decided one evening to forego dinner and have a nap instead. I was barely bedded when the phone rang. Maria had broken out in spots and no understudy was ready. An hour later I was on stage in Maria's dress and bonnet. Next day I came out in spots.

Boston, March 23rd

So now I have German measles and can stay at home and write you more letters. This morning's message swept me through rehearsals with great gusto, well spotted out as I grew momentarily. Katya is now having acute nervous indigestion. Terry is in bed with ice bags on her head. Mr. Hammerstein runs a temperature that won't stop. But there are others nothing happens to. If only this were real measles, I'd have a brand-new skin all over me and when you saw me in that you'd die—brand new all over, pale, translucent, pink, like a baby's stomach.

I'm going to read a detective story now and then I'm going to fall asleep dreaming of the clothes I shall buy to ravish you with. I want your battalion to gape with envy and Prude's Ag to become synonymous with all that's provocative, an Omaha byword. Mamoulian said to me last night at dinner, "Why is it all great dancers never give a damn how they look?"

Boston, March 26, 27

I've had three beautiful days doing nothing, sleeping, eating, with Katya and Johnny, reading the Constitution of the United States and a Perry Mason mystery, sleeping, trailing around the Ritz in my brown velvet dressing gown to midnight conferences with the bosses who wanted to cut my work without my concurrence, sleeping, thinking of meeting you in ten days—afternoon or evening and this time could you meet the train? And what should I wear to delight you the most? Receiving phone calls from my kids, hourly reports— Margit had fever but Vivian had done extremely well in her place, Marc had bruised the bone in his foot, Ray would do the "bells" for him, Marc was proceeding very well with rehearsals on "Kansas City" (phone call from Marc as I write this—Joan McCracken passed out cold during performance). So I continued doing nothing. Tomorrow I go back to the slaughter. All the bosses (except Johnny and I) believe we have a smash hit. I sit by the window and hear a wonderful old bell tolling the hours in a beautiful old church tower. And April seems imminent in the buds on Boston Common.

March 27

Thank you for breakfast gay and good because of your wire. I rushed to the theater in singing spirits. Marc had all but fractured his foot and was ordered not to dance for a week. McCracken's attack had been nervous exhaustion resulting in suffocation—no less. Margit fainted every time she jumped, two of the leads and one of the best girls out of every number.

The matinee went on today in good order. This is a remarkable troupe. The actors are dumfounded. They've never seen such stamina before; they've never worked with real dancers.

My memory of this time is chiefly a sense of well-being and excitement, lying in my luxurious Ritz bedroom, listening for the sound of the wheels on the little serving tables as breakfast arrived, possibly with the letter from the West. The snow fell lightly. There were daffodils and apple blossoms in the lobby and the old bell tolled in the church near the Common. Much was going to happen—very much. I was going to be married, for one thing.

During the last dress rehearsal in New York, some musician struck a wrong note—Diana Adams's face contracted with pain. It was not annoyance or amusement, it was agonized concern. Richard Rodgers saw the expression and marveled. That look had never crossed a chorus girl's face; he was aware (as were not all of us?) that responsible artists had entered the ranks. Diana's expression marked the beginning of a new era. I remember going up to the Ballet Arts School the day of the opening and finding her and Bambi Linn sweating through two classes. I ordered them home to rest but I had to enlist the help of the teacher to make them leave the floor.

The first night was by no means sold out. The Guild subscription had fallen very low. I had ten front-row balcony seats and I didn't know whom to give them to. I think a couple remained empty. They stood alongside of me, Rodgers and the staff. Oscar, who was calm, sat with his wife.

Marc's foot was very bad, but he said if he lost his leg he would dance the opening so a doctor anesthetized it. He danced on a frozen leg and foot. He had to be cut out of his boot afterwards.

I stood at the back in Margaret's black evening dress. Rodgers held my hand. The curtain went up on a woman churning butter; a very fine baritone came on stage singing the closest thing to lieder our theater has produced. He sang exquisitely with his whole heart about what a morning in our Southwest is like. At the end, people gave an audible sigh and looked at one another— this has seldom happened before. It was music. They sat right back and opened their hearts. The show rolled.

At intermission, I bucked the tide of spectators and fought my way to the stage door. Marc's leg was in a terrible state. I got a bottle of brandy for him. Upstairs Kate Friedlich was crying because she had torn two ligaments from her heel but she insisted on continuing. I got some brandy for her too. Luckily Marc's doctor was on hand to cope.

The barn dance opened Act II. Marc Platt in an ecstasy of excitement rode the pain to triumph. Virile, young, red-headed and able, he looked like Apollo and moved like a stallion. The audience roared. "Oh, Agnes," said Rodgers, "I'm so proud of you. I hope this opens the doors."

"Dick, Dick," I said, melting into his arms, "I love you. Thank you." Then the rehearsal accompanist started beating us on the back and shrieking, "Will you two stop courting and look what's happened to the theater?"

They were roaring. They were howling. People hadn't seen girls and boys dance like this in so long. Of course, they had been dancing like this, but not just where this audience could see them.

I took Mother to Sardi's for a sandwich. Some critic, I think it was Wolcott Gibbs, crossed the restaurant to shake hands. "I want to congratulate you. This was most distinguished." I chewed on in a sort of stupor.

The morning press next day was only fair. *Brigadoon*, for instance, got better. I was back in the theater at noon rehearsing Marc's understudy. I left for the West without knowing what had happened.

In Omaha, while making my wedding plans, the phone started ringing, Hollywood calling. "Have you signed with M-G-M? Well don't. Paramount is interested." The lieutenant and I tried to talk about things engaged people talk about. New York calling: "Sam Goldwyn is really interested."

"How much was that last for?" he asked.

"Seven hundred and fifty dollars a week to begin with."

"That's a lot of money," said the lieutenant. "I don't think I can keep pace with this."

"But I only want to be with you and do good dances. I don't think I'll do such good dances at Paramount."

"That's a lot of money to say no to," said the lieutenant. The phone rang again. He said, "It's likely I'll be busy for some time. While I'm away you might as well keep occupied. Do one more show. Get it out of your system. Then you'll be ready to quiet down."

I spoke to my mother. First I told her I was going to get married soon, and then I told her about the Hollywood money. "I can pay you back everything. I can help now. I can be a real help."

"What are the terms?" she asked.

"A seven-year contract . . ."

"Never," she shouted through the phone. "Never, not for any money. Your freedom is not to be bought for anything in the world. Not for money. Keep your freedom. It is beyond price. You must be able to choose. Do not consider the money. Think only of the kind of work you want to do. Don't ever speak to me about paying back."

Oh, Annie! Spoken like your father's girl! She had done without every possible luxury to keep me going, a woman aging and sickening fast. I listened to her as I had grown used to doing. When she spoke, the bugles called. That she gave advice that was also profitable was not known to either of us at the moment.

When I returned to New York, the deluge was upon me. Everyone in New York and Hollywood wanted me to do the *Oklahoma!* ballet for his new show or picture. But I was buying a trousseau.

This was the first time in my life I had taken more than a sporadic interest in clothes. They piled on my bed now, white on snowy white, ruffle on starched ruffle, crisp ribbons, button on silk—Mother was sewing petticoats and dressing jackets—the kind of lingerie she had had—not costumes.

All through my packing I heard the phone ringing. Agents, reporters, pressmen, musicians, dancers—all now wanted to talk to me urgently. My number was, of course, listed as it had been for years. How was I going to get time to study? To plan my new good works? To keep to myself and think? The clamor was frightening.

The ship had come to port—but to what port? Was this what I had intended and wanted?

I saw *Rodeo* again. Due to lack of rehearsals and replacements, it was unrecognizable. I had succeeded all right. Now I did the cold reckoning without the hysteria of failure to underscore my concern. The work wasn't good enough. All changed, all passed. There was no way of ensuring lasting beauty. Verily, I wrote in water and judging my work with a dreadful dispassionate vision, perhaps it was as well. I spoke to Martha Graham on the pavement outside of Schrafft's restaurant. She bowed her head and looked burningly into my face. She spoke from a life's effort. I went home and wrote down what she said:

"There is a vitality, a life-force, an energy, a quickening that is translated through you into action and because there is only one of you in all of time, this expression is unique. And if you block it, it will never exist through any other medium and be lost. The world will not have it. It is not your business to determine how good it is nor how valuable nor how it compares with other expressions. It is your business to keep it yours clearly and directly, to keep the channel open. You do not even have to believe in yourself or your work. You have to keep open and aware directly to the urges that motivate you. Keep the channel open. As for you, Agnes, you have a peculiar and unusual gift and you have so far used about one third of your talent."

"But," I said, "when I see my work I take for granted what other people value in it. I see only its ineptitude, inorganic flaws, and crudities. I am not pleased or satisfied."

"No artist is pleased."

"But then there is no satisfaction?"

"No satisfaction whatever at any time," she cried passionately. "There is only a queer divine dissatisfaction, a blessed unrest that keeps us marching and makes us more alive than the others. And at times I think I could kick you until you can't stand."

I kissed her and went west to my bridegroom. (320–335)

One Touch Of Venus (Dances by Agnes de Mille)
("Show Biz," And Promenade Home)

An account—the first of two in *And Promenade Home*—of some of the personalities who worked with de Mille on the 1943 Broadway musical *One Touch of Venus*. Although the events chronicled are theatrical, the World War creeps in, as during a conversation de Mille relates between herself and dancer Sono Osato, in which one finds reference to de Mille's new husband, Walter Prude, serving in the military, and the fact that Osato's new husband had been rejected for military service. The mention of the "Petty calendar" is quite topical. The illustrator of female pulchritude George Petty (1894–1975), especially well-known for his pin-up calendars, had just had two such calendars published by *Esquire*, one in 1955 and one in 1956, the publication year of *And Promenade Home*. The widely influential humorist Sidney Joseph Perelman (1904–1979), author of the book for *One Touch of Venus*, is best known for his many contributions to *The New Yorker* and for his explosively funny screenwriting (the Marx Brothers' *Horse Feathers* and *Monkey Business* and *Around the World in 80 Days*, for which Perelman's screenplay won an Oscar). With chilling exactitude and wicked understatement, de Mille outlines his egregious insensitivity to people, which fueled his brilliant humor. The lyricist Ogden Nash (1902-1971), beloved for his light verse, had an outstanding gift for rhyming, often inventing rhyme words that were multiple puns. Howard Bay (1912-1986), the luckless scenic designer for the show, went on to design for many more Broadway musicals and dramas, as well as for opera and television. A winner of four Tony Awards for scenic and/or costume design, he served as a longtime president of United Scenic Artists. The costume designers de Mille discusses are Kermit Love (1916–2008), who had collaborated with her on *Rodeo* and who would go on, as a puppeteer, to design for Jerome Robbins, George Balanchine, and Jim Henson, for whose Muppets he perfected the character Big Bird, and Paul Du Pont (1906–1957), who went on to design many plays and several revivals of *Porgy and Bess*, as well as to work as a stage manager and performer. The conductor Maurice Abravanel (1903–1993), a native of Greece from a family of Sephardic Jews, was a boyhood friend of another theatrical conductor, Ernest Ansermet, and, at one point, a music student of Kurt Weill's. "Trude" was the German-born concert pianist and arranger of choral and dance music Trude Rittmann (1909–2005), who worked on the scores of many Broadway classics by Rodgers and Hammerstein, Lerner and Loewe, Irving Berlin, and others, including, with de Mille, *Carousel* and *Brigadoon*. De Mille devoted a chapter of homage to her ("Trude") in *And Promenade Home*, republished in this collection.

A good part of the success of a musical comedy depends, I should say, on three elements: first, a strong skeletal plot line; second, good songs and dialogue; and third, someone who can coordinate all the disparate ingredients—dialogue, singing, dancing, acting, clowning and spectacle. This will not necessarily be a great director, but a man of experience with the ear and eye to maintain style, to balance and to edit. He must know what is possible in his medium and, most important, he must know how to organize the various lines of work, all of which have to proceed simultaneously. He is, in effect, a kind of train master. No one element can succeed without the other two.

A musical comedy begins when composer, lyricist and book writer agree on an idea, or rather, more often, an adaptation of someone else's idea. They compose a series of songs which presumably include two or three smash hits, several funny pieces and, in the case of the most sophisticated authors, a couple of numbers so special that they pertain only to the play on hand. These last are luxury items because, although they undoubtedly heighten the dramatic effect, they cannot be performed indiscriminately on other occasions, and it is in repeated performance on records, television and radio that the big money lies.

By the time three quarters of the songs are written, a producer and a star have been approached and the plot and dialogue will be more or less complete. It is unlikely, however, that the book or play which goes into rehearsal will closely resemble the book that opens in New York. The songs will undergo smaller alterations; metrical verse and music are harder come by and require substantial time in the composing—also, any alterations that involve an orchestra are expensive—just how enormously expensive, I will shortly make clear.

When the show, or at least a hopeful blueprint, is on paper, scene and costume designers, a director, a choreographer and orchestrator are summoned.

Cheryl Crawford, our producer, had assembled what her press agent, Jean Dalrymple, termed "The Brain Trust," top people in each field, Ogden Nash, the best-known light-verse writer in America; S. J. Perelman, a leading humorist; Elia Kazan, the coming director (he had long had a name as an actor with the Group Theatre, and had now directed his first hit, Thornton Wilder's *Skin of Our Teeth*); Mainbocher, the *couturier*; Howard Bay, the scene designer; Kurt Weill, internationally known opera composer and author of two smash Broadway successes, and me. "How can you go wrong?" demanded Crawford complacently, "with these people? Just reading over the list of names makes one begin to chuckle and rub one's hands in anticipation."

But this was the first creative venture in the musical theater for Nash, Kazan, Mainbocher and, with the exception of a revival of *Porgy and Bess*, for Crawford.

Perelman has since described himself as "button-cute, rapier-keen, wafer-thin and pauper-poor." All these epithets were exact except the last. He was charming, brilliant and slender; a slouch made him look thicker. He seemed inadvertent, both hopeful and startled either by what he couldn't believe he was hearing or by what he couldn't believe he was about to say. And his expression alternated between professorial dignity and raffishness. He spoke in a sententious monotone, and there was always a raising of the eyebrows behind the round glasses, an intake of breath and a clearing of the throat as though in preparation for public address or a Noel Coward song. His most casual observation was delivered in rounded periods of incisive misquotation. Through every deliberation his staccato laugh cut like the signal given by deer when alarmed, like the ejaculation of a fencer before the thrust to the heart. "Ha!" he would warn us, roll off a couple of balanced and slightly soiled Addisonian phrases and then lie in ambush behind his glasses. He never failed any occasion. There was always an appropriate cliché which could be rubbed up and have its neck screwed around. Technical discussions and the dialogue of the play were decorated with these wry and disheartening observations. "They broke the mold before they made Perelman," he said.

Ogden Nash appeared quieter and younger (although he was not), like a bashful and nicely reared college boy. He brought in superb lyrics from day to day and seemed happy and surprised if we liked them. The two went around together through our rehearsals like visitors on a vacation, bubbling with curiosity and an enthusiasm which lasted a good three weeks. Unfortunately, first-class light verse and racy irony do not always make effective dialogue nor does all verse sing well. The lyrics of songs are a special art. There is the disturbing fact that no amount of humorous detail strengthens plot.

There are the peculiarities of musical comedy construction, of a piece that must play without pause, with only one interval between the two long acts. For this reason, scenes requiring large sets must alternate with scenes playing at the front of the stage before a curtain or in "One." When the script of *Venus* was handed to designer Howard Bay, the novice playwrights had made no provision for the changing of any sets, no dialogue or songs before the curtain in "One." In perplexity about the practical mechanics of scene changing, Bay suggested a series of arches with curtains that could be rolled up and down (by motor) at any depth on stage. The staff agreed with alacrity.

The plot of the show is hard to remember. It had to do with the coming to life in modern suburbia of an antique statue of Venus. There was a gang of thieves who turned out not altogether reliably to be comedians, and there were several leading men who responded to the Goddess of Love in the expected ways.

In support of the star, Mary Martin, I had engaged two splendid dancers, Sono Osato, of Ballet Russe and Ballet Theatre, and, from the Carnegie Ballet Arts Studio, Diana Adams.

Osato was the happy result of a Japanese father and an Irish mother. With great good fortune, she had been born with a tall slender body and not, as might have been expected, with the low-waisted torso characteristic of the Japanese. She was slim as a houri, and like a houri she danced, although her strong sinews had been trained by Russian ballet masters. Blessed with the figure of a Petty calendar and the manner of a minor deity, she danced secretly with no apparent effort, ivory bones and sleek flesh functioning smooth as an animal's. Her spell lay in her delicate but proud posture, in the sense of antique refinement and the discretion of mouth, in the ceremony of hand and wrist, in the display of torso which seemed to be—how shall I say?—ready. It lay also in the black lightning of mischief and perception that escaped from time to time from her opaque pupils.

Thanks to her fastidiousness, she was able to perform comedy no lesser actress would attempt, managing most wonderfully to be irresistible and outrageous, sensual and funny at the same time.

Wolcott Gibbs was to write in his review in *The New Yorker*: "Sono Osato is a marvelously limber girl of cryptic nationality, who led the dancers and alarmed and fascinated me almost unbearably."

Sono was plain-spoken in six languages and she talked in a flat Omaha voice and took no nonsense from anyone. She was brave and sweet, but she was not stupid. She trusted where she could trust, which, in the theater, is very seldom. This combination of mystery, courage, sportsmanship and magic drove people, I mean men, stark mad. She had just married a handsome young Moroccan, given up touring, and in an attempt at compromise, decided on a Broadway career to help the family budget. Because she was a bride herself, and because she was a dancer, she was able to understand my plight. We had long girl-talks over sodas and sandwiches.

"Oh, Lord, Sono," I said. "I suppose it's important I make a success of this."

"It is," she said, "for all of us."

"But nothing I do seems to have any meaning now except in relation to him. I only see and feel in order to tell him about it later. He's right beside me in the rehearsal hall, and that's funny because he's never seen a rehearsal. I don't see how I can possibly stick it out for two and a half months."

"It's lousy," she answered gently. "I'm lucky that my Pash was rejected. But it's imperative for both of you that you clinch this success. Top *Oklahoma!* and you're fixed for life."

The days weren't too bad. They went along. There were problems right from the first to take my mind off personal matters.

The other soloist, my pupil and protégée, the sixteen-year-old Diana Adams, was working as an Equity chorus girl in *Oklahoma!* at forty-five dollars per week. I asked for her release, offering a solo role, double the salary and real opportunity. I was promptly informed by the management that taking a performer from one of my shows for the benefit of another would be regarded as a form of "incest." My rivals could pick and choose among my discoveries and, quite naturally, they did, recognizing a good thing when they saw one. But I was forbidden to. I must think of the Good of the Show. When professionals talk about the Good of the Show they mean the Good of their end of the Show and it is generally not the dancers who do the talking.

Managements, I noticed, made quite free to transfer their employees from one of their shows to another when it suited them and there was never any inconsequential babbling about incest. At the time, Diana, who was a girl of high conscience and delicacy, was treated as though she had broken with all fine feeling. After three weeks of censor and chivying, her nerves began to give way.

I suggested that if the child was so valuable, a higher salary was in order, maybe even fifty-five dollars per week, and a run-of-the-play contract. But this seemed to be out of the question.

Diana was desperate for opportunity. She and her folks were by no means sure of her gifts. Several times her father took me to tea and begged me with deprecations for advice on the matter, believing there was no point in her continuing unless she had a chance at real success.

She thought she was ugly and this made her shy. As a result, she tended to be overlooked in spite of her height. She was very tall, five feet eight, and when on pointe topped most partners by two or three inches. This can be a disaster and is always a disadvantage, but so impeccable was the child's deportment that there was never a hint of aggression. Her height appeared a yearning up and out rather than a dominating and she seemed strangely most to yield when stating the full expanse of her gesture. She had a waiting face and a cloud of dusky hair that tumbled from her dollar-fifty beret. She looked, as Oscar Hammerstein said, like everyone's younger sister.

But when she took the stage, when the lights were on, behold, there was the huntress, chaste and cruelly strong, every gesture absolute as though there were no possible other gesture. Like a great sea bird, wild and mysterious, she balanced on the exact compass points of definition. Her whole life's effort and hope were hazarded on her skill.

We began rehearsals in the great studio rooms of the American Ballet School, now officially closed for the summer. The heat was overpowering. Sono showed up for rehearsal in the white cotton wrap-around pants and shirt which is the native garment of the Mexican peon, neat, cool and, on her lovely legs, startlingly attractive. Her waist-long, thistle-silk hair was braided Mexican style with colored yarns and her waxen skin glowed amber under the ink-black plaits. The staff, on hand to wish me luck, surveyed her outfit and drew me hastily aside. "You're planning to use this girl quite a lot, aren't you?" they inquired.

"That was my intention."

There were other beauties—Pearl Lang, Nelle Fisher, Allyn McLerie—all young and appealing in their black woolen tights, worn even in August for the practicalities of warm muscles, light sweat and no floor burns. (Diana got free at last after weeks of negotiation—none of us wanted hard feelings—and I composed her a number about adolescent love whose essence was bewilderment, which she performed most touchingly. Her father came to a rehearsal and laid his fears to rest forever.) And, of course, there were some men, good ones—Peter Birch and Robert Pagent—but no one except me paid any attention to them. The staff had eyes only for the white peon pants.

"Maybe we'll have to revise our ideas about ballet dancers," they murmured as I pushed them reluctantly out of the room. They marched off to watch Elia Kazan, who didn't mind the attention. Cheryl Crawford, our lady producer, swung her great leather pouch pocketbook over her shoulder, adjusted her summer seersucker suit, winked at me and stamped out in her sensible shoes. "We've got a winner there, kid," she said in her low even voice. The door closed on what they foresaw would be magic communion with delicious creatures. This was a misapprehension. No dance rehearsal is delicious; not, certainly, in its preliminary stages. I rolled up my sleeves, Sono rolled up her pants, and we got at it.

I was working in a studio instead of on stage because I need privacy and because I prefer sunlight and air to union light, excruciation and migraine. Furthermore, there is no advantage to rehearsing on stage. We may not use sets or any exact props of any kind. If we rehearse with any equipment whatever, even hand props necessary to the dance that will eventually be used in actual production, we have to call not only house heads of departments—head electrician, property man and carpenter—but our own special head stagehands, and these latter, once hired, must be retained for the duration of rehearsals. We work, therefore, with token props, never anything of the exact weight, shape, size, or material.

We began, accordingly, in a studio, more or less in privacy, without props and with only space approximations marked out on the floor. The respacing of dancers to the actual sets and props would be one of the grueling jobs waiting for us in the out-of-town dress rehearsal. If we were lucky, we would be allotted before curtain two hours of uninterrupted stage time in which to make all necessary choreographic adjustments.

Kurt Weill, the composer, sat at the piano, bright eyes gleaming behind thick glasses. Maurice Abravanel, the conductor, sat beside him. Weill had composed a stunning six-minute bacchanal which they now played for the cast four-handed. It was a grand encouragement and it is the only show music of any development or length that has ever been handed me at rehearsal's start; we usually have to put our feet forward to nothing but the bare melody. This piece was, in Weill's opinion, the finest orchestral composition he had turned out since he had come to America from Germany, on a par with his great early work, *The Three-Penny Opera, Mahagonny.*

I always thought this gentle-voiced little German suggested a gnome from a Grimm fairy tale. He was short, with a head unnaturally large in proportion to his body, and his balding skull and glittering eyes behind thick double lenses gave him a slightly underwater appearance. His smile was sudden. He seemed to peer through decorum and lean against every idea as though he were pressing his mind to the windowpane of thought. But his intelligence was so apt, his knowledge so wide, that one was flattered if a trifle abashed. He had a wry sense of humor and viewed all matters, even his own music, with sardonic appraisal. Weill was one of the very few who did his own orchestrations and he used to score in the rehearsal room and later in the theater through the chaos of shouting, counting, orchestral reading and rows. He never faltered; his concentration was absolute. He composed on the back of the Steinway, standing up, or sitting in an empty box, inking in freehand the nineteen staves of the conductor's sheets. He composed and orchestrated in ink because he made no mistakes. What's more, he was always aware of everything going on in rehearsal around him, whether musical, scenic, vocal, choreographic, or emotional.

Weill insisted on being part of the active workshop. At first, as a matter of course, I begged him to leave, according to my morbid custom, but he was so sympathetic, so wise and experienced, that I soon got over my terror and became grateful for his help. He stood quietly at the piano, his back to the mirror, eyes gleaming behind his thick glasses, and when he spoke, it was with the authority of a doctor. Trude had the keyboard now and kept it for the duration. Weill came and went, for he had also to supervise the rest of the score and all the songs in another theater.

We blocked through two ballets in a week and then our star, Mary Martin, was ushered in to be placed and taught her role. She was just back from

Hollywood and looked like the Sugarplum Fairy, a pretty, rather unimposing Southwestern girl with a straight body and a flat Texan voice as carrying as someone calling cows, almost unsexed like a choir boy's, of trumpet clarity. Whenever she spoke or sang, there was a sense of distance, and that is why, I think, she could later sing beside opera voices like Ezio Pinza's and hold her own.

Hollywood had just finished glamouring her up. The Western experts had curled and fluffed her hair, covered her with ruffles and ribbons, hidden her long neck under froufrou, persuaded her to wear enormous heels for height and sexiness, taught her to dip her knees and slouch for grace, and to purse her lips and to pout for humor.

When she came to rehearse, she was extremely nervous and shy. It is no easy thing, whatever one's reputation, to walk into a room full of professional dancers, many of them soloists with the great companies. Miss Martin was accompanied by her husband, Richard Halliday, and she wore a special little rehearsal suit, a sort of romper that showed off her lovely unmuscled legs. She had taken off her spike heels and now paddled across the floor childishly in flat ballet slippers. She was irresistibly charming. She was sweet and eager and dear and pretty and she was a very real problem. She couldn't walk. She walked like Miss Atlantic City 1927. She couldn't stand. She couldn't raise an arm simply or directly. She could do all these things to please and catch the eye of Daddy but not, I felt, of Jupiter Omnipotens.

The next day she literally couldn't walk because she could not put her heels to the floor; having worn high heels for so long, her Achilles' tendon had shrunk. She limped for a week, but she was hellbent on continuing. It was her husband who forbade further practice except in heels. He didn't want her opening in a wheelchair.

Our black-woo. led athletes regarded her with interest and speculation. She had to take her place in front of them, dominate and lead them. None of us were fools—least of all our star.

"I'm not very good at this," said Miss Martin to me simply as she put on her beautiful costly hat before leaving that first day. "I'm going to need lots of help."

Sono and I looked at each other over a soda at the end of the rehearsal. I was disheartened.

Sono spoke crisply. "I've made a decision. I'm going to be a gentleman. I could dance, I could move so that Miss Martin would look very poorly. Why, my God, we've spent our lives learning just how to walk across a stage! But what good would that do? I'm going to fix it so that she looks better than all of us. I'm not going to be an ass, of course, and dance down, but I'm going to help her if she'll let me. Do you think she'd mind if I coached her a little?"

Over my chocolate malted, I gazed at Osato with something close to awe. Sono had spent her teens with the Ballet Russe de Monte Carlo. "Sonotchka," as her colleagues called her, had learned theater entirely with the Russian dancers, whose second technique is chicanery. They expect nothing else and they give nothing else. From the outright criminal compassing of planned accidents (broken glass and slashed slipper ribbons) to constant ungrounded suspicion, they never, under any circumstances, practice anything but deviousness. Trust and mutual help occur only in emergencies. They do occur then, I must admit, and as these are chronic, the companies often present to the casual eye the aspect of hearty camaraderie, but this impression is inadvertent and against intention. Sono, however, was gallant and, as she said, a gentleman.

So she approached Mary Martin and the coaching began very gently and unobtrusively.

"Why do you stand like that," said Sono, so honestly and decently that Mary, who was equally honest, could not fail to accept the question as a disinterested challenge, "with your knees all slack and your chest caved in?"

"They told me to in Hollywood," said our star meekly.

"Never mind Hollywood. This is Olympus. My goodness," Sono said, "you've got a fine body. Be proud of it. Throw out your chest—and here, tuck your tail in. Stand on your feet. Put your heels down and stand hard. Be proud."

"I can see you're right," said Mary, gazing in surprise in the mirror. "I wish I could move the way you do."

"You're going to move like yourself," said Osato, "and it will be dandy. But you've got to have confidence."

And thereafter every day I could see, from the corner of my eye, Sono take her quietly aside to work out their problems. Mary straightened, Mary walked and stood like a deity, and it didn't take her very long to learn. Beside her were five veterans of the Ballet Russe, two future leading ladies and one future prima ballerina, standing and walking right beside her, and she did, as Sono had promised, dandy. Mary has never scorned coaching since. Today she dances creditably and moves with real authority, freedom and expression.

Great theater figures of various categories differ widely, but they all have this in common: they do not tire, they do not flinch, they never give up, and they never become discouraged, or if they do, like Martha Graham, they never tell.

Some stars acquire what they know by instinct, some by paying attention. The latter, I believe, was Mary Martin's method. She might be called the Great

Learner. No one ever said anything useful to her twice. She was pretty always; she took advice: she invented a style. She found the man to dress her and now is one of the world's fashion leaders. If she crops her hair close, as in *South Pacific* (and at the time this was without precedent except in cases of typhoid), a whole generation of women do likewise.

Mary epitomizes the average American girl, her gusto and unlimited force being her only startling characteristic—and her enormous skill (but this is hidden and not apparent). She seems like anybody's sweetheart, just usual folks. And as there is a legend that any mother's boy can become President, so Mary seems to prove that any man's sister or cousin can become an International Star, and everyone's bosom swells with vicarious pride. She appeals straight to good sense and liking. She is neither mysterious, nor unfathomable, nor dangerous, nor maddening. She is effective, and whatever she plans to do she succeeds at with bull's-eye proficiency. Behind this knack is intellectual and emotional machinery as intricate as a Packard motor—and a life of dedication and of undeviating service shared by her husband, Richard Halliday, and now lately, to some extent, by her daughter Heller. Together, they plan every move; together, they try to sense whether it is right for Mary or not; together, they succeed.

As she studies a new role, absolutely no nerve is spared, and the whole family bends its efforts to the cause. The whole family usually triumphs. It is a composite effort, but Mary carries the flag and her arm never falters.

When Mary knew her part in the dance we showed it to the company and she proudly displayed the considerable amount she had learned in one week. We then repaired to her hotel suite, where Lotte Lenya, the great *chanteuse* (Mrs. Kurt Weill), discussed singing techniques. Mary listened to all carefully. Mary continued to profit. Mainbocher discussed costumes. He had just finished dressing the female members of our Navy, the WAVES, to look as though history and not he had designed the cut of their coats, and he had been chosen by our producers for the dissimilar but equally tricky task of making a Hollywood star look like a divinity whom men still do not wholly disbelieve in. He attacked the problem drastically. He peeled everything off little Miss Martin—curls, bows, ginghams, flowers. He cut classic gowns in classic materials. He bared the wonderful long throat and, contrary to Hollywood's doubts, advertised it by lifting her hair away neat and high and by tying a small ribbon about it. The fine little skull balanced on the wand of her neck with nobility. He gave her a back which is strong as a boy's and flawless, and he gave her lovely free arms, the trim waist, the hips and the fine legs, the sprightly and elegant figure we know now as Mary.

Mary's five Mainbocher costumes cost ten thousand dollars, and there were additional charges for suggestions and corrections for other clothes in the show. But they were worth every penny, and although the backers may have opened their eyes at this time on the statement, what they bought for the sum was a new star, Mary Martin, and an overall style. This show could well have been tacky; it had, as it turned out, great chic.

After two weeks came the first run-through—always an evening of horror. Here were the numbers unshelled, out of the protection of the studio and the studio atmosphere and placed as they must be in the middle of dialogue and songs and jokes—all their values altered, before a jury with special powers of life and death. It is invariable on these occasions that the authors discover that they have furnished too much material and that, consequently, the dances must be cut. This is axiomatic and the dancers and choreographers expect it.

To this run-through came as expert witness Moss Hart, who had, with Kurt Weill, created the prodigiously successful *Lady in the Dark*. He didn't think Diana's pretty dance had anything to do with the plot and he was, unfortunately, quite right. Kazan had thought so too, and besides, he had never understood it. He could not see why adolescent love should be in any way bewildered. Sex, he said, was gay and confident. (It is since this conversation about gay and confident sex that he has devoted his strength with such distinguished effect to *Streetcar Named Desire*, *Cat on a Hot Tin Roof*, *Camino Real*, *Flight into Egypt* and *Baby Doll*.) So five minutes after it had been seen for the first time on stage, the dance was out of the show.

"How shall I tell Diana?" I asked.

"Oh, she's strong," said Kazan. "Don't pity her. She's got real talent. Don't underestimate her strength. Treat her like an artist."

She learned the news, of course, immediately somehow, and before I could find her, disappeared. I went all over the empty theater hunting and crying her name. Finally, sticking out from under a low wooden platform on the darkened stage, I saw the sole of a foot. I pulled on the ankle. She was crying silently. I hauled her out by the legs, and she lay, dust-covered, sweaty and weeping, in my arms. I remember men were loading in cables and electronic equipment past us. I sat on the floor and tried to tell her it was not very important, that Kazan was right, that she was young and very gifted. She wept without answering. Behind her disappointment lay eight years of daily practicing, no games after school, and history and English learned under hanging practice clothes in a dressing room that smelled of sweat and old malted milks, and a young back, weary every night when it went to bed with a weariness like old age. Behind it lay the fear that if she didn't justify herself quickly, the family could not continue the expenses of her career. Behind it lay the fear that if she didn't hurry, she'd never make the grade: a ballerina must be well on her way by twenty.

I got her to wash her face and took her out to tea. She rehearsed her chorus bits the next day like a veteran and the matter of her solo was never mentioned again between us. Although she lost her dance, I had the consolation of knowing she was doing her chorus work at double the salary she had earned in *Oklahoma!*

Diana Adams is now one of the ranking ballerinas with the New York City Center Ballet, an internationally known figure—but only after years of penury and effort. Diana made good. I can name you three with equal talents who have not.

After that run-through Kazan took me aside. "You don't appreciate Sono."

"I don't what?" I gasped in blank incredulity.

"You're not using her enough. The authors want more of her. They've made a place for a solo dance and another bit."

They had, it seemed. They had asked for more dancing, a demand unique in my theater experience.

Our producer, Cheryl Crawford, was sorry about Diana and glad about Sono but unwilling to go against the men in anything and worried about money, an attitude characteristic of her trade. A producer's occupation is one of unrelenting stress, the rewards uncertain, and the creative satisfaction intermittent. Smash hits pay off handsomely; failures net absolutely nothing in return for considerable outlay of time and worry. And always one does business inside a cage where it is unwise to turn one's back on any of the performers. The terrible wear and tear would seem to unfit the job for a woman except that two of the requirements are tact and patience and these women are apt to have. Crawford added another of her own, humor. She also proved, as rehearsals progressed, steadfast and kind, but she seemed determined to persuade all business associates that she was nothing of the sort, apparently wishing to be thought a woman of iron with decisions as irrevocable and fearsome as edicts from the Supreme Court. From her manner, one would suppose that she lived in a house with solid brick furniture. She wore square-cut suits of durable tweed, or, in summer, unmodified seersucker. Her hair went straight back and no nonsense. Glasses unsuccessfully screened off her piercing eyes. Her voice was a controlled soft baritone, her speech laconic.

Actually she proved, on acquaintance, to be everything she strove so hard to belie. She was vague, girlish, giggly and changeable, and because she must have been aware of all this and considered it weakness, at least in her field of operations, she usually entrenched herself behind a business manager of formidable habits and vague scruples. These remarkable associates were given their head until stopped by Cheryl's conscience.

Mary's clothes were, thank God, Mainbocher's concern. The rest of the costumes were designed by two men, Paul and Kermit. Paul did the bulk of the show, but for the ballet costumes I demanded Kermit, having a great admiration for the *Rodeo* costumes which he had designed for me the previous year.

He was a long slender creature of indeterminate age, sandy hair cut *à la brosse*, a moon countenance with a long chin, a small precise mouth, thick nose, and expectant bright eyes browless and behind glasses. His voice stayed high with constant excitement and seemed to wail even when expressing pleasure or enthusiasm. His manner was amiable and mollifying. He had an amusing gift for mimicry, always, however, an octave in alt, and nothing about him could be predicted but uncertainty. He was gone like the morning dews when needed. He appeared regularly and conscientiously at all appointments not his own. His promises were heartwarming, his views of his capacities unlimited, likewise his willingness to undertake everything mentioned, his tendency to disappear thereafter reliable.

He had a diffuse and watery charm, a character transparent in the sense that it was invisible. There was an iridescent sheen of manner but no discernible form. You knew something was there because of the reflection of humor, but you were damned if you knew what; uncertainty or absence had filmed over the impression. The Dusty Wraith the scene executant called him. During the *Rodeo* preparations I had learned that patience with him paid off, for in the end, his costumes turned out to be works of art.

The other designer's work I was not familiar with.

"But then you realize, my dear," said Kermit with the liveliest enthusiasm, "he's copying everything out of *Harper's Bazaar*! Everything, my dear!"

"Oh—surely not."

"Yes, I swear. He hasn't done one dress himself—except—but they're hideous!" His voice reached treble with sensuous excitement in this tribute to his colleague. "And let me tell you about the direction—" He proceeded to outline what he thought were Kazan's morning mistakes. He worried about the casting and the musical arrangements. He worried a lot about me. He was always present, interested, noticing, advising and fretting.

"Kermit," I said, beginning to be rather worried myself, "how is your work coming along? Who is supervising the execution of your costumes?"

"Being done. Being done!" he sang. "No cause for alarm. And, my dear, they're lovely. But when I see what Paul is up to and when I realize how his things are going to hurt your wonderful work, my heart breaks."

The authors and director were also getting a little nervous about his constant prowling. "Dammit," said Kazan, "has the man nothing to do? If I throw him out again, it will be out of the show." And, indeed, Kermit's behavior was unusual. Costume designers barely get a production ready in their allocated span, working sixteen hours a day.

I finally insisted on seeing with my own eyes. So I was reluctantly summoned to Eaves' costume house. Kermit chose to model the satyr's outfit himself. He stood on a podium under a spotlight surrounded by mirrors and his glasses winked joyously. He was a very pleased exhibitor.

"Not many people have seen my legs. They're good, aren't they?"

It wasn't the legs that held my attention.

"Kermit," I said, "I'm shocked."

"Oh, my dear, no! Not really! Do you mean it?" He became as gravely solicitous and respectful as a drugstore clerk selling an unmentionable. "You see, I've emphasized all the virile parts of the male body with dark plush to simulate hair. I think it's very strong."

"It does give an unusual piebald effect, but I think it's also pornographic."

"Oh, my dear, I do so hope not."

"Possibly I'm naïve. Let's ask Sono. She's cosmopolitan."

Sono stopped as though struck. "Oh, no, Kermit, certainly not. Take it off. Those things! Those things! Have you lost your mind?"

"Are you girls quite sure?" said Kermit, turning wistfully in front of the glass. "I thought we really had something here. And it was difficult to sew!"

"Kermit," I said as kindly as I could, "don't strain so hard. The less a dancer wears, the better. Just let's have plain bare arms and legs and the trunk as bare as the law permits. Let's not try to reinforce them sexually. They do very nicely let alone."

"Oh, dear!" said Kermit. His glasses had misted opaque and he ran a tender hand over the strong plush.

"There, there now! I'll go see Sono in the dress Paul has fixed for her."

"You won't like that, I can tell you," said Kermit, his spirits rising immediately.

Alas, he was right. Paul had turned Hebe into a fat frump. And our Sonotchka looked at us ruefully over a mass of wrinkled velvet, every line in her beautiful body cut and obscured.

"You know, Sono," I said musingly, "there won't be a costume ready for opening night in Boston?"

"Here's a nymph," said Kermit, thrusting Ann into our curtained enclosure.

"Now, isn't she lovely? You see, she doesn't look like anything at all you've seen before. Quite unworldly. Where you'd expect a breast, there is just sea foam. Extraordinary! You didn't like Sono's dress, did you?" he whispered in a piercing parenthesis sibilant with satisfaction. "I wanted to warn you about that. But I thought it would be better to let you all see for yourselves."

"About the nymph, Kermit. There seem to be breasts under her arms and on her back too."

"That's the mysterious part. But as she dances, you won't know where they are. The spangles will make just a film of light, sea spume, or cloud iridescence. You wouldn't want ordinary anatomy on nymphs, surely!"

"What I want—" my voice rose a fraction—"what I want is to see the dances for what they are. I don't want you to put spangles where the boys have to place their hands for lifts or you'll cut the flesh off their fingers."

Kermit put down the scissors and gazed fixedly out the window.

"I simply will not be banal. Nobody can make me be." He threw down the scissors and retired in dignified misery behind the screen.

Paul's costumes were all finished in time, but they presented difficulties. Part of the dramatic point as well as the rhythmic accompaniment of "40 Minutes for Lunch" was nervous finger snapping. He put the entire cast in gloves, long gray velvet ones on the girls at forty dollars a pair, thereby rendering all finger work inaudible, snapping or clapping. The boys were in Madison Avenue suits of green and rust red and lavender.

Kermit always tried to do what was inventive and original, experiments that required a great deal of time and effort, and the successful costumes were fine, but so many of them seemed to remain unfinished. The good ones, we kept reminding ourselves, were the reason we'd hired him. Everyone worried a lot. Oh, we did a peck of worrying.

Throughout all this, a never-failing source of strength was Elia Kazan, who, notwithstanding his inexperience in musicals, brought humor, zest and insight to every situation, and a sense of command which made these ridiculous disturbances bearable. I fought him off my work, as I did everyone, at the start. He later told me that when he entered the theater or rehearsal hall, he could see from across the auditorium all the muscles of my shoulders and neck tighten as I withdrew inside my core. But he teased me out; he treated my work with tenderness and respect. He was not so polite about the book, which was his special province. The authors complained, with some reason, that he distorted their intention.

"Their plot!" he moaned with his head on my shoulder. "Their plot! They have asked me to study their character development! Oh, my God!" and he leaned, rocking with laughter, against the walls of the outer lobby and wiped tears from his eyes.

This was not quite fair. The plot was, as Ogden Nash said, as substantial as *Puss in Boots*. They wanted style and fantasy. Style is a very tricky business, and the realistic method of the Actor's Studio, in which Kazan had trained, proved no help. Our particular brand of nonsense needed a technique as developed and ritualistic as Noh dancing. The authors, nonetheless, behaved like gentlemen, and were friendly throughout. Kazan had said at the start that he saw no reason for confusion; there was none in the nonmusical theater. He kept repeating the opinion for quite some days. Confusion and terror, however, mounted steadily throughout the rehearsal period according to tradition.

It must be remembered that musical comedy is not an art form but a compendium of many art forms, collected and smashed into pattern during rehearsal. {A real synthesis of the ingredients has since been attempted with only partial success in Rodgers and Hammerstein's *Allegro*, with more notable results in the Robbins-Bernstein-Laurents *West Side Story*.} The work is largely improvisation on the spot. There are no known recipes for success and when those that have proved most useful are copied, the resulting form seems stale. Work proceeds, therefore, freely, in anguish, doubt, foreboding and conflict, with lighter moments of true creative inspiration and recurrent bouts of hope.

One Wednesday at 2 P.M. the cast met at Grand Central at Gate 51 and entrained for Boston and the tryout period. They left gay and hopeful—in spite of history, they were hopeful. The staff was, as was fitting, riddled with apprehension.

Cheryl Crawford and Kazan, who had preceded us by two days, were finishing their early dinner in the Ritz dining room when I found them.

"Well, rest easy on one score," said Cheryl. "We've seen the sets and they're fine. In good taste, beautifully built. They're very successful."

Kazan nodded agreement.

"Thank God," I breathed, and sinking down before my roast beef, I ate with a quiet stomach for the first time in ten days.

Most of the scenery in any show is designed for purposes quite outside dancing and the ballets are fitted into limited floor space, broken levels, furniture and props which may aid book scenes and songs but provide real hurdles to movement. The same applies to the costumes. The difficulties cannot always be corrected. Very few professionals and no layman can diagnose the precise reason a number fails to make effect. It may lie in the size of the floor, in the lighting, in the cut of the coats, in their color, in the color of the background, in the placement of the dance within the act, in its length or shortness, in the orchestration, even in the rhythmic sequence and duration of the final chords, in tempo (every conductor holds the dancers' and choreographer's fate in his right hand). It may also very well be that the choreography is poor. Even directors do not always know where the trouble lies. But the dance stands or falls on its audience effect and the choreographer must diagnose and correct immediately or his work will be scrapped no matter what the reason. {The ballets are always lit last because the singers and actors have to go home to rest. It has happened, not once but several times, that when all else was done and the turn allotted to the ballet finally arrived, time was up and the electricians walked off the controls and went to bed themselves. Many dance numbers have been premièred without a light cue of any kind.}

So the news about the sets was to me good news. Kazan and Crawford went off for a dialogue rehearsal. Trude and I repaired hopefully to the Shubert, where we were to open forty-eight hours later. We entered together at the back of the auditorium and walked down the aisle and there we stopped stock-still. In the single naked watch light there was revealed the permanent masking frame of the play behind which the painted drop would be slipped. This frame was composed of a series of gray velvet arches, extending back like a dark subway tunnel, from which hung cobwebs and frills of velvet looped in a kind of mortuary-parlor elegance. These curtains were run by motors and could be dropped at any depth on stage. They were Bay's solution to the authors' failure to invent any cover for scene changes. Whatever the backdrop, these would never be removed. I thought of my nymphs lifted against the stars and peering up into those drab and dirty-looking skirts. I thought of the hurrying crowds in "40 Minutes for Lunch" rushing about under shawls instead of blue New York weather.

"We are lost," I said.

Trude set her lips and marched down to the piano. She slipped into the pit and tried to adjust a light for herself.

"Try to work, Aggie. We face the other problem later."

"I can't work. This is defeat. What is the use of all we've tried to do? This is pompous and permanent. We cannot for one minute get the impression of fresh air and sky."

"Have a try at Sono's dance. Plainly they must fix the set. That is obvious. Now, how would it be if we started like this? The piano is not precisely in tune either. And the orchestra coming in at nine tomorrow morning! What are they thinking of? Stop looking at the stage. It will do you no good. Do you like this rhythm? Or not? I don't like it myself, come to think of it. I dish something better." She tore up the paper. I dove to retrieve the pieces and we were off!

They found me rehearsing steps between the seats and up and down the aisle when they came in at midnight to resume lighting. Trude was asleep, sitting at the keyboard with her head on her folded arms. Her glasses and the new piece rested at her side.

They came in force, the entire staff, and sat down in a group. The designer switched on his talk-back box and the crew climbed into position, on ladders, catwalks and in the balcony.

The lighting rehearsal resumed. As each scene was revealed, the staff sank lower in its chairs. There was no sound of applause or comment. After a bit, Nash and Perelman and their wives moved to the other side of the house. Kurt Weill and his wife, Lotte Lenya, joined them shortly, then I. Kermit roved the background, wringing his hands and moaning and rolling his eyes to heaven behind his glasses. Halfway between the camps sat Mainbocher, silent in his smart gray raincoat, looking with a sort of benign incredulity at the spectacle before him.

These sets were exactly what had been approved in sketch. The designer had made no alterations. But few people in the theater have the gift of visualization. Naturally Bay was surprised and hurt that we were surprised. There had been no secrets. In the face of our cold disappointment he struggled to bring order from backstage chaos and get the lighting charted. It is a tedious and slow process and therefore our hopes did not crush; they slid downwards ponderously for three hours.

Then we came to the ballet. I put my head in my hands. Here I knew I was partly to blame, for, although I had not liked his original sketch and had said so, I had not been able to give him specific suggestions. Not knowing what else to do, he had gone ahead and executed it. Perelman jumped up and spoke for me.

"Look here. Do you think this has anything to do with the choreographer's intentions? Do you think this helps her work?"

Kurt Weill was on his feet also. "None of this will do. This is disaster. Plainly and simply disaster."

Nash rose. "I'm a mild agreeable sort of fellow usually, but I think we might as well not open."

Then Kazan, who remained seated, spoke firmly, forcefully and with the voice of complete authority. "We open. We open tomorrow night and with the scenery because that is all we have. We know that it is not all in order.

Corrections will be made later. Now, I suggest you all leave and let us get on with our work."

We left in a body. Kazan, Crawford, designer Howard Bay and the crew maintained the death watch. We walked, muttering and exclaiming, along Boston Common (it was now two o'clock) to Childs' and had coffee.

"You do realize, don't you," said Weill, "that this is just plainly catastrophe—two years' work thrown away?"

We all nodded. We realized. We walked on to the Ritz and got into the elevator. Kurt raised his hand.

"Look, friends, we're deserting. Back to the theater."

We returned. This time in taxis, posthaste. Nobody's head turned as we entered. We continued to sit in a small clump on one side of the house, quiet now with despair. At eight o'clock in the morning (a lovely September day) we went home. The musicians came in at nine.

Later that day we had dress rehearsal. The rehearsals for the past few days had been mounting steadily in nerve tension, hubbub and confusion. The last two weeks of any musical are a hell of conflicting disturbances—book rehearsals are undermined by music consultations and music rehearsals by costume conferences. Everyone stamps in and out of dance rehearsals talking—mainly about possible cuts. But hardly anyone seems to think silence might be a help.

Singers, for instance, always arrive for work in full cry and their approach can be heard corridors away as they enter any situation full of head resonance, breakfast and gossip. So firmly have they come to identify sound with working effort that they cannot bring themselves to believe that thinking is sometimes done quietly. When attention is diverted from them for one second, they hum, chew, stroll, chatter and munch.

Dancers are quiet partly because they have little breath to squander, but mainly because all their training has been in group work and by imitation and rote; and under these conditions, silence is rewarding. Unique among theater people, they respect other artists' working efforts, an appreciation they have learned from having to stand by during actual creative spasm.

When to the usual rehearsal distraction is added the cacophony and uproar of instruments and their owners, nerves really stand still. Notwithstanding, this must be the moment of our major effort. Once the pitmen are with us, any change in the show is preluded by full orchestral cooperation. Of all the theater workers, the musicians are the noisiest, and I don't mean by virtue of their art. Twenty minutes before any rehearsal they have to build the pit and furnish it, moving chairs and pianos, and even commandeering the boxes when necessary. Also, they have to test every instrument to see if it still works, and they sort out an entire music library. This is necessary. But due to various union restrictions, we are forced to overlap our rehearsals and compose and invent through chaos, until the baton is raised. The musicians' time is bought in blocks of an hour, and a ten-minute delay is prohibitively expensive. A prolongation or stretch for anything under an hour (or one hundred and sixteen dollars) is not allowable.

The last half hour of our final preparation for any orchestra rehearsal will therefore be in pandemonium. Sometimes the fire curtain is lowered to help us. But an English horn makes itself known even through asbestos; besides, the carpenters and electricians, with the sounds appropriate to their trades, are walled up on our side.

All dress rehearsals begin alike. The theater is dark and it is, for a blessed wonder, at least quiet. The pit is full of silently attentive musicians. In the front three rows sit arrangers and usually orchestrators. Unseen before this moment and usually unseen again, they live holed up in some hotel suite working around the clock and ghosting for one another in a tacitly admitted anonymity. Only one man's name will be on the score; but the work may represent a compendium of the best talent in the country. During the *Venus* rehearsal Weill himself is in the stage box scoring the finale and in the front row are the music copiers and their piles of new sheets ink-wet. Midway in the orchestra, seated at a desk with telephone and two-way talking box, works Bay in direct constant communication with the stage manager, the spotlight booth and the backstage switchboard, where four or five electricians are manning the 268 levers and where the head electrician reads from his notes and briefs the men on the catwalks and up in the flies. They are all wired for sound. Close beside Bay sits Kazan and Crawford. Weill finishes and goes to the back of the auditorium where he can hear a balanced sound from the orchestra and voices. This will not be exact because a full audience will change all the acoustics, but he knows how to correct for the difference. He will instruct the stage manager which of the singers to amplify on the overall sound system. He will edit on the spot orchestration for audibility of speech and vocal balance. The authors and their wives sit quietly in a cluster midway. I am seated on the tops of the seat backs, my legs stretched out before me. This gives me a good vantage point and makes it easy for me to run in any direction quickly. Beside me is the dance captain with a notebook and a flashlight. Trude is in the front row, hanging over the pit rail, conferring with conductor, copier and musicians. She runs up and down the front row, jumping over piles of music to check mistakes at each desk.

Kermit and Paul and the Eaves costume executants sit near an exit where relays of seamstresses and tailors can shuttle conveniently between them and the backstage army of dressers. The cast, as they are ready, take places in costume and make-up in the empty seats. And this is the last time that any member of the cast will be permitted to see the show from the front.

A new unknown group of men, scene shifters and grips, now take over, the crew in whose hands the entire well-being of the production rests. They have not seen the play, and the actors have never seen them. The stage manager captains all. He knows who they are—we don't. He gives them orders—we don't. Not even author or producer or director or theater owner can speak on the other side of the proscenium arch. The stage manager takes and transmits orders from the staff in front; backstage his power is absolute.

Everyone, front and back, holds a stop watch. There will be no halting for anything except technical production matters. We, the show people, are supposed to be perfect. This rehearsal is for the mechanics and technicians.

The lights go down. The house curtain goes up, revealing the specially designed show curtain. The boys and girls, sitting with their arms around one another and their feet up over the backs of the seats ahead, applaud and snuggle excitedly, that is, they usually do. The *Venus* group is unhappily not very responsive. The orchestra starts on the temporary overture; there will be another and presumably better one written before the New York opening when it is discovered just which songs must be dropped and which are likely to be hits. Everyone looks at his stop watch and makes a note. Bay's voice is heard droning monotonously over the telephone. "Bring up the blue balcony rail to five. Take down your pinks. Take them out. Take the first pipe Fresnels to two. What's the matter with the Fresnel on the first boom? It's winking. Peter, get a ladder and fix that. I said the blue balcony rail down to five."

The assistant stage manager appears at the entrance behind the boxes and signals. "Company on stage for the opening."

Abravanel lifts his baton.

This is the moment of transfiguration. This, only theater can give. Close to fifteen hundred people have been working all over New York City in separate workshops, without checking or comparing or testing, never knowing their collaborators or understanding the plan or even the purpose of their work, and within this hour the groups come together, the purpose becomes distinct and effective. A show emerges.

The real professional knows nothing better. It is our wine and bread and comfort. It is our time of power.

We had better savor it, for within two hours this theater will become an arena wherein will assemble fellow professionals who have gone to the most remarkable trouble to judge their colleagues' work in an unfinished state. They will come with no thought of mercy. (70–99)

Fall River Legend (Agnes de Mille)
(Excerpts from Lizzie Borden: A Dance of Death)

At least since the tragedies of Aeschylus, the willingness of a creative artist to explore characters capable of monstrous acts has served as the definition of the very greatest dramatic art, or, at least, of the greatness of an artist's ambitions. During the 1940s, two female choreographers took up the challenge: Martha Graham, in the 1946 *Cave of the Heart*, a ballet about Medea's murders of her children and her husband's new young bride, and Agnes de Mille, in the 1948 *Fall River Legend*, a ballet about the historical Lizzie Borden's murders of her parents. Both works have also provided juicy leading roles: Graham, herself, performed Medea to acclaim, and subsequently Yuriko (Kikuchi), Takako Asakawa, and Fang-Yi Sheu have also triumphed in the part. At Ballet Theatre, Nora Kaye and Sallie Wilson were de Mille's own favorite Lizzies, and Cynthia Gregory and Alessandra Ferri won audiences, too. As de Mille's biographer, Carol Easton, notes, de Mille was also a fan of Virginia Johnson's Lizzie at the Dance Theatre of Harlem.

Although the actual jury at Borden's trial acquitted Lizzie Borden, de Mille doesn't let her off the hook: in *Fall River Legend*, the murderess is hanged. Even so, de Mille went to great lengths to clarify what she saw as Borden's understandable motives for the murders, not only on stage but also on the page, in an eye-popping book of research and interpretation, entitled *Lizzie Borden: A Dance of Death*. At the time of its 1968 publication, Easton relates, this volume was so controversial that the *New York Times* killed the review, owing to the reviewer's invective. Of course, audiences of the 1960s had already been shocked by writers (Truman Capote's *In Cold Blood*, 1965) and filmmakers (Alfred Hitchcock's *Psycho*, 1960; Jean-Luc Godard's *Weekend*, 1967), as well as by many violent real-life assassinations, wars, and genocides. And *Fall River Legend* had been in repertory so long that it was practically old hat. (Indeed, some dance critics find it to be derivative of Antony Tudor's 1942

Ballet Theatre hit *Pillar of Fire*.) However, de Mille's writing, debatably even more powerful than her dramaturgy, touched a nerve—especially, perhaps, her attempts to comprehend oedipal violence.

Below are several excerpts that give a sense of what might have been (and might continue to be) alarming to some readers. Whatever your impression, there is no question that, with the ballet and the book, de Mille—who maintained close and loving relationships with each of her parents, even after their divorce—proved that she had gone way, way past her girlhood unhappiness at being deemed insufficiently pretty for the theater. Edward Weeks (c. 1897–1989), who is discussed in the preface, was de Mille's empathetic longtime book editor at the Atlantic Monthly Press/Little, Brown; Weeks's tenure as editor of the *Atlantic Monthly* (1938–1966) was the longest in the magazine's history. Edward Brewster Sheldon (1886–1946), who gave de Mille the idea for her Lizzie Borden ballet, was a successful dramatist during his twenties—many of his plays were made into feature films, with such stars as Greta Garbo—but rheumatoid arthritis crippled him and compromised his sight during his thirties, and he had to give up writing, serving instead as an unpaid consultant to many theatrical luminaries.

Preface

There are two themes in this book; the meaning of each derives from the other; together they spell out the process of emotional discovery inherent in the making of any work of art. In this case, it was a theater piece, a tragic mime. The choreographer was bound to learn unsuspected and dubious aspects of her own character, and to establish strange relationships with her collaborators. This is true of any work, but in the theater these discoveries are made in public and in concentrated time. For this reason the experience, while instructive, is often punishing. Nevertheless the difficulty encountered in translating the crime into a ballet was as nothing compared to the bafflement in changing the ballet back to a prose story.

The plan for the book was suggested by Edward Weeks, who persisted in hoping that the form would clarify long after the author despaired. He persisted, one might say, with New England fortitude. It is a fact that Mr. Weeks comes from New Jersey, but he lives and works in Boston. In any case, he has grown adept at hardening the sinews of weak and faltering clients. The writer cannot exaggerate her debt to him, and her gratitude is as profound as it is astonished and admiring.

"The Challenge"

It was Edward Sheldon who first brought the dark matter to my attention, Sheldon, lying blind and paralyzed in his New York penthouse.

To his couch, set high like a catafalque in the large living room above the New York skyline, came hundreds as to royalty. An hierarchic still figure, waxen and shiny-skinned, masked and blanketed in brocade, he received and counseled the creative, the searching, the ambitious, the learned, the godly, and very often the bewildered and distressed. Playwrights brought their scripts for help in construction (he had been a playwright: *The Nigger*; Mrs. Fiske's vehicle *Salvation Nell*; *Romance*, in which Doris Keane and Greta Garbo starred); novelists brought their books for advice; actresses begged at his bedside for the help of his infallible instinct and wonderful ear; composers tried out new scores on the grand piano in the corner. To all he was first audience and discerning enthusiast: Otis Skinner, Charles MacArthur, Ruth Draper, Anne Morrow Lindbergh, Helen Hayes, Ruth Gordon, Katherine Cornell, Thornton Wilder, Alexander Woollcott, Franklin P. Adams, Constance Collier, Edmund Pearson; I came because of his friendship with my mother. I came as a young friend—I went away freighted with ideas and a big project.

When calling on him I always wore silk so that he would hear the rustle and know I had taken the trouble to dress up, and I always found it hard to leave, lingering bewitched at his portal while his words, sounding from the dusk (he needed no light), opened windows in perception until finally a nurse appeared and signed for me to go.

As a young man he had been handsome, dashing and adventurous, endowed with all the charms and with every prospect of a happy career; but his life suddenly warped into tragedy. When still in his thirties he developed arthritis after a cold caught in Rome, and over the years, in spite of all that the medical profession could do, the disease conquered him inch by inch, until in his mid-forties he found himself unable to use even his hands. He had moved into a New York penthouse as into a tomb, attended by trained nurses, and there, motionless for the rest of his life (it is rumored that he had to choose a position to harden in), he devoted himself to an existence of the mind alone.

He had enormous learning and undiminished zest, and no exhaustion or agony subdued his curiosity.

"Tell me about Martha Graham," he said to me in his deep voice. "I've read yesterday's reviews, but how does she really move?" And I had to make him see, without stirring a hand or a foot, I had to make him see in detail and dynamically because he insisted on seeing exactly. And that is precisely how I learned to describe dancing. If I have any skill in this matter, I learned it from Edward Sheldon, lying blind beside and asking, "But what does she do with her feet in these contractions?" and then, "and her neck?"

One night he said, "Your next ballet must be about Lizzie Borden," and he outlined her story briefly with equal appreciation for the gore and the social import.

"You don't need to keep it in New England. You can change the locale. It's the family relationships that must stand," and he chuckled deeply and the forefinger of his right hand, which was all he could move, twitched under the silk coverlet. "Dreadful, dreadful family."

It is not easy to explain why his idea took such hold. So many people have suggested ballets that I could not accept or respond to. But on this gruesome story I grew to be fixed. There was the tantalizing mystery, of course, but beyond that was the search for why, the search for an understanding of the murderer, and eventually, as I got deeper and deeper into the work, a search for me, and my relation to the crime. As preliminary research I read, as he directed, *The Trial of Lizzie Borden* by Edmund Pearson.

When it was known that I was working on Lizzie Borden, letters began to flow in from New England; I kept a dossier and subsequently became acquainted with several of the writers, among them a few who had known Lizzie personally. I further discovered a coterie of Borden sleuths, amateurs of the case who pursued each clue with the excitement of connoisseurs. This group included two Supreme Court judges; foreign criminologists; Edmund Pearson, who wrote the first important treatment (on evidence not then complete); Mrs. Belloc Lowndes; Alexander Woollcott; Elizabeth Bowen; Joseph Welch, the Massachusetts lawyer; and Victoria Lincoln, who when young lived near Lizzie. Lizzie, it seems, entered into the psyche of many lives.

It was eight years before I had an opportunity to mount the ballet, but for me the subject was not exhausted and seven years after the ballet's première I attempted a factual reconstruction of the trial on a TV broadcast. This called for exact knowledge, and I resumed correspondence with my New England enthusiasts.

Among my informants was Eva Kelly Betz, the daughter of the Bordens' next-door neighbors. Mrs. Betz sent me contemporary articles, printed accounts by witnesses, and copious recollections of all she had heard as a child, the somber, curious, salty anecdotes of her parents' experiences.

Mrs. Dwight Jennings Waring, the daughter of the defense attorney, opened her house and her horrible archives. Mrs. Sylvia Knowlton Lewis, the daughter of the prosecutor, was clarifying, as was the novelist Esther Forbes, the daughter of a contemporary Massachusetts judge.

Victoria Lincoln talked to me and wrote at length.

And there were many others who, as children, had known Miss Lizzie, whose parents had known her extremely well.

Joseph Welch was perhaps as great a help as any. He had never seen the heroine, but he was well acquainted with several of the legal protagonists, at least by reputation.

I had not met Mr. Welch, but I grew to venerate him as on the television screen I saw him battling Senator Joseph McCarthy during the celebrated 1954 Army hearings. It seemed logical to suppose that any Massachusetts lawyer who had been alive at the time of the trial would be tantalized by the celebrated puzzle. At the first opportunity, and without introduction of any sort, I accosted him.

"Mr. Welch," I said. "I admire you very much. I think you are a great patriot." He turned to me in noncommittal but courteous boredom. "Are you by chance interested in the Lizzie Borden case?"

His face lit up. He recognized a member of the club.

We fell to comparing our bits of knowledge, raging with enthusiasm as all the Borden clientele do.

"How would you like to make the legal comments on my *Lizzie Borden* TV? Analyze the trial?" I asked eagerly.

He turned slowly and smiled. "How would you like to go with me to Fall River and examine the premises and interview all the people still alive? It's not too far from my home."

In due course we made the pilgrimage together.

He proved a most fortunate and knowledgeable accomplice. All facts of law were naturally within his particular province, filled him with vocal enthusiasm, with wonder, with a kind of love. The Medieval Latin terms breathed history, the struggle toward dignity and identity; the emergence of the individual from the herd. Each legalism, he explained to me, and as he spoke his voice shook with emotion, had been coined in blood; each device, which to the outsider might seem an incomprehensible or even ornamental formality, was to him solemn assurance.

From the racks, from the dungeon-keep, from the pillory and gibbet, came these victories, the promise that innocence should be defended.

He went over the trial with me point by point, explaining why the defense revealed a fact here or strove so mightily to exclude another. Between the contestants in the courtly battle, I saw the accused sweating as he spoke. I saw more. I saw innocence championed until proven guilty beyond reasonable doubt. My opinion of Lizzie Borden didn't matter. She was enjoying her heritage, the English concept of justice built so terribly and wonderfully for a thousand years.

Mr. Welch remembered many things, Lizzie's period being closer to his childhood than to mine. But I was conversant with fashions of household living and manners, economic and sociological considerations, and it is possible my questions may have prodded his curiosity. From time to time I would twitch his sleeve like a junior clerk, and remind him of what we specially wanted clarified.

On one aspect of the case he was remarkably forthright. "My dear," he said, "you don't properly value the New England attitude toward money. It lies at the root of our thinking and feeling. Money is not money to us; it is a gauge, it is also a power. To work for too little, to save too little, is demeaning, a taint on intelligence." He smiled suddenly. "How do you feel about money?"

"I like it. I like as much as I can get without going off the tracks."

"That's a relief," he replied happily. "That is a real bond. I have no false shame. I have a strong New England relation to money."

"I thought you worked on the McCarthy investigation for nothing." (He had worked for over a year for nothing, and his firm had borne all the expenses involved.)

"That was a quite different matter—totally different."

"Patriotism is one thing, business another?"

He winked and patted my hand.

Because of the national televising of the McCarthy-Army hearings, he was recognized wherever we went. Faces turned, faces lit up. At the first sound of his slow and exact speech, heads bared, folk came from out of back rooms and stood attentively, hoping for a chance to serve. He accepted all with gentle and kindly grace. He deferred. He waited, but he usually got exactly what he was after. It was not just that people had no wish to refuse him. He knew, great lawyer that he was, what to ask for and what to provoke.

He saw what was there, but he felt overtones and innuendos. He weighted the precise words, the sound of the voices, and the glances, remembering what he seemed not to have been particularly attending; what was reserved and held back told him as much as what was vouchsafed. He was himself an incomparable actor, and he never scrupled to use all his arts to gain his ends. His favorite role was that of the simple cracker-barrel, country lawyer, whose only wisdom was common sense and a nose for the weather.

"Well, I'll be darned," he would say, with mild surprise, or "By gosh, think of that!"—quietly snapping the trap and regarding the victim in a kind of pleased astonishment. However courtly and deferential, he remained a virtuoso legal performer, and anybody who forgot the one while succumbing to the other was soon helpless.

He had known the fathers or the uncles, if they were in law, of many we spoke to in Fall River. And, of course, our path took us among lawyers' families or their relatives. They got out their best sherry, their best tea sets, and their scrapbooks. He enchanted the whole town. "By gosh," he would say, "this is interesting!" and they held out their hearts. And all the time he was noticing and remembering. And this was helpful because while our informants were generous, they were at the same time curiously guarded; although every statement made in the present retelling was given me as a fact, either witnessed personally or learned firsthand from witnesses, yet where the source has not been named, it has been by direct request. Even today at the long end of a nervous reaction, the desire not to be quoted is still strong. Reputable citizens, doctors, writers, lawyers, and their wives and children drew aside the veils of discretion to disclose the emotional essence of the hideous situation, but they refused to go into print on the matter, and every letter, phone call, and conversation was followed within days by a panicky written demand for caution, so persuasive was the spell of horror put on a quiet community by these sixty-four-year-old crimes. I have checked and cross-checked whenever possible, but because of the enforced anonymity several of the events recorded must be judged as legend.

Mr. Welch and I investigated what facts we could, but others have done this. We scrutinized and re-evoked the atmosphere also which, although not legal or provable, was, we felt, close to the verity.

"This is how it was," said our informants, "not in the trial records, not in the newspaper accounts, but this is how it was. We remember." But they stipulated that they must never be named.

Psychologists will say that such unauthorized statements contain one penetrating truth: that this is how they wish to remember. Wishes are in some ways more telling than facts. It was about these wishes, the black need for sin, that the ballet was formed. It is about the universal need to name a murderer that I am now writing.

In the first draft there were two scenes originally projected that I loved: Lizzie at a church social with the minister, the graveyard white in the moonlight outside, where among the headstones Lizzie's mother appears calling her, laying the hand of her dead love on the young girl's life and on her new romance. For music—Calvinist hymns, and, in counterpoint, wailing violins calling "Lizzie, Lizzie!" as with the ghost's voice. This scene had, I felt, all the rich decay of Poe and Ryder. Inside the church the people singing and outside in the cold blue night the unholy spell of the dead and the beginning of love-hate. But after study I realized that the churchyard scene was dangerous because what was needed was more than a haunting in the graveyard. Lizzie needed a pull toward life to propel the crimes, rather than a pull toward death. The choir singers had to be viewed head-on, not sideways, and they must be robust, affirmative, neighborly, and joyous. Lizzie must nearly be saved; if she runs away from this merely to commune with a headstone she's just loony and neither interesting nor tragic. I yearned for the loss of the Ryder graveyard. But I was firm with myself. It was time for some fresh air. The ballet was getting dank.

So I dropped the haunting in favor of a choir practice full of hopeful, brotherly feeling and the promise of peace, and for a cotillion, the promise of happiness. The scenes of household hate, in the confines of the rocking chairs, shaped up well, as did the scene of Lizzie's perpetual loneliness and longing.

I thought of the heat, and Lizzie sitting every night alone at her window or in the dark garden behind the flowerless lilac bushes, of Lizzie peering through the leaves on the road, the glimmer of a dress; listening to steps down the street, laughter, the creak of a porch swing, a piano through an open window, a train whistle far off, the soft half-heard voices, running feet in the dark, the stirring of a palm-leaf fan. (These were to become in dance terms the light crouching runs, the breathless movement of the girls' hands, the enormous swing balance of the lead couple in the nocturne.) I kept thinking of the heat, the comings and goings; the whole world ready, but Lizzie locked away in the garden; the stars turning overhead while her young life spoiled; and the heat, the heat; and her dreadful parents soundless in the house behind her.

Should I show the murder? Better not. Violence on stage is nearly always silly. How indicate it then? What did the murder mean to Lizzie? It meant freedom, the reestablishment of love, and reunion with all she had lost. We would not show the hitting and chopping. We would show her in her dead mother's arms. . . .

"Dania" here is Dania Krupsa, de Mille's then-chief assistant, who had also worked with her on the Broadway show *Allegro*.

I began rehearsals by telling the Ballet Theatre cast the story. They didn't want to hear the story. They wanted to learn the counts, which were very, very difficult. So Dania and Bob Pagent carefully helped them memorize.

The exact counts, the exact grips, balances, leverages, and positions I leave to my assistants. I take care of the dynamics and nuance of performance and overall pattern. I never count. I proceed by instinct, which is pretty good. My assistants count out after me and teach the others. While this is going on, and it is laborious, I am being instinctive about another piece of music.

The Ballet Theatre dancers didn't know whether the music was good or bad, but they damn well knew they had to stay on it. No two consecutive bars counted alike.

"Must it be this hard?" I finally asked Morton Gould.

"Well, you know," he answered, "I don't think so. I was just trying to impress you," and he drew bar lines in quite different places all down the pages and, behold, we could count in regular fours for half a minute.

"Why didn't you do that in the first place?" I demanded.

"Well," he said, "I've had my fun," and he straightway changed all the time signatures. . . .

The pure dance patterns transferred easily to the new groups, but the pantomimes fared poorly. The dancers were not trained in acting and the dramatic sections seemed thin and obvious; except when our star, Nora Kaye, took the stage as Lizzie Borden.

Kaye had been in the corps de ballet the first year of Ballet Theatre, but had worked her way with relentless energy up to small solo roles and in the second year had been rewarded with the part of the Russian ballerina in Tudor's *Gala Performance*, followed the next spring by her overwhelming Hagar in *Pillar of Fire*. Thereafter she starred.

She was a dark, spare, New York Jewess, with wry New York wit, a flat Bronx voice, a hard, driving plastique, great force and brilliance, and a beauty of phrasing, an ability to suggest more with sparser means than anyone in our time. She could be brilliant in the virtuoso classic parade numbers, although a gross foot and hard relevé barred her from the feather fragility that the romantic heroines demand. Comedy was not for her—she was not sufficiently gentle; she burlesqued. But lyric tragedy she brought to heights very few of us had ever seen. She wore suffering like a flower, and when her arms lifted on a breath, her dark head turned, and her eyes opened, it was with the wonder of a stricken animal. But for all that, hers was a stern and classic world. There was never an iota of sentimentality in her portrayal because she practiced economy like a nun. Not one single irrelevant or frivolous gesture was permitted in her idiom. Her dancing laced about a steel scale. She used just what was necessary, exactly what was necessary—nothing else—nothing for show, nothing for vanity, and against this basic minimum her life beat and throbbed like a musician's hand on a single string. She took the ideas brought her and illumined them, so that I watched rehearsals in astonishment. There was an aura of everlastingness about the way she rocked in a rocking chair, or rolled on the ground in misery. She let a hand drop as though letting fall hope forever. . . .

Postscript

The works, plays, operas, ballets and TV's about Lizzie continue to come. In fact, no one has ever stopped talking about her. Few now live who knew her, or even saw her. . . . But the gossips have never stopped and every six or eight years there is a drama. In 1965 there was an opera by Jack Beeson, premiered by the New York City Opera, and the ballet not only continues to interest but mounts in effect.

One is put in mind of Beaumarchais' Figaro, who kept inspiring opera after opera, play after play.

What then is her fascination? What does she mean to us that we cannot let her alone?

She killed her parents; and because this is America and not Greece, she got away with it. That is the latter-day twist to the tragedy. The community consented to overlook the crime because under Christian ethics there is no excuse for parricide, the revelation and its implication being too terrifying. Admit this is possible and anything can happen. No one is safe. God the Father dims. The crime was expunged and conscience and neighborhood nerves quieted.

But the crime did happen. There were two corpses.

Lizzie is the first heroine of the defiant young. The young are no longer to be put upon to the vile point of extinction. When the mold of life becomes intolerable, the mold is broken. Lizzie's was an act of primal dynamics.

She was undoubtedly touched in the head, but the community was not. The community apparently sighed and remarked, "High time!" and with this toleration fell bastions of tradition. Driven sufficiently one could at last kill, and generation after generation has thought back with horrified relief to that still house in the August heat, the hollyhocks fainting in the humidity outside, and inside vengeance ripe and hate provoked moving steadfastly toward doom and release.

(ix-x, 3–12, 135–137, 162, 164–166, 291–292)

A Lesson in Bowing
(Excerpt from *Reprieve*)

De Mille suffered her massive stroke as she was about to speak on stage at Hunter College in "Conversations on the Dance," a program of lecture and demonstration by her dancers, to which potential funders of her Heritage Dance Theatre had been invited. Following her recovery, which took a couple of years, Robert Joffrey invited her to restage the "Conversations" program using his dancers and to move it from the 700-seat Hunter theater to the nearly 3,000-seat City Center. Although nervous, de Mille accepted. Below is an account of that evening, whose audience included not only representatives from many foundations and de Mille's doctors (George Gorham, Fred Plum, and Caroline McCagg); her close friend and amanuensis, Mary Green; and the saintly Pauline, her caregiver, but also Mrs. Walter Mondale, the wife of the then-vice president of the United States and a former student of modern dance. De Mille's husband, Walter Prude, stood in the wings; her sister, Margaret, then suffering fatally from cancer, conveyed her congratulations by phone. James Mitchell, now known best as an actor for television, was originally one of de Mille's most trusted dancers. James Jamieson (1920–1993), a specialist in Highland dancing, is best known for performing in and restaging the dances of *Brigadoon*. An influential teacher, his students include Tina Fehlandt, of the Mark Morris Dance Group, and the Broadway choreographer Susan Stroman. Charles "Honi" Coles (1911-1992) was a tap dancer of elegance who, in his youth, was considered by his peers to have "the fastest feet in the business." He is especially beloved for his class act with Cholly Atkins, for his star turn in Tommy Tune's Broadway hit *My One and Only* (for which Coles won several major awards), and for his inexhaustible generosity to other dancers and students. De Mille featured him in both her Agnes de Mille Dance Theatre company and her Heritage Dance Theatre.

My eighteenth-century serenity was only now and then, and in between, from instinct and habit, I fretted to be active. Up, up, out of the torpor. To horse and away.

I did not yearn to rejoin the Broadway parade, nor to force my name back in the market, but to rejoin the living, the doers.

Let me try to be clear, because I think this is important. All those capabilities and activities which I was so used to—the freedom to drive myself wherever I wanted to; to go alone where I wished to (the theater, movies, lectures, rehearsals, trips, dinners, shopping, whatever); the ability to do alone whatever had to be done; the policing up of my own house (mending, cleaning, washing, cooking, whatever I wanted to do); as well as those more animal exercises (running, walking, jumping, ah! And, oh yes, dancing), gone, gone. Denied me suddenly and absolutely. I never regretted them except in moments of frustration and irritation. I could accept the loss of these. I never yearned to have them back because I couldn't, simply, and therefore there was no choice. But in those concerns where there was a possibility of achievement, where there was a possibility of choice and an undetermined path, there I yearned to be active, to be alive, to be, as the Buddha said, AWAKE. And I felt that I must not, could not, willed not to just shut my eyes and sleep, accepting in these matters also total cessation.

Robert Joffrey's reconstruction of *Rodeo* having proved thunderingly successful, I approached him with the idea that we do my *Conversations about the Dance*, which had been so abruptly interrupted by the stroke. I proposed that this time we do it with full orchestra and his company and all the resources of his school. It would be a big undertaking. It would also be risky. He agreed....

I was happy to be in the thick again, but, of course, I was also scared. There is always trepidation before a public performance. In this case the hazards were special. I had been off the stage for nearly two years and there was considerable curiosity about how the catastrophe had left me! Had I grown old? White-haired, yes, but decrepit? Was I, in fact, alive?

The City Center Opera House has a capacity of 2,932 seats, very much larger than anything I had ever spoken in before. The Hunter College Playhouse had held less than seven hundred seats and we had filled that with effort. But three thousand! Quite a different problem. My small foundation had some money saved. We raised some more. Joffrey and I pooled our resources.

Everyone of note in New York would be attending, and this time it really would be everyone, including all the press. Expecting what? Also, there would be all the big foundations that I had vainly summoned before, and they were vital to continuance.

Before the stroke I had given one concert and lost six thousand dollars, but

I was enthusiastically persuaded to repeat it by the heads of IBM, who had heard of it and promised to attend this one. They sent their secretaries. The secretaries reported we had a smash hit. The bosses said, "Please do another." But the price had gone up. It was now ten thousand. I didn't have an extra ten thousand and the company had been dispersed. We had had to wait. We had had to wait until May 15, and on May 15 they had all the important viewers assembled in the Hunter College Playhouse.

Now, two and a half years later for this November night in the New York City Center Auditorium, the foundations had agreed to come back; the public television station Channel 13 in New York also said they'd come; and all the heads of the Shubert Foundation, the Rockefeller Foundation and the Ford Foundation. If all went well, the idea was to televise the performance and get it on PBS. This time, in very truth, they were there, but with an attention not only to artistic and professional values but—something new to my experience—clinical considerations, because they were not only looking for talent but durability, for much as they applauded my courage they guarded their investments and they were not going to be enticed into sentimental risk just because I showed a streak of stubborn gallantry.

I had heard on fairly good authority that someone at WNET with high responsibility had stated that I was certainly not up to the concert, nor to making a TV show of the concert, and that anyone who hazarded a penny on such an enterprise was a fool. And doors were closed, very quietly and rather secretly and politely, but firmly and finally.

There were other disturbing considerations. My speech had slurred and thickened. My mind was slower than it had been, my tongue far less nimble. And then there was the question of my stamina. I was now subject to sudden fatigues, fatigues that I had never known before. They came on me as hunger assails a child, after only two hours of effort. It was as if somebody had turned a light off. I didn't begin to get tired. I was suddenly exhausted, had to stop whatever I was doing and lie down. How could I maintain the disciplines with these handicaps?

But the real hazard I did not mention to anyone or even name to myself: I was frightened for my very safety. On the last occasion involving such a speech I had had a massive cerebral hemorrhage, and since that time I had had very bad mental lapses, two or three of them, and the heart prank. With this occasion duplicating in all ways the strains of May 15, 1975, but adding some extra strain under the heading of our grandiose augmentation, would these added challenges produce a tension that would do me down? Would I have a second stroke, possibly a coronary attack? Would I have a mental lapse, so that in the middle of a sentence I would find myself unable to finish and simply babble? The evening was two hours long. I was to be on the stage for the duration. Was I up to it? Could I ask myself to be? And there was to be no complete full dress run-through, no preview, no pretrial, no warm-up. Why not? We couldn't afford it. And I didn't have the energy.

Walter was frightened and said so. He put his entire will against the idea.

"Why must you?" he said. "Why must you risk further? Why disturb the placidity we now know? It's a form of vanity." And, indeed, I suppose it may have been. But as I had to live, I felt I had to function the best way I knew how.

I proceeded by dumb animal instinct, as plants turn to light, as animals to oxygen. I needed activity. I must DO.

Walter suffered.

Passivity is not a man's natural role. This is what I had had to endure during the war. But then, of course, it was *force majeure* and must be submitted to willy-nilly. No choice. Now he was being asked to stand back and let me walk deliberately into danger, to risk incompetence, speechlessness, yes, even death—to gain what? I know, I knew. And it was not just another Broadway success but the sense of living and the rejoining of the active human race.

I had two solo sessions each with Gorham and Plum. Gorham said, "You seem alright to me as far as I can tell. I cannot predict exactly, of course. You're not twenty. You're not even fifty, and you've been through dreadful experiences. But as far as any instruments show, you will be able to do this if you feel you will be."

"I do," I said.

And Plum said, "You cannot live your life as though you were going to die. You will die, of course, and possibly sooner now than before. But you must live as though you will live. This is not a bad risk."

In my stress I phoned Margaret. "If the doctors say Okay, go ahead. What else can you do? I would if I could in your place."

"If I could I would."

Lost, lovely woman! She flashed handsomely by, laughing, making us laugh, dazzling of skin, blue of eye, with the piercing gaze of a child beneath a high, tortured brow; flirting her graces and pretendings and in the very second of the pretty flummery naming herself with honesty, lean and terse. Brave Mag! You never flinched. The grace and stylishness of your courage we shall not look on soon again.

Her death was to be later in the spring, but now she said, "Take your courage in your hands and do it."

Not all my friends and associates were of a single mind. They said nothing, but their worry was very real. Walter's apprehension—no, his terror—remained extreme. Yet he bowed to my need.

"I'll help," he said.

Suddenly I was aware of what I was asking of him, of the courage demanded of his discipline. We never spoke again on this matter, but he knew I knew.

Physically I got stronger. The effort made me stronger and the habit of doing things right. I went to company dance rehearsals every day, promptly, and raised hell for two or three hours and went home and had my tea and slept. And that was a day's work done.

I bought tickets for my doctors, Gorham and Plum and McCagg, and I knew where they were to be seated so that if anything happened they could be summoned backstage instantly. And I asked James Mitchell in Los Angeles to cross the continent to stand beside me in the wings with the extra script so that in case I collapsed he could slip into my chair and simply read and the show would go on this time and would not come to a sickening halt. The audience could be told afterward that I was out of sorts.

But whatever happened, this was to be my golden night! My resurrection. Unique among the thousands I had lived.

I knew this performance would be without match whatever happened, so I asked to have it videotaped for the New York Public Library's archive. The dancers' union, AGMA, balked; not even history was to be recorded without pay. If they got paid the musicians and stagehands wanted full recompense. So this project was abandoned. Accordingly, I asked for an audiotape only and the musicians' union agreed. *Mirabile dictum*! Just before curtain a little man arrived with full equipment and authority he claimed from the dance archives of the Lincoln Center branch of the New York Public Library. Gerald Arpino, codirector with Robert Joffrey, gave up his own seats—the best in the house, front-row balcony center—to accommodate him. At the conclusion of this exercise the little man was to thank everyone courteously and disappear. Forever. And the tape has never surfaced, although we searched illegal and bootleg outlets. All proving that Paradise has leaky ceilings.

The company blessedly knew nothing of my worries. They had seen me in rehearsal and they knew that I was physically unsteady, but they knew nothing more. Also, they had no idea what the performance would be like, not having heard me speak except in rehearsal, informally, muttering and calling. They had never heard me say a finished sentence, so they were rather bewildered by the entire proceedings and probably pleasantly curious in an apathetic way, interested only in doing their dance steps correctly.

Mrs. Mondale, the Vice-President's wife, said that she would come to this hazardous, extraordinary, problematical evening. (She was the key to the National Endowment for the Arts and she meant to help.) Well, it was do or die. The proper seats were procured for her and her party and for her FBI bodyguards, who had to sit directly behind her. And the proper publicity was sent out.

On the big night Walter was white around the lips, but he said nothing and he went off to get ready and I went to the theater.

Pauline and I went to the dressing room, Joffrey's own, and there were flowers there for me, but I ordered them to be brought in afterward. In a certain way this was to be like an operating room.

I went down to the stage very early and sat there; the beloved environment, the beloved country, the dancers in make-up with woolen leggings tied over their tights to keep them warm, warming up and trying steps and trying holds and positions; the stagehands extraordinarily courteous to me for the first time in my whole life, solicitous. "Watch where you step. Look out for this cable. There's a light stand there. Let me have your hand." And flashing torches on wires and braces, Joffrey hovering around like a beneficent bumblebee, small, with a can of hair spray in his hands, pushing loose strands of the girls' hair back into place, patting girls' hair, fixing their dresses, watching. He is not a fusser. This was a nervous release for him and for them, and he was there with them watching every gesture. "Throw your legs higher on that lift. Try to get the balance lower in the hips. Lean forward and you'll spin longer. Have some spray."

Suddenly we were all told that Mrs. Mondale's limousine had turned in from Seventh Avenue and was coming down Fifty-sixth Street, and that she would stop backstage on her way out to the auditorium. We were all lined up and hordes, literally scores of press people came with their official tickets tied on and stood beside police and cameramen. And there were batteries of public media personnel and all I could think of was, dear God, let me keep my wits about me, let me be quiet in my heart.

And then we were told that Mrs. Mondale was indeed turning down Fifty-sixth Street, and then that Mrs. Mondale was at the door of the theater, the back door. And, in fact, she did come up the back steps, the same ones that I had gone up so often with the help of the dear, lame, black guard who made it his business to see that I got properly put in the elevator and looked after by the other guards, and who gave me advice about how to walk and how to protect myself. She came past him and she came past my elevators, and there she was, the good, gentle lady with her immediate entourage. And she came to me and I rose up on the arms of my dancers and made my courtesies. And she said charming things and I answered charmingly. Keep your mind on what you're going to say. Don't be diverted. Don't be disturbed. "Thank you, Mrs. Mondale. You're too kind." What will the opening sentences be? How do you follow up? Supposing they don't laugh. "I hope your sets are alright." Supposing they don't applaud when you enter? Oh, how chilling! You must be sure of yourself, so that you go ahead no matter what happens. Mrs. Mondale was taken into the auditorium and we got about our business.

There were a few minutes more left to become quiet again and acclimated to a professional backstage atmosphere and to forget the press and all the outlanders streaming around. But she was there alright and the evening was official.

We had to get on with it. We did get on with it.

Lights were changing. Lights were being tested with new colored gelatins. "Is this microphone the right height for you?" Jim Mitchell arrived. I gave him one script and asked him to stand at stage right. Walter had given him a thermos of tea just in case my throat closed up. He also had a phial of nitroglycerin in his pocket. Mary Green had another script and was at stage left. But since we had been through the very complicated program only once, she thought she'd better stand there and check the dancers on and off in the proper sequence. She literally called the show like a square dance.

Beyond the curtain was the astonishing rustle of the crowd, which an experienced ear can detect as either a full audience, half an audience or an empty house; and either happy or nervous. This one was full and this one was excited. It murmured and rose. It is an extraordinary sound, muffled by the curtain, unlike any other. Bob Joffrey took my hand and we stood. The stage manager signaled us and the barrier swished up and there was a rush of air. And there was absolute silence and electric emptiness and waiting.

Applause, I guess. And then Bob seated me and I began to speak.

Would I remember? Would I hold onto myself? I said the first two sentences without notes and there was a cracking laugh, as sharp as a blow on my back, as sharp as a hand extended over an abyss. I took the hand. I continued. Another. They were with me. They were ahead of me. They intended that I succeed. They would not let me fail. With that collaboration from the audience I knew I could not show weakness or uncertainty. They expected me to be excellent, and so I obliged them. We did it together. Every hesitation they waited out with humor and courtesy and understanding. They exploded at the amusing points. I had to wait for them to recover. Never ever in my entire life had I experienced such support and caring from a body of people. And when the dancers came out and performed the lovely old Jacobean numbers, they had faces like roses and the boys were gallant and the audience was pleased. And so was I. And so were the performers. And then they got into the meat of the evening and the soloists appeared: James Jamieson and Honi Coles, Gemze de Lappe, and they delivered the way great soloists do.

The company began to hear me talk. They heard the remarks and they heard the astonishing response and they were surprised and delighted and extremely stimulated. They laughed spontaneously.

And we were through the first half and it was intermission.

I changed from the old red dress which I had worn as a talisman. (I wore exactly the same costume I was to have worn on May 15, 1975, jewel for jewel, the beautiful, dark, blood-red dress that Stanley Simmons had designed for me. The shoes were different because I could not wear heels and I had to have a brace on my right leg. That was different.) I put on the new beautiful dress Stanley had made for me, reds of all tones, like the heart of a rose, like flame, my Phoenix dress, and we started the second half and it was simply grand. And at the end, when I shouted

"Honor your partner.

Honor your corner"

I threw out both hands to the audience, *both*, the right as well as the left, extended and held open, a perfectly natural and spontaneous gesture. Caroline McCagg, sitting just below me, drew in her breath so sharply that her neighbors thought she was in pain and looked around concerned. And she burst into tears. I had never used the right arm before.

"'Cos now I'm through

And so are you!"

And the curtain came down.

I couldn't hear and I couldn't see, but the whole cast stood there as planned, as rehearsed, and took their bows and then Joffrey led me out to the center and I'm told the entire audience rose on one count, spontaneously. But I couldn't see or hear because of the lights.

I had gone white since my illness. I could not walk forward and I could not bow. But I could stand and I could acknowledge. And the flowers came. Flowers and flowers. And because I couldn't hold or carry anything, they were laid at my feet. Jim Mitchell came out with a great bunch of roses and laid them at my feet. At this point my agent, Biff Liff of the William Morris

Agency, burst into tears because Jim was a star and he came without announcement or fanfare or place in the line of soloists. Bob Joffrey fixed a tiny, old-fashioned nosegay in my right hand. It was very light and very small, so that he thought that I could hold it and then he suddenly said, "Leave her."

And they scrambled. A voice hissed from the wings, "Be ready to catch her if she falls." David Baker, the pianist, was heard. "She's not going to fall."

I had no cane. I had no arm. I had no support. I had no companions. I was alone out there, absolutely alone. And the curtain went up and I stood exposed. And all I could think of was, "Let me not drop the bouquet." I stood alone and Walter's eyes filled with excitement. Fred Plum bit his lips. I stood without wobbling. I extended my arms again and the right arm did not waver. I held it high. And I did not drop the bouquet. (272–288)

"Preparing for Performance"
(*To a Young Dancer*)

Make-up

You will need to find a proper basic make-up for yourself. Old-timers can help you here. Have a friend check from the front until you have evolved what is best for you. This will be your image, to which changes and additions can supply special effects.

Dancers use heavier make-ups than actors because, for one thing, they often play in larger houses, and for another, they sweat more. You will have to learn from experimentation how your skin reacts to make-up under extremes of exhaustion and heat. Many people have to put on a base and powder and sweat it through at least twice before a performance. Some skins eat rouge; it absolutely disappears with exertion. But in this field, the more experienced performers can advise and they are always generous.

There are schools for difficult or corrective make-up in New York and Hollywood. If you are a boy, be careful of body paint, especially on your hands. It comes off on the girls' clothes. After most *pas de deux*, the female takes her bows with a brown waist while the dresser weeps in the wings.

Costume

Try to have one or two extra of every vital accessory—a prepared extra pair of slippers, extra tights, undergarments, ribbons, pins, etc. If something breaks, there is *no time* for hunting a substitute. Proceed on the assumption that everything is going to break or tear.

Do not alter your costume without the costume designer's or choreographer's permission. Your taste probably is not as good as theirs, certainly not as experienced, and they have the overall picture in mind, a point of view you cannot be expected to share with the same impartiality.

Be neat in your dressing room. You will, at first, have to share dressing space with many other people. You will save yourself hours of useless searching and a great deal of tension if you are clean and tidy and know where all your belongings are. Cleaning and tidying is a wonder antidote for nerves. Alicia Markova spends hours before each appearance cleaning and darning her slippers. They are laid out in rows on a white cloth, like surgical instruments, the afternoon of her performance. She has a dresser, of course, but she chooses to do this. It calms her.

You must not fall to bits on the stage. Your shoes must not come untied, your tights wrinkle or fall down, your clothes unzip, or your hat fall off. As you whirl and writhe, you must not spray out hairpins, flowers, buttons, belts and bows like a lawn sprinkler. With the violence you are going to subject your clothing to, preventatives take real planning. Hair is a special problem, but veterans can show you the secrets. Many ballet dancers, Markova notably, sew themselves into their slippers, and the ribbons are stitched in place around the ankle. Tights used to be a torment, and extraordinary devices of pennies and tapes, crossed elastic bands, and harnessings were resorted to for the sake of smoothness. Now with nylons and Danskin, there is no excuse for a wrinkle. Tights should be washed after every performance; besides the obvious reason of cleanliness, the washing causes them to cling to the skin. Beau Brummell, not a dancer but nonetheless fond of his legs, used to get into his smallclothes wet and allow them to dry to his contours. Don't you try this—but be sure the garments are spotless. A fact known only to the trade is that nightly laundry is part of your daily regimen, and only stars can have help in doing it. It is as inevitable as *pliés* in the morning. It is your cross.

There are fines imposed in most companies for the dropping of accessories onstage, and quite properly. Not only is the dancer exposed as sloppy and irresponsible, and the visual pattern disturbed by unplanned and unwanted variation, but whatever is dropped provides a real hazard underfoot.

Do not ever, therefore, risk an addition or change to your costume in performance that you have not tested in rehearsal; no matter how carefully you think through every possible eventuality, there will be some unforeseen, unremembered exigency that confronts you in mid-flight. It is nice to meet these surprises in rehearsal first.

Performing

Performing is a spiritual experience and is the responsibility of the artist alone. It is a point of view. It is the sum total of his personality. He spends his life in preparation for this—the whole of his life, not just the time he gives to class exercises.

When you enter the stage in the presence of a live audience, everything you have ever learned is suddenly different. You lose your breath where you never did before; you have strength you never guessed; you are more aware of your body and less aware. Headaches and stomachaches disappear, but just keeping your mouth shut has become an achievement. You can see both in front of you and behind you at once. You see the whole stage and the rip under your sleeve. You hear everything—each cough, each musical instrument, the grip dropping a gelatin offstage, your partner's whispered warning, the creak of your shoes; you hear nothing—a fire engine could drive down the aisle and you would still know how many turns there were left to do; that bit of just standing around feels wonderful, but the long lifts are boring; they were fun to work out, but they are boring to watch. How do you know they are boring to watch? You have not seen them. You know. Suddenly you know.

You finish, walled safe by light. And there are the faces and the noise, and it was over so fast, this thing you prepared ten years for. It was completely changed from the way it had been that very afternoon. You are changed. You have not been yourself for some minutes. It was like a rebirth.

And now you want to perform it really! Now you are ready! Now! Now! But it's done. It's over.

And a whole new set of problems and considerations takes over your life.

For the first time you face the problem of projection. This cannot be learned, or even gauged in the rehearsal hall. This is the test of whether or not you are a performer. When the very great enter a stage, a thrill goes over the nerves of all watchers. This tremendous communication has nothing to do with hair-dressing or false eyelashes or high kicking. These are not what get the tribute of silence or the triumphal salute of laughter. The chosen few who have the magic are freighted with power and hope. They know what they are meeting, and they join forces with the waiting audience in high anticipation. The greatest stars have not always been beautiful, but all have had the royal prerogative of commanding with every tiny gesture total, rapt, heart-hungry attention, as have had comedians. (Indeed, there are fewer great comedians than ballerinas or *danseurs nobles*.) Some beginners are blessed this way; the mark is on their foreheads from childhood. These are stars, experienced or not.

As nearly as we can define it, projection mesmerism is a matter of concentration combined with absolute confidence. Every faculty, every nerve is bent on communicating a definite idea. Not one iota of energy is wasted in fear.

It is the self-conscious performer who fails. If you are going to give a performance of a performer in action, you stop giving a performance of the dance, and you become your own worst rival. The audience will sense the fraud, the divided intent, and lose interest. They will forgive a dancer who bets his mother, peddles dope; they may even conceivably forgive him for missing his turns or forgetting his steps, but not for bringing onstage with him his private fears for himself. A show-off pushing to the front of the stage can become almost invisible, while the expert at the back makes himself known through rows of thrashing bodies. A show-off is troubling the waters in order to hide, and what he is hiding is self-doubt. You cannot hide this. It will be perfectly apparent to all. The stage is like an X-ray and reveals what you are, not what you hope you are or wish to be.

Believe in yourself therefore. You cannot hold attention or command others' belief unless you do. The parts you play, no matter how different from your own nature, no matter how carefully felt through, are merely dresses you put on. But the wearer, the actor, is you, and you must be of a piece and eager to say what you believe.

"It is the strange paradox of acting that the more a person disguises himself in another character, the more, to a discerning eye, does he reveal his own," says Tyrone Guthrie.

Do not fool. You may think the audience cannot see your face, but they can tell from the lines of your back and the carriage of your head when the tension of projecting and communicating has stopped. Lydia Sokolova, who was called on to stand with her back to the audience alone on the stage for some four minutes (a phenomenally risky feat), says, "I learned in 'Les Matelots' that even with my back turned, I could command attention simply by concentrating on the character of my role. If my thoughts wandered for a moment, people would begin to cough or whisper or shift about in their seats."

Some stars joke and talk, but they know how and when. Until you can make an audience laugh or cry at will, do not permit yourself this laxity.

No matter how confident you are in your ability, you will from time to time be nervous. That's all right. Nerves are part of the actor's equipment. There are two kinds of nerves. The one that sharpens the edge of perception to cutting point, that ensures the gathering of forces and the expenditure of total energy—that is to performing what light is to color. The other kind is an unraveling of concentration into a tangle of self-pity, at the horrid core of which appears the ugly sore, a fear of performing—in fact, a desire not to perform. This cancer can coexist with talent.

The pseudo or neurotic performer will always fall ill at the time of testing or destroy himself with stage fright. The true pro tries not to go on unless good and ready, but can anyway, if he must. Most ballet dancers learn to meet crisis as gallantly as soldiers, sometimes with little or no preparation. A girl turns an ankle; another soloist is on in twenty minutes with only a verbal briefing in the wings. When the replacements involve stars, the hazards are enormous. Just think of the colossal nerve it takes to walk to the center of a stage before the knowledgeable eyes of three thousand people and calmly start lengthy and repeated spins on the big toe of the left foot. Particularly if at dinnertime one hadn't expected to do anything of the sort.

This steadiness is not learned quickly, although it can be applied in emergency. It is acquired humbly by drudgery over many years. It is built into daily living. It is built into the fibers of character. Few trades require such discipline. It is equal to that of the research chemist or the practicing surgeon.

Training in physical techniques is spiritually good from every point of view. No amount of personality will help you spin or jump. It is very salutary to come to terms regularly with the laws of nature, where the charming giggle has almost no effect, and fight it out on a basis as universal and enduring as gravity. This testing cleanses and clarifies. There is no class of people more severely disciplined than dancers, more regularized as to life habits (excepting always the cloistered religious), or more sensible in practical affairs. This has been largely acquired in the daily exercises.

Applause

Bowing, acknowledging applause, is the only direct or, so to speak, civilian gesture permitted you before an audience.

Here you are on your own, and it would be wise, until you have learned something of stage decorum, to act with quietness and tact. Bow as simply and as graciously as possible, and get directly off the stage. Do not linger; do not try unduly to prolong the clapping. This looks greedy and silly. It is also risky. You might just outlast the applause, which can be embarrassing all around. On the other hand, do not be nervously hasty, and, above all, do not be fancy. After you have bowed, leave briskly, but there is no need to do a variation as you make for the wings, or a repeat of your last good technical stunt.

Keep directly within the mood of the piece. If you have done a dance about starving miners, do not take bows like a swan queen, but it is not necessary to preserve character in total detail and, after a peasant dance, for instance, react with coy astonishment at finding yourself in a theater before an audience and presented with real live flowers. Argentina used to do this, and it was her one lapse of taste. But, then, she was not a very good actress, although a dancer without peer.

Confine all your jokes to the dramatic presentation. Ad-libbing before an audience is for the very experienced and the greatly gifted. It used to take vaudeville comedians half a lifetime to learn how to bring this off effectively. Jack Benny's impromptu asides are about as haphazard as brain surgery.

If your dance is tragic, do not come back bubbling with high spirits and jollity. Conversely, do not scowl after a comedy. Do not scowl at all, even when much has gone to your disliking. It wasn't the audience's fault. Save your storms for the other side of the curtain. Sometimes the audience is hard, cold, indifferent, no matter; sometimes even drunk and unruly, no matter. Be a sport. One superb career was shattered by the star's losing her temper and tongue-lashing a drunken audience. The management never forgave her. You presumably are embarking on a long career, and you will face many audiences in many climates. Take the bitter with the better.

You are not to throw kisses unless you receive a genuine personal ovation, which, it is safe to predict, you will not be accorded until you have been on the stage at least five years.

Generosity is charming to observe. The management and your choreographer will see that you get your due. There is no call to push publicly for applause. Share. The young dancer who crowds in on the soloist is an unforgivable boor. Let the audience find you out. They will, never doubt, if you're good.

It is etiquette for the man to lead the woman onstage, present her to the house, and lead her off. She must for her part not forget he is there and snub him. He is not a footman.

In the ballet world she may receive flowers; in other dance theaters she may not. No flowers are ever presented in America on the opera or theater stage. The male dancer may not receive any publicly, anywhere. One famous Russian male star encouraged bouquets and even fruit after every solo passage, and reversed tradition by presenting his partnering ballerina with a single blossom as a token of approbation. This procedure made a poor impression, although an unforgettable one.

Acknowledging applause can become a fine art. Anna Pavlova and Maria Callas have transformed a reasonable hand into screaming salutes by their coquetry. Puccini rehearsed his surprised, reluctant acknowledgments carefully. But leave this kind of delicious playacting to the experienced.

Do not ever go out into the auditorium, on the sides or in back of the audience, in costume or make-up. Do not wear theater make-up in the street, or your theater clothes to parties. The curtain is magic, and whatever happens behind it must be special and reserved. You must not pass back and forth without transformation. Adeline Genée used to say that the ballet costume, even the tutu, was like a soldier's uniform, to be treated with respect, never displayed piecemeal or under improper circumstances, and worn only in line of duty.

Get to the theater long ahead of time—two hours at least—warm up and make up carefully. Quiet down.

Attitude toward Criticism

What the critics say will probably not concern you directly at first, but you will quickly absorb the nervous apprehension that everyone in the business holds for the printed word, morbidly so in America. This is because, being a former colonial people and deferring always to the old countries as authority in the arts, we have not generally learned to stand by our own judgments or waked up to the fact that we are gifted. Our fear is also due to the abnormal and artificial price of tickets and general theater costs and the consequent lessening of chances to make good. We feel we have to make the grade right away or else—and to a degree this is true. Theater costs are appalling, the chances given brief and hard, and the competition cutthroat.

None of these conditions, although unhappily peculiar to us, alters the fact that the critics are human and frequently mistaken and that they have to make rapid judgments. It is hard for proud men to recant afterwards, but they sometimes do.

The audience reaction is a better test, unless, of course, you are playing to their lower instincts. If people sit in hushed silence, you have reached them. If they weep, you have reached them. If they rise, screaming cheers, it can be taken as a good sign. The same is true if they laugh solidly. But be fastidious about laughs. Women in the presence of men will giggle hysterically, whether they are amused or not. They are merely excited by male presence and showing off. Women also recognize intent and are quick to respond in a kind of nervous sympathy. But an audience of women alone will remain limp and flaccid and show no response of any kind. Men will not laugh unless they are genuinely entertained, so listen for the male laughter. An audience of men alone can become manic. Audiences of families or schoolmates or clubs are obviously special and predisposed to appreciation. The audiences to trust are the ordinary mixed audiences of civilians who have paid for their tickets. It is notoriously true that the hardest people to please are those who have been given their tickets free.

You must learn to sense audience reaction, as a surgeon senses pulse and breath, and to trust to your instinct about this, but never, never set your will or your vanity against proper authority. You must listen carefully to director, choreographer, or *régisseur*. You must not listen to your colleagues, except possibly an older star who advises with the permission of the *régisseur*. You must learn to disregard your family's clamorings. No matter what you are given to do, it will never, believe me, be fine enough to suit your family.

In the end, however, the only real critic is your own taste, your own instinct—but in the end, not at the beginning and only after you have developed discrimination and acquired proper discipline. You must learn to know whether or not you have been good or bad. You must learn to know how best to make your effects. This may take time, and you must not be haughty or arrogant.

Endeavor always to become more and more sensitive, more and more aware, quicker in response, and then—but only then—be loyal to yourself. Stand fast. Never mind what they say in the dressing room or in the dance columns. You must yourself know. When you do, you will have stopped being a student and become an artist.

This advice must be followed soberly. It is quite possible to be absolutely wrong and pigheaded, fighting for a career that should never have been attempted, valiantly breasting unwavering, universal dislike. Such procedure is plainly neurotic. It is possible to become conceited and selfish, pushing away all proper advice and warning. You must be sensitive, aware and strong, not insensitive, unaware and stubborn.

Envoi

In the words of comfort given by the impresario Walter Prude to uneasy clients, "do the best you can the whole of your life, and if you do not succeed, better luck next time!"

You have been told by all your friends that this is a tough and difficult business, and if you have any gumption you have disregarded all such warnings. But when I tell you it's tough, I mean precisely the following: that you may not earn your living for three years; that you may not get beyond a bare earning for six or seven; that the opportunities for frustration and exhaustion are constant, while the chances for quiet and security are small; that in America a career means a direct choice between work and children until such time as you are sufficiently well established to dictate your own terms; and that in the end there is no guarantee that all your sacrifices will not, from a material point of view, have been in vain.

We are not as careful or cherishing of our artists as Europeans; nevertheless, what with television, movies, and shows, it is possible for outstanding dancers to make a living, while choreographers, directors, and dancing actors can make fortunes. The rest pursue, albeit precariously, a career they respect, under stimulating and adventurous conditions. They have to decide whether they prefer to enjoy life this way or by collecting automobiles and refrigerators.

You can accept these statements intellectually perhaps, but let me tell you what it means in terms of daily living. You feel good. You may often feel tired, but you feel good, alive, strong, young, able. You may be in your mid-forties, but that is how you feel when you wake up and when you go to sleep. When you walk down the street, there is a strength in your step. When you sit, you sit straight. You can always sleep—anywhere, under any conditions. You can eat anything. If you are a girl, you will bear children easily, and fail to show age to an almost unnatural degree.

Since you enter the most disciplined branch of the theater, you will have to train every day until you stop performing. You will keep yourself in every department of your life in working order, and this makes for decent working professional relations and self-respect. Dancers are never heard talking down their profession like Hollywood writers or Madison Avenue salesmen.

When you practice each morning, you put yourself through a re-examination and testing, a rededication, like reciting a rosary. This applies to all of you, body and mind. Tensions are released, tempers forgotten, hates appeased. Trouble works itself out through the muscles. Each time you exercise, you strengthen and test your entire self.

And when you rehearse, you alone of all executants share the creative process. You are there when it happens. You work with the best composers, the best designers and painters, the ranking conductors. No dancer is really bored.

American actors often have to play the same role to the point of stupefaction, and their technique is largely concerned with preventing fatigue and satiety from altering the dynamics of performance. You will not be so troubled. In repertory, you may play thirty or forty roles in a season and understudy half as many again. Even in a long-running production the physical changes in cast, the hazards and tests of the work itself, will keep you alert. You will not be bored, and you will not be lonely. You travel the world, and wherever you go, you enter the community as a working member, not as a tourist—you have an international family.

And when you perform—ah, then!—even if you are not a star, even if you have not risen above the ranks, what does your daily stint mean, the equivalent of the office worker's eight hours?

It means this: to step out on the great stages of the world, before thousands of rapt and hopeful people, into pristine space, trained and able comrades on either hand, a symphony orchestra at your feet, a carpet of music spread under you each night, to flash and soar—you, the ordinary one—to ride violins and trumpets, to go through the tremendous patterns set for you and to feel the magic work, to accomplish yourself through your breath and your sinews, your enduring heart muscle and your devotion, and in the bewitched emptiness haunted by excitement and risks, to sense the blocked mass of attention as tangible as fire, to blow on it, to stir it, to bend and play with it, to feel the stillness, the shudder of excitement, the recognition and acceptance at the reach of your fingertips.

You are out of yourself—larger and more potent, more beautiful. You are for minutes heroic.

This is power. This is glory on earth. And it is yours nightly. (99–116)

Life Lines
An Exchange of Love Letters
(*Walter's Book*)

De Mille's public writing is a natural outpouring by an inveterate letter writer for readers who were also, themselves, inveterate letter writers. For de Mille and her circle, letters not only recorded the world factually: they reconstructed it imaginatively. The exchange of letters, below, by de Mille and her husband of a year, Walter Prude, then in military service overseas, exemplifies the touching efforts of the correspondents, separated by thousands of miles and a global cataclysm, to build a private space together, entirely through the literary deployment of the English language. Walter's letter alludes to the Normandy invasion of the day before; to a couple of books, including a mystery novel by Craig Rice; and to several Broadway projects on which de Mille was working, including one—the 1944 *Sadie Thompson*, co-written by Rouben Mamoulian and Howard Dietz and based on the W. Somerset Maugham story "Rain"— whose choreography is now credited to Edward Caton. Agnes's vow at the end of her letter was realized in 1988, when Walter died, forty-four years into their marriage. These letters were part of a book she put together—from tributes at his memorial, candid photographs of him, and journal entries and letters by him—and had printed in 1991, a forever rose garden to Walter Prude.

Dearest Agnes,

I wonder if you were in the country when the hour struck and if you jumped wildly up and down or just sat quietly over your coffee saying "About time!" at intervals like a pint-sized Stalin.

We were all pretty well aware of its imminence as who wasn't?—But I missed my prediction by 8 days, figuring the 14th was the best of all days for starting something big and portentous. I still think my D-Day would have been better, for the weather is extremely bad for operations now; and we need everything on our side, up to and including God.

You're probably much better posted than I am on what's happening now. The only times I've been able to get to hear a radio BBC has been addressing remarks to Europe in German and suggesting ways to Italians and French of confounding the Nazi supply lines. We all knew last week that we wouldn't get in on this phase. Strangely enough—for any reasonable being—it was disappointing. After a certain amount of waiting any kind of change and excitement comes as a relief.

Anyway this will serve to keep you from worrying about me. Until we get on the move I'm certainly as safe here as anywhere in the world.

I'm glad you're finding *The Rain* project interesting. But *Lilliom* (*Carousel*) still sounds like the real thing to me. I have a feeling *Rain* will surely develop a need for another prostitute dance, and you've *done* that. However I must tell the Sandwiches you are collaborating with Howard Dietz. That will interest them. I talked with Faith and Lady A—on the phone last week and planned to go for tea Sunday, but at the last moment I couldn't. They said they'd had a charming letter from you and seemed quite pleased about it. The mystery you sent—*Home Sweet Homicide*—is marvelous, the best of the lot. Please send any Erle Stanley Gardner or Rex Stout (new ones) that you can find. I didn't find *Peace Without Retort* very startling but there is a sort of dreadful parallel-in-the-making to be observed, isn't there? Also I'd like to have a *New Yorker* sent whenever you can get around to it. That's the main piece of reading I miss.

It looks as though my best chance of seeing you dance would be to get myself banged up enough for hospitalization. That's a grand project, darling. (Dancing in hospitals for wounded soldiers.) And I'm very proud of you for taking it on. But couldn't you take off a couple of months first? Do try. I love you so very much—

Walter

Your picture is pinned up and has been the delight of all beholders these many days. (A colored full page from the *New York News*. A jumping pose from "Tally-Ho")

June 14, 1944

Dear Walter,

A year ago today I stood in the porch of the little church on North Rodeo and heard our sturdy fine wedding march and you waited by the altar with Dennis at your right. I have never seen anyone so beautiful as you were at that moment. You looked very young and vulnerable, diffident, almost timid, but resolved and true. I think we both felt that we didn't quite know how we'd maneuvered ourselves into this position. It seemed as though some other girl had taken possession of my life that day and was hurrying me on I didn't actually see where to. But I felt as I saw your nervousness such a need to help you get through the business. It was as though I [was] outside of me—the real me said to you outside of you—"those two are in real trouble. Here, take my hand and let's go steady while they flounder around." And then when the minister placed my hand in yours and I dared look into your face I saw a strange face. I saw my face. I saw my father's face. I saw more deeply into your face than I ever had. When you looked at me that night you left there you were, but strong, integrated, controlling, gathering your forces, but at our wedding when you looked at me you were exposed, astonished, naked, defenseless with the terrible power and wonder of pure hope.

Oh my love, how that hope builds my life to yours! Your face is always strange to me. I never quite believe that you are you and pledged to me, that I know you well. Every time I see it on the pillow beside me, every time I see it over a coffee cup I am surprised that you are there. And every time you make me laugh or meet my eyes at some remark or some tune I am unsurprised because it seems to me I have always known you would be there.

Most of my adult life has been spent quite alone, sleeping alone, walking alone, eating alone. To think of coming home with someone, knowing someone is at work in the next room, being certain that the next day and the next I will have a companion to gossip with, listen to.—It doesn't seem possible to me that I can really have these things. And yet when they happen I shall not be surprised. For there is this about you. I am startled to find you at my side and yet you are well known. Like your letters. I am always amazed to see your handwriting on a letter. It is as though I never expected to receive another, as though I'd never received one before. It has been like this in all our shared experiences—always as though I had never known you before, always as though you were better known than my own mind, as though I were becoming acquainted with some other and better part of myself. And the longer I know you the more striking this grows, this duality of strength. I think this is why although you have often said you believed men and women were of one another physically, with us it will not be so. This is why I think we will not ever get used to one another or our happiness together. I want to grow old beside you, and I believe I shall have all I ask of life.

I believe in all you believe in, Walter. I love what you love. Suffering has pulled us fine. What we are hoping for and living toward takes sturdy nerves and real purpose. But I find with you this is not so hard.

To love.

To honor.

To cherish—These are big words.

Till death do us part—

I will

Agnes

Acknowledgments

Robert A. Gottlieb supported my writing between 1988 and 1992, when I contributed weekly to both the Goings On About Town and Talk of the Town sections at *The New Yorker*, which he then edited. He also included several of my essays, for other periodicals, in his recent anthology, *Reading Dance*. It was in putting together *Reading Dance*, where Agnes de Mille is well represented, that Bob became convinced her essays and memoirs deserved to be back in the marketplace of ideas, and he suggested this to Meredith Babb, director of the University Press of Florida, along with my name as a possible editor. She entrusted the de Mille anthology to me, and it has been a joy to work on, in every way. My appreciation of Bob's generosity is represented by the dedication of this book. With pleasure and deep gratitude, I also thank Meredith and her colleagues at the press for their readiness to help and guide de Mille's work into print once again: Marthe Walters (project editor), Michele Fiyak-Burkley (managing editor), Dennis Lloyd (director of sales and marketing), Allyson Gasso (marketing assistant), and Heather R. Turci (grants coordinator). And thank-yous are tendered to the original project editor, the spirited Jacqueline Kinghorn Brown, and to freelance copy editor Patterson Lamb, with whom it was my pleasure to work several years ago on an earlier book. And my thanks also go to Robyn Taylor (book designer) and Aileen Rieck (editorial intern).

I am also grateful to Jonathan Prude and other members of the Agnes de Mille Estate for giving permission to republish the wonderful writings by de Mille herein. Scott Eyman kindly gave permission for me to publish a passage from his then-forthcoming biography, *Empire of Dreams: The Epic Life of Cecil B. De Mille*.

Through their steady encouragement, the following friends of longstanding made it possible for me to work on this project. Although I list them here together, in my feelings each person commands a separate, unbound page of blessings: Ansie Silverman Baird, Mary Meeker Gesek, Leslie Getz and Don McDonagh, Gail Weinstein Golod and Zvi Golod, Sara Swan Miller and Martin Miller, and Nancy Reynolds.

The de Mille stager Gemze de Lappe and the choreographer and teacher Liza Gennaro granted me extensive telephone interviews about their experiences with the creative work of Agnes de Mille. Diana Byer, the founding artistic director of New York Theatre Ballet, which has devotedly maintained a repertory of de Mille's Broadway dances, arranged for me to speak with them. I give heartfelt thanks to this kind and gracious triumvirate.

Several friends who are also colleagues in the realm of dance history have offered help for which I am continually grateful. Susan Reiter, the critic of dance, theater, and figure skating, lent me a book by de Mille that was not available in the library and went over a substantial portion of the manuscript as a volunteer fact-checker and proofreader. George Dorris, the scholar of dance, literature, and classical music, generously vetted the preface. Both individuals tendered invaluable suggestions. The historians Lynn Garafola and Nancy Reynolds kindly contributed help in picture research. Of course, any errors in the manuscript are entirely my own.

A deep reverence to Elizabeth Souritz, of Moscow, the incomparable scholar of Russian theatrical dancing, who hastened to help with information about the ballerina Eleonora Vlasova.

The irreplaceable New York Public Library for the Performing Arts at Lincoln Center made it possible for me to track down most of the rarities in the de Mille bibliography: I thank especially Jan Schmidt, Curator of the Dance Division; Charles Perrier; and Jeremy Megraw (Billy Rose Theatre Collection). I am also indebted to the Lehman Library of Barnard College and the Butler Library of Columbia University.

One day, my daughter, Ariel Cohen, brought over a huge collection of used dance books, which she'd bought for me just because she thought I'd like them. One of those books was a copy of the first volume I ever read by Agnes de Mille: the imaginatively written and magnificently illustrated one-volume history *The Book of the Dance*. It woke up the little kid who fell in love with theatrical dancing about a century ago, or so it seems. I am so very glad to have it again.

Literary Works

Written or Edited by Agnes De Mille (1905–1993)

"Acrobatics in the New Choreography," *Theatre Guild Magazine*, January 1930.
Dance to the Piper. Atlantic-Little, Brown, 1952.
And Promenade Home. Atlantic-Little, Brown, 1956.
To a Young Dancer. Atlantic-Little, Brown, 1962.
The Book of the Dance. Golden Press, 1963.
Lizzie Borden: A Dance of Death. Atlantic-Little, Brown, 1968.
"Russian Journals," *Dance Perspectives*, 44, 1970.
Speak to Me, Dance with Me. Atlantic-Little, Brown, 1973.
Where the Wings Grow. Random House, 1978.
"Who Was Henry George?," Robert Schalkenbach Foundation, 1979.
America Dances. Obolensky/Macmillan, 1980.
Reprieve. Doubleday, 1981.
Portrait Gallery. Houghton Mifflin, 1990.
Walter's Book: In Memoriam Walter Foy Prude (1909–1988). Memorial Service Reminiscences, Letters, and Journal Entries Compiled by Agnes de Mille Prude. Privately published, 1991.
Martha: The Life and Work of Martha Graham, Random House, 1991.

Secondary Sources

Easton, Carol. *No Intermissions: The Life of Agnes de Mille*. Little, Brown, 1996.
Eyman, Scott. *Empire of Dreams: The Epic Life of Cecil B. De Mille*. Simon & Schuster, 2010.

Mindy Aloff teaches dance criticism and history and First-Year Seminar at Barnard College. She serves as editor of the *Dance Critics Association News* and as a consultant to The George Balanchine Foundation. A past fellow of The John Simon Guggenheim Memorial and Woodrow Wilson Foundations, and a recipient of a Whiting Writers Award, she is the author-editor of *Dance Anecdotes: Stories from the Worlds of Ballet, Broadway, the Ballroom, and Modern Dance*; the editor of *The Unpicturelikeness of Pollock, Soutine and Others*, a collection of essays by the painter Louis Finkelstein; and the author of *Hippo in a Tutu: Dancing in Disney Animation* and of *Night Lights* (a collection of poems).